MEDIA POLITICS

A Citizen's Guide

THIRD EDITION

MEDIA POLITICS
A Citizen's Guide

THIRD EDITION

Shanto Iyengar
Stanford University

W. W. NORTON & COMPANY
NEW YORK LONDON

W. W. Norton & Company has been independent since its founding in 1923, when William Warder Norton and Mary D. Herter Norton first published lectures delivered at the People's Institute, the adult education division of New York City's Cooper Union. The firm soon expanded its program beyond the Institute, publishing books by celebrated academics from America and abroad. By midcentury, the two major pillars of Norton's publishing program—trade books and college texts—were firmly established. In the 1950s, the Norton family transferred control of the company to its employees, and today—with a staff of four hundred and a comparable number of trade, college, and professional titles published each year—W. W. Norton & Company stands as the largest and oldest publishing house owned wholly by its employees.

Editor: Lisa Camner McKay
Project Editor: Jennifer Barnhardt
Editorial Assistant: Samantha Held
Managing Editor, College: Marian Johnson
Managing Editor, College Digital Media: Kim Yi
Production Manager: Benjamin Reynolds
Media Editorial Assistant: Michael Jaoui
Marketing Manager, Political Science: Erin Brown
Design Director: Rubina Yeh
Designer: Margaret M. Wagner/Anna Reich
Photo Editor: Trish Marx
Permissions Manager: Megan Jackson
Composition: Jouve North America
Manufacturing by RR Donnelley—Westford, MA

Permission to use copyrighted material is included on page 367.
Library of Congress Cataloging-in-Publication Data

Iyengar, Shanto.
  Media politics: a citizen's guide / Shanto Iyengar, Stanford University.—Third edition.
     pages cm
  Includes bibliographical references and index.
  ISBN 978-0-393-93779-4 (pbk.)
  1. Mass media—Political aspects—United States.   2. Press and politics—United States.
  3. United States—Politics and government.   I. Title.
  P95.82.U6I94 2015
  302.23'0973—dc23
                                                                                    2015009306

W. W. Norton & Company, Inc.,
500 Fifth Avenue, New York, NY 10110-0017
wwnorton.com

W. W. Norton & Company Ltd., Castle House, 75/76 Wells Street, London W1T 3QT
1 2 3 4 5 6 7 8 9 0

CONTENTS

6. Campaigning through the Media 148

VIDEO ARCHIVES FOR *MEDIA POLITICS*

The Media Politics video archive includes Video Features on the topics listed below. Each Video Feature presents clips that illustrate the discussion in the text. An icon in the margins of the text indicates when a corresponding clip is available. The video archive can be accessed at *mediapolitics.stanford.edu*.

Chapter 6

Chapter 7

Chapter 9

Chapter 11

ACKNOWLEDGMENTS

A substantial part of this book derives from a series of collaborative research projects conducted over the past three decades. The author has had the good fortune to cross paths with several distinguished scholars, including Toril Aalberg, Stephen Ansolabehere, James Curran, Roy Behr, James Fishkin, Franklin Gilliam Jr., Kyu Hahn, Allison Harrell, Simon Jackman, Donald Kinder, Jon Krosnick, Daniel Lowenstein, Robert Luskin, William McGuire, Helmut Norpoth, John Petrocik, Markus Prior, Adam Simon, Stuart Soroka, Nicholas Valentino, and Lynn Vavreck. He thanks them all for their ongoing contributions to the study of media politics.

No less important was the continuous support provided by graduate and undergraduate students at Yale University, the State University of New York—Stony Brook, University of California—Los Angeles, and Stanford. This edition incorporates research by several recent Stanford PhDs including Yphtach Lelkes, Solomon Messing, Gaurav Sood, and Sean Westwood.

The updated video archive was compiled by John Walker, the technical director of the Political Communications Lab at Stanford.

Scott Althaus, Matthew Baum, Jamie Druckman, Steven Livingston, Robert Sahr, James Endersby, and Russell Neuman contributed insightful commentary on individual chapters for the First Edition; the end result was a significantly strengthened manuscript. The Second Edition benefited from commentary provided by Chris Burnett, Matt Eshbaugh-Soha, Paul Freedman, Phil Habel, Paul Harwood, Danny Hayes, Travis Ridout, and John Sides. Daniel Lowenstein not only reviewed but also revised the account of campaign finance reform. For the Third Edition, thanks are due to all of the reviewers who provided feedback on chapter content.

Lisa McKay, my editor at Norton, not only made the book more reader friendly, but also provided several substantive suggestions that strengthened the presentation. Finally, thanks to Marne Evans for her fine copy editing.

Shanto Iyengar
Palo Alto
January 2015

MEDIA POLITICS

A Citizen's Guide

THIRD EDITION

Introduction

Image Is Everything

May 1, 2003—On the deck of the USS *Abraham Lincoln*, President George W. Bush claims victory in the war against Iraq.

August 13, 2010—At a White House dinner with prominent members of the American Muslim community, President Obama announced his support for the proposal to construct a mosque near the site of the destroyed World Trade Center in New York City.

In different ways, these two incidents illustrate a basic maxim of American politics: image is everything. Firstly, as in the case of President George W. Bush's premature claim of victory in Iraq, politicians feel no compunction about making exaggerated (and even false) claims before national television audiences because they understand that it is politically beneficial to associate themselves with successful action and they expect that their claims of success will be taken at face value. Secondly, politicians take great care to avoid supporting unpopular groups or becoming involved with controversial causes. President Barack Obama's advisers understood that the mosque controversy posed unique risks for the president. At that time, approximately 20 percent of the American people (and nearly one-third of all Republicans) mistakenly believed that Obama was a Muslim. Opposition to the mosque was strong among both Democrats and Republicans. In fact, 70 percent of the respondents in a poll commissioned by *Time* magazine believed that the construction of the mosque represented an insult to the victims of the 9/11 attacks. Organizations representing the victims' families condemned the president for desecrating the sanctity of Ground Zero. Republican politicians attacked the president's position as abhorrent. Former Congressman Newt Gingrich compared the proposal to demands by Nazis that the swastika be displayed at the Holocaust Museum. Equally telling, not a single prominent Democratic politician defended the president for his position.

The preoccupation with media imagery is hardly surprising, given that, for most Americans, the media are their only contact with the world of public affairs. On the flip side, from the perspective of the public, events not covered by the news media make no greater impression than the proverbial tree falling in the forest when no one is around to hear it. For the public, what's in the news is all there is to know.

MEDIA-BASED POLITICS IN THE UNITED STATES

Video Archive 1.1
Image is Everything

The power of media imagery reverberates throughout political life. The incidents illustrated in Video Archive 1.1 reflect situations at differing ends of the politician's comfort gradient. President Bush's declaration of victory on board the USS *Abraham Lincoln* was carefully staged to reinforce his own contributions to the successful invasion of Iraq, at a time when the possibility of actual victory seemed plausible. President Bill Clinton's emphatic (and false) denial of a sexual relationship with White House intern Monica Lewinsky was an attempt to stem the rising tide of doubts about his fitness for office. President Obama's support for the construction of a mosque near the site of the destroyed World Trade Center in New York City landed him in political hot water in a debate that had less to do with what was constitutionally allowed and more to do with how the image of the mosque would be perceived. Cultivating favorable media is a politician's major day-to-day focus and preoccupation.

No longer confined to elections and campaigns, media appeals have become standard fare in the day-to-day conduct of government and are used by private interests as well as by candidates. During legislative debates, spokespersons for both sides appear regularly on television news programs and talk shows to cast their individual spin on the policy or problem in question. Rather than relying solely on old-fashioned lobbying methods, private parties now sponsor television ads intended to cue officials about issues such as healthcare, immigration, or Social Security reform.

The habit of playing to the public has even spread to policy arenas not typically associated with partisan politics. The bipartisan Warren Commission, established to investigate the assassination of President Kennedy, conducted its business behind closed doors. In contrast, the Kean Commission appointed by President Bush to investigate the 9/11 terrorist attacks conducted its business in televised hearings (except for the testimonies of President Bush, Vice President Cheney, and some high-level intelligence officials). The substantive jurisdiction of both commissions involved sensitive matters of state, but our expectations about how an inquiry of this type should properly be conducted have changed greatly. Moreover, the media coverage of the Kean Commission's work was not limited to the actual hearings; several members of the commission appeared as regular guests on news programs and talk shows where they were prepared to and did discuss the developing findings in partisan terms. Indeed, their daily media appearances were utterly predictable; Republican members denied that the Bush administration shared culpability at any level, and Democrats seized on the intelligence breakdowns as symptomatic of the general unpreparedness of the administration.

More recently, natural and man-made disasters have become occasions for public posturing. The Bush administration's inexplicably slow response to Hurricane Katrina, which killed 1,833 people in 2005, generated a wave of negative publicity. In an attempt to stem the tide of bad news, the president ended his summer vacation early, dispatched high-profile spokespersons (such as Secretary of State Condoleezza Rice) to the affected areas, and replaced the head of FEMA (the Federal Emergency Management Agency). In addition, the government announced that news organizations would be prevented from covering the recovery of the dead. It was only the threat of a lawsuit by CNN that caused the government to abandon the effort to censor the news.

The lessons of Katrina were not lost on President Obama's advisers. Immediately after the explosion of the BP oil rig Deepwater Horizon in 2010, the president's top energy adviser appeared on NBC's *Meet the Press* and declared that the Obama administration was in control of the situation. President Obama made several visits to the Gulf Coast to signal his concern and intent to deliver relief. After Hurricane Sandy devastated the New Jersey coast, President Obama toured the area with Republican Governor Chris Christie, who was then criticized by Republican leaders for acting as a public relations prop for the opposition party.

In sum, the use—even the manipulation—of the mass media for political purposes has transformed the practice of leadership and governance. Policy makers resort to the very same tactics that are used by candidates running for election. Television advertising, credit taking, blame avoidance, finger-pointing, and other forms of political rhetoric air long after the election is over. Campaigns are continuous.

The effect that the unceasing use of the media to further partisan and self-serving objectives has on the collective welfare is problematic. Electoral victors are those who excel at projecting powerful imagery and symbolism, but not necessarily those who offer substantive expertise, political experience, or pragmatism. The flood of attacks and counterattacks has increased partisan rancor and animosity among leaders and followers alike. The lack of goodwill in Congress and state legislatures makes it more difficult for elected representatives to bargain and compromise. The role of policy maker has devolved from decision making based on bargaining and accommodation to attempts to intimidate and coerce opponents through media exposure. On more than one occasion, the result has been gridlock and paralysis in government. Thus the practice of media politics amounts to a tragedy of the commons: individual participants may be able to manipulate the media to their advantage, but in the long run, both the body politic and the politician are weakened.

OUTLINE OF THE BOOK

In this book we have the following goals:
- To explain the rise of media-based politics in the United States.
- To describe the media strategies used to contest elections and win over policy opponents.
- To document the payoffs associated with these strategies: increases in the candidate's share of the vote on election day, higher approval ratings while in office, and assured reelection.
- To assess the liabilities of media-based politics, most notably, the possibility of intensified party conflict and polarization, which makes it more difficult for leaders to govern.

- To speculate on the emergence of a new, technology-based system of campaigning featuring direct rather than mediated communication between candidates and voters, and to offer some modest proposals for making news coverage of campaigns and governance more substantive and meaningful.

We begin, in Chapter 2, by providing a theoretical perspective. In democratic societies the news media are expected to contribute three important public services. First, they provide an electoral forum in which all candidates can solicit support from voters. In the United States, the forum is a combination of paid and free media appearances, but primarily the former. In most European democracies, on the other hand, the mix favors the latter: free television time is awarded to all the major parties before elections. Second, the news media are expected to erect a public sphere where voters can sample from a variety of perspectives on the issues that concern them. In effect, news and other forms of public affairs programming are expected to facilitate the expression of informed opinion. Third, the press is expected to act as an agent of the public by policing the behavior of government officials. Citizens lack the resources to monitor the actions of their leaders on a daily basis; they delegate this watchdog task to the media. In countries with a free press, the fear of transparency (in the form of media publicity) is supposed to deter public officials from engaging in corrupt behavior (Besley & Prat, 2006). In short, democratic theory casts news organizations as multitasking, public utilities.

Against the standards of democratic theory, most contemporary media systems fall short of meeting their civic responsibilities, but the American media appear especially inadequate. A distinctive feature of the American media system is that virtually all news outlets are privately owned. Private ownership creates an inherent tension between the profit motive and civic responsibility. The need to survive forces owners to value audience size over news content; they deliver content that sells rather than content that informs. Inevitably, infotainment takes precedence over serious coverage of national and international issues.

Most democratic societies deal with the dilemma of civic shirking by providing public subsidies to news organizations. The BBC in the United Kingdom, CBC in Canada, ARD in Germany, and NHK in Japan are major television networks, watched by millions of viewers and financed by taxpayers. Freed from market forces, these organizations deliver more news, documentaries, and other forms of public-spirited programming than their privately owned competitors do.

The American approach to encouraging the free flow of public affairs information has evolved from early regulations requiring public service programming to a more laissez-faire reliance on the market. Supporters of regulation assume that the existence of multiple media organizations does not necessarily create a flourishing marketplace. In the early years of broadcasting, for instance, the FCC (Federal Communications Commission) required all national networks to provide a minimal amount of daily news programming in exchange for their free use of the airwaves. The antiregulation argument, on the other hand, rests on the assumption that the sheer number of news outlets—daily newspapers, national television networks, local television stations, cable networks, Internet blogs, social media sites—provides Americans with ample opportunity to encounter the proverbial marketplace of ideas.

On a more practical level, *media politics*—as exemplified by the American system—requires two conditions. The first is universal access to the media. No matter how independent or civic-minded the press is, societies with low levels of literacy or with relatively few television sets will be characterized by alternative forms of political communication, simply because mass media will not be the most efficient means for politicians to reach voters. When the news media's reach is restricted, those who seek votes through media strategies are disadvantaged. The case of Howard Dean's Internet-based 2004 presidential campaign is revealing. Although he succeeded in raising vast sums of money over the Web, and in so doing established himself as the early front-runner for the Democratic nomination, Dean's use of technology did not translate into even one primary victory. In 2004, most primary voters (unlike donors) remained on the wrong side of the digital divide.

The second necessary condition for the flourishing of media politics is the diminished role of political parties in selecting candidates. In most democratic societies, political parties recruit and sponsor candidates. Parties offer competing policy bundles; voters choose among parties; and, depending on the party's share of the popular vote, some number of the individual candidates running under the party banner are declared elected. When party organizations lose control over the selection of candidates, *free-agent candidates* turn to the media as the most efficient form of communicating with voters. Media politics becomes a substitute for party politics.

In fact, the rise of media politics in the United States coincides with the increased reach of the broadcast media and the weakening influence of party elites over the selection of candidates. Beginning in the 1960s, candidates became less dependent on their party organizations and migrated to the mass media as the principal means of reaching voters. Because candidates for elective office represent a significant revenue stream during political campaigns (in the form of paid television advertising), media owners have been only too happy to encourage this form of cash-on-the-barrelhead electioneering.

BEHAVIOR AND PERFORMANCE OF THE PRESS

In Chapter 3 we examine the performance of the American media in two stages. First, we trace programming decisions to the pull of market forces, and to the professional values and aspirations of journalists. Market forces compromise the public sphere, as we have noted already. Somewhat paradoxically, the independence that is so valued by modern journalism has also exacted a toll on press performance. As professionals, journalists seek autonomy and control over their work product. They are unwilling to act as stenographers for campaigns and actively resist candidates' efforts to use them as mouthpieces. Instead, they prefer to provide their own professional analysis of the candidates' actions. Presidential candidates still tour the country making as many public appearances as possible, but their voices are rarely encountered in news presentations. Instead of the candidates, whose speeches represent bias, journalists have turned to a coterie of expert commentators for objective analysis of the campaign. Interpretive or analytic journalism has largely supplanted the earlier standard of descriptive reporting.

Professional norms are but one element of a broader organizational process model of journalism. In this view, the news is determined by the culture of the newsroom and the routines of the workplace. The importance of authoritative sources makes journalists especially reliant on government officials. The Pentagon, State Department, and White House together account for the great majority of news reports on a daily basis. In the aftermath of the BP oil spill, the press deferred to Admiral Thad Allen's pronouncements on the scale of the disaster, even though many academic scientists had raised doubts about the government's estimates of the rate of oil spillage. (Allen was the official in charge of coordinating efforts to control the spill.) And the pecking order within journalism creates a strong copycat mentality: what is reported in this morning's *New York Times* and *Washington Post* is inevitably repeated in the evening network newscasts.

The second stage of our examination extends the analysis of press performance to the question of adversarial journalism. In Chapter 4 we show that the stylized account of a watchdog press does not fit well with the facts, particularly reporters' heavy reliance on government officials as news sources. Every day, the Washington press corps converges on the White House press office for the official briefing from the presidential press secretary. In the aftermath of the American invasion of Iraq, a similar daily ritual was played out at the Pentagon and, although only briefly, at the Iraqi Ministry of Information in Baghdad.

The dependence on government sources does not necessarily inject partisan bias into the news; after all, Democratic sources can easily be neutralized by Republicans, and vice versa. But the preoccupation of the press with official sources means that incumbents have a sizable advantage over their challengers in gaining access to the press. Some official sources are more newsworthy than others. The president is the prime official source; any presidential event—no matter how trivial or stage-managed—elicits considerable news coverage.

Even though coverage of government policy can be *indexed* to reflect the degree of diversity among the opinions of elites, sometimes elite disagreement is quashed and one particular perspective achieves dominance. The prototypical case of elite consensus occurs during times of military tension or imminent conflict, when opponents of the incumbent administration tend to fall silent as the nation prepares for war. During these periods, the news becomes dominated by official accounts of events, and the press is generally in no position to scrutinize, discount, or otherwise cast doubts on these accounts.

In the aftermath of the shock and awe military campaign in Iraq, news reports from American journalists embedded with the American invading force were overwhelmingly celebratory in tone and devoid of references to the pain and suffering inflicted on Iraqi civilians. Given the one-sided presentation, it was inevitable that a significant number of Americans would come to believe that Iraq did in fact possess weapons of mass destruction and that the Hussein regime was implicated in the September 11 attacks on the United States. As late as August 2004, nearly 30 percent of the public believed that the United States had *found* weapons of mass destruction in Iraq. When opposition sources fall silent, the news becomes a conduit for the official version of events. This is a far cry from watchdog journalism.

In a third and final look at the behavior of the press, Chapter 5 addresses whether the civic capacity of the media has been strengthened or weakened by the revolution in information technology. Paradoxically, public affairs information may flow even less freely in the aftermath of the technology-induced transformation of the media marketplace. In 1968, most Americans got their news from one of the three national network newscasts because they had no other choice. Today, the same newscasts compete with cable and satellite networks, local news programming, a variety of soft news programs, millions of websites the world over, and gigantic online social networks. This bewildering array of media choices makes it almost certain that exposure to the news will be more selective; like consumers of goods and services, people will seek out news from preferred providers or programs and tune out others. Information conveyed through social networks and recommended by "friends" is more likely to attract the receiver's attention. Because people typically prefer being entertained to being informed, the enhanced media environment has substantially reduced the audience for public affairs programs. In 1960, some 60 million Americans—representing 55 percent of the voting-age population—tuned in to the presidential debates between Richard Nixon and John Kennedy. In 2012, the audience for the Barack Obama and Mitt Romney debates averaged 64 million, barely 25 percent of the voting-age population.

The increased fragmentation of media audiences raises important questions about the motives underlying consumer behavior. Some have suggested that the explosion of online news sites encourages consumers to seek out news that reinforces their own opinions, which reduces chance encounters with unknown or disagreeable voices. The increased availability of news sources with a distinct slant on the news (Fox News, for instance) makes it possible for consumers to choose news programs on the basis of whether they expect to agree with the message being presented. No longer will all Americans be subject to the same media messages; instead, they will encounter their preferred candidates or point of view. When a person's exposure to public affairs information is limited to only one perspective, political discord and division are likely outcomes.

Others have suggested, more optimistically, that the increasing use of the Internet will transform the nature of social interaction; people will substitute online for in-person encounters with friends and neighbors. These scholars cite the popularity of online social networks such as Facebook (now with more than 500 million members worldwide) and Twitter (with over 100 million tweets per day) as evidence of the revival of community and public spiritedness. By this account, the increased use of information technology strengthens *social capital* and allows individuals to belong to multiple communities and obtain information on demand rather than be limited by the availability of news programming.

Academic investigations into the effects of new-media use (which we summarize in Chapter 5) suggest that pessimistic reports about the increasing isolation and fragmentation of new-media users may be exaggerated. The fact that Americans can choose from multiple news outlets does not necessarily mean that they tune in only to sources that share their own values. Rather than constructing gated communities to nurture their partisan preferences, consumers can resort to a more utilitarian form of screening by seeking out information on matters that affect their daily life, such as the weather forecast and details about the daily commute. By this logic, local news will trump partisan blogs as a source of information. However, the emergence of huge online social networks (e.g., Facebook) has placed individuals in the path of messages from like-minded "friends," thus inserting considerable partisan bias into the flow of information.

SHAPING THE NEWS: CANDIDATES, ADVOCACY GROUPS, AND ELECTED OFFICIALS

Having dealt with the theory and practice of press performance, we turn next to the second set of players in media politics: the candidates and advocacy groups that seek to shape the news. A candidate's overriding goal is to attract more votes than the opponent. For their part, interest groups seek to promote or prevent the passage of particular policies. Ever since the onset of media politics in the 1960s, political campaigns have become increasingly professionalized with cadres of media consultants, campaign managers, and strategists, all of whom are well aware of the norms and values of journalists, and who hope to capitalize on this expertise to achieve the most favorable media treatment of their clients.

From the perspective of the candidate, there are two sets of media opportunities. *Free media* refers to news coverage, even though it is hardly cost free. In fact, campaigns invest extensively in hiring well-known media consultants and public relations firms to maximize their client's visibility in the news. Candidates also rely heavily on *paid media*, typically in the form of televised political advertisements. The content of the ads, their timing, and even their appearance during specific television programs are all a matter of careful calibration and analysis.

How do campaign managers inject their spin into the news when facing a hostile press corps? Among other things, they take advantage of competition among news sources to identify outlets that are likely to provide the most sympathetic treatment for their candidates. When the national press was hounding presidential candidate Bill Clinton over various allegations of marital infidelity and womanizing, his campaign turned to local news stations and other unconventional outlets, such as MTV, to get out its message. When vice presidential candidate Sarah Palin was criticized for her failure to provide journalists with access, one of her first televised, face-to-face interviews was with Sean Hannity, the conservative commentator on Fox News, whose program shared Palin's right-wing and fundamentalist ideology.

In addition, campaigns adapt to the more aggressive behavior of journalists. Following the 1988 presidential campaign, when reporters decided to take off the gloves and publish hard-hitting ad-watch reports challenging the veracity of campaign advertisements, consultants responded by producing ads with a veneer of objectivity (by citing newspaper reports in the ads, for instance). More interesting, campaigns began to produce ads that were designed as bait to elicit ad-watch coverage, with the aim of generating more free media coverage for their candidates. Because they take a strategic approach to adapting their game to the prevailing actions of the press, campaign consultants generally succeed in getting coverage that is beneficial to their clients.

The continuing struggle between journalists and campaign operatives to control the news provides a classic instance of a collective-action dilemma. Society benefits when journalists and campaigners cooperate: the news focuses on what the candidates say, the candidates focus on the issues, and voters learn about matters of substance rather than strategy. Because presidential campaigns typically feature two evenly matched sides, old-fashioned descriptive reporting guaranteed that the electorate would be exposed to equal amounts of opposing (and offsetting) spin. Today, in contrast, journalists prefer to inject their voices into the news to tear away the façade of the campaign and reveal the candidates' vote-seeking strategies. The end result is that voters come away with a cynical sense of the process.

Dealing with the press is but one element of campaign strategy. Candidates also have access to the paid element of media—namely, advertisements. In the most general terms, all advertising campaigns are idiosyncratic. Advertising strategy varies depending on the stage of the campaign, the persona and reputation of the sponsoring candidate, and the overall state of the political race. Even allowing for these contextual variations, however, there are several tried-and-true tactics in paid-media strategy, including the use of advertising to set the campaign agenda, to focus attention on the candidate's strengths, and to attack the opponent relentlessly. We outline these strategies in Chapter 6 using a series of illustrations from recent presidential and statewide campaigns.

Advertising is the largest expenditure incurred by candidates. No account of advertising strategy is complete without reference to the complex rules governing campaign finance. We close Chapter 6 with a brief survey of federal lawmaking on the subject—from the 1974 amendments to the Federal Election Campaign Act of 1971, which established the system of public financing of presidential campaigns (and associated expenditures and contributions limits); to the Bipartisan Campaign Reform Act of 2002, which eliminated *soft money* (money raised by political parties rather than by specific candidate organizations) and which banned the airing of *issue ads* (ads advocating the passage or defeat of particular legislation) in the weeks preceding the election; to the 2013 decision of the US Supreme Court in *McCutcheon v. Federal Election Commission*, striking down the cap on the total amount individuals could donate to multiple campaigns.

The same media revolution that swept through the arena of campaigns has similarly transformed the nature of executive leadership. In the premedia era, the campaign ended on election day. The president-elect (or governor-elect) would assemble a broad-based coalition consisting of legislative allies and supportive interest groups, who would work together to implement the administration's policy initiatives. The process typically involved bargaining and accommodation between rival camps.

As described in Chapter 7, bargaining with the opposition has fallen out of fashion in Washington and state capitals. Elected officials now prefer to go public. They resort to public relations tactics designed to cultivate the appearance of responsive leadership—through rhetorical posturing, credit claiming, and avoidance of blame. Their key advisers are no longer party or interest-group leaders but the legions of pundits, spokespersons, and media consultants who make their daily rounds on television news programs and the editorial pages of our newspapers.

The acceleration of going public can be traced to the gradual encroachment of election campaigns on the policy process. Elected officials and interest groups have accumulated considerable expertise in the use of public relations strategies while attempting to win elections, and it is only to be expected that they seek to capitalize on this expertise when formulating and debating legislation. Campaign techniques such as television advertising are now used long after election day. The "Harry and Louise" ad campaign mounted by the health-insurance industry proved instrumental in swaying moderate Democrats and Republicans in Congress against the Clinton health-reform package in 1994. More recently, while Congress was considering the Affordable Care Act in 2010, the Chamber of Commerce launched a significant ad campaign (at a cost of nearly $200 million) in an unsuccessful attempt to derail congressional passage of the bill.

Going public is designed to maintain elected officials' popularity. A president who attracts high marks from the American public can use personal popularity as leverage to get policy agendas passed. The premium on popularity has led chief executives to avoid putting themselves on the media firing line. They avoid televised press conferences, where they may be asked tough questions, in favor of the more scripted opportunity of the presidential speech. During the

Bill Clinton and George W. Bush presidencies, the ratio of speeches to press conferences was more than 20 to 1. And President Obama has so far showed a similar aversion to the press conference; as of February 2015, he had held only four during prime time. Naturally, presidential speeches coincide with the color of the electoral map; the great majority of a president's domestic trips are to states that are in play in the next election.

In theory, popular leaders are more able to persuade their opponents. State legislators may defer to a popular governor's legislative proposals, fearing that opposition could jeopardize their reelection. Conversely, when the president's opponents sense that majority opinion is on their side, they seize the opportunity to push their own policy agenda. In the aftermath of the Monica Lewinsky scandal, for instance, congressional Republicans mistakenly assumed that the public would approve of their efforts to remove President Clinton from office. In fact, the scandal did little to weaken public approval of Clinton's performance as president, the impeachment effort failed, and the Republican Party suffered unprecedented losses in the 1998 midterm elections.[1]

MEDIA EFFECTS

Having outlined how candidates and elected officials use the media, we turn next to assessing the consequences of their actions. How do the content and form of news coverage influence public opinion, and do candidates and elected officials who wage more sophisticated media campaigns secure more votes and influence as a result?

We present the evidence in three separate chapters, beginning in Chapter 8, where we take a panoramic view of the entire field of media effects research. Following an initial preoccupation with political propaganda campaigns, the field gradually adopted a more encompassing definition of *media effects* that ranged from influencing what Americans see as the important problems facing the country (*agenda setting*), to shifting citizens' take on public issues (*framing*), to altering the criteria by which voters make their choices (*priming*). And when conditions were ripe—namely, during periods of one-sided news coverage favoring a particular candidate or policy position—the evidence demonstrated considerable change in public sentiment (*persuasion*). Thus the initial expectation of wholesale changes in public sentiment was replaced by a more cautious definition of the effects of political communication. Against this more realistic baseline, study after study demonstrated that the news media exercise considerable leverage over public opinion. We summarize this evidence in Chapter 8, including a set of new studies documenting the intensified state of partisan polarization in American society.

In Chapter 9 we take up the parallel question of campaign effects. Despite the enormous investments in advertising and the scrupulously choreographed nature of every campaign event and utterance, there remains considerable doubt over the capacity of campaigns to sway voters. Political scientists can forecast presidential election outcomes quite precisely (with the notable exception of the 2000 election) using indicators that seem to have little bearing on the candidates' media strategies. The state of the economy and the approval level of the incumbent administration, for instance, are among the factors used to forecast the vote. If the annual rate of growth in per capita GDP (gross domestic product) in 1999 yields an accurate prediction of the vote count in 2000, surely the time and effort committed to changing voters' opinions is of secondary importance!

In fact, we show that the forecasting models are consistent with the arguments that campaigns matter. The so-called fundamental forces used by forecasters—the state of the economy, the level of presidential popularity, or public concern over the continued involvement of the United States in a foreign war—are precisely the issues on which the candidates campaign. "It's the economy, stupid!" became the slogan for the 1992 Clinton campaign because voters expressed pessimism over the national economy. *Multilateral,* used instead of *unilateral* to describe intervention, was a watchword of the Kerry–Edwards ticket (2004) because of widespread concern over continued American military involvement in Iraq. In 2012, as the American economy floundered, the Obama reelection campaign adopted "road to recovery" (rather than the 2008 mantra of "hope and change") as its designated slogan. In short, presidential campaigns are debates about the fundamentals; over time, as more voters encounter the candidates' messages, their opinions on the fundamentals become more closely aligned with their candidate preference.

Campaigns do more than activate voters' positions on the state of the economy or the performance of the incumbent. Voters acquire considerable information about the candidates' personal qualities as well as their positions on the issues. Campaigns also shift the salience of particular issues in the minds of voters. Finally, campaigns can also affect the level of election turnout. On the positive side, get-out-the-vote efforts can mobilize large numbers of voters. Simultaneously, negative campaigning can be used to demobilize voters whose partisan attachments are weak and who might find the spectacle of attacks and counterattacks sufficiently distasteful for them to drop out.

The final collection of evidence that we present on media effects concerns the impact of going public on incumbents' level of public approval (Chapter 10). We evaluate two competing theories. One theory proposes that political leaders are prisoners of events and relatively powerless to shape public opinion on their own. In this view, Ronald Reagan's popularity had less to do with his communication skills and more to do with the fact that he presided over events that reflected well on his leadership. Popularity is simply a matter of good fortune for those who hold office during peace and prosperity.

The opposing argument is that leaders can use the media to insulate themselves from any rising tide of public discontent or to even improve their standing in the aftermath of policy failures. In this view, events do not speak for themselves. In many instances, political events are ambiguous (representing neither a major success nor a debacle) and how the public views an event and the actions of a president or governor very much depends on media presentations of that event and those actions. In 1983, President Reagan was able to justify the American invasion of the tiny island of Grenada as a response to a communist threat. Ten years later, President Clinton convinced Congress and the American people that there were several compelling reasons to send American troops to Somalia. In both cases, the president's ability to command media attention, coupled with the willingness of administration critics to remain silent, created a one-sided flow of news in favor of the administration.

We consider both of these arguments—history versus media management—in the context of recent presidencies. Using polling data extending back to the 1940s, we trace the ebbs and flows of presidential popularity. We show that, over time, popularity varies with the actual state of the national economy rather than news coverage of economic affairs. However, popularity is more sensitive to news coverage of national security issues than to actual security-related events. In the case of President George W. Bush, economic indicators such as the unemployment rate diminished his public approval while the frequency of news reports on terrorism, on the other hand, served to boost his popularity. In the aftermath of 9/11, the president's performance as commander-in-chief appeared to be the major ingredient of his public image. Thus, media management is a significant resource for presidents; all else being equal, the ability to direct and shape news coverage makes a difference to a president's political fortunes.

On the surface at least, the increased importance of public approval to the exercise of leadership suggests a more popularly influenced form of government. On issues for which clear majorities exist—as in the case of law and order—policy makers must converge on the majority position if they are to remain in office. This is why there is bipartisan consensus on the merits of "three-strikes and you're out" criminal justice policies that ensure that repeat offenders are imprisoned for lengthy terms with no possibility of parole.

However, the fact that media politics has made policy makers more sensitive to public opinion does not necessarily mean that opinion drives policy.

Media politics might encourage officials to resort to polling to identify the issues on which they have more or less leeway. On issues for which the public has strong opinions, such as crime, officials may go to great lengths to avoid the wrath of the electorate, even if that means endorsing bad public policy or reversing decisions made by subject matter experts. No doubt many elected officials were moved to support three-strikes laws on the grounds that the public demanded nothing less. But, as we point out in the case of the defeat of Proposition 66 (a measure that would have weakened the provisions of the California three-strikes law), public support for harsh treatment of violent criminals is driven more by hysteria spawned by advertising and sound-bite news than by any well-considered judgment about the pros and cons of punishment versus rehabilitation as elements of criminal justice policy. In California, where the governor has the power to veto or override parole decisions made by the nonpartisan Board of Parole Hearings, between 2000 and 2010, governors exercised this power in more than two-thirds of all paroles granted (Weissberg, Mukamal, & Seagall, 2011). The annual cost of incarcerating a prisoner in California in fiscal year 2010 was $44,688 (Henrichson & Delaney, 2012)—approximately the same as the cost of sending a student to Harvard. Why, then, should they be kept in prison at enormous expense to taxpayers? Elected officials do not raise the question, for fear of providing sound bites that label them soft on crime. Thus one of the effects of media politics is to weaken the ability of public officials to lead—that is, to enact policies on the merits and then persuade voters to concur.

In sum, media politics encourages public officials to engage in cosmetic rather than genuine problem-solving behavior. American society faces any number of deep-seated, structural problems: the massive budget deficit, dependence on foreign oil, degradation of the environment, underperforming public schools, a continuous stream of undocumented immigrants, and increasing economic inequality, to name but a few. A political officeholder cannot take action to treat these festering problems without incurring short-term political costs (such as increased taxes) or arousing the wrath of entrenched interests (such as the pharmaceutical industry in the case of healthcare and the National Rifle Association in the area of firearms control). In this era of media politics, elected officials generally cannot afford to bear these costs.

To close the discussion, in Chapter 11 we consider how society might short-circuit the escalating use of media appeals in public life. Asking public officials to moderate their rhetoric, scale back on attack advertising, and advocate policies that are unpopular with voters is hardly plausible. One possible pathway to reform is to restore political parties to their rightful place as the principal link between voters and policy makers. A campaign featuring extensive televised advertising from the two political parties on behalf of their entire team of candidates would free individual candidates from the burden of anticipating and avoiding attacks on their record, making it more likely that they would tackle rather than sidestep pressing political issues. As in Europe, party advertising would necessarily be less personalized because the message would be an appeal on behalf of hundreds of candidates. By running on their platforms, parties would encourage substantive rather than image-based voting.

No resurgence of parties in American politics appears imminent. The leaders of the campaign reform movement have worked hard to undermine the voice of the party in election campaigns. Just as the national party committees were poised to regain a semblance of influence in presidential campaigns— through their use of soft money—Congress banned soft money. With reforms such as these, the prospects for media-based politics remain excellent.

A more realistic design for reform would reimpose significant public service requirements on the media. Since the 1970s, Congress and the FCC have stripped away the obligations of the broadcast media to contribute to serious, substantive discussions about the issues of the day. In return for unrestricted use of the publicly owned airwaves, broadcasters owe society a minimal level of public affairs programming. Yet, while media revenues from campaign advertising have soared, news coverage of issues has shrunk to negligible proportions. Clearly the media cannot be counted on to voluntarily live up to their civic obligations. Hence it is time for legislation that would require the broadcast media to provide significant amounts of free airtime for all candidates and in a manner that maximizes public exposure. In the case of the presidential election, for example, requiring all major networks to simultaneously air free-media presentations would increase the size of the captive audience.

The revolution in information technology provides the seeds of a more radical solution to the problem of superficial and issueless politics. As tablets and smartphones begin to overshadow the television set as the center of Americans' information universe, politicians and interest groups are regaining the ability to communicate directly with voters. The most recent evidence, summarized in Chapter 5, suggests that voters are increasingly turning to the Web and social media as a source of news coverage, often bypassing conventional media platforms. Facebook now accounts for some 25 percent of referrals to major news sites. Recognizing the vast size of online social networks, candidates, parties, political action committees, and civic groups have all turned to Facebook and Twitter to publicize their candidacies and causes.

The increased use of direct candidate-to-voter communication has the potential to make voter autonomy a more viable reality and will increase the breadth and depth of the policy debate as well as candidates' control over their messages. These gains, significant in themselves, may ultimately be overshadowed by the collective benefit of having a more enthusiastic, informed, and engaged citizenry.

NOTE

1. The Republicans lost only a handful of House seats. However, it is quite remarkable for the party of the incumbent president to pick up House seats in a midterm election—a circumstance that has, in fact, arisen only three times since the Civil War, most recently in 2002.

2

The Press and the Democratic Process

The American System in Comparative Perspective

The news media can, and arguably should, contribute to the democratic process in several important ways. First, the media can provide a forum for candidates and political parties to debate their qualifications for office before a national audience. Second, even when there is no forthcoming election, news programs can contribute to informed citizenship by providing a variety of perspectives on the important issues of the day. Third, acting as agents of citizens, the media can monitor the acts of public officials, thus helping deter them from violating the public trust.

In modern industrialized democracies, the broadcast media reach virtually all adults and provide a national forum for candidates and political parties. From country to country, however, the candidates' practical ability to access this forum varies significantly. In the United States, entry costs are significant barriers; there is no guaranteed minimum level of free access. In most European democracies, access is provided at no cost, and television stations typically provide an equal (or proportionate) amount of free airtime to major political parties shortly before the election.

In the delivery of the electoral forum, the extent to which candidates' messages are unmediated or mediated also varies across countries. American parties and candidates must reach voters through news media that interpret and scrutinize the candidates' rhetoric and actions. In performing this function, the news media have become increasingly hostile and unwilling to permit candidates to speak for themselves. In European countries, by contrast, in part because of free access, party spokespersons have greater ability to reach voters without going through the filter of news organizations; their messages are delivered without accompanying analysis or commentary.

A closely related civic responsibility of the media is to keep the citizenry abreast of public affairs. The news media are expected—again, to a greater or lesser extent, depending on the country—to supply programming that encompasses a broad range of political perspectives and to provide citizens with opportunities for expressing their own viewpoints. This dialogue is viewed as necessary if citizens are to make informed decisions about public issues. As eloquently stated by Peter Goldmark (2001),

> News is for the citizen. The citizen is that dimension of each one of us that is responsible for, contributes to, and benefits from the cooperative endeavor of self-government. The citizen is the basic constituent element of the public dimension of human activity. Without the citizen, there is no self-government, no individual basis for responsibility, choice and values; there is only the state in all its fearful, unchecked power and unaccountability. And without the independent news function, the citizen is starved, paralyzed, neutered, rendered insensate, ineffective, and robotic. (p. 9)

Of course, the democratic ideal of fully informed citizens is rarely realized. Ordinary people are preoccupied with their personal affairs and have little time for keeping abreast of public issues. Indeed, most citizens prefer to watch sitcoms or sports. Naturally, the ability of the media to perform the function of keeping the public informed is compromised when citizens are uninterested. As we show in Chapter 3, the news media cannot be expected to deliver a steady stream of in-depth public affairs programming that no one will watch.

Accordingly, over time, the unrealistic ideal of attentive citizens who scour the media for political information has given way to the notion that democracy can function through "efficient" citizens who either pay attention only to issues of personal importance or rely on a variety of psychological cues, such as a candidate's party affiliation, to compensate for a lack of factual information. A related alternative to the classic ideal of informed citizenship is that citizens do pay attention, but only when the media sound an alarm alerting them to issues that threaten the well-being of society or the nation.

Even if judged by weaker standards, however, the performance of the American media can be questioned. Widespread famine in Ethiopia in the early 1980s went unnoticed until a BBC television report caught the attention of an NBC News producer based in London. The collapse of the American savings and loan industry in the late 1980s was similarly ignored and ultimately cost taxpayers $175 billion in the form of a government bailout. No matter how low one sets the bar for the delivery of public affairs information, the American media do not rate a high grade.

A third important function of the media is to serve as a watchdog on behalf of citizens, scrutinizing the actions of government officials and blowing the whistle when those officials cross the bounds of political propriety. Individual citizens do not have the means to keep abreast of their numerous elected representatives; they delegate this task to the media. Maintaining an adversarial posture toward government is one of the basic principles of modern journalism.

The best evidence of the successful exercise of the watchdog function comes from studies of corruption. Countries with a free press are also characterized by lower levels of corruption. And more generally, the presence of a free press makes government officials more responsive to the needs of ordinary citizens (Besley & Burgess, 2002; Besley & Prat, 2006).

The ability of the news media to deliver on the electoral forum, public sphere, and watchdog functions (or more broadly, civic performance) varies considerably across societies and media systems. Two key factors affect media performance: regulatory policy and market forces. Regulatory policy comes from the applicable regulatory framework. In the United States, the agency charged with regulating the media (the Federal Communications Commission, or FCC) has taken an increasingly laissez-faire approach, arguing that free-market competition is sufficient to ensure the delivery of diverse perspectives on public affairs issues. Most other advanced industrialized democracies, on the other hand—while also moving in the direction of deregulation—have maintained much tighter control over media programming, with the aim of ensuring the delivery of necessary public goods.

Market forces have a significant effect on levels of civic performance. In societies where the broadcast media are predominantly privately owned (as is the case in the United States), competitive market pressures compel media owners to shirk their civic responsibilities. To be profitable, the media must deliver more entertainment than news; and when they do deliver news, they

 IN FOCUS

Three Important Functions of Media in Democratic Societies

- To provide a forum for candidates and political parties to debate their qualifications for office before a national audience
- To contribute to informed citizenship by providing a variety of perspectives on the important issues of the day
- To serve as a watchdog, scrutinizing the actions of government officials on behalf of citizens—most of whom do not have the opportunity to closely follow the actions of politicians and the government

must use formats that are designed to be entertaining rather than to provide information on substantive issues. The alternative to exclusively private ownership is a mixed model consisting of both privately owned and publicly subsidized media. In most European democracies, at least one television network is financed with government revenues. Public subsidies offer broadcasters significant protection from market forces, enhancing their ability to deliver serious (rather than entertaining) news programming. Thus, societies in which media ownership is mixed rather than entirely private are more likely to support informed citizenship.

Both regulatory policy and market forces influence the production of news. The political significance of media programming, however, ultimately depends on the strength of political parties. Countries with strong political parties are less dependent on the news media to provide an electoral forum and guide voters' choices. Parties control the selection of their candidates and can rely on their supporters to cast informed (party-line) votes. In these systems, accordingly, what the media might offer by way of public affairs presentations is likely to be of little consequence to the outcome of elections.

Compared to most other democracies, the United States is characterized by weak political parties. Most notably, party leaders have little say over the selection of candidates. For American voters, candidate and issue considerations compete with party affiliation as important voting cues. Many Americans lack strong ties to a party. In this world of floating voters, electoral outcomes depend especially on what the media offer by way of news programming.

We'll outline the effects of news coverage on voter attitudes and behavior in later chapters; in the rest of this chapter we'll put the American system in perspective by comparing the role of political parties and the media in the United States and Europe. Regarding political parties, we'll focus on American reforms that have undermined the influence of party organization and contrast these with the strong party systems that predominate in Europe. Regarding media systems, we'll compare the American and European models in terms of the extent of government regulation and the structure of media ownership.

MEDIA POLITICS AS THE SUCCESSOR TO PARTY POLITICS

How and why did the mass media become so central to political life in the United States? Certainly the sheer size of the country contributed to the situation. It would be difficult for any presidential candidate to traverse all fifty states to meet and greet each eligible voter in person. Congressional candidates, too, would have a hard time connecting with all their constituents in person; most US senators represent many millions of citizens (over 35 million in California, for example), and the average population of a US House of Representatives district is 710,000 (the US Constitution originally suggested one representative for every 30,000 citizens).

However, the reliance on the mass media is not simply a result of population growth, as candidates relied more on personal campaigning than media until recently, despite the country's size. In the 1896 presidential campaign, for instance, the candidates relied on "retail" politics, crisscrossing the country to deliver hundreds of public speeches to a total audience estimated to exceed five million people" (Iyengar, 1997, p. 143). Certainly the population at that time was smaller and the media options were fewer, but even as late as the 1960s when radio and television were widely available, campaigns relied heavily on teams of volunteers who organized local appearances for the candidate, canvassed neighborhoods, knocked on doors, distributed campaign flyers, and transported people to the polls on election day. What was it, then, that precipitated the switch to media-based campaigns?

The explanation is rooted in the candidate nomination process. As documented by Nelson Polsby (1983), rule changes adopted in the late 1960s weakened the influence of party elites on the selection of candidates and created a void that was filled by the news media. Before 1968, the selection of delegates to the national party conventions, and therefore the nomination of the party's presidential candidate, was controlled by state and local party organizations. Although some states did hold primary elections, the great majority of the convention delegates were selected by the party leadership.

The turmoil that engulfed the 1968 presidential campaign—the unexpected withdrawal of President Johnson as a candidate for nomination, the assassination of Robert Kennedy, the ensuing clashes between supporters of Eugene McCarthy and Hubert Humphrey, and the climactic suppression of the protests outside the convention hall—led the Democratic Party to establish a commission to reform the delegate selection process (for a detailed account, see Polsby, 1983). This commission recommended primary elections as the means of selecting candidates. The widespread adoption of primaries, along with changes in campaign finance regulations after the 1972 Watergate scandal, fundamentally altered the incentives of presidential hopefuls in such a way as to diminish the role of party organizations and increase the importance of the media. By 1972, as Figure 2.1 shows, a majority of the delegates to both party conventions were selected on the basis of primary elections.

FIGURE 2.1

National Convention Delegates Selected in Primary Elections

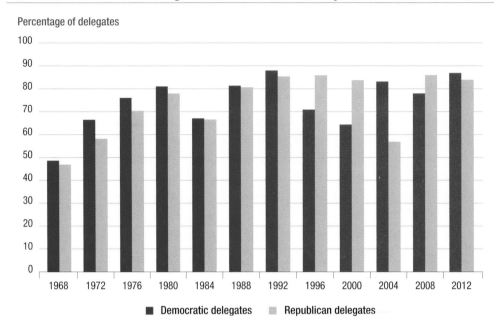

Percentage of delegates

■ Democratic delegates   ▨ Republican delegates

Source: Data from H. W. Stanley & R. G. Niemi. (2010). *Vital statistics on American politics 2009–2010.* Washington, DC: CQ Press. 2012 data compiled from http://www.thegreenpapers.com/P12/events.phtml.

The adoption of primaries meant that, instead of cultivating party activists and leaders, candidates had to appeal directly to the public. At the same time, technological developments—in particular, the widespread proliferation of television—made it possible for candidates to reach statewide and national audiences. By 1963, 91 percent of American households had at least one television set, up from only 45 percent just ten years earlier (see Figure 2.2).

Although radio had been almost as widespread (more than 80 percent of American households had a radio set in 1940) and had also commanded huge audiences, it was no match for television's visual imagery. This new medium allowed its audiences to experience major events (such as the Army–McCarthy hearings and the aftermath of the assassination of President Kennedy, including the on-air shooting of his assassin) in real time, almost as though they were at the scene. It wasn't long before television supplanted radio and newspapers as the public's principal source of information. Politicians could not ignore this new mass medium even if they were inclined to do so, particularly in light of the weakening of political parties and the fact that other social institutions

FIGURE 2.2

TV Penetration, 1950–1978

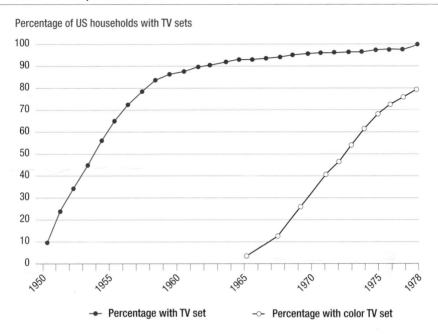

Percentage of US households with TV sets

● Percentage with TV set   ○ Percentage with color TV set

Source: Data from C. Steinberg. (1980). *TV facts*. New York: Facts on File.

(clubs, newspapers, etc.) that had been important in grassroots-type politics were declining at the same time.

The end result of party reform and the rapid spread of television was a shift from party-based campaigns to candidate-based campaigns waged on television. Those who seek elective office covet exposure to large audiences; increasingly it was television that delivered the goods. As the public became entirely dependent on television for political information, candidates altered their campaign strategies to maximize their television exposure.

The most fundamental consequence of party reform was a transformed relationship between candidates and party leaders. Today, after meeting only the most perfunctory requirements, any American citizen can seek a party's nomination for president, senator, or other public office. To qualify for the primary ballot in California, for example, a would-be Republican candidate for president must gather signatures from only 1 percent of the state's registered Republicans (for the Democratic Party, the California signature requirement is 1 percent of registered Democrats, or five hundred—whichever is fewer—in each of the state's congressional districts). In Vermont, a prospective nominee

Media Politics as the Successor to Party Politics　　25

needs the signatures of only a thousand voters of any partisan affiliation. In the primary election system, moreover, any voter who has simply checked a box on a registration form to claim affiliation with a party has a say in selecting the party nominee. In states that have *open* primaries—in which any registered voter can vote in the primary for any party—voters don't even have to be registered with the party to participate in candidate selection. In addition, some states hold *modified open* primaries, in which registered partisans can vote only in their own party's primary, but independents can vote in any primary (in all of these systems, each voter may vote in only one party's primary). Another primary system, long in use in Louisiana and recently put in place by ballot initiatives in Washington and California, is the nonpartisan blanket primary, which consolidates all party primaries onto one ballot. In this system, only the top two vote-getters move on to a general election, regardless of political party, which opens the possibility that candidates of the same political party will face off in the general election.

Although candidates who are not established party figures (and who may lack support from party leaders) may be at some disadvantage when seeking the presidency, they have proven quite capable of winning—or at least seriously competing—for statewide office. Movie star Arnold Schwarzenegger easily won the special election for governor of California in 2003 by using his *Terminator* image to win over California voters. And in 2006, after Pittsburgh Steelers Hall of Fame wide receiver Lynn Swann was endorsed by the Republican state committee, the other Republican candidates for Pennsylvania governor dropped out of the race.

Moreover, because parties now realize that if they want to win in the general election, they are well advised to embrace candidates who are capable of funding and operating an effective media campaign, some party elites may choose to support and endorse candidates who have not played much of a role in the party or whose ideology is inconsistent with that of the party, if they have more resources with which to fight a media battle against their general-election opponent. It is not surprising, therefore, that the 2010 elections produced a freshman class of senators with a median net worth of close to $4 million, while the comparable figure for the freshman House member was more than half a million dollars, according to the Center for Responsive Politics, a Washington-based, nonpartisan think tank that tracks the effect of money on elections and public policy.

In contrast with the American model, party organizations in most other industrialized democracies exercise decisive control over candidate selection. As a result, campaigns are run primarily on the level of the party rather than on the level of the individual candidate. In many cases, candidates are prohibited from making individual appeals separate from the party message and can be sanctioned (or expelled from the party) for doing so.

To maintain rigid control over candidate selection, parties in other democracies impose strict eligibility requirements. In general, only party members can be potential candidates. In most countries party membership represents a much greater political commitment than in the United States. At a minimum, members are required to pay monthly dues to the party organization, but expectations are typically more comprehensive, including representing the party in internal and external organizations and in the community, and campaigning for the party.[1] Often there are additional requirements for candidate eligibility; Hazan (2002) cites the case of the Belgian Socialist Party, which, in addition to requiring party membership for at least five years, specifies that potential candidates must, among other things, have been regular subscribers to the party newspaper and have sent their children to state schools.

Merely meeting the eligibility requirements in no way guarantees selection by the party; would-be candidates still have to survive the selection process. In most democracies, the procedure for selecting candidates is adopted at the discretion of political parties, and the *selectorate* (the group that actually selects the candidate) is much more restrictive than in the United States. In their most inclusive form, selectorates include all registered members of a party (defined, again, in the strict sense, and not in the loose American sense); a slight variation on this model of the selectorate is those parties that require an additional condition to be met by members—such as a minimum length of membership—before they become eligible to participate in the selection of party candidates. However, cases of even more exclusive selectorates—consisting of small party committees—are common, as are *multistage* systems, in which a small body either preselects a group of candidates (from which a broader selectorate, consisting of all party members, selects one) or selects from candidates nominated by a broader selectorate. In many countries (including Australia, Canada, France, Germany, Italy, Japan, and the United Kingdom), some political parties give their national leaders the power to veto or otherwise alter the roster of candidates selected by a broader selectorate.

The degree of party control over candidate selection also depends on the electoral system. Whereas the United States employs a single-member-district plurality voting system[2] (in which whoever wins the most votes in a district wins the office), many other countries use multimember-district and proportional representation systems in which parties compete for multiple seats within a single district and the number of seats each party wins is allocated in proportion to their share of the vote. In the common *closed party list* version of proportional representation, parties determine the order in which the candidates are listed on the ballot, and the voter simply casts a vote for the party. For most major parties, candidates appearing at the top of the list are assured election, and those at the bottom have little chance of winning. Candidates who lose favor with the party leadership may find themselves consigned to the bottom of the candidate list.

Thus, in countries with strong parties, it is important for candidates to defer to party leaders. Accordingly, political campaigns in European and other democracies—and media coverage thereof—are more party oriented than are campaigns in the United States. It is true that the media are becoming increasingly important in campaigns around the world, that there is a growing global cadre of political professionals, and that political parties in more and more countries are adopting American-style campaign techniques. Indeed, there is mounting concern in many European countries about the mediatization or Americanization of political campaigns—the increasing emphasis on party leaders rather than party policies, for example. Nonetheless, traditional methods of campaigning—such as door-to-door canvassing by candidates and party activists—still play a significant role in other industrialized democracies.[3] And perhaps more important, party-centered campaigns are more likely to generate issue-focused news coverage by the media, because campaign events are themselves more issue oriented (such as the release of a party manifesto in Ireland, as opposed to the release of a new attack ad in the United States).

Although weak political parties and universal access to media were both necessary to the development of media-based politics in the United States, they do not alone explain the civic performance of American news organizations. In Chapters 3 and 4 we will describe how a combination of professional norms and economic pressures have severely limited candidates' access to media audiences, constrained both the sheer amount and the range of perspectives represented in news programs, and contributed to the weakening of watchdog journalism. But before we examine the supply and content of news programming, let's take a moment to put the American media system in some comparative perspective.

PATTERNS OF MEDIA OWNERSHIP AND REGULATION

American media differ from most other media systems in two fundamental respects: their autonomy from government regulation and the scope of private ownership. In relation to the media in most other democracies, US media are

IN FOCUS

What's Different about American Media?

- **More private ownership.** Media entities in the United States, including broadcast media, are almost entirely privately owned and operated; most other democracies have at least one government-funded broadcast network.
- **Less regulation.** The regulatory structure governing the behavior of American media is considerably more lax than that in most other democracies.

much less subject to government regulation and are almost entirely privately owned. These differences hold the key to explaining why American media are less likely to make good on their civic obligations.

The structure of the media industry—in particular, whether media are owned and operated by government organizations or by private enterprises—has a major impact on the supply of news because government-subsidized media outlets are typically required (by statute) to provide minimal levels of public affairs content, whereas privately owned outlets are generally free to do as they please. Although the issue of public versus private ownership generally applies only to broadcast media, other regulations governing aspects of ownership apply to all forms of media. In the case of election coverage, for example, explicit regulations may directly spell out the subject matter to be covered, as well as when and where the coverage is to occur.

PUBLIC VERSUS COMMERCIAL OWNERSHIP OF BROADCAST MEDIA

There are three models of ownership of broadcast media: purely public, mixed, and purely commercial. The rationale for publicly owned television (and radio) is that the electromagnetic spectrum, as a scarce public resource, must be utilized for the public good.[4] The concept of public service broadcasting was first put into practice in the United Kingdom with the establishment of the British Broadcasting Corporation (BBC) in 1927 and was soon emulated in some form by most democracies in western Europe and beyond. In most cases, this entailed the creation of a state-owned broadcasting system that functioned either as a monopoly or as a dominant broadcaster. Typically, the public broadcasting network was financed from radio or television license fees or taxes.

Although these publicly owned media entities are generally free from political interference, they are expected to follow certain principles (the exact details of which vary by country), such as providing universal service and informative, educational, and diverse programming.

In 1979, all but three countries in Europe had monopolistic public television channels; and two of the three that did not (Great Britain and Italy) had mixed systems, with both publicly owned and commercial television channels. By 1997, however, as a result of significant deregulation across Europe, only three countries had exclusively public-sector television markets. Still, even in the now dominant mixed model, public television channels enjoy large audience shares. In fifteen of the seventeen European Union countries with mixed-ownership television markets, the public television channels hold the number one market spot and capture larger audience shares than would be expected from the number of commercial channels with which they compete. The audience share enjoyed by public television in Europe ranges from a low of 23 percent for Spain to a high of 67 percent in Denmark (see Figure 2.3).

In return for government financing, public broadcasters are required to provide sustained levels of public affairs programming, and to represent a diversity of regions, cultures, and viewpoints. Sweden's STV (Sveriges Television), for example, is "obliged to carry cultural and quality programming, and 55% of its

FIGURE 2.3

Public Broadcasters' Audience Share by Country

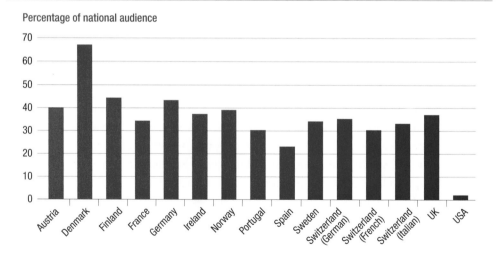

Source: European Audiovisual Observatory (2010). *Yearbook 2010, Volume 1: Television in 36 European States.* Strasbourg, France. I am grateful to Dr. Jose Santana Pereira for making the data available.

programming must be produced regionally outside Stockholm" (Williams, 2003, p. 39). Thus, public broadcasters in Europe tend to produce higher quantities of public affairs programs (which, as we'll discuss, are of higher quality than most programs found on commercial television worldwide). These programs reach large audiences; the early localized evening newscast on BBC ONE in the United Kingdom, for instance, attracts approximately 30 percent of the television audience. European audiences are not disinclined to watch serious news.

~~Unlike the European model~~, the American television market is dominated by commercial broadcasters. Instead of adopting public ownership, US telecommunications policy has followed a trusteeship approach, by which access to the public resource of the spectrum was granted to those who pledged to act in the "public interest, convenience, and necessity."[6] The FCC is the agency responsible for setting and enforcing the requirements that broadcasters must follow to meet that public interest standard.

Initially the FCC set fairly high standards for broadcasters' public interest obligations, requiring them, for example, to "promote the discussion of public issues, serve minority interests, and eliminate superfluous advertising" (Zechowski, n.d.). These standards were quickly abandoned, however, because broadcasters considered them an undue economic burden. The regulations that followed were less stringent and not strictly enforced, and most have since been abandoned.

Contrary to appearances, the United States does not fit a purely commercial model. Congress established the Public Broadcasting Service (PBS) in 1967. However, most PBS funding comes from private corporations and individual donors, and even the small portion of its funding that does come from the government is frequently under threat for political reasons (most often from Republicans in Congress who accuse PBS of displaying a liberal bias). In stark contrast to European public broadcasters, as Figure 2.3 reveals, PBS reaches only 2 percent of the American television audience.

Between 1997 and 2007, the public service networks in Belgium, the United Kingdom, Norway, and Sweden aired an average of eighty-four minutes a day of news and current affairs during prime time (7:00 PM to 10:00 PM), whereas PBS in the United States aired just forty-seven minutes, opting instead to broadcast shows like *Masterpiece Theatre* or fine arts performances (see Figure 2.4). Even commercial television networks in European countries

FIGURE 2.4

Public Affairs Programming during Prime Time

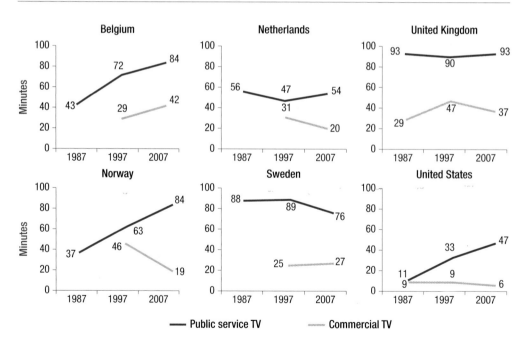

Source: Data from T. Aalberg, P. van Aelst, & J. Curran. (2010). Media systems and the political information environment: A cross-national comparison. *The International Journal of Press/Politics, 15*(3), 255–271.

Note: Average minutes per day devoted to news and current affairs during prime time 7:00 PM to 10:00 PM among public service TV and commercial TV, 1987–2007.

broadcast more than 4 times as much public affairs programming during prime time than their United States counterparts, with an average of twenty-five minutes per day during prime time in Belgium, the Netherlands, the United Kingdom, Norway, and Sweden, and six minutes per day during prime time in the United States. Notice, however, that the average public TV–commercial TV gap in the amount of time devoted to public affairs programming has increased in many of these countries, with commercial television devoting fewer minutes to such programming in the Netherlands, the United Kingdom, Norway, and the United States in 2007 than in 1997, and public service television devoting more time to current affairs programming during prime time in Belgium, the Netherlands, the United Kingdom, Norway, and the United States.

FIGURE 2.5

GDP of Countries Receiving Disproportionate Attention in the News

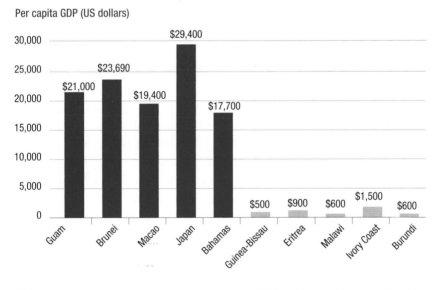

Per capita GDP (US dollars)

■ Countries receiving proportionately more attention from CNN than from BBC   ▦ Countries receiving proportionately more attention from BBC than from CNN

Source: CNN and BBC data from E. Zuckerman. (2003, August). *Global attention profiles: A working paper—First steps towards a quantitative approach to the study of media attention.* Cambridge, MA: Harvard Law School, Berkman Center for Internet and Society. Retrieved March 10, 2005, from the Global Attention Profiles website: http://h2odev.law.harvard .edu/ezuckerman/paper.pdf. GDP data from *The World Factbook.* (2005). Retrieved May 17, 2005, from the CIA website: www.cia.gov/cia/publications/factbook.

Note: Comparison based on multiple years of material on the websites of CNN and BBC, current as of October 2, 2004. The top five countries receiving the most disproportionate attention from each network are included here (only countries that had at least one reference from each network are included).

Not only do public broadcasting systems supply a greater quantity of news programming, but they also produce more substantive, issue-oriented programming than commercial stations do. For example, Krüger (1996) found that 37 percent of the news reports broadcast on the three commercial television channels in Germany could be categorized as *infotainment* (what he called "boulevard" news) compared to just 7 percent on the two public channels. Similarly, a study by Canninga (1994, as cited in Brants, 1998) found that news items on commercial television news in the Netherlands and Belgium were shorter than those on public channels.

Another difference between news programming on public and commercial television concerns the more limited geographic reach of the latter. In his analysis of the proportion of national versus international news in the news broadcasts of sixteen channels across eight countries, Heinderyckx (1993) focused mainly on public television channels. However, the two commercial channels that he examined (French TF1 and Belgian VTM) had slightly lower proportions of international news (39 and 44 percent, respectively) than the average (47 percent) for the public channels.

The restricted reach of international news in the offerings of commercial networks is also evident in a more recent study by Zuckerman (2003), which analyzed the frequency of references to various countries on the websites of major television news outlets (working on the reasonable premise that website stories were an adequate indication of the attention given to those countries by each news organization). This study found that the best predictor of the sheer amount of CNN coverage accorded to any particular country was that country's level of economic development (as measured by GDP; see Figure 2.5). Wealthy countries received more attention from CNN than poor countries. The best predictor of BBC coverage, on the other hand, was the country's population, suggesting a more broad-based allocation of attention to international affairs on the part of the BBC.

These differences in the availability of news between the United States and most European countries have important implications for democracy. Most normative models of democracy depend on an informed citizenry, and it is the news media's responsibility to provide costless information. Rather than upholding their civic duty, owners of American media value ratings and the bottom line first.

The connection between a media system's priorities and levels of public knowledge become apparent when average knowledge levels between countries are compared. As seen in Figure 2.6, Americans compete on level terms with their European counterparts only when it comes to domestic *soft news*—for

FIGURE 2.6

Knowledge of Hard and Soft News in Domestic and International Domains

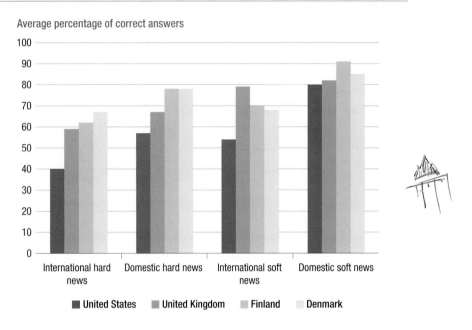

Source: Data from J. Curran, S. Iyengar, A. B. Lund, & I. Salovaara-Moring. 2009. "Media system, public knowledge and democracy." *European Journal of Communication, 24*(1), 5–26.

example, facts about American celebrities. When it comes to knowing about both international and domestic *hard news* as well as international soft news, Americans lag well behind.

An egalitarian society is another important benchmark for democracy, and disparate levels of public knowledge between advantaged and disadvantaged groups translate into disparate levels of political power. In general, differences in hard news knowledge associated with education, income, and ethnicity are much greater in the United States than in European countries. Iyengar and Curran (2009) explain,

> In those societies where the media provide ample coverage of hard news and where the schedule of news programming is adjusted so as to capture the attention of even relatively inattentive citizens, easy access to information can compensate for inadequate motivation. In the Scandinavian countries of Denmark and Finland, for instance, where news bulletins air regularly during

the peak television viewing periods (such as just before a nationally televised sporting event), a sufficient number of citizens who are not especially interested in politics nonetheless find themselves in the path of news reports, thus allowing them to acquire information. Thus, in countries where news programming is more substantive and the delivery of news is scheduled to capture a substantial "inadvertent" audience, we observe a significant narrowing of the traditional knowledge gap. It is in this sense that the supply of news can contribute to civic competence.

Although the evidence is compelling that public television delivers more substantive and global programming than commercial television does, there are shortcomings to the mixed-ownership broadcasting systems common in European industrialized democracies. For example, many Britons object to the mandatory license fee that is imposed on all owners of television sets in the United Kingdom to fund the BBC. Furthermore, the share of the audience reached by public broadcasters in mixed-ownership systems—though still respectable, as noted already—is dropping in response to increased commercial offerings and the proliferation of satellite and cable programming. Some evidence suggests, moreover, that programming quality on public television channels is declining because of the increased competition from commercial channels.

In summary, the structure of media ownership affects news programming. In industrialized democracies where public ownership of at least some television channels is the norm, public affairs programming is more extensive than is the case in the almost purely privately held American media market.

ALTERNATIVE APPROACHES TO MEDIA REGULATION

In addition to the ownership question, different regulatory frameworks have important consequences for the delivery of news programming generally, and for the diversity of political perspectives represented in program content specifically. This is true for broadcast media as well as print media, and we will deal with each in turn.

BROADCAST MEDIA

Although the FCC in its early years issued strict (though not always strictly enforced) requirements for public affairs programming by its licensees, most of these no longer apply. From the beginning, broadcasters regularly challenged the FCC regulations as a violation of their First Amendment guarantees of free speech, but the courts generally ruled in favor of the public trustee basis of broadcast regulations. Eventually, ideological change at the FCC—not any judicial mandate—led to weakening of the public service requirements. Under pressure from President Reagan, the FCC adopted a marketplace approach to the media. In essence, the FCC held that the mere existence of competitive media outlets was sufficient to serve the public interest, making it unnecessary to regulate programming.

The scope of the policy shift was substantial. In 1960, the FCC had published a list of the fourteen major elements necessary to serve the public interest. The list included community-oriented programming, political broadcasts, and public affairs and news programs. In 1976, the FCC issued more-precise standards: stations were required to air at least 5 percent local programming, 5 percent informational programming (defined as news and public affairs), and an additional 10 percent nonentertainment programming. In 1984 the FCC abandoned these requirements in favor of looser guidelines, which stated that it was sufficient for stations to "air some programming that meets the community's needs" (Bishop & Hakanen, 2002, p. 264).

In the aftermath of deregulation, television stations increased their amount of local news programming both because local news attracted large audiences (see Chapter 3) and because this sort of programming proved inexpensive to produce. The typical local newscast, however, lacks meaningful public affairs content.[7] Moreover, local news replaced other forms of public affairs programming. For example, the number of hours per week devoted to nonnews public affairs programming across all TV channels in the Philadelphia market dropped from 57.5 in 1976 (before deregulation) to 28.2 in 1985 (after deregulation), and that number fell even further, to 24, in 1997. Nevertheless, the provision of local news has become increasingly important in the FCC's definition of the public interest standard.

One of the most important shifts in FCC policy eased the restrictions on concentration of ownership. The National TV and Local Radio Ownership Rules, established in 1941, limited the number of television stations that could be owned by a single entity to seven nationwide, only five of which could be VHF stations (the most common commercial format), and set a similar limit on the number of radio stations. The Dual TV Network Rule, issued in 1946, prohibited any major network from buying another major network, and the Local TV Multiple Ownership Rule (adopted in 1964) limited a broadcaster to just one local station per market, unless there were more than eight stations in that market. Further regulations were implemented in the 1970s limiting cross-ownership of TV stations, radio stations, and newspapers in the same market.

Over time, the multiple-ownership restrictions have been removed. In 1985, the FCC raised the maximum number of TV stations that could be owned by any single entity from seven to twelve. The Telecommunications Act of 1996 further eased the rules by allowing ownership of multiple TV stations, as long as the combined audience of the stations amounted to less than 35 percent of the population. In 2003, the FCC proposed to eliminate all restrictions on cross-ownership within a single market, as long as that market had nine or more TV stations, and to further raise the TV ownership cap from 35 to 45 percent, eventually phasing out TV ownership restrictions altogether. However, this FCC proposal was overturned by a series of court rulings that reinstated the previous ownership limitations. The FCC weakened the media ownership rules again in 2007 by eliminating a cross-ownership statute that prohibited a single company from owning both a newspaper and a television or radio station in the same market.

Quite predictably, the relaxation of ownership restrictions has increased the holdings of the largest owners. As Figure 2.7 shows, the top ten local television station companies increased their combined station ownership almost

FIGURE 2.7

Increasing Concentration of TV Station Ownership

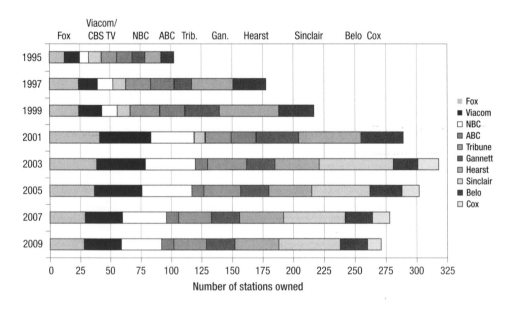

Source: Pew Project for Excellence in Journalism. (2010). *The state of the news media: An annual report on American journalism.*

Chapter 2 | The Press and the Democratic Process

threefold, from 104 stations in 1995 to 271 stations in 2009. Their combined revenue doubled during the same period.

The concentration of media ownership in the United States extends well beyond television stations. Large multinational corporations own all categories of media. Rupert Murdoch's News Corporation, for example, currently owns a large number of US cable networks as well as the terrestrial Fox network, thirty-four Fox-affiliated stations, three movie studios, the Fox Sports Radio network, the *Wall Street Journal* and the *New York Post* newspapers, and several magazines and major publishing houses. Univision, a relative newcomer to the scene, already holds a virtual monopoly on Spanish-language television, owning sixty-three local television stations and over twelve hundred cable affiliates in the United States. As noted by the authors of the Project for Excellence in Journalism (2004) report:

> In radio, the top twenty companies operate more than 20 percent of all the radio stations in the country; one, Clear Channel, dominates, operating stations in 191 of the 289 Arbitron-rated markets. In local television, the ten biggest companies own 30 percent of all television stations reaching 85 percent of all television households in the United States. In network television, the owners are all giant corporations.

With so much of the industry controlled by so few, there are good reasons for concern about the supply and quality of news, and about the diversity of voices represented in media programming. According to one well-known critic of American media, "News reporting and commentary controlled by mainstream media companies are the most politically narrow in the democratic world" (Bagdikian, 2000, p. xii).

Research into the effects of ownership on news programming confirms the suspicion that company size is inversely related to quality journalism—that is, the larger the company, the lower the quality. In a comprehensive five-year study of broadcast news quality, the Project for Excellence in Journalism (2003) found that stations owned by small companies (with holdings of three or fewer stations) were 2.5 times more likely to earn an A grade for news quality than were stations owned by the twenty-five largest companies.[8]

In addition to relaxing ownership rules, the FCC has weakened directives that aim to increase the diversity of perspective in news content. The Fairness Doctrine, which required broadcasters to present opposing sides on controversial issues, was repealed in 1987 after broadcasters mounted legal challenges against it. (Other changes in regulation of content, specifically those that deal

The Rise of Comcast

Comcast was founded in 1963 as a cable television provider with 1,200 subscribers. In 1988, the company acquired Storer Communications and became the fifth-largest cable provider in America. Through further acquisitions in the 1990s, the company became a major provider of broadband Internet. By 2002, Comcast had more than 20 million cable subscribers and 6 million high-speed Internet customers. In 2011, the company acquired NBC Universal from General Electric (along with the cable networks controlled by NBC, including Bravo, CNBC, MSNBC, and Telemundo), making it the single largest source of television programming in the country. The FCC and Justice Department agreed to the merger but imposed several conditions, including that Comcast give up its management of Hulu, a major video-sharing site. Comcast also committed to providing greater local news coverage and expanded Spanish-language programming. In 2014, the company announced plans to acquire Time Warner. If approved by regulators, this merger would create a single telecommunications giant with more than 30 percent of the cable market (33 million subscribers) and nearly as many broadband users. The sheer size of the company would grant it considerable leverage over television production companies in determining which programs are streamed on mobile devices and laptops; its size would also provide Comcast with the market power to set rates for cable-Internet access.

with candidate access to the airwaves, will be discussed in more detail later in the chapter.)

In the wake of elimination of the Fairness Doctrine, broadcasts with a partisan slant have increased in frequency and scope. Corporate interests have begun to exert influence over news programming in a number of subtle ways, such as by encouraging journalists not to pursue stories that reflect poorly on their parent corporations or by imposing programming in keeping with their political preferences. In a recent example, the Sinclair Broadcast Group, whose top executives were major contributors to the Bush 2004 presidential campaign, ordered its sixty-two television stations (which have a combined reach of 24 percent of the national audience) to preempt their regular programming to broadcast an anti-Kerry documentary film a few days before the 2004 presidential election.[9] Sinclair had previously ordered its ABC-affiliate stations not to air an episode (which they denounced as political) of the regular ABC program *Nightline* in which Ted Koppel read the names of all American military personnel killed in Iraq. In similar incidents, the Walt Disney Company refused to distribute Michael Moore's *Fahrenheit 9/11*, and CBS refused to air an anti-Bush ad made by MoveOn.org during the Super Bowl. Thus, media owners increasingly feel free to base programming decisions on their political interests.

Overall, it appears that concern about the impact of deregulation on the quantity and quality of public affairs programming made available to the American public is not misplaced. Clearly, the FCC has transformed American telecommunications policy in ways that significantly decrease the number of voices that have access to the market.

The American experience is hardly unique in this regard; the trend toward broadcast deregulation is global. In Europe, too, ownership rules have been considerably relaxed in recent years, although in most European countries the relaxed regulations are still stronger than those in the United States. In Germany, for example, ownership of television stations is capped at a combined 30 percent of the national audience. In France, no single entity can exercise more than 49 percent control in a company that owns a national television network, with ownership being limited to 15 percent in a second such company, and 5 percent in a third. Furthermore, the presence of public television and radio stations in these countries to some extent counteracts the overall effects of ownership deregulation.

Unlike the American model, the regulatory frameworks of most European countries (and other democracies) take the public service obligations of the media seriously. These countries impose strict programming requirements that apply even to their commercial broadcasters. All European Union countries, for example, have "right-of-reply" laws, which require broadcasters to give people criticized in the media "a right of access to answer criticisms against them" (Hallin & Mancini, 2004, p. 122). In Germany, an internal agreement among all the German states requires any television broadcaster with at least a 10 percent market share to allocate a minimum of 260 minutes of airtime per week to minor political parties. Even in the United Kingdom—which has been criticized for following the US model and dismantling its media regulations in recent years—both the publicly funded BBC and the commercial television stations operate under formal requirements for impartiality and balance in news programming.

Thus, despite the privatization of their broadcast markets, European governments continue to see broadcasting "not simply as a private commercial enterprise but as a social institution for which the state has an important responsibility" (Hallin & Mancini, 2004, p. 161). That responsibility is to ensure that privately owned broadcast outlets, in response to powerful market forces, do not underproduce public affairs programming. This same logic, as we'll see next, is largely mirrored in the regulation of print media.

PRINT MEDIA

In the United States and elsewhere, the print media have never been subject to the same level of regulation as the broadcast media, because the principal rationale for government regulation of broadcasting—that the airwaves are a scarce and publicly owned resource—does not apply to print. Beyond libel laws, regulation of newspaper content has been close to nonexistent. In fact, regulation of American print media has been almost entirely limited to the area of ownership, where the government has applied antitrust laws to promote competition.

Antitrust legislation has been invoked to block the acquisition of one newspaper by another in cases where it has been considered that such mergers or acquisitions would lead to a decrease in competition in the media market, thus potentially harming consumers. In *United States v. Times Mirror Co.* (a case decided in 1967), for example, the court blocked the acquisition of the *San Bernardino County Sun* by the larger *Los Angeles Times* on the basis of the government's argument that the deal would harm competition. Antitrust laws have also been used to prevent newspaper companies from taking anticompetitive measures, such as employing predatory pricing, in which a company prices its product "below cost, usually to run another firm out of business, with the plan of making up the losses later through higher prices" (Lacy & Simon, 1993, p. 200).

The occasional application of antitrust laws has had little impact on the general trend toward concentration of ownership. The lack of effect is partly because the laws have not been rigorously enforced and partly because Congress has exempted newspapers from antitrust provisions in certain situations.[10] Over the years, the newspaper industry has become one of the most monopolistic markets in the American economy.

Historically, American newspaper markets developed on a local level, while those in other Western democracies (most of which are considerably smaller than the United States) developed on a national scale. Only a handful of American newspapers—such as *USA Today* and the *Wall Street Journal*—reach a level of distribution that might be described as national; the vast majority are distributed locally. Because the total readership in local markets is small, American newspapers cannot subdivide the market into narrower segments. The importance of advertising to the newspaper industry adds further impetus to reduced competition. Local advertisers, the major source of revenue for newspaper owners, benefit from monopolistic newspaper markets because they reduce the cost per reader. Thus economic pressures push toward a single newspaper per local market with a catchall audience.

The combination of the inherent tendency toward monopoly in newspaper markets and the lack of a strict regulatory framework (along with the development of the Internet, a factor we discuss in Chapter 5) has had predictable consequences—namely, a significant drop in competition. Between 1910 and 2008, the number of daily newspapers fell from 2,202 to 1,408. As Figure 2.8 shows, the percent of cities with competing daily newspapers dropped sharply during the same period, from 43 in 1920 to just 2 in 1986. Recent technological changes coupled with a poor economy have sounded the death knell for many newspapers. Companies that publish the *Chicago Tribune, Los Angeles Times, Baltimore Sun, Philadelphia Inquirer, Chicago Sun-Times, and Star Tribune* of Minneapolis have declared bankruptcy. The *Seattle Post-Intelligencer* and the *Christian Science Monitor* have stopped publishing a printed daily and have moved to a Web-only format.

FIGURE 2.8

The Decline of Competition among Daily Newspapers in US Cities, 1880–1986

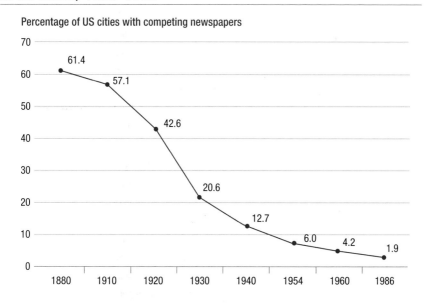

Percentage of US cities with competing newspapers

Source: Data from D. C. Hallin & P. Mancini. (2004). *Comparing media systems: Three models of media and politics.* Cambridge, England: Cambridge University Press.

Only limited research has investigated the effects of ownership concentration on the content of newspapers, and the pattern of results to date is inconsistent. However, the prima facie evidence suggests that the sheer number of voices being represented in the newspaper marketplace has been reduced.

In general, regulation of the print media in Europe has not been as strong as that of the broadcast media. However, some European countries have ownership requirements substantially stricter than those in the United States. In France, for example, a company may not acquire a new publication if the acquisition will push the total daily circulation of all its publications over the 30 percent mark.

An even starker difference between the American and European approaches to print media regulation is the proactive support for diversity in the newspaper market that is provided by European governments, many of which grant direct subsidies to newspapers with the specific aim of increasing diversity. These subsidies seem to have slowed anticompetitive pressures in the European newspaper market. Host (1999, cited in Hallin & Mancini, 2004) estimates, for example, that without subsidies, not a single Norwegian city would have more than one newspaper; with the subsidies, half the cities that had more than one paper in 1972 still had more than one in 1999. It is important to note that, as in the case of public broadcasting, the evidence indicates that newspapers receiving public subsidies are no less likely to play the watchdog role than are newspapers receiving no such subsidies.

Another explanation for the greater competitiveness of European print media markets is the willingness of European newspapers to adopt *self-regulation* practices. In many European countries, there exist strong, institutionalized, self-regulatory bodies that monitor content, and investigate and respond to complaints. These agencies have the power to develop and enforce codes of press ethics. Although some US newspapers have appointed public editors or ombudsmen, there is no formalized interorganizational agency to regulate behavior or serve as a public forum for concerns about the press. To date, American news organizations have proved reluctant to submit their content to outside review.

In sum, although newspapers are generally subject to less regulation than broadcast media in both the United States and in Europe, the same pattern that holds for broadcasting—stronger regulatory frameworks in Europe aimed at promoting the public good—also applies to the print media. As we'll discuss in the next section, this pattern is repeated in the cross-national rules governing media coverage of campaigns and elections.

REGULATING THE NEWS MEDIA'S COVERAGE OF CAMPAIGNS

As is the case with public affairs programming more generally, the regulatory treatment of the news media has a significant impact on their ability to fulfill the function of providing an electoral forum. And once again, the United States falls short of other industrialized democracies in establishing a regulatory framework that ensures candidate and voter access to the electoral forum.

The equal-time and equal-access rule, which was intended to ensure that the public would have roughly equal opportunity to encounter the perspectives of opposing political candidates (by requiring radio and television stations to treat candidates equally when providing them airtime), have been rendered meaningless because the FCC now interprets the rule as requiring broadcasters only to make available time to candidates on equal terms, whatever those terms may be.[11] Thus whenever a candidate cannot afford to buy the same amount of ad time on a given station as the opponent can (as is often the case for challengers running against congressional incumbents), the rule does not require the station to broadcast the lesser-funded candidate's advertisements for free. The public is effectively denied the opportunity to learn about underfinanced candidates.

In other industrialized democracies, by contrast, access to the electoral forum is not contingent on ability to pay. In every industrialized member of the Organisation for Economic Co-operation and Development (OECD) *other than the United States*, political parties are granted blocks of free airtime for "party political broadcasts" during campaigns. The allocation of airtime is based on an objective formula that differs depending on the country. In the United Kingdom, for instance, the amount of airtime is based on the number of candidates being fielded by each party; in France, broadcasters are obliged to grant equal airtime to candidates, regardless of their prominence or electoral strength. This means that in other democracies, smaller parties, which typically do not have the financial resources available to major parties, are not disadvantaged and still have the opportunity to reach a wide audience through the mass media.

In some instances (such as in the United Kingdom), the party election broadcasts are required to be carried not just by public channels, but also by commercial stations. Moreover, all five British television networks are required to air the party election broadcasts on the same day (although not at the same time), thus increasing the size of the audience. In 2001, 58 percent of the respondents in a British panel survey reported that they had seen at least one party election broadcast, and 37 percent said they had seen one from each of the three major parties. The numbers dropped in 2010, however: 50 percent of the British public said they saw at least one party broadcast, and 19 percent said they saw broadcasts from all three parties.

Not only are political parties guaranteed free airtime, but many countries (including the United Kingdom, France, Ireland, Belgium, Denmark, Spain, and Switzerland) prohibit candidates and parties from advertising on television. However, the European Court of Human Rights recently ruled that the ban on political advertising in Norway is a violation of the EU Charter of Fundamental Rights, and legal experts question whether bans in other countries will withstand court challenges as well. There is a stark contrast between American-style media campaigning and the campaigning in countries with free party broadcasts. Setting aside candidates' attempts to influence the content of news in their favor, broadcast campaigning in the United States consists almost entirely of thirty-second paid television ads. In countries with free election broadcasts, in contrast, the blocks of time for campaign messages tend to be considerably longer.

Video
Archive
2.1
The Ameri-
canization of
British Party
Election
Broadcasts

In the United Kingdom in 2001, for example, parties could choose between time slots of two minutes and forty seconds, three minutes and forty seconds, or four minutes and forty seconds. Indeed, British party election broadcasts would seem quite strange to an American audience. They range from plain, straightforward, no-frills presentations—typically featuring the party leader speaking directly into the camera—to more amusing, offbeat presentations from well-known comedians such as John Cleese. Over time, however, as illustrated in Video Archive 2.1, the parties have increasingly resorted to American-style campaign commercials that focus on image and style rather than on the issues.

It is worth noting that election-time media regulations in other democracies apply to more than just broadcast advertising. Many countries regulate the balance of content within television newscasts and election-related special programs. In France, for example, news programs are required to ensure equality between the amount of airtime allocated to members of the government and the amount allocated to opposition parties. In the United Kingdom, all broadcasters (commercial and public) are required to be impartial in their election coverage and to provide for "balance in viewpoints" (McNicholas & Ward, 2004, p. 156). These regulations contrast sharply with the situation in the United States, where "all news outlets, whatever their means of distribution, may cover elections in any way they deem appropriate" (Kaid & Jones, 2004, p. 33).

Candidates and parties in European democracies are thus guaranteed access to the public, and the public, in turn, is guaranteed the opportunity to learn about the full range of available choices. Furthermore, by eliminating the need for candidates to raise money to purchase airtime, the European model allows candidates to focus on more traditional, grassroots forms of campaigning that strengthen, rather than weaken, the role of political parties. And even in the case of broadcast campaigning, the length of the party political broadcasts provides a greater opportunity for candidates to provide important and substantive information to the public, at least in comparison with what is made available in the average thirty-second American political advertisement.

CONCLUSION

It is clear that there are two conditions under which news media in democratic societies are more likely to make good on their civic responsibilities. The first is a more stringent regulatory framework that requires the media to provide a certain level of public affairs programming. This is the approach adopted in most European democracies, and the evidence shows that European media typically deliver a more robust version of the public forum than that realized in the American market-based approach. Although the laissez-faire approach to media regulation is gaining influence around the world, most industrialized democracies persist in viewing the media in general, and broadcasting in particular, as "an institution whose influence on society is too great to be left under the control of private interests and that must be run under the authority of the state as a representative of the general interest" (Hallin & Mancini, 2004).

The second key condition for helping ensure that the media meet their civic responsibilities is to afford broadcasters some protection from the ravages of the market. Publicly funded television networks have the necessary cushion to deliver a steady flow of substantive, hard news; they need not constantly look at their market share when making programming decisions. Societies in which public television reaches a significant share of the audience are thus more likely to have relatively well-informed and engaged electorates.

Neither the regulatory framework nor market protection conditions hold in the United States. It is not surprising, then, that American media tend to fall short of expectations; they generally deliver programming that is more entertaining than informative, and instead of acting as a restraint on the actions of government, they frequently toe the official line. The next two chapters will address the weaknesses of contemporary American journalism. In Chapter 3 we'll show how market forces and the norms of professional journalism have combined to undermine the quality of news programming. In Chapter 4 we'll analyze the factors that have undermined the media's ability to play the role of watchdog.

SUMMARY

1. Mass media in democratic societies serve three important functions:
    - Providing an electoral forum for candidates and political parties to debate their qualifications for office before a national audience.
    - Contributing to informed citizenship by providing a variety of perspectives on the important issues of the day (the public sphere function).
    - Serving as a watchdog scrutinizing the actions of government officials on behalf of citizens.
2. The centrality of the media's role in the political process depends on universal access to media and on the relative strength of other political institutions—political parties in particular.
3. The media became central to US politics in the 1960s, at a time when major changes in the candidate nomination process were weakening political parties. These changes were made possible by the almost universal spread of television occurring at the same time.
4. The American media system (particularly with respect to broadcast media) differs from that of most other industrialized democracies in two respects:
    - It is almost entirely privately owned.
    - Its regulation is relatively weak.
5. Print media, in the United States and elsewhere, have never been subject to the same level of government control as broadcast media.
6. The United States also has weaker regulatory standards governing the coverage of elections. Whereas politicians in the United States must purchase access to the broadcast media (usually in the form of thirty-second campaign commercials), many other democracies grant free airtime to candidates in the run up to elections. Some also have rules governing the balance of viewpoints presented in news during political campaigns.

FURTHER READINGS

Aalberg, T., van Aelst, P., & Curran, J. (2010). Media systems and the political information environment: A cross-national comparison. *The International Journal of Press/Politics, 15*(3), 255–271.

Bagdikian, B. H. (2000). *The media monopoly* (6th ed.). Boston: Beacon.

Bennett, W. L. (2003). The burglar alarm that just keeps ringing: A response to Zaller. *Political Communication, 20*, 131–138.

Besley, T., & R. Burgess. (2002). The political economy of government accountability: Theory and evidence from India. *Quarterly Journal of Economics, 117,* 1415–1451.

Besley, T., & A. Prat. (2006). Handcuffs for the grabbing hand? Media capture and government accountability. *American Economic Review, 96*, 720–736.

Curran, J., Iyengar, S., Lund, A. B., & Salovaara-Moring, I. (2009). Media system, public knowledge and democracy. *European Journal of Communication, 24*(1), 5–26.

Dalton, R. J., & Wattenberg, M. P. (2001). *Parties without partisans: Political change in advanced industrial democracies.* New York: Oxford University Press.

Djankov, S., McLiesh, C., Nenova, T., & Shleifer, A. (2001, June). *Who owns the media?* (Working Paper No. 2620). Washington, DC: World Bank, Office of the Senior Vice President, Development Economics. Retrieved March 14, 2005, from World Bank website: http://econ.worldbank.org/files/2225_wps2620.pdf.

Hallin, D. C., & Mancini, P. (2004). *Comparing media systems: Three models of media and politics.* Cambridge, England: Cambridge University Press.

Holtz-Bacha, C., & Norris, P. (2001). To entertain, inform and educate: Still the role of public television? *Political Communication, 18*, 123–140.

Iyengar, S., & Curran, J. (2009). Media systems, news delivery and citizens' knowledge of current affairs. Retrieved October 1, 2010, from http://publicsphere.ssrc.org/

O'Hagan, J., & Jennings, M. (2003). Public broadcasting in Europe: Rationale, licence fee, and other issues. *Journal of Cultural Economics, 27*, 31–56.

Polsby, N. W. (1983). *Consequences of party reform.* New York: Oxford University Press.

Schudson, M. (1998). *The good citizen: A history of American civic life.* New York: Free Press.

Stanley, H. W., & Niemi, R. G. (2010). *Vital statistics on American politics 2009–2010.* Washington DC: CQ Press.

Zaller, J. R. (2003). A new standard of news quality: Burglar alarms for the monitorial citizen. *Political Communication, 20*, 109–130.

NOTES

1. Note, however, that several studies have found that levels of party membership, and levels of activity by party members, are declining all across Europe.

2. The United Kingdom uses the same system. In a handful of cases in the United States, alternative electoral systems are used. For example, San Francisco voters approved a ballot measure in 2002 to bring in the use of instant runoff voting (where voters can specify second preferences that are distributed if no candidate wins a majority) in city elections. Many other cities, including Minneapolis and St. Paul, Minnesota, and Aspen, Colorado, have adopted similar systems since then.

3. Denver, Hands, Fisher, and MacAllister (2003) report, for example, that in the 2001 British general election, fully 17 percent of the electorate reported that they were canvassed on their doorsteps. As noted earlier, however, partisan activism is declining around the world, and this figure represents a substantial decline from the 28 percent who were canvassed in 1992.

4. The rationale for the regulation of broadcast media lies in the very technology of broadcasting. Operation of a newspaper printing press does not interfere with any other press. Radio and television, by contrast, are broadcast through signals of a specific frequency and power. Televisions and radios receive these signals on a fixed number of channels, each of which corresponds to the frequency of the signal. The channels have to be sufficiently far apart to avoid interference among the signals. Unlike newspapers, the production of which is not exclusive, with broadcast media "one person's transmission is another's interference" (Krasnow, 1997).

5. It is estimated that approximately 5 percent of televisions in the United Kingdom are unlicensed. Licenses are enforced, on behalf of the government, by private companies, who maintain a database of all addresses in the United Kingdom. It is assumed that there is a television at every address, so any address that does not have a television license is likely to be visited by enforcement agents. In addition to the address database, enforcement agents use electronic detectors to search for unlicensed TVs (by picking up the small amount of energy radiated by traditional television sets), and electronics retailers can be fined if they do not report the addresses of people buying televisions.

6. The public interest stipulation was built into the Communications Act of 1934, enacted in response to the increasing congestion of the radio airwaves. Any person who wished to build and operate a transmitter needed to get a license first. The act also created a new agency, the Federal Communications Commission, to regulate all interstate broadcast communication. The agency was to grant licenses free of charge either on a one-year provisional basis or for a three-year term. At the end of the term the station could apply for renewal. The FCC could deny or modify a license if the station failed to live up to the commission's standards of the public interest. However, the act said little about what constitutes the public interest.

7. For an example of the categories and styles of stories that dominate local news coverage, see Gilliam and Iyengar (2000).

8. The quality measure was based on performance on a number of criteria: "Cover the whole community; be significant and informative; demonstrate enterprise and courage; be fair, balanced, and accurate; be authoritative; be highly local; presentation; sensationalism" (Project for Excellence in Journalism, 2003).

9. In the aftermath of intense public criticism, threats of viewer boycotts, and a significant decline in Sinclair's stock price, the company reversed course and aired a "news special" called *A POW Story: Politics, Pressure and the Media*, which dealt with "the use of documentaries and other media to influence voting, which emerged during the 2004 political campaigns, as well as on the content of certain of these documentaries" (Sinclair Broadcast Group, 2004).

10. The Newspaper Preservation Act of 1970 permitted two or more newspapers publishing in the same area (at least one of which is failing) to combine advertising, business, circulation, and printing operations, as long as the news operations (meaning both staff and editorial policy) remained separate.

11. In one example of equal terms, the lowest unit rate rule requires that stations offer advertising time to candidates at the lowest rate that they have charged other commercial advertisers during the preceding forty-five days (Kaid & Jones, 2004).

3

The Media Marketplace

Where Americans Get the News

Historically, where Americans get their news has depended on the development of new technologies for transmitting information. The earliest newspapers were affiliated with political parties. Their news offerings were unabashedly slanted in the direction of their partisan sympathies. During the latter part of the nineteenth century, however, major improvements in the technology of printing lowered the costs of production. Publishers could reach mass rather than niche or localized audiences, and revenues from advertising far surpassed the subsidies provided by political parties, thus spelling the doom of the partisan press. In 1870, nearly 90 percent of all dailies were affiliated with one of the two major parties. Thirty years later, the figure had been cut in half.

As newspapers began to demonstrate both profitability and political independence, civic-minded publishers and editors began to push for the formal training of journalists. They subsidized the establishment of journalism schools at major universities. By the 1930s, journalism had become professionalized, with appropriate "canons of conduct," including the pronouncement that "news reports should be free from opinion or bias of any kind" (Stevens, n.d.).

The continued success of large-circulation daily newspapers led to gradual consolidation of the industry as local newspapers were acquired by regional and national newspaper chains. Today, most American newspapers are owned by a chain. The six largest newspaper chains (see Figure 3.1) account for nearly 38 percent of the total circulation of 40 million.

With the development of radio in the 1920s and the immediate popularity of radio news (spawned by radio's relatively fast-breaking coverage of World War II), newspapers began to surrender their position as the major source of news. The arrival of television in the 1950s accentuated this trend, and broadcast news gradually replaced print outlets as the major carriers of news. The national newscasts aired by the three major television networks (ABC,

FIGURE 3.1

Circulation of the Top US Newspaper Companies

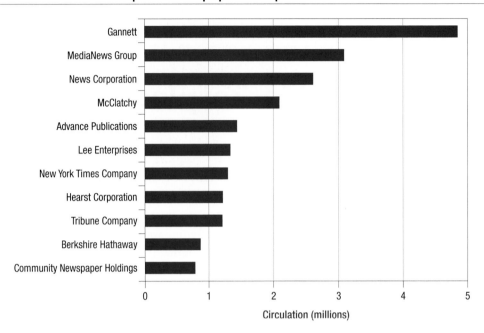

Source: Project for Excellence in Journalism. (2012). *The state of the news media 2012. An annual report on American journalism.*

CBS, NBC) soon emerged as the dominant source of daily news. In 1969, at the height of their dominance, the combined audience for the three newscasts accounted for three-fourths of all American households. More people (approximately 25 million) tuned in to any one of the network newscasts in the late 1960s than subscribed to the top twenty daily newspapers combined.

The development of cable broadcasting in the early 1980s weakened the major networks' monopoly hold on the television audience. CNN, the first all-news cable network, was formed in 1980 and was soon followed by Fox, CNBC, and MSNBC. By 2009, 90 percent of American households had access to cable news channels.

A more significant threat to the dominance of network news was the increasing proliferation of local and soft news programming. Responding to the low cost of producing local news and the substantial audience demand, station owners began to air multiple local newscasts and hybrid entertainment–news programs each day. In the 1960s most stations broadcast a single evening local newscast; today the ratio of local to national news programming on television is tilted overwhelmingly in favor of the former. In the Los Angeles area, for instance, the three network-affiliated television stations air a total of 5.5 hours of local news each day between 4:00 PM and 7:00 PM (see Figure 3.2).

The recent breakthroughs in digital technology have further transformed how we get our news. With the adoption of the personal computer and mobile devices as gateways to the outside world, the competition for news audiences has intensified. Today, all news organizations—big and small—provide their news offerings online, giving consumers instant, on-demand access to the news. We will discuss the implications of information technology for the consumption of news in Chapter 5. For the moment, note that the major Internet portals all provide access to online news sources, but their content is derived almost exclusively from conventional outlets (newspaper, wire services, or television news). In some cases, such as MSNBC, media and technology companies have joined forces, hoping to create synergy between established providers of news content (such as NBC) and technological giants (such as Microsoft).[1]

FIGURE 3.2

TV Listings for Network-Affiliated Channels in New York and Los Angeles (July 3, 2014)

Los Angeles

	4:00 PM	4:30 PM	5:00 PM	5:30 PM	6:00 PM	6:30 PM
KCBS	Judge Judy		CBS 2 News at 5		CBS 2 News at 6	CBS Evening News with Scott Pelley
KNBC	Ellen DeGeneres Show		Channel 4 News at 5		Channel 4 News at 6	NBC Evening News with Brian Williams
KABC	Eyewitness News at 4		Eyewitness News at 5		Eyewitness News at 6	ABC World News with Diane Sawyer
KTTV	TMZ Live		Studio 11 LA		TMZ	Dish Nation

New York

	4:00 PM	4:30 PM	5:00 PM	5:30 PM	6:00 PM	6:30 PM
WCBS	Judge Judy		CBS 2 News at 5		CBS 2 News at 6	CBS Evening News with Scott Pelley
WNBC	Ellen DeGeneres Show		News 4 at 5		News 4 at 6	NBC Evening News with Brian Williams
WNYW	The Dr. Oz Show		Fox News at 5		Fox News at 6	TMZ
WABC	Eyewitness News		Eyewitness News		Eyewitness News	ABC World News with Diane Sawyer

■ National news ■ Local news ■ Entertainment

Source: Data from TVGuide.com, 2014.

In the rest of this chapter we will describe the evolution of the national audience for news and changing patterns of news consumption. We will also track changes in the public's evaluations of news; for example, do people believe what they read? Then we'll address the major factors that shape the news. First and foremost are market forces. In a competitive market, audience size is paramount and all news organizations are in a race to increase their market share. Thus news is produced to entertain rather than inform. Second, the professional norms and values of journalists shape the content of news. The desire to maintain autonomy, for example, has led journalists to cover campaigns from a more interpretive perspective. Rather than simply summarizing the candidates' speeches and advertisements, reporters now focus on the state of the horse race and the candidates' strategies and tactics for winning over voters. Third, the news is inevitably a reflection of organizational processes and routines; the beat system, for instance, by which reporters are assigned to particular subjects, ensures a regular supply of news reports from major government agencies.

AUDIENCES

Audience size is everything in the world of news. Since all news outlets (with the exception of National Public Radio and the Public Broadcasting Service) are privately owned, their survival depends on maintaining a loyal audience. Advertising represents the principal source of revenue for publishers and broadcasters. The price of advertising depends on the number of people reached by any given newspaper or television news program. Statistics on newspaper circulation are compiled by the Audit Bureau of Circulations; television news audiences are measured by the A. C. Nielsen Company.

Unlike the situation in Europe, where individual newspapers often command a large share of the national audience, American newspapers circulate on a more modest scale. Today the most widely read American newspaper is the *Wall Street Journal* (with a combined print and digital circulation of 2.4 million), followed by the *New York Times* with 1.9 million daily readers. (*NYT* also enjoys the highest Sunday circulation at 2.3 million.) *USA Today*, the only truly national newspaper, is in third place with a print circulation of 1.7 million. In order to boost revenue, most newspapers have recently introduced online "paywalls" and digital subscriptions. The *Wall Street Journal* has 795,000 digital subscribers, and the *New York Times* even more (896,000), but no other paper has yet to reach 200,000.

Unlike most nations, where newspapers reach a national audience, American dailies are limited to local or regional audiences. The *New York Times* publishes Midwest and West Coast editions, but the majority of its readers are residents of New York. In general, American newspapers can reach only as far as their advertisers, most of whom are local businesses. New York City department stores have little interest in advertising in the West Coast edition of the *New York Times*.

The historical trend in newspaper circulation is not promising. Unlike broadcast media, newspapers require the audience's undivided attention. Americans' lifestyle and use of time changed dramatically in the latter part of the twentieth century. The marked increase in dual-worker households and the increasing amount of time devoted to work-related activities led to significant declines in newspaper circulation. Between 1990 and 2012, newspaper circulation numbers dropped by about 20 million and several newspapers went out of business, partly due to declines in advertising revenue (see Figure 3.3). Readers are turning away from classified ads, once a major source of revenue, and using online sites like Craigslist and Monster.com instead. Major corporations and local businesses are also increasingly opting to advertise online. Today the audience for the ten largest newspapers is approximately 9 million. This figure is less than half of the combined daily audience for the television shows *Wheel of Fortune* and *Jeopardy* (18.3 million for the week of October 15–21, 2012).

Unlike newspapers, network television has a nationwide presence. Television programming produced by a network is transmitted across the country by local stations affiliated with that network. Measuring just how many people watch a particular program is the mission of the A. C. Nielsen Company. Nielsen developed the concept of television *rating points*. One rating point generally translates to 1 percent of the viewing audience. Nielsen compiles information from two sources: television diaries maintained by a large and representative sample of households (over five thousand households) and twenty-four-hour metering of television sets (among a smaller subset of households). Each television program broadcast in the United States is identifiable by a unique digital fingerprint. Nielsen's metering system captures this identifying information, making it possible to estimate precisely the number of television sets tuned in to any particular program.[2]

The audience for broadcast news exists at two levels: local and national. The broadcasting industry consists of hundreds of local outlets, many of which are affiliated with a national network, thus enabling them to relay network programming. In exchange, station owners must pay the networks a subscription fee for access to their programming. The three major television networks (and their corporate parents) are ABC (Disney), CBS (Viacom), and NBC (Comcast). More recently, Congress granted Fox a network license in 1986. Controlled by Rupert Murdoch's News Corporation, Fox has aggressively purchased local stations across the country.

FIGURE 3.3

Status of US Newspapers

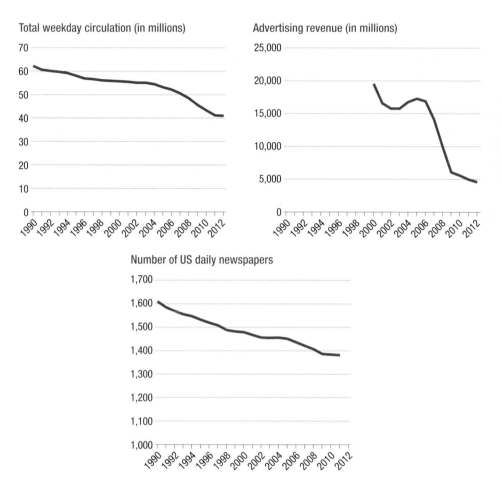

Total weekday circulation (in millions)

Advertising revenue (in millions)

Number of US daily newspapers

Source: Pew Research Center. (2013). *The state of the news media 2013. An annual report on American journalism.*

On a smaller level, the country is divided into 210 local television markets known as *designated media areas*, or DMAs. In many cases the DMA corresponds to a metropolitan area, but in less urban parts of the country a DMA may include multiple counties. Whereas California has twelve DMAs, the entire state of Montana has only one. Each DMA consists of a set of antenna-based local television stations licensed by the FCC and assigned to a specific channel.

By the late 1960s, the thirty-minute evening newscasts produced by the major networks had emerged as the industry leader. At the height of their popularity, the three network newscasts attracted a combined daily audience in excess of 60 million viewers. The introduction of cable television, however, inaugurated a period of greater competition within the world of broadcasting. CNN emerged as a reputable supplier of news in the 1980s, employing well-known journalists (many of whom had been let go by the networks) and reaching viewers across the globe.[3]

Although the American audience for CNN (and the other cable networks) is typically less than four gross rating points (GRPs), the market share of cable news providers increases during periods of international tension or conflict. Immediately after the start of Operation Desert Storm in January 1991, CNN reporters Bernard Shaw, John Holliman, and Peter Arnett found themselves the only American television correspondents in Baghdad. As the US bombing of the city began, they broadcast live from the terrace of the Al-Rashid Hotel. Their dramatic reports of the bombing raids were watched by a worldwide audience of more than a billion people, including President George H. W. Bush, Saddam Hussein, and other major participants in the conflict, thus guaranteeing the network a place in broadcasting history.

With the institutionalization of cable television, the audience share of network news has gradually declined. Since their heyday, the three nightly newscasts have experienced a ratings decline of nearly 60 percent. The network television audience share fell from 85 percent of households in 1969 to under 30 percent in 2012 (see Figure 3.4). The most dramatic declines occurred in the 1990s, considerably after cable television had come of age. Between 1980 and 2012, for instance, the combined audience for the three evening newscasts fell from 42 million to 17 million. It was precisely during this period that the production of local television news surged.

Despite the increasing competition from cable providers, network news remains the single most watched national news source in the United States. In 2012, the combined audience for the three evening newscasts equaled the circulation of the top forty newspapers.

For decades, CBS was considered the premier network newscast. Under the leadership of Edward R. Murrow, the network recruited a stable of distinguished correspondents, including Walter Cronkite, Howard K. Smith, and Eric Sevareid. During much of Cronkite's long tenure as anchorman, the *CBS Evening News* emerged as the perennial ratings winner. Cronkite's retirement in 1981, however, created a more competitive environment, and by the early 1990s the network had fallen to third place in the ratings, trailing both ABC and NBC by a substantial margin. In 2004 and 2005, the long-standing anchors for NBC and CBS (Tom Brokaw and Dan Rather, respectively) both retired, and ABC's Peter Jennings died (having retired several months earlier),

FIGURE 3.4

Evening News Household Ratings for ABC, CBS, and NBC, 1980–2012

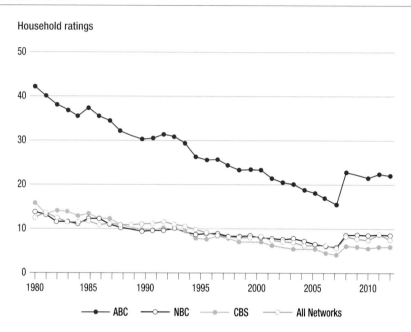

Source: Pew Research Center. (2013). *The state of the news media 2013. An annual report on American journalism.*

prompting speculation that the network news audience would once again be up for grabs.

Since then, the leadership of the evening news has been in relative flux. Brian Williams anchored the *NBC Nightly News* from 2004 to 2014. Bob Schieffer took over the *CBS Nightly News* after Rather's retirement and was replaced by Katie Couric shortly thereafter. Couric was replaced by Scott Pelley in 2011. Charles Gibson replaced Peter Jennings on ABC and then Diane Sawyer took over in 2009 after Gibson retired. Sawyer announced her retirement in 2014 and will be replaced by David Muir.

It is important to place the audience for network news in context. Although millions of people watch the evening news, the newscasts are small-fry when compared to reality programming, sports, or prime-time drama. *American Idol*, *CSI*, or *Monday Night Football* outdraws any of the nightly newscasts by a substantial margin. In comparison with entertainment, the demand for public

TABLE 3.1

Top Ten Rated TV Programs, 1961–2014

Program	Episode	Network	Date	Ratings	Share (%)	Number of Households
Superbowl XLVI	Giants vs. Patriots	NBC	2/5/2012	47.1	71	53,910,000
Superbowl XLVIII	Broncos vs. Seahawks	Fox	2/2/2014	46.4	69	53,727,000
Superbowl XLIV	Saints vs. Colts	CBS	2/7/2010	45	68	53,600,000
M*A*S*H	Final episode	CBS	2/28/1983	60.2	77	50,150,000
XVII Winter Olympics	Women's Figure Skating	CBS	2/23/1994	48.5	64	45,690,000
Superbowl XX	Bears vs. Patriots	NBC	1/26/1986	48.3	70	41,490,000
Dallas (series)	"Who Shot J. R.?"	CBS	11/21/1980	53.3	76	41,470,000
Superbowl XVII	Redskins vs. Dolphins	NBC	1/30/1983	48.6	69	40,480,000
Superbowl XVI	49ers vs. Bengals	CBS	1/24/1982	49.1	73	40,020,000
Roots	Part 8	ABC	1/30/1977	51.1	71	36,380,000

Source: Data from Nielsen Media Research, unpublished data. Retrieved July 11, 2014 from www.nielsenmedia.com.

Note: Rankings based on surveys taken from January 1961 through February 7, 2014; only sponsored programs seen on individual networks are included, and programs scheduled for less than thirty-minute duration are excluded.

affairs programming is weak. The ten most popular regularly scheduled television broadcasts ever (see Table 3.1) do not include a single news or public affairs program (although very large numbers of people watch soft news events such as the O. J. Simpson low-speed chase through Los Angeles and the funerals of Princess Diana and Michael Jackson).

The most serious threat to network news today is local news. Station owners have discovered that local news programming can be delivered more or less continuously, and at relatively low cost. Moreover, millions of people tune in because local news provides information that is closer to home, more usable (such as the weather forecast), and entertaining (such as the latest sports results). In market after market, stations have increased the number of programming slots devoted to local news. As Figure 3.2 shows, local news runs on a continuous basis during the late afternoon–early evening time slots in big-city markets. Across the country, the audience for evening local news aired by the network local affiliates generally equals or exceeds the audience for the network's own national newscast. In fact, as we'll describe later in the chapter, the rise of local television news is a compelling case study of how media economics determines media programming.

Ratings are the lifeblood of the broadcasting industry. Advertising revenues for specific television programs fluctuate on the basis of how many people they reach. Nielsen conducts quarterly ratings "sweeps" during the months of February, May, July, and November. The size of the audience during each sweeps period locks in advertising rates for individual programs and stations until the next period. Programs that suffer a decline in their ratings thus stand to lose significant revenue, so broadcast news providers do their utmost to maintain or improve their ratings.

Efforts to monitor online audiences are still in their infancy. The analytics firm comScore has emerged as the market leader for online metrics. The company maintains a global sample of Web users whose computers are equipped with monitoring software that enables the company to track online behavior. The panelists also complete surveys on a regular basis allowing the company to combine consumers' online behavior with their attitude and demographic profiles. Internet traffic is dominated by social networking sites (such as Facebook), online search engines (such as Google), and major portals (such as MSN and Yahoo). As we will discuss in greater detail in Chapter 5, the emerging audience for public affairs information online is not nearly as large as the number of people who engage in online shopping, interpersonal communication (e-mail), pornography, and other browsing activities.

One final point about the supply of news concerns the gradual increase in joint ventures or *cross-media sources*. We have already noted the emerging partnerships between technology and content providers in the case of online news and entertainment. Thus, Microsoft, Verizon, and Comcast have partnered to enable video streaming through Xbox. Similar partnerships have been initiated within conventional media because the FCC has relaxed its cross-ownership limits—that is, the limits on the number of different news outlets operating within a media market that can be owned by a single entity. In many media markets, the same owner operates both the major newspaper and the top-rated local television station.[4]

The Tribune publishing company became Tribune Broadcasting when it acquired television station WGN (whose call letters stood for the Tribune-owned *Chicago Tribune*, or "World's Greatest Newspaper"). Currently, Tribune Entertainment owns stations in several of the top media markets, including KTLA in Los Angeles, KPIX in New York, and CLTV, the Chicago area's first and only twenty-four-hour all-news local news channel. As the sister station of the *Chicago Tribune*, CLTV quickly became a model for content sharing and cross-promotion, with stories and reporters moving seamlessly from print to broadcast outlets.

CREDIBILITY

Audience size is one measure of the demand for news. But does size also imply credibility? Source credibility (believability) is an important indicator of media status and influence; when people perceive news reports to be unbiased and trustworthy, they are more likely to take them seriously (see Chapter 8). Media scholars have tracked the American public's evaluations of media credibility for several decades.

Given the freedom of the American press from government controls and journalists' commitment to objective reporting, we would expect consumers to view the news as generally unbiased. The behavior of practitioners suggests that they take their credibility seriously. A few years ago, CBS anchor Dan Rather agreed to speak at a fund-raising event for the Democratic Party. The ensuing controversy over the appearance of partisan bias led Rather to issue an immediate apology for demonstrating "a lapse of judgment."[5] More recently, *NBC Nightly News* anchor Brian Williams was suspended without pay for six months following revelations that he exaggerated his experiences as a war correspondent during the 2003 Iraq War.

An approximate indicator of media credibility is the level of overall public confidence in the press. The General Social Survey, conducted annually by the National Opinion Research Center (NORC) at the University of Chicago, asks a representative sample of Americans for their level of confidence in the media. In 1973, the first year the question was asked, only 10 percent of the public responded "hardly any." By 2008, however, this group had grown to 45 percent of the sample. Although it is true that public confidence in just about every public institution has declined substantially since 1973, in comparison with other institutions the press has taken a much bigger hit. As shown in Figure 3.5, today there are considerably more Americans who say they have "hardly any" than have "a great deal" of confidence in the press. In contrast, confidence in education shows a much slower decline over time with a plurality of Americans expressing great confidence. The audience may be listening, but it is also increasingly skeptical.

The generic confidence-in-the-press question is likely to underestimate the credibility of particular outlets for the well-known reason that people rationalize their own preferences. Many people deride Congress as a corrupt institution but revere their own congressperson as honest and hardworking. Similarly, when people are asked to rate the credibility of the news outlets they rely on, their evaluations are more favorable. The Pew Research Center (2010) asked Americans to indicate whether they "believe all or most" of the programs offered by well-known news organizations. As Figure 3.6 shows,

FIGURE 3.5

Confidence in the Press versus Confidence in Education

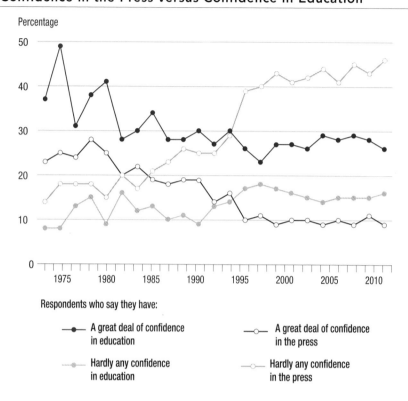

Percentage

Respondents who say they have:

—●— A great deal of confidence in education

—○— A great deal of confidence in the press

—●— Hardly any confidence in education

—○— Hardly any confidence in the press

Source: Data from T. Smith and J. Son. (2013). *Trends in public attitudes about confidence in institutions*. Chicago: National Opinion Research Center.

by this measure a majority of Americans rate most outlets with skepticism. Relatively speaking, television news enjoys a clear credibility advantage over print sources;[6] in fact, CNN and the three major networks are the most credible sources in the United States. Surprisingly, Fox News, widely recognized as a pro-conservative source, enjoys *higher* credibility than the *New York Times*, the *Wall Street Journal*, and the newspaper you are most familiar with. It is not surprising that people are also attached to their local news programs (and to a lesser degree their local newspaper); just as many people believe their local station as believe network news.

Although the level of believability accorded to broadcast news is impressive (if we combine the two highest categories of believability, a majority of Americans find network news believable), the trend line is consistent with the downward trend in confidence in the press. In nearly every case, more

FIGURE 3.6

Believability Ratings

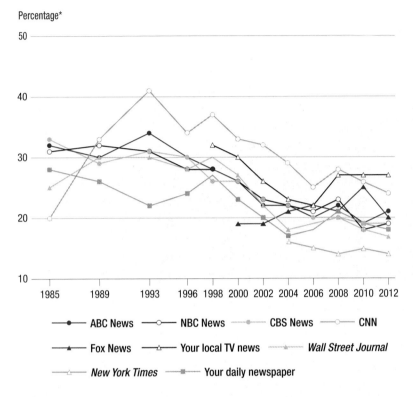

Percentage*

ABC News ⬤ **NBC News** ◯ **CBS News** ⬛ **CNN** ◯

Fox News ▲ **Your local TV news** △ **Wall Street Journal** ✱

New York Times △ **Your daily newspaper** ⬛

Source: Pew Research Center. (2013). *The state of the news media 2013. An annual report on American journalism.*

*Y-axis shows percent who "believe all or most" of the reporting by particular media sources.

Americans believed the news in 1985 than did in 2004. The only exceptions to this trend were the two newcomers to the industry—CNN and Fox News—both of which were insufficiently known when survey respondents were first asked about believability to elicit high ratings. For network news, the average decline in believability between 1985 and 2008 was 10 percentage points. For print media, the decline was even steeper.

A different measure of credibility is the demand for news during times of national or international crisis. When important news stories break, where do people turn first? In the case of the 2003 Iraq War, the data show clearly that people gravitated to more-familiar sources (see Figure 3.7). By a margin of greater than 2 to 1, Americans relied on CBS, NBC, and ABC rather than CNN, Fox, or MSNBC. By this measure of viewer loyalty, the national networks retain a significant advantage over their younger competitors.

FIGURE 3.7

Breaking-News Audience, First Night of 2003 Iraq War

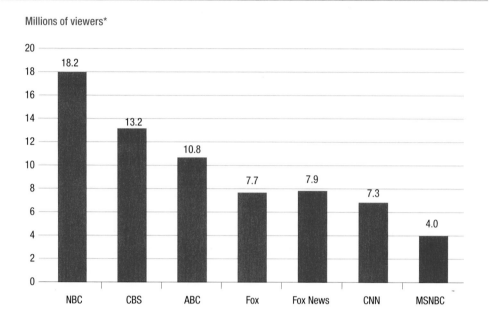

Millions of viewers*

*Number of viewers between 9:30 PM and 11:00 PM on March 19, 2003.

Source: Data from J. Hamlin. (2003, March 22). NBC declares victory in TV ratings battle. *San Francisco Chronicle*, p. W2.

Studies of media credibility show one consistent pattern: people who tend to hold strong political views, such as those affiliated with a political party or cause, are especially likely to view the news as biased. Enthusiasm for the party line makes partisans dubious of news presentations designed to present a balanced perspective on the day's events. The tendency to believe that so-called objective coverage is biased is directly proportional to the intensity of one's political commitments. In fact, research has shown that people with opposing viewpoints, when shown the exact same news report, will each believe that the report is biased in favor of the other side! This is called the *hostile media phenomenon*. Recent research by Goldman and Mutz (2011), however, demonstrates that most people view the media they use most often as favoring their own views. This *friendly media phenomenon* highlights the difference between a person's beliefs about the media in general and the media that he or she uses regularly and puts a new twist on the hostile media phenomenon.

In the United States, perceptions of media bias tend to be tilted in one direction; many Americans view mainstream news organizations as favoring liberal–Democratic points of view. Prestigious newspapers such as the *New*

IN FOCUS

The Hostile Media Phenomenon

Research has consistently shown that, in general, people who are highly committed to a point of view—strong Democrats or Republicans, for example, or those who are strongly pro-Israeli or pro-Palestinian—perceive impartial news stories to be biased in favor of their opponents.

York Times and *Washington Post* are especially likely to be viewed as biased. Since Fox News has staked out a clearly conservative identity, it is not surprising that beliefs about the credibility of Fox are clearly divided according to viewers' party affiliation. Republicans trust Fox a great deal and distrust all other news sources. For their part, a majority of Democrats distrust Fox while trusting most mainstream outlets.[7] As we note in Chapter 5, strengthened party polarization and the increasingly acrimonious relations between Democrats and Republicans have made providers of news more susceptible to allegations of political bias.

WHAT GETS REPORTED?

News is meant to be a reflection of reality. The major events and issues occurring in the world at large that are deemed to have consequences for Americans are the events and issues one expects to encounter in the news. This mirror-image definition of news stipulates close correspondence between the state of the real world and the content of news coverage. During times of rising joblessness, the news focuses on unemployment; when thousands of Sudanese civilians are massacred, the spotlight shifts to Sudan and to US policy on Africa.

Implicit in the mirror-image definition of news is the well-known asymmetry between newsworthiness and the normal course of events. Events are judged newsworthy only when they deviate from anticipated (everyday) outcomes. Planes that land safely are not news, but planes that land safely on rivers are front-page news. In general, negative events or outcomes tend to attract greater coverage, for the simple reason that they indicate a deviation from normalcy. News coverage of the economy is sparse during periods of prosperity but abundant during recessions. Politicians who behave as law-abiding citizens attract little attention; the few who break the law elicit volumes of coverage. As in economics, there is a Gresham's law which stipulates that negative information always drives out positive information.

The expectation that news organizations behave as mirrors of real-world events is unrealistic on a variety of grounds. Practical considerations make it impossible to cover events at every remote location across the globe, and many issues (such as global warming) do not manifest themselves in the form of observable, concrete events. In other policy areas, indicators of reality (such as the level of threat to US national security) are simply unavailable.[8] In these cases, it is impossible to assess the level of correspondence between reality on the one hand, and *mediality* (the "reality" portrayed by the media) on the other.

In the final analysis, the mirror-image definition of news is unrealistic because the practice of journalism rests on fallible and culturally determined human judgments. On any given day, thousands of potentially important events occur. It is physically impossible to cover all of them. Editorial selection (gatekeeping) is the hallmark of news: events are granted coverage in proportion to their newsworthiness. Judgments of newsworthiness are inherently subjective; what's newsworthy to CBS News may be of little interest to All India Television or, for that matter, to the *New York Times*.

Explaining the content of news, therefore, is very much an exercise in understanding journalists' professional values, career incentives, and decision-making processes, all of which affect their behavior and work product. This perspective is generally referred to as the *organizational process* account of news, meaning that the standard operating procedures of news organizations influence what's reported and what's ignored. Thus, to the degree that news reports deviate from reality, the discrepancy is attributable to organizational procedures and news-gathering routines and not to the political preferences of journalists.

The major competitor of the organizational process account of news is the standard market-based account of profit-maximizing behavior. As we have noted repeatedly, the media industry in the United States is privately owned. Consumers are free to choose from a wide array of news providers. Facing competition, rational owners prefer to further their own interests rather than to provide public service to the community. The content and form of news coverage are subject to the same logic that drives all other economic activity: minimize costs and maximize revenues.

MARKET PRESSURES

Consider the following facts from the world of broadcast journalism. The award-winning television news program that delivers the most detailed, substantive, and wide-ranging discussion of policy issues is the hour-long newscast produced by the Public Broadcasting Service. This newscast is watched by fewer than 3 million Americans each evening. *Entertainment Tonight*, the thirty-minute program focusing on Hollywood celebrity news, attracts a daily audience in excess of 5 million viewers. Soft news and reality television programs attract much larger audiences than does serious news.

The message for news organizations is obvious: make news reports more interesting. In the last two decades, no matter what the medium, the public affairs content of news has been substantially diluted. Slattery and Hakanen (1994) found, for instance, that news about government and policy fell from 54 to 15 percent in a sample of Philadelphia local newscasts between 1976 and 1992. Even the *New York Times*, which features "All the News That's Fit to Print" as its motto, has had to chart a similar course.

Market pressures are especially intense in the world of broadcast news, where survival must take precedence over informative news reports. Substantive news content and audience size are inversely related. Obviously news producers have to adapt to the competition from soft news, sitcoms, and cable talk shows. They do so by making their own news programs more entertaining and less serious. Patterson's (2000) research shows that one-half of all network news reports broadcast in 2000 had no policy content; in 1980 the figure was approximately one-third. Of the network news reports that aired in the 1980s, 25 percent were sensationalized; by 2003 the figure was 40 percent. Clearly, news organizations have learned that fluff is more profitable than substance.

This can be seen most clearly when the content of the news from countries where media are driven primarily by market pressures is compared to the content of the news in countries where financial considerations are less important. Curran and his coauthors (2009) recently found that 37 percent of television news content from the bottom-line-oriented US media is soft compared with only 17 percent for the public service–oriented Finnish media. From a demand-side perspective, a focus on soft news also makes sense. Patterson (2007) found that Americans were more likely to recall soft news stories than hard news stories, and a study of news interest between 1986 and 2006 (Robinson, 2007) found that people were almost as likely to closely follow soft news stories (18 percent) as they were to closely follow political news (22 percent) and foreign news (17 percent).

Journalism was not always so sensitive to the bottom line. In the early days of television news, most senior managers were themselves journalists, with the view that their news programs were to be the very best rather than the most economical. All three network news divisions were loss leaders during the 1970s, yet they employed large staffs, maintained bureaus in several countries, and provided what was considered top-notch reporting. In effect, the networks used the vast profits generated by their entertainment programs to subsidize their news divisions. William Paley, the founder of CBS, is said to have remarked to a journalist concerned about the rising costs of the *CBS Evening News*, "You guys cover the news; I've got Jack Benny [a famous entertainer at the time] to make money for me."

As the networks were acquired by conglomerates, the corporate culture changed. The news divisions were expected to make a profit and sink or swim within the parent company. The amount of time reserved for news in the thirty-minute newscast was cut by 10 percent, from twenty-one minutes in 1990 to nineteen minutes in 2009. All three networks were forced to reduce the number of correspondents and close most of their international bureaus. With the end of the Cold War, foreign affairs no longer had a compelling story line ("Could we get along with the Russians?"), and news organizations felt free to scale back their overseas coverage. These measures have created a serious lack of access to international events. In the case of breaking overseas events, American networks typically purchase footage from freelancers or from European network correspondents, with voice-over from the nearest network correspondent. Cost cutting also ushered in the end of serious documentary programming. Hard-hitting investigative documentaries were transformed into up-close interviews with celebrities.

Accentuating the new economic logic was the gradual breakdown of the rigid boundaries in the daily television programming schedule, which restricted local news programs to one thirty-minute slot in the early- and late-evening schedules. Once stations began airing local and soft news programs in multiple time slots, the pressure on network news only intensified.

When the networks were created, their rationale for airing news programs was hardly selfless. Rather, they were required by the FCC to provide a minimal level of public affairs programming in exchange for free use of the broadcasting spectrum. As we documented in Chapter 2, these public service obligations have long since been weakened or altogether ignored, making it possible for networks to exist as all-entertainment entities. A first-rate news division was once a symbol of a network's commitment to public service; today it is a mere cog in the entertainment machine. News is what sells. Several of the most basic principles of serious journalism—worldwide news coverage, multiple correspondents working the same story, and the commitment to getting the story right—all became victims of the new economic logic.

Further compromising the quality of journalism was the acceleration of the news cycle. In the current twenty-four-hour cycle, news organizations face intense pressures to deliver the news faster than their competitors do. The race to be first often requires loosening the standards of journalism; rather than confirming a story with multiple sources, editors routinely accept reports that are poorly substantiated. In a well-known instance of the risks of maintaining rigorous standards, in 1998 *Newsweek* decided to delay printing its report about new evidence concerning the alleged affair between President Clinton and Monica Lewinsky (the semen-stained dress) because its reporter on the story (Michael Isikoff) had not yet confirmed the material with multiple sources. While *Newsweek* waited, the Drudge Report published the story online. It does not pay to be right, if you're last.

Although the conflict between cost-driven journalism and the delivery of hard news is especially pronounced in the world of broadcast journalism, where the financial stakes are much higher, print media have been no less affected. Newspapers have reduced the size of the daily "news hole"—space allocated to current events—in favor of features. On any given day, the reader of the *New York Times* is presented with sections on technology, food, entertainment, real estate, travel, and more. Newspaper design has been visualized with the use of color photography, graphics, and other eye-catching devices. The very same economy measures implemented at the networks—staff cuts, bureau closings, and softening of news content—have been adopted at leading newspapers across the country. The editors of the *New York Times*, for instance, did not notice any conflict between their motto, "All the News That's Fit to Print," and their assigning a full-time correspondent to cover the O. J. Simpson case in 1995. All news organizations, no matter what their prestige or rank in the world of journalism, converged on the O. J. story because it attracted readers. The *Times* simply had no choice; it could either provide intensive coverage of the event or lose readers.

In short, the economic realities of the media business create strong pressures on journalists to cater to the tastes of the median viewer or reader. Programs that are heavy in policy content or in-depth expert analysis will find that their audience has migrated within minutes to the next episode of *Jeopardy*, or to *Action News at 6 PM*. The proliferation of broadcast outlets and the resulting competition for the attention of the viewing audience spelled doom for the previously held standards of serious journalism. A new genre of news programs, focusing on the lives of the wealthy and famous, and dwelling incessantly on the mayhem and violence on local streets, created the appropriate fit (for owners and publishers) between economic interests and the delivery of public affairs information.

A CASE STUDY OF LOCAL TELEVISION NEWS

The rapid emergence of local news programming in the decade of the 1980s is a compelling case study of the responsiveness of news programming to economic constraints. In the 1960s, station owners typically aired old episodes of popular sitcoms (such as *Hogan's Heroes* and *The Beverly Hillbillies*) in the programming slots just before or after the national newscast.[9] Naturally, they paid a significant fee to the syndication company holding the rights to these programs, and the programs tended to attract only modest audiences, so the resulting profit margin was less than station owners hoped it would be.

In the more competitive media markets (Los Angeles and New York), owners noticed that the thirty-minute local newscast proved quite popular with the audience, often drawing in more viewers than the national news. Moreover, the local newscast was inexpensive to produce. The typical local newscast can be staffed by four or five all-purpose correspondents, an anchor or two, a weather forecaster, and a sports correspondent. Local news correspondents, in contrast with their network news counterparts, do not command extravagant salaries. Infrastructure costs for local news programming are similarly limited; for the typical news station, the single most expensive budget item is the monthly lease of a helicopter (to provide immediate access to breaking news). All told, the cost of putting together a local newscast is trivial.

Cost is only half of the programming equation, however. Local news is especially enticing to station owners because they can present the program in ways that bring in large audiences. Not only is local news close to home and the source of both useful (weather forecast, traffic reports) and personally engaging (latest baseball scores) information, but even the public affairs content can be structured to appeal to viewers. It is no accident that the signature issue of local news coverage is violent crime. From armed bank robberies to homicides, home invasions, carjackings, police chases, and gang wars, violence occurs continually in local newscasts. Conversely, little time is devoted to nonviolent crimes such as embezzlement, fraud, or tax evasion, because they lack the action to command the attention of the viewing audience. Thus local news is essentially a televised police blotter: "If it bleeds, it leads" is the motto of local news directors.

Stories about crime focus on concrete events with powerful impacts on ordinary people, convey drama and emotion, and above all, provide attention-getting visuals. The power of this formula is apparent to station owners and news directors in media markets across the country. English-language commercial television stations operating in the Los Angeles market aired a total of 3,014 news stories on crime during 1996 and 1997, of which 2,492 (83 percent) focused on violent crime. The crime of murder, which accounted for less than 1 percent of all crime in Los Angeles County during this period, was the focus of 17 percent of crime stories. In fact, the number of murder stories (510) was equal to the total number of nonviolent crime stories (522) during the period sampled (all figures are taken from Gilliam & Iyengar, 2000).

Although brutal acts of violence are understandably newsworthy, this level of overrepresentation of violent crime is extraordinary. Overall, the Los Angeles study found that the typical thirty-minute local news segment included three distinct reports on crime, totaling to approximately four minutes of coverage (out of twelve minutes devoted to news). The results were identical across all six television stations whose offerings were examined. Moreover, violent crime was equally newsworthy in late-afternoon, early-evening, prime-time, and late-night newscasts.

In their preoccupation with violent crime, Los Angeles television stations are not especially distinctive. A study of fifty-six different cities by Klite, Bardwell, and Salzman (1997) found that crime was the most prominently featured subject in the local news, accounting for more than 75 percent of all news coverage in some cities.

Local news generates nearly half the total revenue for the typical television station, according to a survey of station managers done by the Radio and Television News Directors Association. The strong profitability of local news accounts for the steady increase in the number of programming hours. On average, local stations aired more than five hours of local news per day in 2011, representing an increase of more than one hour a day from 2007. In sum, low costs and high interest value make local news a winning combination. More generally, the law of supply and demand has shifted the content of news programming away from relatively serious subjects. Publishers cannot eat Pulitzer Prizes and Peabody Awards; to maintain their competitiveness, they must provide news offerings that attract an audience. Hard news about government and political issues made up 14 percent of all local news programming in 2012, while crime, accidents, traffic, or weather-related reports and other human interest subjects accounted for 76 percent of the coverage (Pew, 2013).

ORGANIZATIONAL PROCESSES AND ROUTINES

Although the brutal logic of the bottom line goes a long way toward explaining recent trends in the practice of journalism, a fuller understanding of the production of news entails more than a simple exercise in economic determinism.

IN FOCUS

Influences on What Is Reported

- **Market forces.** As commercial enterprises, news organizations are subject to the same logic that drives all other economic activity: minimize costs and maximize revenues. Soft news attracts much larger audiences than does serious news, so producers are under pressure to make their programs more entertaining.
- **Journalistic norms.** Professional norms of autonomy and objectivity in journalism lead journalists to interpretive forms of coverage, emphasizing ad watches, candidate strategy, the horse race, and scandal stories.
- **Organizational processes.** The routines and procedures followed by news organizations—deadlines in the news cycle, the assignment of reporters to beats, and reliance on official sources—have substantial impact on the content and form of news, as do the accessibility and appropriateness of competing stories.

Although news organizations must make ends meet, journalists continue to have considerable leeway to exercise choice, discretion, and control over their work product. Like other professions, journalism has a culture that guides everyday practice. There is a right way and a wrong way. Journalists also pursue professional advancement and recognition. Above all, they rely on a set of conventions or standard operating procedures for uncovering and reporting the news. As we will describe, all these factors leave an indelible imprint on the content and form of news coverage.

AUTONOMY AND OBJECTIVITY AS DOMINANT VALUES

Modern political journalism rests on two dominant values: objectivity and autonomy. In the particular case of election news, as campaigns have become more choreographed and expert at using the press to recirculate their messages, autonomy has upstaged objectivity as the guiding principle of journalists' behavior. In the era before media politics, the press maintained an objective stance on the campaign by providing regular opportunities for *both* candidates to reach their audience. Objectivity simply required equal exposure; the candidates' partisan rhetoric canceled each other out.

In the aftermath of the 1988 campaign, however, the press decided that merely reprinting both candidates' words compromised journalistic autonomy. In that election, the media made the Bush campaign's use of racial imagery in a television commercial (the "Willie Horton" ad) to attack Governor Duka-kis's record on crime the major story line of the campaign. The coverage met the standard definition of objectivity: the Bush and Dukakis campaigns were both quoted extensively on the subject of crime and prison furloughs. By their actions, however, journalists elevated the importance of crime as a campaign issue, thus handing Bush (who was more widely seen as tough on crime) a significant edge.

Thus, after the 1988 campaign, leading reporters argued that recycling the candidates' message of the day was an inappropriate form of campaign jour-nalism because it made reporters captive to the agenda of campaign consul-tants. To protect their autonomy, reporters turned to a more analytic form of news coverage that centered on interpretations and analysis of the candidate's actions. Not only was this more aggressive scrutiny of the candidates designed to reduce the likelihood that reporters would be captivated by campaign spin, but it also amplified the voice of the journalist. The campaign correspondent was now a solo author of the news, whose own analysis was more newsworthy than what the candidates had to say.

INTERPRETIVE JOURNALISM

The manifestations of the switch from descriptive to interpretive reporting of elections were many. In the first place, reporters were more apt to debunk the candidates' pronouncements. Campaign ads were no longer described exactly as they were; instead, journalists adopted a new genre of reporting—the ad watch or reality check—in which they dissected and enumerated the spe-cific errors, exaggerations, or undocumented allegations contained in ads or speeches (see Video Archive 3.1). Ad watches soon became a staple of election coverage, with all major news outlets dedicating a full-time correspondent to the task of analyzing the candidates' rhetoric and ads. As noted in Chapter 6, ad watches also changed the behavior of advertisers, but sometimes in a coun-terintuitive direction.

Video Archive 3.1
Policing Campaign Ads

The emphasis on resisting simple regurgitation of the candidates' ads spilled over into daily coverage of the campaign. To a great extent, the older, descrip-tive mode of coverage consisted of reporting the events of the day, often includ-ing verbatim reports of significant amounts of candidate speech. The newer, interpretive journalism also reported on daily events, but in a much different way. Journalists were generally less interested in describing the event and more inclined to use the event as a means of divining the candidates' motives and tactics. Because the focus is no longer on the candidates' positions, reporters today bypass the candidates and turn to a coterie of experts. The task of the expert is to act as an agent of the reporter and provide the necessary analysis of such questions as why President Obama did not respond more assertively to Mitt Romney's criticisms of his economic record and whether Romney's "binders full of women" comment would weaken his standing among women.

Thus the *strategy frame*—analysis of the rationale and strategy underlying the candidate's rhetoric and positions—has emerged as the single most frequent theme in coverage of the political campaign. News is no longer limited to what the candidates say; it also reports *why* they say it. The pouring of campaign resources into battleground states, fund-raising tactics, the tone of the advertising campaign, whether going negative will help or harm the candidate—all become the stuff of election reports.

The most popular element of interpretive reporting is the state of the horse race. Reporters invariably frame the election not as a contest of ideas or policy platforms but as a race between two teams, each bent on securing more votes than the other. The bottom-line question at the end of the day is "Who's ahead?" or "Who's scoring more points with the electorate?" Reports on the latest polls or behind-the-scenes efforts to improve the candidates' electoral prospects far outnumber reports on the candidates' worldviews, policy pledges, or previous records of decision making. In fact, the state of the horse race now accounts for more news reports than any other category of news. During the 2008 presidential campaign, reports on the horse race outnumbered reports on the candidates' policy positions by a factor greater than 2.5 to 1 from September 8 to October 16 (see Table 3.2). The only time that reports on policy positions outnumbered reports on the horse race was during the week when the economic crisis began. Four years later, during the Republican primary campaign, the ratio of horse race to policy news reports was even greater (6 to 1). Between November 2011 and April 2012, there was only one month in which the level of horse-race coverage dropped below 60 percent (Rosenstiel, Jurkowitz, & Sartor, 2012).

What is especially revealing of the new genre of campaign journalism is the synergy between the professional aspirations of journalists and the competitive pressures of the market. Horse-race coverage appears to be a dominant strategy because it satisfies the journalist's need for autonomy and objectivity, it is easy to report, and it sells! All major news organizations now administer their own surveys of public opinion, often once or twice a month. Poll-based coverage is entirely objective; after all, reporters are relaying the results of their own (rather than the candidates') polling, the results are based on representative samples of likely voters, and the journalist or someone in the news bureau

TABLE 3.2

Percent of All Campaign-Related Stories

	Overall (Sept. 8 – Oct. 16)[a]	Postconvention Week (Sept. 8–14)	Economic Crisis Begins (Sept. 15–23)	McCain Temporarily Suspends Campaign; First Presidential Debate (Sept. 24–28)	Vice Presidential Debate (Sept. 29–Oct. 5)	Second Presidential Debate (Oct. 6–10)	Third Presidential Debate (Oct. 12–16)
Political horse race	52.7%	52.1%	30.5%	50.1%	66.6%	65.0%	53.9%
Advertising fund-raising[b]	9.8%	13.3%	10.4%	13.7%	8.5%	8.2%	6.2%
Public record	5.5%	13.1%	8.3%	0.6%	2.5%	5.8%	0.5%
Policy	20.4%	11.9%	43.6%	28.7%	11.5%	12.7%	15.1%
Personal	5.4%	6.1%	4.4%	3.3%	5.4%	1.2%	10.1%
Other	6.3%	3.6%	2.9%	3.5%	5.5%	7.1%	14.1%

Pew Research Center, 2008.

[a] N = 2,412 campaign stories.

[b] Also includes stories about the treatment of candidates by the press, the electoral calendar, and endorsements.

with survey and statistical expertise is responsible both for determining the questions to be asked and for tabulating the results (most major news organizations employ a full-time survey researcher to design and interpret their election polls). From the perspective of the reporter, examining the latest poll results on computer and then telephoning a pair of competing experts to get their take on what the results mean for the eventual outcome is much less labor-intensive than following the candidate across the country to extract the message of the day.

Polling also helps make the election more interesting to the audience. The idea that the election is a close race with each side making momentary gains, only to find the race still deadlocked, capitalizes on voters' curiosity and uncertainty over the outcome. People abhor uncertainty; the less clear-cut the eventual result of the election is, the more often they will tune in to news about the race. In fact, some critics have alleged that during the closing stages of the campaign, media organizations deliberately frame their survey results so as to tighten the race and increase the interest value of their election news.

As the horse race has come to dominate news of the election, coverage of issues has receded into the background. Conventional wisdom holds that issues do not interest the audience. News-reporting organizations cannot protect their market share by covering the candidates' positions on tax cuts or defense. More compellingly, issue information is typically old news. Early in the campaign, once a candidate has announced an economic plan, there may be some ripple of news coverage, but as the campaign progresses, the plan is no longer of interest. A candidate's policy stances are never a fresh news item unless there is some discrepancy between the candidate's stated position and the rhetoric, or if the candidate suddenly reverses position.

Finally, issue-based coverage also weakens the journalist's autonomy from the campaign. Issues are difficult to cover objectively and often leave the reporter open to charges of biased coverage. A spokesperson for the Romney campaign is liable to complain about a story on the Obama healthcare plan on the grounds that the story cited a lower total cost than that estimated by the Republicans. Alternatively, the Obama camp might demand equal time to correct an error in the original report. Given the ambiguity inherent in most policy platforms, virtually anything the reporter says may be disputed as inaccurate or biased. For these reasons, issues are not high-priority items for reporters on the campaign trail.

There is good evidence that the horse race plays well with the audience, while issues do not. Using a multimedia CD as the medium, Stanford University researchers gave a representative sample of online American voters a large number of typical news reports (from broadcast and print-based sources) about the 2000 presidential campaign three weeks before the election. The CD was programmed to enable usage tracking—that is, recording the specific pages that participants accessed, the number of times they used the CD, and the length of their CD sessions.

The CD usage data revealed that news stories focusing on the horse race were the most popular. After adjusting for the location or placement of the news story within the CD (stories that appeared first or second received much more attention than stories that appeared in the hundredth position), the section on the horse race was found to be the most visited section (with an average of nineteen page visits per respondent). Polling-related stories even attracted more attention from CD users than stories focusing on the candidates' personal attributes. In contrast, issue-based stories attracted virtually no attention; the average number of visits to reports covering the candidates' positions on the issues could not be distinguished (with statistical reliability) from zero (see Iyengar, Norpoth, & Hahn 2004).

The inevitable consequence of interpretive reporting and the associated fixation on the horse race is a reduced role for the candidates themselves in daily news reports. The candidates still crisscross the country making four or five campaign speeches each day, but their appearances on network television amount to a bit role. The disappearance of candidates' voices from daily news coverage of the campaign is striking; in 1968, a viewer of network news could listen to the opposing candidates for over a minute each day. By 2004, the average duration of a candidate's sound bite was 7.7 seconds. Over the same period, the size of the journalist's sound bite has steadily increased.

Video Archive 3.2 Candidates' Own Voices in the News

COMBAT STORIES

Interpretive journalism demands that reporters do their utmost to keep campaigns off message—to cut through the spin cycle and expose the unrehearsed candidate, warts and all. The 2012 Mitt Romney campaign provided journalists ample opportunity to engage in interpretation when a video of the candidate speaking at a private fund-raiser was provided to *Mother Jones* and the Huffington Post. On the video, Romney made comments to the effect that nearly one-half of the electorate would vote for President Obama no matter what because they "believe that government has a responsibility to care for them, who believe that they are entitled to health care, to food, to housing, to you-name-it. That that's an entitlement. And the government should give it to them." The comments were especially compelling not only because they were unscripted and spontaneous, but also because they appeared to confirm the stereotype of Romney as a plutocrat unable to relate to ordinary people.

Other opportunities to keep campaigns on the defensive include publicizing inconsistencies between a candidate's record and rhetoric. During the 2008 Democratic presidential primary campaign, Hillary Clinton described landing in Bosnia in 1996 under sniper fire. Her image was severely tarnished when a video of the trip was released that showed her calmly walking down the tarmac, stopping on the runway to shake hands and to listen to a young girl read a poem. On the Republican side, Sarah Palin was ridiculed for supporting a policy toward Pakistan that was in direct opposition to John McCain's position. To use former presidential candidate Ross Perot's apt characterization, "gotcha" journalism is the order of the day.

A candidate can neutralize a feeding frenzy by mounting a strong counter response. During the 2008 campaign, Barack Obama initially denied ever hearing incendiary comments by his former pastor, the Reverend Jeremiah Wright, but then backtracked. To deal with the media storm that ensued, Obama severed all ties with Reverend Wright and delivered a major speech on racism in America. These actions proved sufficient to distance the candidate from the controversy.

The degree of conflict between the national press corps and the presidential candidates has reached the point that alternative news programs have emerged as significant outlets for the campaigns. Bill Clinton discovered he could avoid the constant gaggle over the state of his marriage by making the rounds of soft news programs, where questions were friendlier and he could more effectively control the message. The wisdom of the Clinton strategy is evident from studies that compare the tone of mainstream and nonmainstream news outlets. In the 2000 campaign, Matthew Baum (2005) tracked the coverage of the candidates in national newscasts, interviews with the candidates by serious journalists, and interviews by entertainment-oriented talk show hosts. As expected, he found that both Gore and Bush received much "kinder, gentler treatment" in the nontraditional venues. Candidates have realized the advantages of appearing on entertainment-oriented shows. Between 2004 and 2008, candidate appearances on late-night talk shows, such as *The Tonight Show with Jay Leno*, increased dramatically (see Figure 3.8).

The one area where the press typically achieves total control over the story line, and in many cases inflicts terminal harm to a campaign, concerns allegations of personal misconduct or other signs of unsuitability for office. From 1988, when Colorado Senator Gary Hart was exposed as an adulterer, to 1992, when Bill Clinton faced multiple news reports about his womanizing, to 2012, when

FIGURE 3.8

Avoiding Mainstream Media Negativity

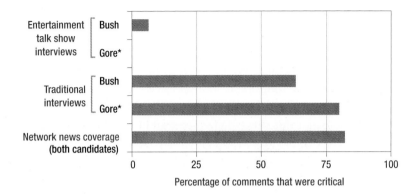

Percentage of comments that were critical

Number of Visits to Nontraditional Sources**

2004		2008	
John Edwards	5	John Edwards	5
Al Sharpton	5	John McCain	17
Howard Dean	4	Mike Huckabee	16
Carol Moseley Braun	3	Barack Obama	15
Wesley Clark	3	Hillary Clinton	7
		Joe Biden	6
		Dennis Kucinich	4
		Fred Thompson	3
		Chris Dodd	3

Source: Data from M. Baum. (2010). *Preaching to the choir or converting the flock? Presidential communication strategies in the age of new media.* Unpublished manuscript, Kennedy School of Government, Harvard University, Cambridge, MA.

*Gore gave no interviews on entertainment talk shows.

**Nontraditional sources* refers to programs such as *The Daily Show* and *Colbert Report.*

allegations of sexual harassment forced Herman Cain to withdraw from the presidential race, the press has held candidates accountable for their personal behavior. Bill Clinton faced multiple stories describing his womanizing; to 1998, when a young White House intern was sexually linked with President Clinton. More recently, New York Governor Eliot Spitzer was forced to resign after he was linked to a prostitution ring. During the early weeks of the 2012 Republican primary campaign, little-known business executive Herman Cain registered strong gains in the polls on the strength of his unconventional background (he had never held elective office) and his proposals to introduce a flat income tax. Cain's bubble was burst by revelations of sexual harassment

Video Archive 3.3
Feeding Frenzies

and awards of severance pay to women employees who filed the complaints. On December 3, Cain withdrew from the race.

As in the case of horse-race news, sex and scandal meet both the economic and the professional aspirations of journalists. Ratings go up, the journalist makes the front page, and the candidate is weakened. Unlike inconsistencies in a candidate's voting record or policy preferences, which might conveniently be attributed to changed circumstances or other complex excuses, it is impossible for candidates to evade responsibility for their personal misconduct. News coverage of the character issue is especially damning because the personal responsibility is unavoidable. All these ingredients, as Howard Kurtz (1999), the media critic for the *Washington Post*, pointed out, made Monica Lewinsky the perfect subject for news coverage when it emerged that President Bill Clinton had an affair with Lewinsky:

> And then along came Monica. When Monica Lewinsky first burst into public view on January 21, 1998, the journalists were presented with more than a juicy scandal. It was a chance to convince the public at long last that Clinton was a liar. Whitewater was too arcane? Fundraising too complicated? Here at long last was a plot everyone could understand—a president having a tawdry affair with an intern half his age. And the journalists were right on one fundamental point. The president was lying. It was a legitimate story. The president was under criminal investigation by the independent counsel. But the press went crazy, bonkers, totally over the top. All Monica on the nighttime cable shows with the same cast of characters, all Monica on the Sunday shows, all Monica on the front pages and the magazine covers. And yes, pretty close to all Monica on my CNN program, *Reliable Sources*, where we would critique the all Monica coverage of the other all Monica outlets.

The prominence of the character issue in recent history raises an important historical question: why were reports about the candidates' personal lives missing from the news coverage of campaigns in the 1950s and 1960s? It is implausible that the nomination process in those decades produced candidates of such impeccable moral strength that there was simply no basis for questions over their character and integrity. The well-known *New York Times* correspondent R. W. (Johnny) Apple describes his first assignment for the paper as watching the elevators going up to President Kennedy's suite in a New York City hotel. Among the president's visitors was a well-known Hollywood actress. Apple dutifully informed his editor, who showed little interest. By 1980, it would have been impossible to keep this story off the front page!

The character issue was not big news in 1960 because the all-male press corps did not deem womanizing as especially unethical or immoral. The values of the newsroom led journalists to believe that they had better things to do than investigate the bedroom. The media began to consider marital infidelity unacceptable behavior only after journalism opened its doors to women. The culture of the newsroom changed to acknowledge that candidates' bad treatment of a spouse could be thought to reflect poorly on their candidacy.

As the nonappearance of character stories in the 1950s and 1960s suggests, the fact that journalists are trained to suppress their own values when covering elections does not guarantee that these values will not eventually creep into news reports. It is well known that journalists are more likely to identify as Democrats than as Republicans, and critics of the right have long attacked the mainstream media for providing a liberal slant on the news. In fact, however, as we note in the conclusion to this chapter, these fears are misplaced. Most careful analyses of campaign news find few traces of one-sided coverage. For not only are partisan values easy to suppress (by providing candidates equal time), but reporters are especially eager to debunk the liberal-media hypothesis.

If campaign coverage in the 1950s and 1960s reflected the culture of an all-male press corps, more recently the effects of an all-white newsroom were clearer still. Despite some progress, journalism remains a field that underrepresents people of color. Overall, minorities made up less than 15 percent of all journalists (compared with 37 percent of the national population), meaning that few media outlets can match the populations they serve in racial or ethnic background. Tellingly, the absence of diversity is clearest where it matters most, at top management. The most recent American Society of Newspaper Editors survey reports that 86 and 91 percent of television and radio news directors respectively are Caucasian (Radio Television Digital News Association, 2013).

The insensitivity of reporters to issues of racial bias is especially clear in local television news coverage of crime. We have already noted that local TV stations converged on crime as a means of strengthening their audience appeal. In doing so, they focus on particular episodes of crime, which means that, more often than not, the audience is given information about a suspect. In the previously cited Los Angeles study of local news, crime stories provided footage of the suspect—in the form of either a live arrest or a photograph or police sketch of the suspect at large—in more than half the instances. Generally the suspect was either Hispanic or African American.

Even in the absence of a debate about the accuracy of racial profiling of the crime issue by local newscasts, the daily association of criminal activity with the minority community constitutes strong evidence of racial bias. As community advocates have noted, often vehemently, there is much more to the minority community than violence and crime, but these more positive elements are not news. The all-consuming focus on crime to the exclusion of other activities is equivalent to university administrators' informing the news media only about minority dropout rates while ignoring the awards and distinctions achieved by minority students. Why, then, have local news stations persisted in presenting a clearly one-sided view of racial minorities? The answer is simple: the television newsroom across the country is disproportionately white. The lack of diversity in the newsroom translates into habitual acceptance of news reports that stereotype minorities.

ACCESSIBILITY AND APPROPRIATENESS

Turning to more mundane elements of the organizational process model, the news must often be tailored to the specific needs of news organizations. Accessibility generally refers to the ability to cover stories in timely fashion. In terms of everyday news, there is good reason that Washington, DC, is the center of the universe for most major news organizations. This is where they station most of their correspondents. The *Los Angeles Times* and *New York Times* both assign more correspondents to Washington, DC, than to their respective state capitals. As national news organizations, both papers have more interest in the US Congress than in the New York or California legislatures. National news most frequently emanates from the seat of the national government, and news organizations allocate their resources accordingly.

The need for accessibility works as a disincentive for news organizations to cover international news. Most news organizations are hard-pressed to cover developments in Outer Mongolia. In the case of television, the share of international news in the national newscasts has fallen significantly since the end of the Cold War. The likelihood of a newsworthy event occurring in Bangladesh is insufficiently high for the *New York Times* to station a correspondent in that country.

The importance of accessibility to news organizations is a particularly compelling argument against the news-as-mirror-image argument. If the news were indexed to an objective indicator of importance, one would expect that, in the case of natural disasters, coverage would be proportional to the number of people who die. Traditionally, the level of coverage of international disasters by the American press was less responsive to the scope of the disaster and more dependent on the distance of the event from Washington, DC: the closer the disaster to the United States, the greater the coverage.[10] But more recently, the development of portable communication devices (most notably the videophone) has reduced the costs of overseas coverage. Much of the live coverage of the 2010 Haitian earthquake and the uprising in Iran in 2009 was in the form of Twitter messages and videos posted on YouTube.

Potential news stories vary not only in their accessibility but also in their appropriateness, or fit, to the particular mission of news organizations. Developments in the stock market are of greater interest to outlets with a focus on the economy; stories involving nuclear waste are especially newsworthy to news audiences in close proximity to nuclear dump sites. Many news outlets are, in fact, aimed at niche audiences; these outlets necessarily rely on different criteria for judging the newsworthiness of stories. And, as noted already, news organizations treat international, national, regional, and local events differently. A traffic accident is not news for the *New York Times* but may be a candidate for the lead story on New York City local newscasts.

An alternative definition of appropriateness is independent of subject matter or geography. Some news stories are more likely to be covered to a greater or lesser extent, simply depending on the medium. Broadcast outlets emphasize certain issues and ignore others, and print media reveal a different set of preferences. In the case of television news, issues that generate compelling visual images are especially appropriate. From the perspective of a television reporter, the presence of a clear story line and the ability to convey the report within two minutes are additional pluses. Conversely, issues that have fewer concrete referents, or episodes, and that require talking heads are unlikely to be judged broadcast worthy. Dueling mathematical models of budget deficits and economists' views on macroeconomics may be covered by PBS's *News Hour* but will almost certainly be ignored by network television.

The particular needs of television create a demand for action news. During the 1980s, the three networks covered two policy areas—crime and terrorism—more often than any other. This pattern was evident well in advance of the current preoccupation with terrorism. Both issues provided a steady supply of dramatic visual images, a story line consisting of the forces of good versus evil, and an ample supply of individual victims for gut-wrenching interviews. Although the networks aired hundreds of stories on crime and terrorism, they broadcast fewer than fifteen reports on the subject of global warming. The more complex the subject matter is, the less likely it is that the issue will be sufficiently telegenic.

ROUTINES AND PROCEDURES

News organizations rely on well-developed routines as a means of anticipating the location of newsworthy events and facilitating their reporters' ability to cover the stories in a timely manner. These routines include establishing deadlines, assigning reporters to news beats, and relying on authoritative sources.

News reports require considerable editing and revision before they see the light of day. Before the Internet, the daily news cycle made it imperative that reporters finalize their stories in time for the publishing deadline. In the case of the evening news, the report had to be filmed, edited, and transmitted to New York well in advance of the 5:30 PM broadcast. In practice, events occurring in the late afternoon were necessarily ignored. Today such late-breaking events still do not make the newscasts, but instead they are posted immediately on the networks' websites. As news organizations have replicated themselves online, the news cycle has become compressed. In the views of many, this acceleration of the news cycle has contributed to sloppier journalism. The rush to print or broadcast is often accompanied by an inadequate level of background research and fact checking, as evidenced by the *New York Post*'s mistaken revelation in its July 6, 2004, issue that Congressman Gephardt was Senator Kerry's running mate in the presidential election.

The beat system developed as a way of acclimatizing reporters, allowing them to gain expertise with a particular area or subject matter, and giving them the opportunity to schmooze and develop good relations with key newsmakers. Beats could be defined geographically (such as the West Coast) or topically (for example, healthcare). In some cases, beats reflect career trajectories; the prestige beats are those that guarantee the occupant a regular presence in a paper or broadcast. For national organizations, the three premier beats are the White House, State Department, and Pentagon (sometimes referred to as the Golden Triangle); given the newsworthiness of their location, these reporters become household names in a hurry.

Another standard operating procedure of news organizations is to examine and mimic the offerings of the competition. A fixture in any broadcast newsroom is the panel of television monitors playing the newscasts of other stations. As in any other profession, there are leaders and followers. On any typical day, the stories printed on the front page of the *New York Times* invariably appear in the network newscasts. The term *pack journalism* refers to the tendency of high-prestige news organizations to define the daily agenda. Traces of pack journalism are especially visible during the early stages of primary campaigns, when uncertainty over the outcome is the greatest and inexperienced journalists often follow the lead of well-known veterans. In 1968, for instance, in the aftermath of a chaotic Iowa caucus, the scene in the Des Moines newsroom was this:

> Johnny Apple of the *New York Times* sat in a corner and everyone peered over his shoulder to find out what he was writing. The AP guy was looking over one

shoulder, the UPI guy over the other, and CBS, ABC, NBC, and the Baltimore *Sun* were all crowding in behind. . . . No one knew how to interpret these figures, what was good and what was bad, and they were taking it off Apple. He would sit down and write a lead, and they would go write leads. . . . When he wanted quiet to hear the guy announce the latest returns, he'd shout for quiet and they'd all shut up. (Crouse, 1972, p. 84)

Although *pack journalism* generally refers to a top-down process of influence, at times the logic is reversed and the prestige press chases after purveyors of soft news. Dominick Dunne, who covered the O. J. Simpson case from day one for *Vanity Fair*, emerged as an authoritative source and was quoted extensively in major print and broadcast national outlets. The *New York Times*, in its coverage of the case, saw fit to cite information published in the *National Enquirer*.

As we will discuss in Chapter 5, the emergence of new media has led, at times, to a reversal of conventional pack journalism. Bloggers and other online sources can be the first to break a story. This was the case with the Drudge Report and the Monica Lewinsky scandal, and it occurred more recently, when the Huffington Post posted an audiotape of Obama's comments about voters who "get bitter, [and] cling to their guns and religion."

SOURCES

Sources are perhaps the most critical elements of the news-gathering process. A basic principle of modern journalism is that news is whatever public officials say it is. As Sigal (1973) states, "Even when the journalist is in a position to observe an event directly, he remains reluctant to offer interpretations of his own, preferring instead to rely on his news sources. . . . In short, most news is not what has happened but what someone says has happened" (p. 69).

Where do reporters go to get the news? In most cases, they do not assemble at the scene of an event, but gravitate instead to sources that can provide authoritative accounts of the event. This practice translates into a dependence on government officials. Most newsworthy issues are the province of government agencies or departments. An exodus of refugees fleeing the civil war in Syria sends reporters straight to the State Department, the latest figures on the trade deficit make the Department of Commerce the news hub, and so on. Even by a conservative count, the overwhelming majority of news stories each day emanates from official sources. In the case of the White House, virtually anything the president does (or fails to do) is news.

Reporters are well aware that official sources often have a vested interest in shaping the news. In the case of obviously partisan sources (such as the chair of the Republican National Committee), reporters maintain their objectivity by relying on counter sources from the opposing side of the partisan divide to ensure that the bias is cancelled out. However, objective and balanced coverage requires dissent and conflict among official sources. When official sources all speak with one voice, then the press becomes a tool of government. As we will describe in the next chapter, periods of international tension and impending or actual military conflict are typically devoid of open partisan dissent. As a result, at such times reporters become spokespersons for the administration.

The relationship between reporters and sources is complex, often subject to elaborate rituals. In some cases a government official provides information but does not wish to be identified (so the journalist cites "a highly placed source"). In other cases, officials seek out reporters to provide information in an attempt either to weaken their policy opponents (the typical case of a leak) or to test the waters over an impending policy proposal (the trial balloon). Shortly before the 2004 Republican National Convention, for example, several news organizations reported that the Bush administration was considering a new space initiative aimed at exploration of Mars. Reaction to these reports was swift and derisive; commentators noted that space exploration seemed an unlikely priority, given that the US budget deficit was at an all-time high. The Bush staff got the message; the president's acceptance speech contained no reference to space exploration initiatives.

In still other cases, the reporter–source relationship becomes a matter of litigation, as in disclosures of information that may threaten national security. The controversy over the revelation by the syndicated conservative columnist Robert Novak in 2003 that the wife of a well-known critic of the Bush administration was a CIA agent prompted a grand jury investigation into Novak's source, the conviction of Lewis Libby (an adviser to President Bush) on perjury and obstruction of justice charges related to the case, and considerable public speculation about the identity of Novak's highly placed source. We defer further discussion of the ways in which official sources attempt to manipulate reporters to Chapter 4.

CONCLUSION

Contrary to the assertion that the news is simply a mirror-image reflection of what happens, we have shown that news content reflects a complex set of interactions between the imperatives of the marketplace and the professional aspirations of journalists. The economic model is by far the more straightforward account: the news is simply what sells. Although there is considerable evidence that economic pressures leave their imprint on the news, there is more to news than the desire to protect the bottom line. No matter what they might say to the contrary, journalists have an agenda; they strive to cover campaigns in ways that maximize their autonomy and, happily for them, increase their own professional visibility.

No one who watches television talk shows will be surprised at the revolving door between the regularly invited guests and the list of reporters covering the campaign. Interpretive coverage is defended on the grounds that journalists have a responsibility to protect the public from the machinations of campaign strategists, but it provides considerable side benefits as well. Campaign journalists who project their voices into the news every day not only appear on *Washington Week* or *The Situation Room;* they also command significant book advances from publishers.

One factor conspicuously absent from the commercial-organization process account of news is partisan intent. Politicians, interest groups, and commentators—especially those employed by Fox News—regularly allege that there is ideological bias in news coverage. Conservatives claim that the mainstream media—print and broadcast—are staffed by Democrats whose reporting reflects their personal politics. The media's relentless pursuit of the Watergate scandal led many Republicans to suggest that journalists were motivated by their hostility to the Nixon administration. Nixon's vice president (Spiro Agnew), for instance, attacked broadcast journalists as "nattering nabobs of negativity" who were out of touch with the "silent majority." (Twenty-five years later, when journalists pursued President Clinton with equal vigor in the course of the Lewinsky scandal, Democrats made much the same argument.) The fact that journalists and editors at the most prestigious outlets identify themselves as Democrats lends credence to the charges of liberal bias. The *New York Times* last endorsed a Republican presidential candidate in 1956.

For their part, liberal critics see American journalists as captives of their conglomerate owners. The overriding financial interests of corporate owners, in this account, act as disincentives for journalists to write stories exposing questionable business practices, even when these practices harm consumers. Thus, the American media were reluctant to publicize the public health consequences of smoking, for fear of offending an industry that was a major source of advertising revenue. And in some cases, these critics allege, the conservative views of corporate owners also affect coverage of political issues and candidates. In 2004, for instance, the Sinclair Broadcast Group—a company that owns some sixty local television stations—ordered their ABC affiliates not to broadcast a special issue of *Nightline* produced by the ABC Network in which the show's anchor, Ted Koppel, read the names of American servicemen and women killed in Iraq. Later that year, the same company announced that their stations would air a documentary critical of Senator John Kerry two weeks before the presidential election. It was only after consumer groups threatened to boycott Sinclair's advertisers that the company backed down and decided not to air the program.

Notwithstanding the hue and cry over allegations of conservative or liberal bias in the news, the fact remains that political motives are less important determinants of news content than are commercial and organizational pressures. The evidence indicates that the American media have performed quite well according to the criterion of balanced political coverage. Issues and events are typically covered in point–counterpoint fashion so that the audience invariably gains exposure to the Democratic and Republican perspective on any given story (see D'Alessio & Allen, 2000). Newspaper coverage of American governors, for example, treats incumbents of both parties similarly, providing favorable coverage during periods of falling unemployment and crime rates but turning critical when real-world conditions deteriorate.

In the post-Internet era, however, there are clear signs of a revival of partisan journalism. As the number of news sources increases, offering news coverage with an overt partisan slant may be an effective strategy for getting ahead in a competitive market. The conservative Fox News Channel consistently ranks as the most watched cable news channel, the conservative commentator Rush Limbaugh hosts the highest-rated talk radio show in the United States, and liberal-oriented programs on MSNBC (such as the *Rachel Maddow Show*) have increased their ratings. News coverage of politics on cable news is very much polarized; during the 2012 presidential campaign MSNBC's coverage of Mitt Romney was 76 percent unfavorable and 3 percent favorable (Pew Research Center, 2012). Fox was only slightly less one-sided in the opposite direction providing coverage of Obama that was 46 percent unflattering and 6 percent positive.

In addition to the growth of partisan commentary on cable TV, online news sources offer similarly biased offerings. The liberal Huffington Post is among the most popular online news sites. In fact, the political blogs with the largest online audiences all offer overtly partisan news and analysis. As we discuss in Chapter 5, the growing reach of cable and online sources that deliver partisan news is testimony to the importance of consumers' political views as a determinant of who they turn to for information. Given their increased ability to select from multiple providers, consumers with strong partisan preferences will gravitate to the news source that provides coverage and commentary they find agreeable rather than disagreeable.

Notwithstanding the ongoing debate over media bias, the real problem facing American journalism is less the intrusion of political motives into editorial decisions but more the fact that journalism has become less motivated by the need to inform the public and more intent on offering programming that entertains. There is no shortage of compelling factoids on the extent of media shirking. Nationwide, broadcast media offerings in 2013 included less than 1 percent that could be considered (even by a generous definition) public affairs programming. In the case of local news—admittedly the most deficient outlet—the results are mind-boggling. In 2002, more than half of the top-rated local stations aired newscasts in the seven weeks preceding the election that contained absolutely no reference to the election! In the 2004 congressional elections, the amount of time taken up by campaign ads in local newscasts exceeded the amount of political news coverage by a ratio of more than 10 to 1 (Kaplan, Goldstein, & Hale, 2005). When elections are newsworthy, it is for the wrong reasons. During the closing stages of the 2012 presidential campaign, as both candidates focused their efforts on debating the issues before the American people, horse-race news exceeded issue-oriented news by a factor of more than 2 to 1.

The fixation on the horse race and strategy catches the attention of the audience while simultaneously providing journalists an edge in their continuing clash with the campaigns to shape the content of the news. In the end, the new style of reporting presents the campaign as theatrics rather than as a genuine clash of ideas. Major campaign events such as debates and conventions are ignored altogether by news organizations with significant market share. Thus, by any stretch of the imagination, modern journalism does not deliver the marketplace of ideas that is so vital to the exercise of informed and engaged citizenship. Unfortunately, the verdict is equally pessimistic when we turn to journalism's second potential contribution to the democratic process—namely, serving as a watchdog over the actions of government officials.

SUMMARY

1. Historically, where Americans get their news has depended on the development of new technologies for transmitting information. In the 1920s, radio began to supplant newspapers as the main source of news for most Americans, and radio was itself supplanted by television in the 1950s.

2. The spread of cable television—and more recently the Internet—has transformed the news landscape, but the most serious threat to network news today is local news.

3. The credibility of the media in the eyes of the American public has declined sharply in recent decades.

4. Market forces influence the form and content of news. Market pressures are especially intense in the world of broadcast news, where soft news, sitcoms, and reality television shows attract much larger audiences than serious news does. News producers adapt to the competition from soft news, sitcoms, and cable talk shows by making their own news programs more entertaining and less serious. The current twenty-four-hour news cycle has also increased pressure, as news organizations strive to deliver the news faster than their competitors do.

5. Organizational processes and the professional principles of journalists also influence what is reported. Modern political journalism rests on two dominant values: objectivity and autonomy. In attempting to protect their autonomy, reporters tend toward a more analytic form of news coverage centered on interpretation and analysis. Ad watches, candidate strategy, the horse race, and scandal stories feature prominently in this kind of coverage.

6. Accessibility and appropriateness also shape news coverage. In terms of everyday news, Washington, DC, is the center of the universe for most major news organizations and that's where most of their correspondents are stationed (and hence have access to stories). The appropriateness of a story for a particular news outlet also determines whether it will receive coverage; a car crash in Dallas is not news for the *New York Times*, for example. In addition, a story is more likely to be covered by a television news outlet if it generates compelling visual imagery.

7. Finally, the routines and procedures followed by news organizations have substantial impact on the content and form of the news. The pace of the news cycle means that events are more likely to be covered if they occur at some times of the day than at others. Assigning reporters to news beats ensures a steady flow of stories on those beats. And, in covering an event, reporters gravitate to sources that can provide authoritative accounts of the event, which means that they rely on government officials for their information.

FURTHER READINGS

Bagdikian, B. H. (2000). *The media monopoly* (6th ed.). Boston: Beacon.

Baker, C. E. (2002). *Media, markets, and democracy.* New York: Cambridge University Press.

Baum, M. (2010). *Preaching to the choir or converting the flock? Presidential communication strategies in the age of new media.* Unpublished manuscript, Kennedy School of Government, Harvard University, Cambridge, MA.

Baum, M. A. (2005). Talking the vote: Why presidential candidates hit the talk show circuit. *American Journal of Political Science, 49,* 213–234.

Crouse, T. (1972). *The boys on the bus.* New York: Random House.

Curran, J., Iyengar, S., Lund, A. B., & Salovaara-Moring, I. (2009). Media system, public knowledge, and democracy: A comparative study. *European Journal of Communication, 24,* 5–26.

D'Alessio, D., & Allen, M. (2000). Media bias in presidential elections: A meta-analysis. *Journal of Communication, 50,* 133–156.

Gilliam, F. D. Jr., & Iyengar, S. (2000). Prime suspects: The influence of local television news on the viewing public. *American Journal of Political Science, 44,* 560–573.

Goldman, S. K., & Mutz, D. C. (2011). The friendly media phenomenon: A comparative study of media environments and news consumption gaps in Europe. *Political Communication, 28,* 22–46.

Hallin, D. C. (1986). *The uncensored war: The media and Vietnam.* Berkeley: University of California Press.

Hamilton, J. T. (2003). *All the news that's fit to sell: How the market transforms information into news.* Princeton, NJ: Princeton University Press.

Iyengar, S. (1991). *Is anyone responsible?* Chicago: University of Chicago Press.

Kalb, M. (2001). *One scandalous story: Clinton, Lewinsky, and thirteen days that tarnished American journalism.* New York: Free Press.

Kaplan, M., Goldstein, K., & Hale, M. (2005). *Local news coverage of the 2004 campaigns: An analysis of nightly broadcasts in 11 markets.* University of Southern California: Norman Lear Center.

McChesney, R. W. (1999). *Rich media, poor democracy: Communication politics in dubious times.* Urbana: University of Illinois Press.

Patterson, T. (2007). *Young people and news.* Cambridge, MA: Joan Shorenstein Center for the Press, Politics and Policy, Kennedy School of Government, Harvard University.

Rosenstiel, T., & Jurkowitz, M. (2012). Winning the media campaign 2012. Pew Charitable Trusts. Retrieved from http://www.journalism.org/2012/11/02/winning-media-campaign-2012/.

Sigal, L. (1973). *Reporters and officials.* Lexington, MA: Heath.

NOTES

1. After nine years of partnership and the limited success of MSNBC in attracting an audience, Microsoft finally pulled out of the joint venture (Carter, 2005).

2. Nielsen has had to defend itself against charges of racial bias in audience counts. African American and Hispanic activists have complained that their communities are underrepresented by Nielsen's metering system, thus resulting in an undercount of the size of minority-oriented programs. The controversy is symptomatic of a more widespread debate provoked by Nielsen data

showing that network audiences are diminishing. Naturally, the networks would prefer to see data suggesting the opposite.

3. CNN maintains news bureaus in thirty-three countries and can be seen in more than two hundred countries.

4. Most media markets resemble oligopolies, with small numbers of news providers controlling the vast share of the market (Baker, 2002; McChesney, 1999).

5. This incident came back to haunt Rather during the 2004 presidential campaign. CBS aired what turned out to be an inaccurate report on President Bush's National Guard service. Critics immediately attributed the report to partisan bias. The blue-ribbon commission that investigated CBS's actions (at the network's own request) concluded that the report was a product of sloppy journalism rather than political bias. Immediately after the release of the report, Rather announced his intention to retire (see Chapter 5).

6. Respondents are provided with a four-point scale with endpoints of "believe all or most" (of what they encounter in the news source) and "cannot believe." Figure 3.6 shows the sum of the contiguous "all or most" and "almost all or most" categories.

7. Polling data are from a January 2014 poll conducted by the Public Policy Institute. Retrieved from http://www.publicpolicypolling.com/pdf/2014/PPP_Release_National_130.pdf.

8. In the post-9/11 environment, the US Department of State has attempted to compile statistics on the number of terrorist attacks and casualties on a worldwide basis. As noted in Chapter 4, the department's 2004 report (published in advance of the election) had to be retracted because it was found to underestimate the true level of terrorist activity by a substantial margin.

9. As some scholars have noted, the huge audiences for network news in the 1970s included a nontrivial inadvertent component: people who watched the *CBS Evening News* only because they were waiting for their favorite sitcom, which followed.

10. The tsunami coverage of 2004–2005 represents an exception to this pattern. The scope of this disaster was so unprecedented that it was the major news story across the world for several weeks.

4

Reporters, Official Sources, and the Decline of Adversarial Journalism

In 1974, Bob Woodward and Carl Bernstein, two enterprising reporters at the *Washington Post*, brought about the resignation of an incumbent president. Their systematic exposure of the Watergate cover-up represented the epitome of investigative journalism: a newspaper had single-handedly enforced the standard of honesty in government.

Twenty-four years later, President Clinton emphatically denied allegations that he had had a sexual relationship with a White House intern. His denials were met by an increasingly skeptical press corps, who proceeded to dig deeper into the story and whose efforts ultimately led Congress to initiate impeachment proceedings against the president.

In 2003, the Bush administration decided to invade Iraq, even without the support of key allies and the United Nations. The rationale for American unilateral action rested on two key premises: first, that the regime of Saddam Hussein had the capacity to develop and deliver chemical and biological weapons "in ways that can cause massive death and destruction" (in the words of Secretary of State Colin Powell, speaking at the United Nations in 2003); and second, that the regime was an active collaborator with the Al Qaeda terrorist organization.

What the Bush administration asserted, the press dutifully reported. American journalists accepted the guilty-as-charged claims against Saddam Hussein with little hesitation, despite the opinions of credible international experts to the contrary. One of the country's leading newspapers, the *New York Times*, published a series of reports that supported the administration's position and used Iraqi expatriates as corroborating sources. These same sources (Ahmed

Chalabi, for instance) were in fact either employed by American intelligence or harbored aspirations of political power in a post-Hussein Iraq.

The successful invasion of Iraq and overthrow of the Hussein regime was followed by several months of frenzied American efforts to find the Iraqi weapons of mass destruction. Gradually, it became apparent that the weapons did not exist. As for the second alleged threat posed by Iraq—the close relationship with Al Qaeda—the 9/11 Commission and other experts ultimately concluded that, although there were isolated contacts, these did not amount to a collaborative relationship. Thus, both key premises of the policy of unilateral intervention proved erroneous. Two leading American daily newspapers—the *New York Times* and the *Washington Post*—issued public apologies for their failure to investigate the Bush administration's case against Iraq.

More recently, the clandestine surveillance of foreign leaders, officials of international organizations, and the tracking of the electronic communications of millions of American citizens by the National Security Agency was exposed by former NSA employee Edward Snowden. As an NSA contractor, Snowden had access to the relevant documents and leaked them to the British newspaper *The Guardian*. Had Snowden not acted, the press (and the public) would have remained in the dark about NSA's widespread violations of fundamental privacy rights protected by the American Bill of Rights.

What accounts for the striking contrast between the performance of the press during the Watergate and Lewinsky scandals and today? Why was the press instinctively skeptical when Nixon and Clinton denied wrongdoing, but passively willing to accept the Bush administration's misleading claims concerning the necessity of war with Iraq? The explanation, as outlined in this chapter, is that in matters of national security, the press has been stripped of its ability to act as an adversary of government. Where domestic political events are concerned, the presence of vocal and authoritative critics grants journalists the necessary leverage to question official accounts. On matters of foreign policy and national security, however, critics of government policy tend to fall silent; the press is left with only official sources.

INDEXING THE NEWS

Inevitably, reporters depend on official sources. Nevertheless, they seek to maintain objectivity in coverage. High-ranking officials, for their part, have a strong political stake in eliciting coverage that reflects favorably on their performance. During political campaigns, these sometimes divergent interests create a basic tension between candidates and journalists that profoundly shapes not only the news coverage of campaigns but also the content of everyday news, as government officials seek to promote their policies while reporters attempt to provide objective and balanced news.

For the press to act as a fourth branch of government, journalists must necessarily treat official pronouncements with skepticism. Because they are typically trained as generalists, journalists lack the substantive policy expertise to question or rebut government sources on their own. For critical analysis, they turn to authoritative sources that may provide a fresh perspective on official policies. If the supply of opposition sources dries up, journalists have no real choice but to defer to official accounts. The availability of opposition sources generally dwindles in the arenas of foreign policy and national security, especially during periods of national crisis or international conflict. During the heat of crisis, journalists tend to cover the story exactly as it is given to them.

In a news system based on official sources, the reality of public policy is the state of official opinion. Reporters attempt to mirror this reality by adjusting their coverage to be in line with the level and intensity of debate among the elites. The higher the level of elite dissent, the easier it is for the reporter to pit competing sources against each other.

In practical terms, indexing the news means that the press can represent an adversarial posture only when opponents of government policy outnumber (or prove more vocal than) proponents. On occasions when opponents with stature are not to be found and the government speaks with one voice, the

 IN FOCUS

Indexing the News

Indexing is the process of adjusting coverage of an issue according to the level of disagreement and debate about that issue among policy elites. Indexing is due in large part to the journalistic norms of using official sources and of seeking objectivity by reporting different sides of a debate. If there is conflict among officials, there are opposing viewpoints on which journalists can report and which they can use as a starting point for open debate of the policy in the news. If there is consensus among officials—as there tends to be in foreign policy issues, and particularly during national security crises—there is no reportable conflict, and coverage, when it happens, tends to be deferential.

watchdog role falls entirely on reporters. Because reporters have neither the time nor the expertise to critique the views of their sources, elite consensus inevitably slants the news in favor of government policy.

In practice, the indexing system works well for domestic issues (in the sense of allowing reporters to maintain their autonomy from any particular source), but in the domain of foreign policy and national security, it results in near-total official control over the news. For most domestic issues, there exists a variety of politically viable policy alternatives and a corresponding network of competing official sources. Arguments over affirmative action, for instance, range from the complete elimination of race-based preferences to government-funded compensation for the victims of discrimination (such as reparations). Any Republican initiative on affirmative action will be met by a chorus of Democratic dissents. Economic issues provide an equally competitive set of sources; as soon as President Obama takes credit for the latest decline in unemployment, the media immediately turn to Republican officials for the appropriate antidotes (for example, Republicans might point out that there are more Americans living in poverty than ever before).

One layer removed from government, the press can call on a second team of sources drawn from various think tanks, with their stables of former officials, policy entrepreneurs, and academic researchers with special expertise. On August 4, 2010, addressing the recovery from the BP oil spill, the head of the National Oceanic and Atmospheric Administration announced that "at least 50 percent of the oil that was released is now completely gone from the system. And most of the remainder is degrading rapidly or is being removed from the beaches." Reporters were quick to interview researchers who disputed these claims. MSNBC, for instance, interviewed Samantha Joye, a marine sciences professor at the University of Georgia, who stated, "I have not seen data that leads me to conclude that 50 percent of the oil is gone." In the case of domestic politics, therefore, journalists have no difficulty resisting official spin. The level of elite disagreement and availability of competing sources is sufficient to ensure balanced, objective reporting.

When foreign policy and national security are the issues of the day, the indexing system breaks down, and officials attain substantial control over the flow of news. Traditionally, foreign affairs have not excited partisan divisions; the executive branch enjoys wide latitude to formulate and implement American foreign policy. During the era of the Cold War, for example, there was general bipartisan support for policies designed to resist the spread of international communism. The president exercises tight control over the foreign policy process; White House, State Department, and Pentagon officials offer up a coordinated, uniform take on the events of the day. Moreover, foreign policy events typically occur beyond the geographic reach of most news organizations. Foreign correspondents are few and far between.

The ethnic massacres in the Darfur region of Sudan became a relevant story for US news organizations only after Secretary of State Colin Powell toured the region in September 2004 and accused the Sudanese government of "genocide." Seven years later, President Obama made front-page news when he announced to the nation that US Special Forces had found and killed Osama bin Laden in Pakistan. Both these examples illustrate how incumbent officials are typically able to orchestrate the news coverage of foreign affairs.

Although American officials are the principal sources of information in the foreign policy and national security arenas, journalists can introduce a semblance of balance into their reporting by seeking out foreign leaders—especially those who disagree with US policy—to offset White House or Pentagon accounts. In the weeks leading up to the Iraq War, for instance, prominent European critics of the Bush administration policies were frequently quoted in major American newspapers (see Hayes & Guardino, 2013).

The state of play between the American press and the foreign policy establishment is exemplified by the treatment accorded the State Department's annual *Patterns of Global Terrorism* report. This report purports to document both the frequency and the severity of terrorist incidents. At the press briefing to announce the release of the 2003 report, Deputy Secretary of State Richard Armitage was on hand to declare, "You will find in these pages clear evidence that we are prevailing in the fight." The data revealed a stunning 40 percent decline in the frequency of terrorist incidents since 2001. According to the numbers, 2003 was the safest year on record since 1969. This rosy assessment of the war against terrorism made big news across the country. In its April 29, 2004, news story (see Figure 4.1), CNN suggested that the Bush administration was winning the war on terrorism. The following month, in a *Washington Post* op-ed column, two scholars (Alan B. Krueger and David Laitin) identified numerous flaws in the State Department's report. All the observed decrease in terrorist activity had occurred within the category of nonsignificant events. Significant terrorist attacks (defined as those causing injury and loss of life) had in fact *increased* by about a third—from 124 incidents in 2001 to 169 in 2003. This revised scorecard obviously reflected less favorably on the administration.

In response to the Krueger–Laitin rebuttal, the State Department was forced to acknowledge the errors and prepare a corrected report. The revised report conceded that the level of terrorism had in fact risen since

FIGURE 4.1

CNN Coverage of the State Department Report on Iraq and Terrorism

---

Worldwide terrorist attacks down in 2003

Report: Iraq now 'a central battleground' in war on terror

From David Ensor and Elise Labott
CNN Washington Bureau

WASHINGTON (CNN) -- International acts of terror in 2003 were the fewest in more than 30 years, according to the U.S. State Department's annual terrorism report released Thursday.

The Patterns of Global Terrorism report said ˉ90 acts of international terrorism occurred in 2003 — a slight drop from ˉ98 attacks the previous year and the lowest total since 1969.

The figure marked a 45 percent decrease in attacks since 2001, but it did not include most of the attacks in Iraq, because attacks against combatants did not fit the U.S. definition of international terrorism.

Cofer Black, the State Department's ambassador at large for counterterrorism, told a news conference that he attributed the decrease to "unprecedented collaboration between the United States and foreign partners to defeat terrorism."

Source: Data from CNN. (2004, April 29). *Worldwide terrorist attacks down in 2003.* Retrieved July 26, 2005, from www
.cnn.com/2004/US/04/29/terror.report.

2001. To the highest-ranking counterterrorism official in the department, Ambassador J. Cofer Black, the errors represented database problems, not political spin:

> I want to be very clear: we here in the Counterterrorism Office, and I personally, should have caught any errors that marred the *Patterns* draft before we published it. But I assure you and the American people that the errors in the *Patterns* report were honest mistakes, and certainly not deliberate deceptions as some have speculated. (US Department of State, 2004)

The case of the botched terrorism report epitomizes press performance in the national security area. The evidence in question was a simple list of events, not complex statistical analysis. The fact that the report failed to include major terrorist attacks that occurred after November 11 (such as the bombing of the

British consulate and HSBC bank headquarters in Istanbul, in which twenty-five people died) should have been obvious to anyone with access to a calendar. Reporters initially failed to ask appropriate questions or engage in elementary background research; instead, they deferred to the credibility of the US State Department.

NATIONAL SECURITY NEWS: THE TRIUMPH OF OFFICIAL JOURNALISM

In comparison with foreign policy, national security matters provide officials with even more control over the press. When the United States resorts to military force, opposing elites generally close ranks behind the president. For fear of appearing unpatriotic, leaders of the out party choose not to criticize the administration's actions. The nation—at least as far as the media are concerned—stands united behind the men and women in uniform. Because potential opponents of the use of military force fall silent, the press becomes completely dependent on official spokespersons. In the aftermath of the September 11 attacks, nobody in Washington was willing to question the decision to overthrow the Taliban regime in Afghanistan. And when the Bush administration proposed the USA PATRIOT Act, a measure that would significantly erode Americans' civil liberties, it passed the US Senate by a vote of 99 to 1.

NEWS COVERAGE OF THE VIETNAM WAR: A CASE STUDY OF INDEXING

During the early period of media politics in the 1960s, the first real test of the media's ability to challenge official accounts was the war in Vietnam. In August 1964, the Johnson administration claimed that American navy vessels cruising in the Gulf of Tonkin had been deliberately attacked by North Vietnamese gunboats in two distinct incidents. The president ordered retaliatory air strikes and requested a joint resolution of Congress granting him the power to "take all necessary measures to repel any armed attack against the forces of the United States and to prevent further aggression." The Gulf of Tonkin Resolution, passed in 1964 by overwhelming majorities in the House and Senate, became the principal legal basis for expanding US military involvement in South Vietnam.

The news media did little to question the administration's account of the North Vietnamese attacks, instead deferring entirely to the Pentagon.

The major American news magazines, for instance, described the attacks as follows:

> As the "night glowed eerily," wrote *Time*, the Communist "intruders boldly sped" toward the destroyers, firing with "automatic weapons," while *Life* had the American ships "under continuous torpedo attack" as they "weaved through the night sea, evading more torpedoes." Not to be outdone, *Newsweek* described "US jets diving, strafing, flattening out . . . and diving again" at the enemy boats, one of which "burst into flames and sank." (Karnow, 1997, pp. 386–387)

Later it was revealed that there was only one torpedo attack and that the Vietnamese gunboats had, in fact, been provoked.

As American military involvement in South Vietnam increased, news organizations assigned reporters to file stories from the immediate vicinity of the conflict. These reporters found themselves relatively free to roam the country in search of news stories. Despite firsthand access to events, press accounts of the war in the early and mid-1960s proved entirely consistent with official US policy. Reporters suggested that the strategy of training the South Vietnamese to defend themselves (Vietnamization) was working effectively, that heavy losses were being inflicted each day on the communist Vietcong, and that American bombing of North Vietnam was necessary to disrupt the flow of supplies and personnel down the Ho Chi Minh trail.

Not only was the coverage supportive of stated American policy, but in a harbinger of what would occur later, news reports also avoided details and depiction of military combat. According to Braestrup's (1977) systematic compilation of network news coverage of the Vietnam War, less than 5 percent of all stories that aired on the evening news showed images of battle or American casualties. As described by media critic Michael Arlen (1969), the nightly news provided a

> stylized generally distanced overview of a disjointed conflict which was composed mainly of scenes of helicopters landing, tall grasses blowing in the helicopter wind, American soldiers fanning out across a hillside on foot, rifles at the ready, with now and then [on the sound track] a far-off ping or two, and now and then [as the grand visual finale] a column of dark billowing smoke a half mile away invariably described as a burning Viet Cong ammo dump. (p. 113)

Thus, the viewing audience had little reason to be concerned.

As the war continued and the American death toll mounted, the Washington consensus over Vietnam unraveled. Senator Eugene McCarthy, the most vocal critic of the war, challenged President Johnson for the 1968 Democratic presidential nomination. McCarthy's competitive showing in the New Hampshire primary (he received 41 percent of the vote) signaled unambiguously that his antiwar message was politically viable. In mid-March, Senator Robert Kennedy entered the presidential race. On March 31, realizing that the unpopularity of the war had made it increasingly difficult for him to wage a winning campaign, President Johnson announced that he would not seek reelection (see Video Archive 4.1). Suddenly Vietnam had transformed the American political landscape.

Video archive 4.1 LBJ Announcement

The emergence of multiple critics of the war was prompted not merely by the reading of the New Hampshire "tea leaves." There was also high drama in Vietnam. In January 1968, with apparent impunity, the Vietcong launched a full-scale military offensive, including a major assault on the US embassy in Saigon and coordinated attacks on major American military bases across the country. The Tet offensive and the American counteroffensive became huge news stories; images of napalmed villages, dead and maimed civilians, and American troops under intense enemy fire began to air regularly on television news, as illustrated in Video Archive 4.2.

Video Archive 4.2 Vietnam Coverage, 1968–1970

The Tet offensive and resulting images on the television screen cast serious doubt on the official accounts of the war. Reporters began to question Pentagon officials more aggressively in an effort to contrast the clinical tone of the daily Pentagon briefings with the bloody chaos on the ground. An increasing number of elected officials from both political parties defected to the antiwar position. Mirroring the shift in elite opinion, news reports from Vietnam became less tied to information provided by the US mission in Saigon (whose daily briefings came to be ridiculed as the "Five O'Clock Follies") and more focused on communist successes on the battlefield and the rapidly growing antiwar movement in the United States. By late 1968, the indexing process had kicked in and was producing full-fledged adversarial news.

In summary, news coverage of the Vietnam War provides a clear case of elite opinion leading the news in situations of both consensus and dissent. When Presidents Johnson and Nixon encountered minimal resistance to their military policies, press coverage toed the official line. As soon as well-known Americans made public their opposition to the war and the course of events on the battlefield began to clash with statements from Washington, deferential reliance on official sources gave way to coverage that was more aggressively critical of official policy.

THE LESSONS OF VIETNAM: RESTRICTED PRESS ACCESS

To policy planners in the Department of Defense, the lessons of Vietnam were clear: unrestrained battlefield coverage by the media—and especially by television news—could hamstring US strategy, primarily by weakening public support for military conflict. In the future, military officials would need to orchestrate the news more carefully.[1] The first step was to deny reporters access to the war zone, thereby forcing them to rely on official briefings. This more controlled approach was first exercised in 1983 with the American invasion of Grenada.

In October 1983, the elected government of the tiny Caribbean island of Grenada was overthrown by a group of leftist rebels. The former prime minister and several of his associates were killed. The new leaders declared themselves Marxists and appealed to Fidel Castro for assistance. American reaction to the coup was swift and predictable. Washington condemned the developments and declared that the installation of a communist government within the Americas was a violation of the Monroe Doctrine and incompatible with US national security interests. The administration cited the presence of Cuban military advisers and their efforts to expand the runways at Point Salines Airport as evidence of the new regime's hostile intent.

The fact that the leaders of the Grenada coup were communists was not the sole basis for intervention. A more urgent concern was the presence of American civilians on the island. St. George's University School of Medicine in Grenada, although unaccredited in the United States, attracted a substantial enrollment of American students. With lingering memories of the 1979 hostage crisis in Iran, the Reagan administration decided to preempt a potential hostage situation by invading Grenada (see Video Archive 4.3). American marines landed on October 25, 1983 (accompanied by a small contingent of soldiers from neighboring Caribbean nations) and arrested the rebel leaders with minimal loss of American life. The original constitution was reinstated.

Major news organizations reacted to the events in Grenada by hurriedly assembling news crews to report from the scene. Hundreds of American reporters attempted to make their way to Grenada. The Pentagon refused to give them access, citing national security concerns. Some newspapers then chartered their own boats in a last-ditch effort to get reporters to the front line. Most of these boats were intercepted and turned back by the American navy. The four American reporters who were based in Grenada accepted an offer from military commanders to file their reports from the USS *Guam*, anchored off the coast of Grenada, only to find that the offer was a hoax. The reporters were prevented from leaving the ship for two days.

In response to mounting media pressure, the Pentagon granted access to fifteen reporters, but they were not permitted to file reports from the immediate

▶ Video Archive 4.3 Reagan Speech on Grenada

area of the fighting. Thus, in the first few days of the conflict, the only information delivered to the American public consisted of official briefings and film clips produced by the military. Finally, five days after the invasion, the military granted general press access to all locations in Grenada.[2]

By preventing the press from covering the invasion and then spoon-feeding images and information that depicted American actions in the most favorable light (such as video of rescued American students kissing American soil on their return), the Reagan administration maintained complete control over the story. For the entire period before the president announced on national television that the threat to American security had been removed, American news organizations had been kept in the dark, unable to file independent reports on the situation in Grenada. The president appeared on national television accompanied by the prime minister of one of the neighboring islands, who enthusiastically commended the decisive action taken by the United States. In the days that followed, President Reagan's popularity increased by some 5 percentage points.

Some months after the invasion, several elements of the administration's story line came into question. The airport development was funded by a consortium of European and American companies, as well as by the Cubans. The runway expansion was designed to permit the landing of jumbo jets, thus increasing the volume of tourist traffic. It turned out that the number of Cuban troops in Grenada was less than half that claimed by the administration. The urgent request for US intervention from Grenada's neighbors was solicited rather than spontaneous. Several of the American medical students came forward to state that they had never been at risk. By the time these discrepancies came to light, however, the press had turned its attention to other matters and no real harm was done to President Reagan's credibility. From the perspective of the White House, the strategy of restricting press access had its intended effect; the Reagan administration's account of daily events held sway. In the words of former ABC Pentagon correspondent John McWethy:

When you are in a situation where your primary source of information is the United States government and where, for three days, basically your only source of information except Radio Cuba is the Pentagon, you are totally at their mercy and you have to make an assumption that the US government is telling the truth. You report that Caspar Weinberger, then the Secretary of Defense, says "the fighting was heaviest here," or Weinberger says "the barracks are under siege." Well, you believe it. What are you going to do? You report what he says. (Ansolabehere, Behr, & Iyengar, 1993, p. 197)

THE LESSONS OF GRENADA: MEDIA POOLS

In the aftermath of Grenada and the venting of considerable outrage over censorship of the press, the Pentagon was asked to undertake a review of its press-access policies. The government appointed a blue-ribbon commission consisting of military and press representatives to study the issue of press access to military combat. The panel recommended a pool system for covering future military operations. The press would be granted access, but only in the form of closely supervised *media pools*—small groups of reporters representing several print and broadcast news organizations who would work under close supervision of the Department of Defense. One camera crew, for instance, would provide all the video footage for the major networks.

Initially used in the 1989 American invasion of Panama, the pool system became fully institutionalized in 1991 with the onset of Operation Desert Storm, the campaign to liberate Kuwait from Iraqi occupation. Pool reporters were allowed to cover events in Kuwait, but because they were not permitted to stray from Kuwait City, their independent news-gathering ability was limited to question-and-answer sessions after the daily military briefings. Pooled reports were subject to military approval; in several cases (for example, a story about American pilots watching pornographic videos before their missions), stories were censored or altered. In a telling acknowledgment of the power of visual imagery, photographs and footage of body bags or coffins were prohibited.

In addition to rationing access, the Pentagon gave more careful attention to its choreographed daily presentations for the press. The military officers responsible for briefing the press put on a multimedia performance each day. Not only did film of American smart bombs or missiles hitting their intended targets with unerring accuracy demonstrate the military's concern for

---

 IN FOCUS

Media Pools

In an effort to limit media access without incurring charges of censorship, the Pentagon revised its policy about media access to war zones in 1989. The press would be granted access, but only in the form of closely supervised *media pools*—small groups of reporters representing several print and broadcast news organizations who would work under close supervision of the Department of Defense. The pool reporters' coverage is made available for use by all recognized news organizations.

---

minimizing Iraqi civilian casualties, but the images also provided compelling material for television newscasts. By relaying the official videos as news, television news spread the message of a clinical and sanitized war effort, devoid of all civilian suffering. In the words of one media critic, "The emphasis was on the nuts and bolts of a sophisticated war machine, but the consequences were never made plain. In other words, television portrayed the war as a war without victims. . . . Indeed, the press as a whole bought into the notion that this was somehow a kinder and gentler war" (Dorman, 1997, p. 121).

Another objective of the Pentagon media managers was to elicit news coverage that followed the official story line of Iraq as the transgressor, Kuwait as the victim, and the United States as the law enforcer. Saddam Hussein was depicted as a modern-day Hitler whose occupying forces had engaged in wanton destruction of Kuwaiti natural resources (such as setting oil fields ablaze) and brutal atrocities against Kuwaiti civilians. Adding to the Pentagon's media management efforts, the exiled rulers of Kuwait retained the well-known public relations firm of Hill and Knowlton to spread the word of numerous Iraqi violations of international law during the occupation. In one particularly vicious case, Iraqi soldiers were alleged to have looted a pediatric hospital in Kuwait City and disconnected hundreds of infants from life support equipment. Hill and Knowlton even produced an eyewitness who described the incident in detail to a congressional committee. In contrast to the Iraqis, who were depicted as demonstrating minimal concern for endangering civilian life, the American and coalition forces were portrayed as minimizing collateral damage in their bombing of Iraq. Thus, on all fronts, news coverage of the war accentuated the positive (see Video Archive 4.4).

Video Archive 4.4 Coverage of Operation Desert Storm

Once again, official accounts of the war went unchallenged. It was not until several months later that reports surfaced of the failure of several smart-weapons systems. During the war, the administration claimed that its Patriot missiles had intercepted and destroyed forty-one of forty-two airborne Iraqi Scud missiles. But an independent study by MIT professors Theodore Postol and George Lewis concluded that the missiles had failed to disable the Scud warhead in every instance. Contrary to what the videos that were played at the press briefings implied, the coalition bombing campaign had inflicted significant damage to civilian areas of Baghdad. An estimated thirty-five hundred Iraqi civilians were killed (Conetta, 2003). In addition, Hussein's alleged mass murder of Kuwaiti children was retracted; instead of the three hundred alleged victims, only one could be confirmed.

The various "corrections" to the official record were reported by the press, but only long after the war had receded from national attention. The 1992 presidential campaign was under way, and stories about the failing American economy and the surprisingly strong candidacy of an unknown governor from Arkansas took precedence over revised claims of American military and technological prowess or fabricated eyewitness testimony concerning the behavior of Iraqi soldiers.

A REFINEMENT OF MEDIA POOLS: EMBEDDED JOURNALISTS

In the most recent iteration of the national security media script, the Pentagon decided that it was no longer politically feasible to deny American reporters firsthand access to the 2003 invasion of Iraq. In a modernized version of pooled coverage, a select group of American and international correspondents were to be embedded with the invading forces. While accompanying the coalition forces into battle, the embedded reporters would be subject to strict limitations on the content of their reports; they could not, for instance, discuss operational details, nor could they make any slight reference to information that might be of strategic value. These guidelines were enforced; Geraldo Rivera, one of the embedded correspondents for Fox News, was expelled from Iraq for drawing a map of the mission in the sand.

Video Archive 4.5
Coverage of the Iraq War

As anticipated by the Pentagon, news reports filed by the embedded correspondents provided close-up and often dramatic footage of American troops in action. The public was given a live progress report of the invasion from the perspective of American soldiers, but without coverage of Americans killed in action or of civilians caught up in the fighting. The Project for Excellence in Journalism (cited in Entman, 2004, p. 116) studied embedded correspondents' reports on the major networks; not a single report showed images of people being killed by American soldiers (see Video Archive 4.5).

Once hostilities commenced, the inability of the press to counter official accounts of daily events was understandable: the Pentagon exercised its monopoly control over information. Briefings by the secretary of defense and other high-ranking military officials were the major sources of news. In the case of American television newscasts, the coverage was thoroughly dominated by current and former government officials. The media watchdog group Fairness and Accuracy in Reporting (FAIR) tracked all references to Iraq in four daily network newscasts (aired by ABC, CBS, NBC, and PBS) over a two-week period that ended one week after Secretary of State Colin Powell's speech at the United Nations in which he insisted that Iraq possessed weapons of mass destruction. During this period, broadcast news reports made reference to 393 sources. As expected, the great majority (68 percent) of the sources were Americans. Even more striking, three-fourths of the Americans interviewed in these programs were current or former government officials. Only one official (Senator Edward Kennedy) was opposed to the war. In a 2008 editorial (published on April 26), the *New York Times* dubbed the Pentagon's public information campaign in which former military officers, who were now working as consultants for news organizations, were given special access to information as a "kind of media Trojan horse—an instrument intended to shape terrorism coverage from inside the major TV and radio networks." Even when the networks invited non-Americans, they were drawn overwhelmingly (75 percent) from countries that supported the Bush administration's position on Iraq. Only 4 percent of the foreign sources expressed opposition to the war.[3]

In recruiting their nonofficial sources, the American networks showed only slightly less pro-administration bias. Of the ninety-six private citizens who commented on Iraq, 26 percent expressed skepticism about the war—a level of opposition that considerably understated opposition among the public at large. In contrast to the government sources, who were generally high-ranking officials, half of the nonofficial skeptics were unidentified persons in the street.

In short, network news coverage of the war during the period when many Americans were uncertain of their position was skewed in the direction of official policy. Even PBS, the network lampooned by conservatives as a leftist news source, featured a 4-to-1 ratio of war proponents to opponents in their coverage of Iraq. Given the daily exposure to such one-sided coverage, it's no wonder that American public opinion became increasingly supportive of the administration's war plans.

Still more glaring press failures occurred before the onset of hostilities. The Bush administration's policy of unilateral intervention rested on the premise that the regime of Saddam Hussein represented a significant military threat to the international community. According to American intelligence accounts, Iraq possessed significant stockpiles of chemical and biological weapons. As Secretary of State Colin Powell stated in his February 2003 address to the UN General Assembly,[4] "There can be no doubt that Saddam Hussein has biological weapons and the capability to rapidly produce more, many more. And he has the ability to dispense these lethal poisons and diseases in ways that can cause massive death and destruction." Powell's remarks were part of a pattern. A 2008 report by the Center for Public Integrity found that the Bush administration issued 935 false statements about the threats posed by Saddam Hussein between September 11, 2001, and a few months after the invasion of Iraq.

What is especially troubling is that these claims went unchallenged by the mainstream press, despite vociferous challenges from credible, international experts. For instance, on the very same day that President Bush referred to Iraqi efforts to obtain uranium for use in the production of nuclear weapons (a claim that was later acknowledged to be false), the deputy head of the UN inspections program held a press conference to debunk the alleged evidence of a renewed Iraqi nuclear program. More generally, months of sustained UN inspections had turned up no traces of the Iraqi weapons of mass destruction. David Kay, one of the UN inspectors later recruited to head the postwar American detection effort (euphemistically titled the Iraq Study Group), resigned in January 2004, stating that he did not believe Iraq had stockpiles of chemical or biological weapons.

In short, in the period leading up to war and continuing thereafter, the press had several opportunities to subject the administration's rationale for war to greater scrutiny. For the most part, these opportunities were squandered. Later, as the true extent of the discrepancies between the facts and official accounts became transparent, the *New York Times* and the *Washington Post* issued hard-hitting apologies for their generally one-sided coverage. In indicting their own judgment, the *Times* editors were brutally honest: "Editors at several levels who should have been challenging reporters and pressing for more skepticism were perhaps too intent on rushing scoops into the paper" ("From the Editors," 2004).

CONCLUSION

The outcome of the indexing system of calibrating the news to represent the state of elite debate depends on several circumstances. Clearly, when the focus is on the imminent use of American military force, the president's views are especially likely to dominate. Reporters feel free to ignore congressional leaders or foreign officials as sources because they know that the relevant decision makers are located at the White House and Pentagon. But when war is not imminent, when there is no clear security threat, or when American military power is used to facilitate humanitarian foreign aid (as was the case in Somalia in 1992), reporters are able to spread their news nets more widely and the coverage is less biased in favor of the administration.

The outcome of the indexing process also depends on elites' political calculations. When the country is on the verge of war and the conflict has been broadly portrayed as involving the national interest, critics of the president risk being seen as unpatriotic. A 1994 study by Zaller shows that congressional

Democrats were reluctant to openly question the George H. W. Bush administration's aggressive response to the Iraqi invasion of Kuwait because they feared reinforcing the stereotype of their party as soft on national defense. However, when the president undertakes actions that do not fit the standard script of good versus evil or when the president's actions meet with strong international opposition from our traditional allies, as was the case with the Reagan administration's decision to bomb targets in Libya, press accounts tend to be more critical, both because opposing elites are more willing to speak out in opposition and because the press can cite the views of disgruntled American allies.

At other times, despite the prevalence of indexing, the press is able to express muted criticism of official policy. Despite elite consensus on the need for American military action, the press can resort to horse race–type handicapping of the impending hostilities. In the case of the 1991 Persian Gulf conflict, for example, news reports were rife with accounts suggesting that President Bush's political standing and reelection prospects might be seriously jeopardized if Iraqi forces offered stiff resistance or if Kuwait became a quagmire. Similarly, journalists offered a variety of contextual critiques focusing on possible unintended outcomes of war in the Middle East (such as the elevation of Saddam Hussein to martyr status). However, these manifestations of press objectivity did not venture so far as to question the basic premises of US policy. As Althaus (2003) notes, "No journalist ever questioned the demonization of Saddam Hussein. No journalist ever hinted that the United States had taken an inappropriately aggressive posture toward a regional conflict. . . . At no time did a journalist question whether Iraq's chemical, biological or nuclear capability presented a real threat to the Western world in the foreseeable future" (p. 396).

Finally, there is the possibility that technology may compromise political elites' ability to manage the news. We noted in Chapter 3 that widespread use of videophones has provided reporters with immediate access to breaking events in far-flung locales. And the equally widespread use of digital photography has increased the number of eyewitnesses who may serve as news sources. The graphic photographs of prisoner abuse at Abu Ghraib were taken by American service personnel, who transmitted them via cell phone. Once the photographs had been obtained by the press, the Department of Defense was forced to acknowledge the atrocities and begin an official investigation. More generally, immediate access to the scene of an event strengthens journalists' ability to resist the official story line. If event-driven reporting becomes more common, the indexing process will no longer produce a one-sided pattern of international and defense-related news.

No matter how balanced the outcome of the indexing process, news coverage that is pegged to official sources threatens the ability of the press to maintain an adversarial stance toward government. During periods of military conflict, the silence of opposition sources inevitably results in a "journalism of deference to the national security state" (Dorman, 1997, p. 124). Even worse, "journalism that indexes debate in Washington violates not just the watchdog ideal, but also the mirror ideal. For under the indexing rule, the journalistic mirror is held up not to reality, but to official interpretations of reality" (Mermin, 1999, p. 145).

We began this chapter by contrasting Watergate with the war against Iraq. The differences between domestic politics and foreign policy are undeniably responsible for the wide gap in press performance in these two instances. International issues have generally proved to be of little interest to Americans, thus encouraging editors to place more emphasis on stories that sell. But the diminished adversarial capacity of the press can also be attributed to the general development of media politics. That is, the relationship between reporters and government sources has changed substantially since Watergate. Officials in all branches of government have become sensitized to the importance of the media to their ability to govern. Press secretaries, media liaisons, and public relations specialists are now ensconced in every government agency or office. Officials seize every opportunity to present their actions in the most favorable light possible. When news coverage or the course of events is not to their liking, they resort to various strategies (such as leaking information or staging events) for regaining control over the message. These strategies are the subject of Chapter 7.

Before we take up media strategy, however, we must first examine a major change in the media landscape: the proliferation of media sources brought on by the rapid spread of information technology. Chapter 5 will examine the consequences of the revolution in information technology for the practice of media politics. How does the availability of more media choices affect the public's exposure to public affairs programming, and does the rapid spread of the Internet and new forms of mass media change the way in which political organizations mobilize their supporters for political action?

SUMMARY

1. As coverage of the 2003 invasion of Iraq illustrates, the media tend to be less adversarial in dealing with national security and foreign policy than in dealing with domestic issues.

2. One explanation for the media's less adversarial stance is indexing. In a news system based on official sources, reporters' coverage of issues mirrors the level and intensity of elite debate. The higher the level of elite dissent, the easier it is for the reporter to pit competing sources against each other. Where domestic political events are concerned, the presence of vocal and authoritative critics grants journalists the necessary leverage to question official accounts. On matters of foreign policy, however, critics of government policy tend to fall silent and the press is left with only official sources.

3. National security matters provide officials with even more control over the press. When the United States resorts to military force, opposing elites generally close ranks behind the president, for fear of appearing unpatriotic. Because potential opponents of the use of military force fall silent, the press becomes completely dependent on official spokespersons.

4. After the Vietnam War, the Pentagon and the Department of Defense strove to restrict media access to areas of US military action. There was considerable outrage over censorship of the press after it was discovered that the Reagan administration had misled the media and the public about the invasion of Grenada. As a result, the Pentagon revised its policy about media access to war zones; the press would be granted access, but only in the form of closely supervised media pools.

5. In contrast to its approach during the 1991 Gulf War, the Pentagon decided that it was no longer politically feasible to deny American reporters firsthand access to the 2003 invasion of Iraq. In a modernized version of pooled coverage, a select group of American and international correspondents were to be embedded with the invading forces. The embedded reporters, however, were still subject to severe restrictions on the content of their reports.

FURTHER READINGS

Aday, S., Livingston, S., & Maeve, H. (2005). Embedding the truth: A cross-cultural analysis of objectivity and television coverage of the Iraq War. *International Journal of Press/Politics*, *10*, 3–21.

Althaus, S. (2003). When news norms collide, follow the lead: New evidence for press independence. *Political Communication*, *20*, 381–414.

Bennett, W. L. (1990). Toward a theory of press–state relations. *Journal of Communication*, *40*, 103–125.

Cook, T. E. (1994). Domesticating a crisis: Washington newsbeats and the network news after the Iraq invasion of Kuwait. In W. L. Bennett & D. L. Paletz (Eds.), *Taken by storm: The media, public opinion, and U.S. foreign policy in the Gulf War* (pp. 105–130). Chicago: University of Chicago Press.

Dorman, W. A. (1997). Press theory and journalistic practice: The case of the Gulf War. In S. Iyengar & R. Reeves (Eds.), *Do the media govern? Politicians, voters and reporters in America* (pp. 118–125). Thousand Oaks, CA: Sage.

Frenznick, D. A. (1992). The First Amendment on the battlefield: A constitutional analysis of press access to military operations in Grenada, Panama and the Persian Gulf. *Pacific Law Journal, 23,* 315–359.

Hayes, D., & Guardino, M. (2013). *Influence from abroad: Foreign voices, the media, and U.S. public opinion.* New York: Cambridge University Press.

Mermin, J. (1999). *Debating war and peace: Media coverage of U.S. intervention in the post-Vietnam era.* Princeton, NJ: Princeton University Press.

Sigal, L. (1973). *Reporters and officials.* Lexington, MA: Heath.

Zaller, J. R. (1994). Elite leadership of mass opinion: New evidence from the Gulf War. In W. L. Bennett & D. L. Paletz (Eds.), *Taken by storm: The media, public opinion, and U.S. foreign policy in the Gulf War* (pp. 186–209). Chicago: University of Chicago Press.

Zaller, J. R., & Chiu, D. (2000). Government's little helper: U.S. press coverage of foreign policy crises, 1946–1999. In B. L. Nacos, R. Y. Shapiro, & P. Isernia (Eds.), *Decisionmaking in a glass house: Mass media, public opinion, and American foreign policy in the 21st Century* (pp. 61–84). Lanham, MD: Rowman & Littlefield.

NOTES

1. In fact, conclusions about the pivotal role of television news in turning public opinion against the Vietnam War are mistaken. In the first place, as described earlier, coverage faithfully reflected the state of American elite opinion. Second, as Mueller (1973) has documented, trends in public support for war were no different for Vietnam and Korea, despite the lack of television coverage during the Korean War.

2. This account rests on David Frenznick's (1992) authoritative history of military–press relations in the United States.

3. The sheer number of sources may underestimate the degree of pro-administration slant in the news. For instance, a 1996 study by Althaus, Edy, Entman, and Phalen of *New York Times* coverage of the 1986 US air strikes against Libya found that foreign sources and American government sources were equally represented in the news. However, the same study documented a more subtle indicator of pro-administration coverage: opposition sources were consistently positioned after administration sources within the same news report.

4. Reproduced at www.whitehouse.gov/news/releases/2003/02/20030205-1.html.

5

New Media, New Forms of Campaigning

The frenetic pace of technological innovation over the past two decades has revolutionized the transmission of information, with dramatic consequences for the news media. News is updated instantaneously, there is more competition among news providers, and each provider has a smaller audience share. The array of programming choices now available bears little resemblance to the network news–dominated environment of the 1980s.

The revolution in information technology has altered not only the form of the media landscape but also the very concept of communication. The traditional forms of communication were either *point-to-point* (between a single sender and recipient) or *broadcast* (between a single sender and multiple recipients). Most senders did not have ready access to broadcast forms of communication and could not reach a significant audience. Traditional media were also limited to a single form (print, audio, or video).

The development of the Internet permitted simultaneous point-to-point and broadcast forms of communication for the first time and provided individual users with easy access to a huge audience. Every individual on the network of computers making up the World Wide Web is both a sender and a receiver. Any user of the Internet can direct e-mail messages to individual recipients and at the same time communicate with a worldwide audience by hosting a website or posting a message, video, or tweet. Moreover, unlike conventional media, Internet-based communication is multichannel, allowing the free transmission of text, voice, still images, and video.

Our goal in this chapter is to describe how information technology and the proliferation of new media have transformed both the behavior of individual information seekers and the strategies used by politicians and political organizations to reach and mobilize their supporters. At the level of the individual, the age of the Internet is the age of information overload—hundreds of thousands of information sources, ranging from prestigious news organizations to little-known bloggers, compete for the consumer's attention. The sheer volume of information available forces individuals to rely on a handful of preferred providers. We will explain how individuals choose among programs and providers.

At the level of candidates and organizations, the big story about new technologies is the reduced cost of collective action. The popularity of social networking sites (Facebook now has more than a billion users worldwide) and the development of near-instantaneous forms of communication such as Twitter have given politicians brand-new platforms. Social media make it possible for news reports, campaign ads, and other forms of political messaging to be recirculated on a vast scale. The ability to reach voters is no longer restricted to candidates with deep pockets. In addition, candidates and groups can now communicate directly with potential supporters, bypassing the news media entirely. Politicians can speak directly to voters when and where they please and on subjects of their own choosing. It is no wonder, as we describe in this chapter, that candidates and political parties are enthusiastically embracing new forms of campaigning.

THE DIFFUSION OF TECHNOLOGY

The pace of proliferation of information technology has astonished all observers. The Pew Research Center has regularly tracked Americans' use of the Internet since 1995. Survey respondents are asked if they "ever go online to access the Internet and receive e-mail." Even allowing for some inflation in self-reported results, the increase over time in the percentage of Americans who say they go online is striking. In 1995, a mere 14 percent of adult Americans said they used the Internet. By the turn of the century, the figure had more than tripled to half the population. Continuing on this trajectory, between 1999 and 2010 the share of the online population reached 79 percent. In the span of a decade, self-reported Internet use increased by a stunning 560 percent.

Since the Internet became accessible to the larger public in the early 1990s, the percentage of Americans who get their news online has exploded. In 2001, only 13 percent of Americans named the Internet as their main source for news, while 74 percent cited television. Twelve years later, 50 percent relied on the Internet. Among those under the age of 30, the Internet was the primary news source, outstripping television by a wide margin. The rise of Internet news and the simultaneous decline of traditional news platforms, such as radio and newspapers, suggest a pattern of product substitution. That's not to say that online news has totally replaced other forms of news. Rather, online news supplements consumers' use of other platforms: overall, across both Internet and traditional media, Americans these days are spending more time listening, reading, or watching news than they were twenty years ago.

In an attempt to get accurate estimates of media use, the Pew Research Center often asks respondents to gauge how much time they spent on various activities "yesterday." Figure 5.1 displays the total time respondents reported spending with various forms of news media. The graph reveals two important trends. First, self-reported media use (across all "old" media) has remained steady or declined over the past two decades. Second, use of online news sites is up. People now spend more time every day reading online news than they do reading newspapers.

The use of new media platforms isn't constant across demographic groups. In general, younger people are more fluent in the use of technology. For instance, they are the most likely to access news through their cell phones and also the most likely to encounter news reports on social media. Differences in new media use are also pronounced between other demographic groups. Figure 5.2 shows differences among various groups in the percentage that report getting

FIGURE 5.1

How Much Time Americans Spend Following the News

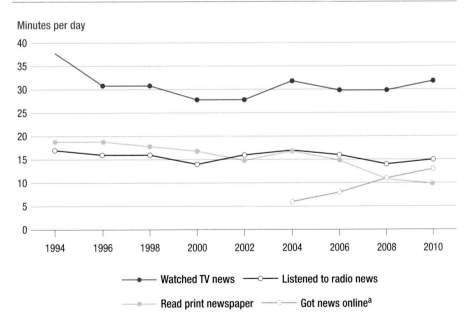

[a]Online news includes newspapers read online. Online news "yesterday" was not asked before 2004.
Source: Data from Pew Research Center, 1994–2010. (2010). *Americans spending more time following the news*. Retrieved December 18, 2014 from http://www.people-press.org/2010/09/12/americans-spending-more-time-following-the-news/.

FIGURE 5.2

Composition of the Online News Audience

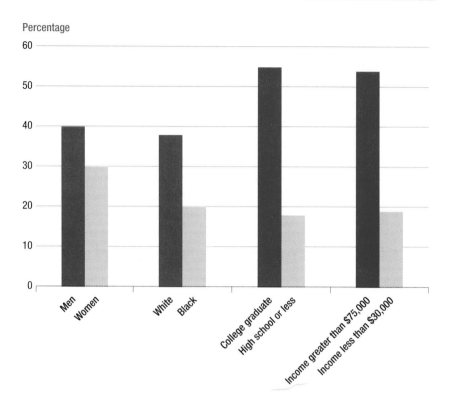

Percentage

Source: Data from Pew Research Center (2010). *Americans spending more time following the news.* Retrieved December 18, 2014 from http://www.people-press.org/2010/09/12/americans-spending-more-time-following-the-news/.

news online. In general, socially advantaged groups are more likely to report accessing online news than are disadvantaged groups. For example, the poor and the less educated are much less likely to report accessing news online than are the rich and more educated. Although these group differences in online news consumption are partially driven by interest in public affairs, access to the Internet is also part of the explanation. According to the 2010 US Census, while more than 75 percent of white non-Hispanic households have home Internet access, fewer than 60 percent of Hispanic households do.

News represents a tiny sliver of the information available online—the Internet provides access to everything from vital health information to job listings. Internet access has become so important in today's world that it's now labeled a "fundamental human right" in several countries, and these countries have passed legislation to ensure Internet access for all. A related issue concerns access to bandwidth. Those with regular access to broadband Internet have a tremendous advantage over those with a slower, less stable connection. In the United States, there are wide gaps in broadband access between the young and the old, the less and the more educated, and the rich and the poor as well as between urban and rural dwellers. In an attempt to reduce inequalities in broadband access, Congress appropriated $7.2 billion as part of the 2009 Economic Recovery Plan for increasing broadband coverage to rural and disadvantaged communities.

The availability of information technology to a majority of the population has created a booming Internet economy. In the case of media organizations, thousands of news sites now compete with each other and with the offerings of political parties, candidates, interest groups, think tanks, and virtually anybody with anything to say about politics. Figure 5.3 lists the news sites with the largest weekly traffic, as measured by Nielsen/NetRatings. The top ten list is a mixture of news aggregators, such as Yahoo–ABC and AOL news, major legacy (pre-Internet) news organizations, and purely online news outlets such

FIGURE 5.3

Top Ten US News Sites, 2012

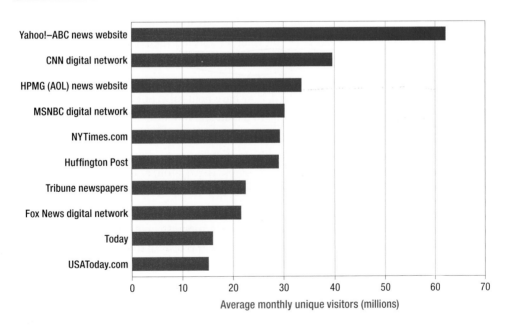

Source: Data from A. C. Nielsen Company. *Top U.S. brands and news websites, May 2012.* At http://www.nielsen.com/us/en/insights/news/2012/may-2012-top-u-s-web-brands-and-news-websites.html.

as the Huffington Post. Websites connected to cable news networks are among the most popular online news sources. The Fox News website not only makes the top ten list, but readers also tend to spend more time on that site compared to the other sites on the list.

Although the numbers suggest that the legacy news organizations now attract a much larger audience online than in their conventional forms (in the case of the *New York Times*, online circulation is 13 times greater than its print circulation), it is difficult to know the actual extent of online news consumption. Readers of the online edition of the *New York Times* spend an average of four minutes per session on the site. Whether this usage is more or less extensive or efficient than traditional readership and whether it displaces traditional readership is unknown (as we will discuss).

The proliferation of Internet technology and use is not, of course, confined to the dissemination of news. Any of the major Internet search engines, for instance, records weekly traffic that far exceeds the online audience for CNN or the *New York Times*. Time allocation shows the same pattern. While visitors to nytimes.com spend about nineteen minutes a month on the site, Facebook users spend nearly seven hours.

Given the speed with which information technology has spread, research into the effects of new-media use on individuals, markets, and institutions is still in its infancy. For scholars of media politics, there are three central questions. First, how has increased access to the Internet affected the behavior of consumers of news? Second, what is the potential impact of the vast online social networks such as Facebook on the recirculation of news or commentary and individuals' exposure to diverse points of view? Third, how have political candidates and organizations attempted to harness technology to recruit and mobilize individual supporters? In the discussion that follows, we will address each of these questions in turn.

EFFECTS OF NEW MEDIA ON CONSUMERS

There are two schools of thought concerning the potential impact of new media on the end user. *Optimists* see technology as a means of revitalizing the public sphere. By providing direct and immediate access to diverse political perspectives, the Internet should enhance the ability of ordinary people to follow events and to participate in the political process. The hope is that easy online access to public affairs information will build civic awareness and engagement. Former Vice President Al Gore epitomized this view when he predicted (in a 1994 speech to the International Telecommunications Union) that the coming Internet age would bring about "robust and sustainable economic progress, strong democracies, better solutions to global and local environmental challenges, improved health care, and—ultimately—a greater sense of shared stewardship of our small planet."

Skeptics, on the other hand, warn that information technology is no panacea for the limitations of conventional news programming and the weak demand for political information. If serious news coverage cannot attract television viewers, why should it draw people online? If Americans are not inclined to read newspapers or watch foreign media, is there any reason to suppose that they will suddenly access the BBC or Xinhua News just because it's possible to do so? Skeptics think not. They believe that the Internet will in fact discourage consumers from pursuing news (whether via Internet or conventional platforms) in favor of more engaging online pursuits, such as shopping, dating, watching movies, or keeping in touch. As people become more fluent in the ways of the Web, they may become more personally isolated, preferring surfing alone over community involvement or face-to-face social interaction. Quite possibly, on balance, technology may weaken community and civic engagement.

Quite apart from the question of whether Internet technology will increase or decrease the average time devoted to public affairs content is the question of whether the Internet will, in practice, be used to broaden users' political horizons. Although an infinite variety of information is available, individuals may well sample selectively, limiting their exposure to news or sources that they expect to find agreeable. There is no doubt that the Internet makes available an ample supply of news that is not screened for accuracy or objectivity. By turning to biased but favored providers, consumers may be able to "wall themselves off from topics and opinions that they would prefer to avoid" (Sunstein, 2001, pp. 201–202). The end result could be a less informed and more polarized electorate.

INTERNET USE AND CIVIC ENGAGEMENT

Representing the optimists, some scholars believe that the Internet will expand the universe of political participation by reducing costs. Rather than having to write a check, address an envelope, find a stamp, and mail in a political donation, one can simply go online and pay with a credit card. And it's not only making a financial contribution that is easier; creating membership rosters, sending out announcements of upcoming meetings, and signing petitions are all simplified.

Optimists also cite the potential of the Internet to draw in individuals who hold a wide variety of ideas and perspectives. Unlike the mainstream news media, which is constrained by the norms of professional journalism and consumer demand, websites can target smaller audiences with more specialized interests, making it possible to create greater numbers of online networks and discussion groups.

Technology not only facilitates conventional forms of participation, but it has also spawned new forms of civic engagement. People can contribute comments to blogs, view and post YouTube videos, and reach out to like-minded others on Facebook and Twitter. These innovations are already influencing the conduct of campaigns. During the 2008 and 2012 presidential primaries, news organizations (including CNN and Fox News) sponsored candidate debates in which Internet users across the country submitted questions to the candidates over YouTube.

Despite the potential of the Internet to foster new forms of political engagement, the skeptics respond that the Internet has had little impact on the actual level of political participation. A recent meta-analysis (a quantitative research methodology that summarizes past research findings) found that Internet use has exerted little positive effect overall (Boulianne, 2009).

A parallel debate concerns the potential impact of technology on inequalities in civic participation. Optimists assumed that the Internet would draw in hitherto inactive groups and level the playing field. Pessimists, however, argued that the costs of going online, in terms of both money and skills, would only exacerbate existing disparities in participation. Since technology use is significantly correlated with social class, it is unlikely that the voices of the poor and less educated will be heard online. In fact, as shown in Figure 5.4, the evidence shows that online activists, like their offline counterparts, are drawn disproportionately from high-status groups. For instance, the participation gap between college and high school graduates is almost identical (around 25 percent higher for college graduates) for offline and online participation (Bimber & Davis, 2003; Smith, Schlozman, Verba, & Brady, 2009).

The overrepresentation of higher-status groups as online activists suggests that new forms of participation simply replicate the old. But some skeptics go even further and argue that that Internet use can displace conventional forms of civic life and lower the overall level of participation. Just as the advent of television sounded the death knell for visually oriented magazines such as *Life*, these scholars argue that time spent surfing the Web will gradually diminish face-to-face social interaction. We might become sufficiently preoccupied with our private online spaces to have few opportunities to visit with the neighbors, write letters to the editor, or even converse with anybody on a face-to-face basis. Because technology use is an inherently isolated rather than social experience, it has the potential to weaken the bonds between the individual and the community.

FIGURE 5.4

Group Differences in Participation

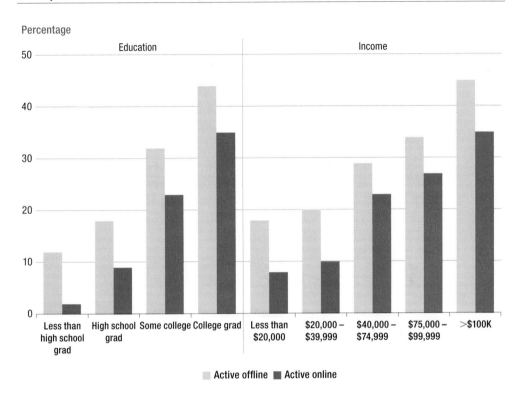

Source: Data from A. Smith, K. L. Schlozman, S. Verba, & H. Brady. (2009). *The Internet and civic engagement*. Pew Research Center, Washington, DC.

To date, the scholarly verdict on the question of displacement is inconclusive. An early study (Kraut, Lundmark, Patterson, Kiesler, Mukopadhyay, & Scherlis, 1998) focused on a group of Pittsburgh-area residents who were given computers and Internet access. Over a two-year period, the researchers found that study participants became less involved in social activities and expressed a higher level of loneliness. More recent studies seem to contradict these findings, especially among youth. Adolescents who use social media frequently, for instance, also report closer friendships and other beneficial psychological outcomes (Valkenburg & Peter, 2007, 2009). However, none of these studies is in a position to disentangle selection effects—whether people who are already sociable and well-adjusted choose to spend more time online—from whether using the Internet makes users less anxious or depressed.

Thus at the level of individuals' self-reported exposure to conventional media and other discretionary activities, the consequences of increased Internet use are unclear. For some, Internet use may free up time for other pastimes; for others, the effect may be the opposite.

For one group in particular, however, it is clear that the Internet has dramatically increased participation. Young adults are the least likely to engage in traditional forms of political activity but the most likely to take advantage of technologically enhanced forms of participation. The young, for instance, are more likely to post comments on blogs and organize for political causes through social networking sites. As shown in Figure 5.5, the age gap in the use of social networking sites for political purposes and posting political content online favors those between the ages of eighteen and thirty-four by a substantial margin. College students are especially likely to engage in online political activity.

With the notable exception of the young, the advent of new technologies has done little to raise the overall level of involvement in civic or community affairs. Civic participation requires motivation, and the motivated are more likely to take advantage of both new and old forms of participation.

SELECTIVE EXPOSURE TO ONLINE NEWS?

The single most important consequence of the Internet is the increased flow of information. In a world dominated by conventional news sources, the supply of campaign information hardly burdens the typical voter's attention span. As noted in Chapter 3, the average candidate sound bite in the networks' evening newscasts runs for less than ten seconds. In the new-media environment, consumers face information overload—hundreds of information providers all capable of delivering much larger chunks of campaign information. Individuals can cope with the overload because new media also provide greater user control, thus facilitating consumers' ability to attend to information selectively. The audience for conventional news programs is hard-pressed to avoid coverage of the candidate they dislike, because news reports typically assign equal coverage to each. When browsing a website, on the other hand, users can filter or search through masses of text more easily than with conventional media. Rather than examining the complete collection of speeches found on the John McCain for President website, users could instead seek out McCain's references to issues of special concern. In short, as candidates, interest groups, news organizations, and voters all converge on the Internet, the possibility of selective exposure to political information increases. Given the availability of so much information and so many news providers, the audience must make choices or be overwhelmed. Exactly how do Internet users decide whether the information they're getting is worth considering or if it should be passed over?

FIGURE 5.5

Online Political Engagement by Age and Education

Age

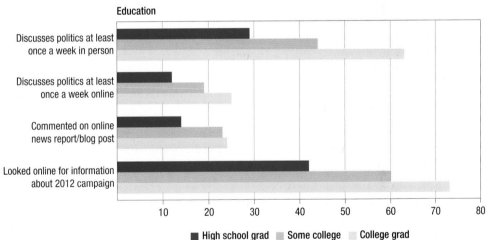

Education

Source: Data from Pew Research Center, 2013. *Civic engagement in the digital age.* Retrieved December 18, 2014 from http://www.pewinternet.org/2013/04/25/civic-engagement-in-the-digital-age/.

There are three main possibilities. First, as we have just seen with the question of civic engagement, exposure to political information online may be simply a matter of generic political interest (the *attentive public hypothesis*). Political junkies will seek out news and political commentary, whereas the apolitical majority simply tunes out all things political, except when major events generate a torrent of coverage that is impossible to ignore. From this perspective, multiplying the number of information sources only widens the information gap between the more and the less interested.[1] Second, among those with some level of political interest, people may prefer to encounter information that they find supportive or consistent with their political beliefs (the *partisan polarization hypothesis*). For example, Republicans may visit drudgereport.com, Democrats dailykos.com. We use the blogosphere as a case study of polarization; the great majority of bloggers participate in completely homogeneous (in-party) discussion networks. Third, people may seek information not on the basis of their anticipated agreement with the message, but because of their interest in particular issues (the *issue public hypothesis*). For example, the elderly seek out information bearing on Social Security or healthcare legislation simply because these policies have an immediate impact on their welfare.

The Attentive Public Hypothesis

According to the attentive public hypothesis, the act of seeking out political information, online as elsewhere, is simply a matter of generic political interest. People captivated by politics tune in to all forms of news, whereas the apolitical majority tunes out politics in favor of online bargain hunting or keeping up with friends. The increased availability of media channels and sources makes it possible for people who care little about political debates to evade the reach of news programming altogether. As a result, this group is likely to possess very little information about political issues and events. From this perspective, therefore, the Internet will simply widen the information gap between the more and less interested.

In the case of conventional media use, a study by Price and Zaller (1993) reported evidence consistent with the rich-get-richer pattern. They found

 IN FOCUS

Theories of Selective Exposure

- **Attentive public.** People interested by politics tune in to all forms of news, whereas the apolitical majority pays very little attention to news in any medium.
- **Partisan polarization.** People prefer to encounter information that supports their beliefs and avoid information that is inconsistent with those beliefs.
- **Issue public.** People seek out information about subjects that are particularly important or interesting to them and tune out information about other subjects.

respondents with a higher level of education (education is an indicator of political attentiveness—that is, people who are more educated tend to be more interested in politics) remembered all news stories better. These investigators concluded that "someone who is generally well-informed about politics will tend to be well-informed about whatever the news media also cover, whether the trials of Hollywood celebrities or the latest arms control proposals" (Price & Zaller, 1993, p. 157). Other studies (Delli Carpini & Keeter, 1996) reach similar conclusions, suggesting that people who attend to political information are generalists, soaking up whatever is available—rather than ideologues looking for ammunition to strengthen their arguments or specialists interested in particular issues.

In the case of new-media use, we would expect the more educated to be especially overrepresented. Virtually every study of Internet use has documented that educated and affluent Americans enjoy greater online access than do their less advantaged counterparts. Since the educated and affluent also tend to be more interested in politics, they will be especially likely to pursue political activities (e.g., signing a petition, contacting a government official, or posting news links) online. Table 5.1 shows that the voters most likely to report engaging in such online political activities were college graduates and the young. In fact, the education advantage in online political participation shown here is almost identical to the parallel advantages in offline participation.

There is one group of Americans, however, for whom the "rich get richer maxim" may not hold. Young people are generally less interested in politics than the middle-aged and seniors but are experts with technology. In the Pew survey reported in Table 5.1, respondents were asked questions about a variety of online civic activities including signing a petition, contacting a government official, and expressing their political views. People in the 18–34 age group registered the highest level of online civic involvement. In the case of the exact

TABLE 5.1

Civic Engagement Online and Offline

	Less than BA	Some college	College graduate	18–34	35–54	55+
Online civic engagement	25	40	51	41	33	27
Offline civic engagement	29	44	50	35	39	42

Data from Pew Research Internet Project, 2013. *Civic engagement in the digital age*. Retrieved December 18, 2014 from http://www.pewinternet.org/2013/04/25/civic-engagement-in-the-digital-age/.

same set of civic activities, but this time carried out offline, older Americans were considerably more engaged than the young.

The Partisan Polarization Hypothesis

Before the advent of television, campaigns were conducted primarily through partisan channels. Candidates would travel across the country delivering their stump speeches and greeting voters in person. Voters were thought to simplify their choices by relying on the candidates and positions of their preferred political party. Selective exposure on a partisan basis was considered the principal means by which candidates reached the public; voters were motivated to seek out information that supported rather than challenged their political beliefs.

The notion of partisan polarization is grounded in the theory of cognitive dissonance, which posits that the acquisition of information at odds with one's preexisting beliefs is uncomfortable and therefore to be avoided. Instead, people are thought to prefer acquiring information that reinforces their beliefs and attitudes. By this theory, for example, Republicans would be expected to avoid news stories supportive of President Obama and seek out stories presenting him in an unfavorable light.

Early studies of political campaigns documented the tendency of partisan voters to report greater exposure to appeals from the candidate or party that they preferred. This pattern of motivated exposure to congenial information sources was thought to explain the surprising finding that campaigns reinforced rather than changed the attitudes of voters. (We will address this finding in greater detail in Chapter 9.) In what would prove to be an early incarnation of concern over the "*Daily Me*" (a concept we'll discuss in a moment), researchers condemned the preference for congenial information as antithetical to the democratic ideal of informed choice:

> In recent years there has been a good deal of talk by men of good will about the desirability and necessity of guaranteeing the free exchange of ideas in the market place of public opinion. Such talk has centered upon the problem of keeping free the channels of expression and communication. Now we find that the consumers of ideas, if they have made a decision on the issue, themselves erect high tariff walls against alien notions. (Lazarsfeld, Berelson, & Gaudet, 1948, p. 89)

As party-based campaigns were replaced by media-based campaigns, the opportunities for encountering partisan sources gradually disappeared. Television news became the dominant source of public affairs information. The norms of objective journalism meant that no matter which network voters tuned in to, they encountered the very same set of news reports, according balanced attention to parties, candidates, or points of view (see Robinson & Sheehan, 1983). In the era of old media, accordingly, it made little difference where voters obtained their news. The flow of news amounted to an information commons. Americans of all walks of life and political inclination encountered the same stream of information.

Given the difficulty of seeking out politically congenial news, research on selective exposure during the era of old media yielded equivocal results. In several instances, what seemed to be motivated or deliberate selective exposure turned out to occur on a de facto or by-product basis instead: for instance, Republicans were more likely to encounter pro-Republican information as a result of their social milieu rather than any active choices to avoid information that seemed to favor Democrats (see Sears & Freedman, 1967).

It is not a coincidence that the revolution in information technology and the increased availability of news sources has been accompanied by increasing political polarization. Over time, polarization appears to have spread from the elite level to the level of mass public opinion (Abramowitz & Saunders, 2006; Jacobson, 2006; for a dissenting view, see Fiorina, Abrams, & Pope, 2005). As we will document in Chapter 10, Democrats' and Republicans' negative evaluations of a president of the other party have steadily intensified to the point that polarized assessments of presidential performance are higher today than at any other time in the history of polling.

The increased level of interparty animus may reflect increasingly segregated flows of political communication and more-polarized news audiences. People who feel strongly about the correctness of their cause or policy preferences are more likely to seek out information they believe is consistent with their preferences. But while as recently as twenty-five years ago these partisans would have been hard-pressed to find overtly partisan sources of information, today the task has been simplified. In the case of Republicans, all they need to do is tune in to Fox News or access the Drudge Report. Viewers on the left can seek out credible yet sympathetic news programming on MSNBC or the Huffington Post.

There is a growing body of evidence suggesting that politically polarized consumers are motivated to exercise selectivity in their news choices. In the first place, in keeping with the well-known hostile media phenomenon (discussed in Chapter 3), partisans of either side have become more likely to impute bias to mainstream news sources (Smith, Lichter, & Harris, 1997). Cynical assessments of the media are most widespread among conservatives who are twice as likely as Democrats to rate major news outlets (such as the three network newscasts, the weekly news magazines, NPR, and PBS) as biased in favor of liberals (Pew Research Center, 2012). Republicans' hostility toward the mainstream media is sufficiently intense that any press criticism of Republican candidates typically boosts their standing among Republican voters. In the aftermath of the *New York Times* front-page story on Senator McCain's alleged affair with a lobbyist (Rutenberg, Thompson, Kirkpatrick, & Labaton, 2008), the McCain campaign was able to capitalize on this "liberal attack" to raise significant amounts of campaign cash. In recent years, especially after the election of Barack Obama, perceptions of media bias (against Democrats) have risen among Democratic voters (Pew Research Center, 2011). Given their perceptions of hostile bias in the mainstream media environment, partisans of both sides have begun to explore alternative sources of news. During the past decade, Republicans have become especially reliant on Fox News and talk radio, while Democrats have avoided Fox and tuned in to late-night "alternative" news such as the *Daily Show* with Jon Stewart (Lelkes, Sood, & Iyengar, 2014; Pfau, Houston, & Semmler, 2007).

Experimental studies of online news consumption further confirm the tendency of partisans to self-select into distinct audiences. In one study administered on a national sample in 2006, the researchers manipulated the source of online news stories in five different subject matter areas ranging from national politics and the Iraq War to vacation destinations and sports (Iyengar & Hahn, 2009). Depending on the condition to which participants were assigned, the very same news headline was attributed either to Fox News, NPR, CNN, or BBC. Participants were asked which of the four different headlines they would prefer to read, if any. The results were unequivocal: Republicans and conservatives were much more likely to select news stories from Fox, while Democrats and liberals avoided Fox in favor of NPR and CNN. Especially striking was the finding that the conservatives' preference for Fox applied not only to hard news (such as national politics, the war in Iraq, and healthcare) but also to soft news stories about travel and sports. The polarization of the news audience extends even to nonpolitical subject matter.

There is reason to believe that the polarization of politically inclined news consumers is increasing. For example, the news selection study reported earlier revealed substantial evidence of partisan polarization in 2006, yet six years earlier, in a similar study of exposure to campaign rhetoric, the researchers could detect only modest traces of partisan selectivity (see Iyengar, Hahn, Krosnick, & Walker, 2008). In this earlier study, the investigators compiled a large selection of campaign speeches by the two major presidential candidates

(Al Gore and George W. Bush) along with a full set of the candidates' television advertisements. This material was assembled on an interactive, multimedia CD and distributed to a representative sample of registered voters with Internet access a few weeks before the election.[2] Participants were informed that they were free to use the CD as they saw fit and that their usage would be recorded on their computer. Following the election, they were provided instructions for downloading and transmitting the data to the market research firm from which they received the CD.

The CD tracking data in this study showed only weak traces of a preference for information from the in-party candidate. Although Republicans and conservatives were somewhat more likely to seek out information from the Bush campaign, liberals and Democrats showed no preference for speeches or advertisements for Gore over those for Bush. These findings suggest either that the intensity of partisan identity was higher among Republicans in 2000 or that selective exposure had already become habituated among Republicans because they were provided earlier opportunities than Democrats (with the launch of Fox News in 1996) to engage in biased information seeking. The data from both the 2006 news selection study and a 2012 follow-up suggest that Democrats are now keeping pace; in 2000, very few Democrats in the CD study showed an aversion to speeches from Governor Bush, but by 2012 virtually no Democrats selected Fox News and a plurality opted for MSNBC or Huffington Post as their preferred providers (see Lelkes, Sood, & Iyengar, 2014).

Although there is no doubt that the Internet has increased the availability of partisan news sources, it is important to acknowledge that the overall level of selective exposure is still small because the news organizations with the largest offline and online audiences offer nonpartisan (objective) and entertainment-oriented journalism (see Gentzkow & Shapiro, 2010) rather than biased commentary. In a recent study that tracked use of smartphones to receive news, local news proved to be the dominant source (LaCour, 2012); news you can use thus appears to trump news you find politically agreeable.

The Issue Public Hypothesis

The third and final account of selective exposure to information is based on differing levels of interest in particular political issues. In their original review of selective exposure research, Sears and Friedman (1967) identified *utility-based selectivity* as a viable alternative to partisan consistency as a motive for seeking political information. They argued that what individuals paid attention to would depend on how useful they perceived the different pieces of information to be rather than on how much they anticipated agreeing with

Case Study:
THE POLARIZATION OF THE BLOGOSPHERE

In the early days of the Internet, discussion forums generally took the form of bulletin boards or newsgroups. People interested in a particular subject—from arthritis to zoology—could join an appropriate group, often moderated by an organizer, where they could read and post messages. Later, as more people began to use the Web to acquire political news, individual commentators established their own blog space for the purpose of expressing their political views. These blogs now serve as forums where like-minded individuals can post and circulate comments by linking to others' sites. Since 2000, political blogs have emerged as major sources of news and political commentary.

According to Technorati, a website that tracks blog traffic, there are more than six thousand blogs that offer content related to American politics. Some of the most visible blogs are maintained by mainstream news organizations (e.g., CNN's Political Ticker), but the great majority represent the views of individuals. Table 5.2 lists some of the most frequently visited blogs that are not affiliated with major media organizations.

Although the sheer number of blogs might suggest the existence of a diverse array of political perspectives, in fact almost all major political blogs represent either the Democratic (liberal) or Republican (conservative) slant on issues and events. Prominent conservative online sites include RedStates, TheBlaze, and The Foundry. On the left, the more frequently cited sites include Daily Kos, Think Progress, and Huffington Post.

TABLE 5.2

Most Frequently Visited Political Blogs

	Blog/Website	Partisan Slant
1	CNN Political Ticker	None
2	Huffington Post	Democratic
3	Mediaite	None
4	Think Progress	Democratic
5	TheBlaze	Republican
6	Daily Kos	Democratic
7	The Foundry	Republican
8	Business Insider	None
9	RedState	Republican
10	Right Wing Watch	Democratic

Data from Technorati.com, May 21, 2014; Technorati suspended their blog rankings in July 2014.

Although the audience for political blogs is relatively small, at least in comparison with nonpolitical blogs, their significance extends well beyond the numbers. For one thing, blog postings can reverberate around the blogosphere through a process of cross-linking (different blogs linking to a particular post). Second, blog posts often become major news stories. This occurred in 2004, when conservative bloggers revealed that a *CBS News* report suggesting, among other things, that President Bush's attendance record as an Air National Guard pilot in Texas was not exemplary, was based on fake documents. The blog posts were immediately picked up by the Drudge Report and the *National Review* (both with conservative inclinations) and eventually spread to the mainstream media.

The *Washington Post* and *New York Times* ran front-page stories noting the errors within the CBS report. Eventually, CBS was forced to retract the report, the network appointed an independent commission to investigate the affair, and Dan Rather, who was the lead correspondent on the story, retired.

In a more recent case of bloggers setting the mainstream media's agenda, Mayhill Fowler, a blogger for the Huffington Post, broke the story relating Obama's comments about "bitter voters who cling to their guns and religion." That post became headline news across the country and was seized by Hillary Clinton as evidence that Obama was out of touch with mainstream America. (In an interesting footnote, Fowler attempted to use the visibility of the bitter voters story to demand a paid position at the Huffington Post. Her request was denied and she resigned.) Clearly, bloggers have the potential to influence the behavior of both candidates and journalists.

The circulation of blog posts is limited by two major constraints. First, as is the case with websites in general (Hindman, 2008), the most widely visited blogs are also the blogs that receive the most links from other bloggers. In effect, less than 1 percent of the blogosphere receives all the attention, while the remaining 99 percent is completely ignored. The second constraint is not size related, but ideological. The blogosphere is almost perfectly polarized along partisan–ideological lines. Cross-linking occurs only among like-minded groups; liberal bloggers cite liberals, while conservatives link to fellow conservatives. In a comprehensive mapping of blog links during the 2004 campaign, Adamic and Glance (2005) documented that virtually all exchanges of opinion occur within rather than between partisan groups. In effect, the blogosphere consists of two isolated echo chambers.

The most recent evidence suggests not only that the political blogosphere is polarized but also that it is a venue frequented primarily by people interested in politics. Researchers administered a survey during the 2010 campaign in which they asked respondents to write in the names of the blogs they followed. Close to 34 percent of the sample listed at least one blog and 14 percent reported they followed a political blog (Lawrence, Sides, & Farrell, 2010). Those who read political blogs were drawn almost exclusively from the ranks of the politically attentive. In fact, 100 percent of political blog readers reported they were "very much interested" in politics. In keeping with the Adamic and Glance analysis, this study also demonstrated very high levels of polarization in the blogosphere. Less than 10 percent of blog readers chose to read posts that did not match their political sentiments; 94 percent tuned in to commentary they found agreeable.

Clearly, the evidence on cross-linking within the blogosphere does not accord with arguments concerning the democratizing potential of new media. The fact that online networks represent homogenous gated communities rather than a marketplace of ideas indicates that people will rarely encounter unfamiliar and controversial views they might find disagreeable. If some minimal level of exposure to opinions that are different from one's own is a necessary condition for the development of political tolerance and open-mindedness, the blogosphere is no breeding ground for democratic citizenship.

the implications of the information. In this view, people who derive special benefits from particular government policies are expected to be more inclined to prick up their ears when news programs mention developments concerning these policies (such as senior citizens or those nearing retirement in response to mention of Social Security).

A considerable body of evidence suggests that people do, in fact, allocate their attention according to the personal relevance or utility of information. For instance, Krosnick (1990) found that people express greater interest in policy issues that touch them directly and toward which they have developed attitudes of great personal importance. To attach importance to a particular policy attitude is to become a member of that policy's issue public. For instance, the issues of gay rights and abortion motivate evangelical Christians to become active in political campaigns (Han, 2009).

The role of issue publics in the consumption of conventional news was examined in the previously cited study by Price and Zaller (1993), who carried out several tests of the hypothesis that people whose personal background suggested they might belong to an issue public were more likely to recall news stories bearing on their issue of importance. The results indicated only limited support for the hypothesis: in only about half of the tests, the group identified as the issue public had higher recall of stories bearing on that issue.[3]

In a related investigation of issue publics by Iyengar (1990), recall of television news reports about Social Security and racial discrimination was significantly higher among older and minority viewers, respectively, than among younger and white viewers. In addition to recalling more stories about race, African Americans proved more informed about matters of civil rights than whites were, despite the latter group's significantly greater knowledge of overall political information. Other scholars have uncovered a similar pattern with gender: on women's issues, women tend to be better informed than men.

The importance of issue public membership to the use of new media was one of the main lessons of the 2000 CD tracking study. The researchers identified eight different issue publics. The "defense issue public," for instance, was identified as all study participants who had served in the military, and the "Social Security issue public" consisted of all retired participants. In six of the eight tests, members of the issue public visited greater numbers of CD pages concerning the issue of interest. When compared with nonmembers, members of issue publics registered more page visits on an order of magnitude ranging from 50 percent (for the "education issue public") to 80 percent (for the "abortion issue public").

As a case in point, Figure 5.6 shows the number of visits to CD pages concerning healthcare by a variety of healthcare-related issue publics. The x-axis corresponds to the average number of visits to health-related pages, and the y-axis divides the "health issue public" into five subcategories: occupation (those who work in the health field versus those who don't), insurance coverage (participants whose health insurance coverage was less than continuous during the preceding year versus those who were continuously insured), membership in a health maintenance organization (HMO members versus non-HMO members), age (participants sixty years and older versus those younger than sixty), and age of parent (those with elderly parents versus those with younger parents). In every comparison, the number of accessed health pages was higher among members of the group more affected by healthcare policy.

To sum up, the evidence suggests that exposure to political information is determined by multiple factors: the desire to keep up with politics generally, to acquire information that is consistent with existing political preferences, and to learn about issues of special interest. In the case of cable and online news, the evidence suggests that party identification is becoming a more important ingredient of consumers' source preferences among both Democrats and

FIGURE 5.6

Selective Exposure to Healthcare Information

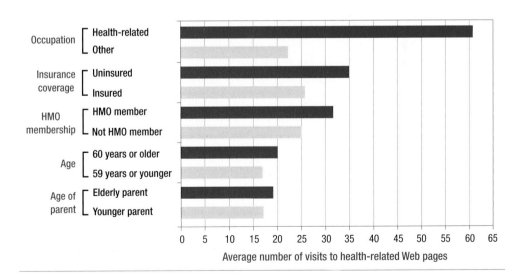

Republicans. News organizations now have some incentive to cater to their viewers' political preferences (Mullainathan & Schleifer, 2005). The emergence of Fox News as the leading cable news provider is testimony to the viability of this niche news paradigm. Between 2000 and 2010, Fox News increased the size of its regular audience by some 50 percent, while CNN, which remains committed to point–counterpoint journalism, found itself mired in last place. MSNBC, after deciding to position itself as the network of the left, has used programming that features the liberal commentators Keith Olbermann (until his resignation in early 2011) and Rachel Maddow to overtake CNN in the ratings. During the 2008 campaign, there were days when *Countdown with Keith Olbermann* was the most watched cable news program. Thus the emerging market for cable news features competition between red and blue providers (Sherman, 2010).

SOCIAL MEDIA AS A NEWS SOURCE: IMPLICATIONS FOR SELECTIVE EXPOSURE

Perhaps the most transforming aspect of technology has been the creation of huge online social networks. Facebook, which was founded just over a decade ago in 2004, now has more than 150 million users in the United States alone. Two-thirds of American adults are on Facebook and half of them say they encounter news there according to a 2014 Pew survey. For our purposes what is especially important is that Facebook users not only exchange personal information but also share news and other forms of media. The Pew data (Pew Research Center, 2014) show that 50 percent of Facebook users report having reposted a news story, video, or image. In fact, there is so much recirculation of media reports that Facebook has emerged as a major source of traffic to the websites of news organizations. For years, the major news sites depended on the big search engines (e.g., Google and Yahoo) for a major share of their Internet traffic. Since 2010, however, Facebook users make up an increasing share of the visitors to news sites, by some estimates providing as much as 25 percent of the referral traffic (Anburajan, 2013; McGee, 2014). Thus, for many Americans, Facebook is a significant source of news (see Messing, 2013; Pew Research Center, 2014).

Similar to interpersonal networks, online social networks are politically homogenous; a study of the composition of friendship groups on Facebook found striking levels of ideological agreement. Liberals have many more liberal than conservative friends and the level of agreement is even greater— around 60 percent—for conservatives (Messing, 2013). Since Facebook users' encounters with political information reflect the content that is shared by their friends, there is a clear partisan bias to information exposure. Democrats tend to be exposed to more left-leaning content, while Republicans encounter more right-leaning content. In many respects, this process of news recirculation matches the classic concept of *de facto* selectivity, the idea that people encountered congenial information not because they actively sought it out, but because the people they conversed with most often shared their political views. Facebook users do not deliberately seek out information that conforms to their political preferences. Instead, they find themselves in the path of news stories that their friends choose to circulate. Furthermore, the data from Facebook suggest that news reports from partisan sources are more likely to be circulated. In fact, the two news organizations with the highest recirculation rates on Facebook are Fox News and the Huffington Post, both offering a distinct partisan slant on events (see Messing, 2013).

While the political composition of online social networks facilitates exposure to agreeable information, news exposure via social media is also shaped by powerful nonpartisan cues. One such indicator is related to topics or subject matter considered trendy or momentarily popular. Research on Facebook news consumption suggests that popularity cues (the number of people who "like" a particular story) are just as powerful determinants of attention, if not more so, than ideological agreement (Messing & Westwood, 2014). Other experiments show that in the context of the Facebook News Feed, individuals are more likely to select news shared from a strong tie versus a weak tie (see Messing & Westwood, 2013).

IMPACT OF THE INTERNET ON POLITICAL ORGANIZATIONS

In democratic societies, it goes without saying that candidates are attracted to media outlets in direct proportion to the size of their audience. In the early days of the Internet, most campaigns felt it unnecessary to establish a Web presence. As the technology spread and innovative new forms of online networking attracted large numbers of users, so too did the incentives for Internet-based campaigning. By 2008, the payoffs of Internet-based campaigning were sufficient to allow a relatively unknown candidate to capture the Democratic presidential nomination.

In principle, campaigns can harness the immense networking power of the Internet to accomplish multiple campaign objectives, including fund-raising; producing and distributing information that increases the candidate's visibility and likability; and most critically, recruiting and mobilizing a cadre of activists. To date, the impact of new media has been greatest on the goal of mobilization. Although other facets of the campaign remain grounded in conventional (especially broadcast) media because there are still more voters to be reached in front of their television sets than at their computers, the development of video-sharing sites and the rapidity with which campaign videos now circulate around the Web means that candidates can deliver campaign messages at their own discretion. (Exactly what campaigns do to influence public opinion is the subject of Chapter 6.) Nonetheless, as described later in this chapter, the ability to organize and communicate with online networks of supporters has transformed the conduct of campaigns.

Before the Internet, candidates recruited volunteers and raised money by making phone calls, sending mass mailings, or going door to door. These low-tech forms of mobilization and fund-raising were both capital and time intensive; successful campaigns had an existing organization, professional (paid) staff, and access to phone banks or mailing lists of prospective supporters. Candidates themselves might spend long hours on the phone with prospective donors. The amount of time between the initial contact and receipt of a financial contribution might take weeks or even months. These infrastructure costs made it nearly impossible for lesser-known candidates to develop and manage a hard-core group of activists.

By lowering the cost of communication, the Internet has opened up the political arena by enabling any group, no matter how large or small its electoral constituency, to assemble a network of supporters. Any candidate with the ability to mount a basic website can instantly sign up volunteers and send them assignments for upcoming events, thus developing the nucleus of a viable field organization. Once formed, these groups become smart mobs—capable of acting in a coordinated manner, despite the absence of any face-to-face contact. (For examples of smart mobs in action, see Rheingold, 2002.) In effect, the Internet has lowered the eligibility requirements for groups to engage in collective action.

In this country, the first instance of a campaign organization using the Internet to organize its supporters was Jesse Ventura's 1998 campaign for governor of Minnesota. Running as the Reform Party candidate, Ventura was heavily outspent by his Republican and Democratic opponents (Norm Coleman and Hubert H. Humphrey III, respectively). But Ventura's campaign launched a website in early 1998 (at a monthly cost of under thirty dollars) and began to develop a statewide e-mail list of volunteers. The list was used to publicize

Case Study:
NEW MEDIA AND REGIME CHANGE

In nondemocratic countries, the reduced costs of collective action have worked to the disadvantage of authoritarian rulers seeking to suppress dissent. In recent years, several dictatorships have been toppled, mainly because anti-regime groups were able to mobilize thousands of their supporters to take to the streets. In what came to be known as the Arab Spring, authoritarian rule was ended in Tunisia, Egypt, and Libya, leading some to speculate that cell phones and text messages have become necessary ingredients of regime change. This is certainly the view taken by dictators, who typically disrupt Internet and cell-phone service during periods of mass unrest. However, as a study of the 2011 Egyptian revolution suggests, such shutdowns made Egyptians living in urban areas more likely to take to the streets so that they could acquire information face-to-face, thus creating a cascade of protest activity which eventually forced President Mubarak to resign (Hassanpour, 2014). Of course, in countries without densely populated urban centers, where the population is dispersed across a wide area, the strategy of disrupting cellular communication may prove effective in neutralizing protest.

China provides an especially interesting case study of the technological challenges facing authoritarian governments. With the diffusion of the Internet, large numbers of Chinese have become active on popular blog sites where they regularly post messages critical of government officials and voice displeasure with the Communist Party. The Chinese authorities, in response, have implemented a vast censorship operation (Shambaugh, 2007), taking down blog posts they deem objectionable (i.e., those identified as potentially destabilizing). A systematic analysis of the content of the blog posts that attract censorship demonstrates that the messages most likely to be censored are not those criticizing the regime, but messages referring to any form of collective action (King, Pan, & Roberts, 2013).

information about local organizational meetings; one such meeting drew a standing-room-only crowd of more than 250 people.

Despite being outspent and outstaffed by his opponents (the campaign had only one paid staff member, the campaign manager), Ventura was elected governor. It is difficult to say precisely how much difference Ventura's use of technology made to the upset victory. After all, his unusual persona and career as a professional wrestler combined to make him a highly visible candidate, and his antigovernment, populist platform resonated well in a state with a long history of supporting progressive reformers. In one respect, however, the payoff of using technology was clear: young people, who are most likely to be reached online, turned out to vote in large numbers. Over half of them voted for Ventura—more than enough to account for the margin of his victory.

The success of the Ventura campaign made it clear to campaign operatives that the Internet could and should be exploited for political action. By 2000, all reputable candidates had elaborate, interactive websites and e-mail lists of prospective supporters. Among the presidential contenders, it was John McCain who became the poster boy for use of the Internet. Capitalizing on McCain's special appeal to the young, his campaign went online to recruit some fifteen hundred volunteers in advance of the 2000 New Hampshire primary. The campaign scheduled regular online chat encounters with the candidate. In one such session, five hundred people each paid a hundred dollars for the privilege of submitting an e-mail question to McCain. The McCain campaign set a new record ($4 million) for electronic fund-raising.

Despite McCain's stunning victory in the New Hampshire primary, his candidacy proved short-lived. George W. Bush rebounded from New Hampshire and soundly defeated McCain in South Carolina. Shortly thereafter, McCain withdrew from the race. But once again, an insurgent candidate had demonstrated competitiveness with the help of a relatively modest investment in new media.

It was during the 2004 campaign that Internet campaigning came into its own. Governor Howard Dean tied his presidential candidacy inextricably to the Internet. Although Dean was eventually forced to withdraw from the campaign for lack of support, his campaign's innovative use of technology contributed to his meteoric rise from the relatively unknown governor of a small state to the front-running contender for the Democratic nomination. The Dean campaign hired a full-time Internet consultant. The first step was to use the networking portal Meetup.com to recruit supporters from across the nation. The Dean campaign used Meetup to schedule events, several of which were attended by the candidate himself. For the campaign, mailing out campaign materials was the only cost of maintaining this network of activists.

The most significant accomplishment of the 2004 Dean campaign was its ability to raise funds online. In one instance, the campaign responded to a Bush–Cheney $2,000-a-plate dinner (which raised $250,000) by hosting an online eat-in challenge featuring a Web page with an image of Dean eating a turkey sandwich, and a "Contribute Now" button. In response, 9,700 people visited the page, and the campaign netted over $500,000. In the second quarter of 2003 alone, the campaign took in more than $7 million.

Given the Dean campaign's effective use of the Internet to mobilize supporters, why did he fail to win even one primary? Dean's extensive network of online volunteers did not translate into an outpouring of primary votes. In the language of social scientists, the Dean campaign was doomed by a self-selection bias. The American technoliterati, most of whom were eager to drive Bush from the White House and who seized the opportunity to volunteer for Dean, were much too small a group to swing even a small-state primary. In other words, the Deaniacs were not representative of Democratic primary voters. A Pew Research Center survey of Dean activists found that 54 percent had attended graduate school (for all Democratic activists, the comparable figure was 11 percent) and that they were significantly more liberal and anti-Bush than mainstream Democrats (Pew Research Center, 2005). Dean's candidacy itself was clearly faithful to his supporters, but it also made Dean less appealing to most Democratic voters.

Thus, the main lesson of 2004 was that although the Internet provides a cost-efficient means of developing a network of campaign workers and donors, it was not yet the best platform for candidates to appeal for votes. It is one thing to develop an electronic network of enthusiastic supporters; it is quite another to attract enough votes to win a primary election. In 2004, the Internet was not yet competitive with television as a way of communicating with rank-and-file voters. In 2008, however, the story was quite different; it was now possible for the Internet platform to be harnessed not just to mobilize activists and raise money, but also to win votes.

Internet Campaigning Comes of Age

The 2008 presidential election was, in the words of the *Wall Street Journal*, "the first real Internet election" (Rhoads, 2008). And no one used the power of the Web more effectively than Barack Obama's campaign. According to Joe Trippi, the architect of Dean's ground-breaking campaign, "the tools [for elections] changed between 2004 and 2008. Barack Obama won every single caucus state that matters, and he did it because of those tools, because he was able to move thousands of people to organize" (Miller, 2008).

From the day he declared his candidacy in Springfield, Illinois (February 10, 2007), the campaign's sensitivity to online marketing was evident. Blue State Digital, the Democratic consulting firm that had handled the Dean campaign, managed Obama's online campaign. The website barackobama.com was designed for a general audience; it attracted more than 2.6 million unique visitors, while visitors to the McCain website numbered fewer than half that number (Rhoads, 2008). Another site, my.barackobama.com, was designed to provide resources (scheduling, call lists, fund-raising scripts) to volunteers and to encourage blogging (see Figure 5.7). Eventually, more than 2 million individuals posted user profiles at my.barackobama.com, 200,000 campaign events were planned, and 35,000 volunteer groups were formed. All the major social networking sites from Facebook and MySpace to BlackPlanet and AsianAve were actively engaged. More than 3 million Facebook users became fans of Obama's Facebook page.

In contrast with previous presidential campaigns, all of which had maintained separate organizations corresponding to online and traditional efforts, the Obama campaign integrated the new- and old-media teams into one overarching organization under the control of campaign manager David Plouffe. Both forms of the campaign operated with the same priorities and emphasized similar themes (see Figure 5.8).

Given the interactive nature of online communication, the Obama campaign was able to compile a massive database of supporters by requesting

FIGURE 5.7

Screenshot from My.BarackObama.com

Source: Courtesy of MyBarackObama.com/The Democratic Party.

FIGURE 5.8

Organizational Structure of the Obama Campaign

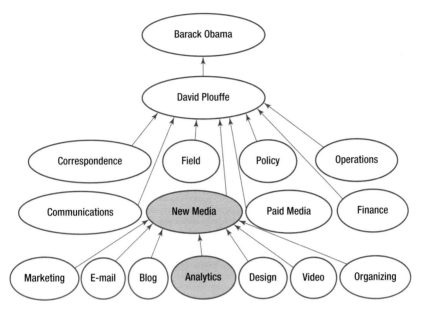

Source: Data from D. Siroker. (2009). *How we used data to win the presidential election.* Retrieved January 23, 2011, from www.siroker.com/files/ses/dsiroker.pdf.

e-mail addresses and phone numbers whenever a person visited the website. Using cookies, the campaign tracked the Web-browsing behavior of online supporters. Based on the browsing profile of a particular voter, the campaign would have a good idea of that voter's interests and then could e-mail her messages or banner ads of likely interest.

In developing a vast network of supporters and volunteers, Obama's use of the Internet was no different from other candidates'. But where the campaign broke new ground was its systematic use of online campaign communication. The video-sharing site YouTube played a critical role in the dissemination of campaign messages. The ability to reach a large Internet audience made it possible to counteract or rebut critical media commentary, a capability that proved especially useful in the aftermath of the controversy surrounding Obama's friendship with the Reverend Jeremiah Wright.

The Reverend Wright story threatened to derail Obama's candidacy. Fox News and other news organizations replayed excerpts from Wright's incendiary comments on a daily basis. Hillary Clinton pointedly commented that "You don't choose your family, but you choose what church you want to attend."

Video Archive 5.1
Obama Race Speech (Introduction)

Faced with an impending political crisis, the Obama campaign decided to meet the uproar over the Reverend Wright head-on in a prime-time speech on the subject of race relations (see Video Archive 5.1). Obama used the speech both to distance himself from Wright and to call for racial understanding and reconciliation. The speech was posted on YouTube and immediately viewed by more than a million people. By the end of the campaign, the entire speech had been viewed 7 million times online (Hill, 2009).

The Obama campaign went on to produce more than a thousand videos, which were watched for over 14 million hours. As Joe Trippi pointed out, an advertising buy on a similar scale would have cost the candidate $47 million (Miller, 2008). In addition to the official campaign videos, Obama supporters created their own videos. Two of the most popular were titled "I Got a Crush . . . on Obama" and "Yes We Can." "I Got a Crush" was posted on June 13, 2007 (see Video Archive 5.2), and by the next day had become a news item; by Election Day it had been seen 12 million times. The woman in the video, dubbed "The Obama Girl," became an Internet celebrity, frequently appearing on mainstream media programs (see Figure 5.9).

Video Archive 5.2
"I Got a Crush . . ."

FIGURE 5.9

Screenshot from "I Got a Crush . . ."

Source: SplashNews/NewsCom

"Yes We Can," posted on February 2, 2008, proved even more popular (see Video Archive 5.3). The video, which was produced without the involvement of the Obama campaign, featured the celebrities wil.i.am, Kareem Abdul Jabbar, John Legend, Herbie Hancock, and others singing the words to Obama's New Hampshire primary concession speech over the audio of the actual speech. It had been viewed 22 million times by election day and was eventually awarded an Emmy for Best New Approaches in Daytime Entertainment.

Video Archive 5.3 "Yes We Can"

The most recent development in the gradual encroachment of technology into campaign management is the incorporation of sophisticated data metrics into day-to-day decision making. As Jim Messina, who managed the 2012 Obama team, stated, "We are going to measure every single thing in this campaign" (Scherer, 2012). A major data analytics firm worked on fundraising, testing the persuasion potential of TV ads, and developing detailed profiles of voters in swing states based on their likelihood of voting for Obama. These profiles became the basis for targeting voter mobilization efforts on Election Day.

In sharp contrast, the Romney campaign's data project—code named Project ORCA (in response to the Obama team labelling their voter profile project Narwhal)—proved relatively ineffective. Campaign volunteers were unable to log in, and the campaign's Internet service provider (Comcast) suspended service, mistakenly interpreting the thousands of log in attempts as a denial of service attack.

In the final analysis, the 2008 and 2012 campaigns indicate that the Democrats have been quicker than Republicans to embrace new forms of online campaigning. In 2008, Obama had 4 times as many Facebook friends as McCain, about 3.5 times as many unique visitors to his campaign sites, and roughly 6 times as many official YouTube videos that attracted 300 times more viewers as his competitor's videos. In 2012, Obama's Facebook friends outnumbered Romney's by 3 to 1, and the number of people downloading the Obama Facebook app exceeded the number with the Romney app by a margin of 30 to 1. The Obama team brought in $690 million online (up from $500 million in 2008), more than 3 times the amount raised digitally by the Romney campaign. Given the far-reaching consequences of online campaigning, it is quite likely that Republicans will make every effort to achieve parity with Democrats in their ability to harness these powerful new tools.

Our brief survey of Web-based campaigns suggests several broad generalizations. First, the Internet makes it possible for campaigns to mobilize supporters at relatively low cost. Second, the Internet is a rich lode of campaign cash. Third, new sources of data and sophisticated data analyses make it possible for campaigns to target potential supporters with high levels of precision. And finally, new forms of communication make it possible for candidates to produce and distribute campaign materials online, thus making them autonomous from the news media. We will elaborate on the possibility of unmediated political campaigns in the concluding chapter.

CONCLUSION

The scholarly evidence concerning the emerging role of the Internet in public life suggests that the audience for news is becoming more fragmented. Given the availability of unlimited choice, Americans with limited interest in politics prefer to avoid news coverage entirely. For those who care about politics, the amount of information and increased availability of news sources forces them to exercise choice. Since online media outlets deliver partisan messages, consumers can choose based on their partisan affiliation. In the case of the blogosphere, what people see or read is driven primarily by the desire to encounter opinions with which they are likely to agree. In the case of news sources, partisan choices are limited to cable outlets with relatively small audiences and the level of motivated exposure to news is thus not nearly as extensive as in the case of the blogosphere. Social media, an emerging new platform for news consumption, also provides opportunities for partisans to encounter information supportive of their political preferences.

Even though partisans still encounter objective, nonpartisan news coverage from mainstream news organizations, they are nonetheless apt to ignore or discount highly publicized facts when these facts are at odds with their political preferences. In 2004, for instance, Republicans refused to acknowledge that President Bush's decision to go to war in Iraq was based on inaccurate intelligence, despite an avalanche of news stories calling the intelligence reports into question. This form of partisan bias in interpreting objective news reports is discussed in Chapter 8.

Quite apart from the ambiguous verdict of the scholarly literature concerning the effects of the Internet on civic engagement or exposure to diverse points of view, there is a different reason to feel optimistic about the potential impact of technology on the political process. We have already documented that media-based campaigns fail to deliver substantive information. In place of the candidates' positions and past performance on the issues, news coverage gravitates inevitably toward the more entertaining facets of the campaign: the horse race, the strategy, and, whenever possible, instances of scandalous or unethical behavior. Against this backdrop, technology at least makes it possible for voters to bypass or supplement media treatment of the campaign and access information about the issues that affect them.

Rather than waiting (typically in vain) for news organizations to report on the issues they care about, voters can take matters into their own hands and seek out information about the candidates' positions on these issues. This form of motivated exposure is hardly an impediment to deliberation: paying attention to what the candidates have to say on the issues facilitates issue-oriented voting; paying attention to the media circus does not. Thus, there is some reason to hope that the spread of new forms of unmediated communication will provide a better way to inform and engage voters.

Finally, the brief case studies of candidates who have successfully exploited technology and the success of pro-democracy movements overseas make it clear that technology, in this respect at least, has leveled the political playing field. Even the poorest candidate has the capacity to publicize his or her candidacy and solicit support online. Grassroots protest movements are able to mount serious challenges to entrenched and ruthless dictators. As the experience of the 2008 and 2012 Obama campaigns suggests, an Internet presence is critical to running a viable campaign. As technology spreads even further, and the next generation of software makes possible even closer contact and cooperation among like-minded individuals, we may expect the Internet to play a pivotal role in American campaigns.

SUMMARY

1. The development of information technology and the spread of new media have changed the communication landscape. Traditional forms of communication were either point-to-point (between a single sender and recipient) or broadcast (between a single sender and multiple recipients). New media—particularly the Internet—have broken down those distinctions. Any Internet user can send e-mail messages to individual recipients and at the same time communicate with a worldwide audience by, for example, hosting a website. Moreover, unlike conventional media, Internet-based communication is multichannel, allowing the intermingling of text, voice, still images, and video.

2. The Internet has greatly increased both the amount and the variety of material available to the public, as well as consumers' control over the information to which they're exposed. There are three main arguments about how people choose which political communications they will attend to:
   - The *attentive public hypothesis* suggests that the act of seeking out political information is simply a matter of generic political interest. People captivated

by politics tune in to all forms of news, while the apolitical majority tunes out politics.

- The *partisan polarization hypothesis* suggests that people prefer to encounter information that they find consistent with their beliefs. Some fear that if partisanship is the dominant basis of selectivity, the spread of new media will lead to political polarization, since liberals and conservatives will both have greater ability to select information sources that they agree with, and ignore others.
- The *issue public hypothesis* suggests that people seek out information about subjects that are particularly important or interesting to them and tune out information about other subjects. Evidence for this type of selectivity has been more consistent than that for partisan polarization.

3. Online social networks such as Facebook have become major carriers of political information. Because individuals' online networks are politically homogeneous, they are more exposed to news and commentary consistent with their partisan leanings.

4. The widespread proliferation of the Internet has increased its use to mobilize individuals for political action. It has been used to great effect by protest groups seeking to topple authoritarian rulers and by campaign organizations to raise funds and target electioneering activities. The widespread use of video-sharing sites makes it possible for candidates to reach voters without first going through the news media.

FURTHER READINGS

Adamic, L. A., & Glance, N. (2005). *The political blogosphere and the 2004 U.S. election: Divided they blog.* Paper presented at Annual Workshop on the Weblogging Ecosystem, WWW2005, Chiba, Japan, May 10–14.

Gentzkow, M., & Shapiro, J. (2010). *Ideological segregation online and offline* (Working Paper 15916). Retrieved August 15, 2010, from the National Bureau of Economic Research. website: www.nber.org/papers/w15916.

Hassanpour, N. (2014). Media disruption and revolutionary unrest: Evidence from Mubarak's quasi-experiment. *Political Communication, 31*, 1–24.

Hindman, M. (2009). *The myth of digital democracy.* Princeton, NJ: Princeton University Press.

Iyengar, S., & Hahn, K. (2009). Red media, blue media: Evidence of ideological polarization in media use. *Journal of Communication, 59*, 19–39.

Iyengar, S., Hahn, K., Krosnick, J., & Walker, J. (2008). Selective exposure to campaign communication: The role of anticipated agreement and issue public membership. *Journal of Politics, 70*, 186–200.

Matsuba, M. K. (2006). Searching for self and relationships online. *CyberPsychology & Behavior, 9*(3), 275–284.

Miller, C. C. (2008, November 7). How Obama's Internet campaign changed politics. Retrieved November 21, 2008, from the *New York Times* blog website: http://bits.blogs.nytimes.com.

Morgan, C., & Cotten, S. R. (2003). The relationship between Internet activities and depressive symptoms in a sample of college freshmen. *CyberPsychology & Behavior, 6*(2), 133–142.

Pew Research Center. (2014). *How social media is reshaping news.* Retrieved August 15, 2014, from http://www.pewresearch.org/fact-tank/2014/09/24/how-social-media-is-reshaping-news/.

Sears, D. O., & Freedman, J. L. (1967). Selective exposure to information: A critical review. *Public Opinion Quarterly, 31*, 194–213.

Smith, A., Schlozman, K. L., Verba, S., & Brady, H. (2009). *The Internet and civic engagement.* Pew Research Center, Washington, DC.

Sunstein, C. (2001). *Republic.com.* Princeton, NJ: Princeton University Press.

NOTES

1. It is well known that interest in politics and other indicators of engagement in civic life are strongly correlated with education and socioeconomic status. In one sense, then, political interest is an indicator of access to and proficiency with information technology.

2. Production of the CD was made possible through the generous support of the Pew Charitable Trusts, the Carnegie Corporation, and the active cooperation of the Bush and Gore campaigns. Produced by the Political Communication Lab at Stanford University, the CD was titled *Vote 2004: Presidential Candidates in Their Own Words* and was distributed broadly to the general public as well as to the study participants. The CD is available at http://pcl.stanford.edu/campaigns.

3. Some of the authors' indicators of issue public membership were, at best, approximations. For example, "reading a great deal of international news in the newspaper" was treated as indicating membership in the issue public for international events.

6

Campaigning through the Media

In the weeks leading up to the 1948 election, President Truman crisscrossed the country on his campaign train, making daily appearances before enthusiastic crowds of voters. Shaking hands, kissing babies, and greeting voters were standard practice in the era of in-person, retail politics.

By 1960, the rapid spread of television had altered the behavior of candidates. In-person appearances were time-consuming for the candidates and attracted only the most faithful of partisans. Most Americans, especially those lacking a strong party affiliation, stayed away from campaign events. These same people, however, watched lots of television. Candidates soon realized that television provided efficient access to a national audience. Unlike personal appearances, with their idiosyncratic hit-or-miss quality (attendance at an event might be cut in half by bad weather), televised news programs attracted a more predictable audience.

As a campaign medium, television provided still further advantages, including the ability to deliver different messages and appeals, depending on the needs and interests of particular television markets. Most notable, the medium of television advertising guaranteed campaigns maximum control over the content and form of their message. Unlike with live public speeches, there would be no hecklers interrupting an ad and distracting voters from the candidate's appeal. Unlike news coverage, there would be no editor selecting the particular sound bites actually aired. Unlike debates, there would be no hovering journalists probing for weaknesses, or opponents standing ready to pounce on any misstatement of fact. From the perspective of candidates, television seemed to have it all.

Beginning in 1952, presidential campaigns began to experiment with different forms of television-based campaigning. The first political ads appeared in that year. During the 1960 presidential campaign, John Kennedy and Richard Nixon debated each other on four occasions before an average audience amounting to 60 percent of the US population. By 1968, campaigns were designed explicitly for television, and no serious campaign was without its cadre of full-time, highly paid media strategists. As Roger Ailes, the well-known Republican consultant (now the CEO of Fox News) declared, "This is the beginning of a whole new concept. This is it. This is the way they'll be elected forevermore. The next guys will have to be performers" (Diamond & Bates, 1992, p. 398).

Candidates perform on two parallel stages, corresponding to *free media* (news coverage) and *paid media* (advertising). In most statewide and congressional races, advertising tends to dominate news as the principal stage, for the simple reason that these campaigns attract only sparse news coverage. In recent contests for governor of California, for instance, less than 1 percent of all local news that was broadcast in October focused on the election to be held that next month. Unable to crack the newsworthiness barrier, gubernatorial candidates are forced to invest heavily in advertising. In the 2010 race for governor of California, Meg Whitman, the Republican candidate, spent more than $150 million of her own money, most of it on television ads.

In contrast to statewide or congressional races, presidential races enjoy virtually unlimited news coverage, making the ad campaign only a small trickle in the cumulative message stream. This does not mean that advertising strategy is unimportant in presidential races. Far from it; the continuous and often acrimonious conflict between journalists and candidates over the content of news coverage has only intensified the importance of advertising as the one truly unmediated form of campaign speech.

In this chapter we will address three forms of contemporary media campaigning: the candidates' efforts to exploit press coverage, their advertising strategies, and their performance in televised candidate debates.

STRATEGIES FOR MANAGING THE PRESS

In the ideal campaign, each candidate hopes to enjoy a regular stream of favorable news coverage while his or her opponent either suffers from inattention or is portrayed in unflattering terms. In this scenario the news media would play the role of a credible spokesperson for the campaign. The professional norms governing journalism make it almost certain that reporters will refuse

IN FOCUS

Strategies That Candidates Use to Manage the Press

- Avoid behavior that calls into question your suitability for office.
- Don't waffle or flip-flop on the issues.
- Make sure journalists have low expectations concerning your chances of victory.
- Schedule events strategically to maximize their newsworthiness.
- When leading in the polls, restrict journalists' access.
- Go local to avoid critical coverage from national news organizations.
- Feed the press titillating but critical information concerning your opponent.

to act as campaign agents. As we noted in Chapter 3, the practice of interpretive journalism requires journalists to dismiss the candidate's rhetoric out of hand. The need to make news entertaining and eye-catching is a further drag on the candidates' ability to insert their messages intact into the news stream. The latest position paper on combating international terrorism might contain myriad specific proposals, none of which can be conveyed in a ten-second sound bite.

In the real world, a variety of factors influence the ability of a campaign to spin the press. We begin with the worst-case scenario and then describe a series of specific strategies that provide campaigns at least some leverage over the content of the news.

AVOIDING FEEDING FRENZIES

The ability of a campaign to influence the press is at a low ebb in races in which the media scent evidence of personal misbehavior or character issues. When candidates demonstrate obvious personal flaws, they are completely at the mercy of the media. Given the premium value of the character story, the ensuing feeding frenzy can prove fatal. Former vice presidential candidate and senator John Edwards was forced to suspend his 2008 run for the presidency after the *National Enquirer* published a series of stories alleging an extramarital affair with a campaign worker while his wife was fighting cancer. As mentioned in Chapter 3, Herman Cain's 2012 presidential campaign effectively ended the day *Politico* broke the news that two female employees of the National Restaurant Association had filed complaints of inappropriate behavior against the candidate. One year later, Congressman Anthony Weiner resigned his seat after revelations he had tweeted a sexually suggestive photograph of himself to a twenty-one-year-old woman.

In less scandalous circumstances, it is imperative that the candidates not behave in ways that raise doubts about their personal makeup. The storm of critical news coverage aimed at Governor Howard Dean after the Iowa caucuses was self-inflicted. His impassioned concession speech—dubbed the "Dean Scream"—was replayed incessantly in the following days and interpreted by the pundits as symptomatic of Dean's unstable personality and lack of self-control. Four years later, Hillary Clinton's claims to have come under sniper fire while on an official visit to Bosnia dominated the news for several days and reminded voters of her penchant for self-promotion.

Video Archive 6.1
Herman Cain Feeding Frenzy

DEALING WITH THE OBJECTIVITY IMPERATIVE

On the substantive or performance side of the ledger, it is rare for a candidate to eke out an edge in news coverage. Unlike character issues, which tend to be viewed in black-and-white terms (a candidate is either an adulterer or happily married), the candidates' credentials and positions on the issues represent a gray zone—there are no clear winners and losers. Journalists purport to be self-consciously objective in their discussion and take pains to provide point–counterpoint reporting. The rare occasions when the norm does not preclude one-sided coverage arise either when one candidate has a clear-cut advantage over the opponent or, as we will discuss here, when a candidate makes a major misstatement of fact or reverses course on a matter of public policy.

The coverage of the 2004 presidential candidates' war records provides an example of the infrequently experienced comparative advantage scenario. During the 2004 primary season, Senator John Kerry enjoyed a favorable balance of news over President Bush because of their contrasting records on Vietnam. Kerry had volunteered for a particularly dangerous assignment (patrolling the Mekong River, one of the deadliest war zones) and won several awards for heroism and bravery under fire. For his part, President Bush had joined the Texas Air National Guard, but the actual extent of his weekend service remains unclear.

Kerry's advantage on the war record story proved short lived. The commitment to balanced coverage is so compelling that this phase of reporting was followed almost immediately by several reports highlighting Kerry's later involvement in the antiwar movement. The *New York Times* and other major newspapers published photos (which later turned out to be fake) of Kerry in close proximity to "Hanoi Jane" (the actress Jane Fonda, then a leading antiwar activist). The call of objectivity had been answered.

As in the case of character-related news, the candidate's pronouncements on policy issues may provide journalists with a convenient excuse to attack. A candidate whose words and deeds are inconsistent or who revises a previously stated position is a ripe target for critical scrutiny. Senator George McGovern, the Democratic presidential candidate in 1972, was widely criticized for dropping Senator Tom Eagleton as his running mate after the press revealed that Eagleton had once been treated for clinical depression. A similar media cloud enveloped Hillary Clinton during the 2008 campaign when she said she had opposed the North American Free Trade Agreement. Journalists were quick to point out that Clinton had actually worked for its passage while serving as First Lady.

PLAYING THE EXPECTATIONS GAME

Recognizing the difficulty of directly influencing the content and tone of news coverage, the candidates have recently turned to more subtle media strategies. One approach is to try to influence reporters' treatment of the candidate's electoral prospects. We have seen that the state of the horse race is the foundation of campaign news. In the early stages of the primary campaign, favorable coverage of the candidate's position in the race can prove pivotal; candidates thought to be doing well (thanks to press reports) can use their standing to attract additional financial contributions and, as several scholars have documented, to attract even more voters in upcoming primaries.

Even more important than favorable horse-race coverage is the surprise factor. Candidates who "beat the odds" and surpass journalists' expectations benefit from electoral momentum. Consider the case of Senator Kerry in the 2004 presidential race. In the months before the Iowa caucuses, Kerry was dismissed as an underachieving contender whose national poll numbers remained steadily in the single digits and whose finances were so shaky that he had to take out yet another mortgage to compete in Iowa. Given this baseline, Kerry's victory in Iowa was equivalent to a home run: he had defied journalists' expectations. The Iowa results elicited a wave of favorable coverage, and Kerry went on to win New Hampshire; eventually he captured the Democratic nomination quite handily (see Chapter 9).

Setting journalists' expectations is crucial during the early days of the primary season. High expectations for Hillary Clinton's 2008 presidential bid hurt her campaign. As the presumptive nominee, she was the target of attacks by both Democrats and Republicans, and the media subjected her campaign to an extra level of scrutiny. While the other candidates could get away with the occasional stumble, even a minor slip by Clinton was front-page news.

Campaign spokespersons typically downplay poll results that show their candidate comfortably ahead in Iowa or New Hampshire, in the hope that the outcome will be more surprising and hence covered more extensively and favorably by the media. Conversely, campaigns sometimes attempt to persuade reporters that the opponent has a substantial lead—when they know that the poll numbers represent a short-term blip that will inevitably wear off. Before the 2008 Democratic National Convention, Sarah Simmons, the director of strategy for the McCain campaign, released a statement to the press claiming that they expected to be trailing in the polls by as much as 15 points after the Democratic convention. Not to be outdone, David Axelrod, Obama's senior strategist, told newspapers that he expected little or no bounce after the convention. Both Simmons and Axelrod knew full well that the increase in a candidate's support after the convention is a short-term bubble effect and that the two conventions generally neutralize each other, restoring the status quo that existed before the conventions.

The expectations game can also apply to debates between candidates. Fearing that Sarah Palin would be given underdog status in the coverage of the 2008 vice presidential debate, the Obama campaign hyped Palin's abilities, with one spokesman stating that Biden is "going in there to debate a leviathan of forensics, who has debated five times and she's undefeated in debates" (CNN, September 29, 2008). In what might be described as an expectations-setting race-to-the-bottom, Romney strategist Beth Myers called President Obama "one of the most talented political communicators in modern history" (ABC News, September 27, 2012) prior to the first 2012 presidential debate only to have the president declare that "Governor Romney, he's a good debater. I'm just okay" (Politico, September 30, 2012).

MANAGING EVENTS

The nuts and bolts of press management is the strategic scheduling of events. Put simply, events must be designed and scheduled to attract maximal news coverage. In the days of old-fashioned descriptive journalism, the selection of the vice presidential candidate was delayed until the convention because the presidential nominee was assured adequate coverage in advance of the convention. The increased resistance of the press corps to campaign spin has forced candidates to use the announcement of the vice presidential selection as a media opportunity.

Rather than wasting the vice presidential selection by announcing it during a period of ordinarily high media coverage (the party's national convention), the announcement is now made considerably in advance of the convention so as to capitalize on the news and analysis that follows. John Kerry announced his selection of John Edwards on Monday, July 5, 2004, three weeks before the Democratic National Convention. The duo immediately left on a multistate bus tour, riding a crest of publicity sparked by the surprise announcement. Romney's selection of Paul Ryan fit the same timeline, the announcement coming sixteen days before the opening of the Republican National Convention.

Nominating conventions were once significant opportunities for the candidates and their allies to posture at length before a nationwide audience. Since the advent of primaries, however, conventions have become ceremonial occasions with no possibility of delegations walking out in protest or the eruption of heated arguments over the platform—either of which might pique the media's attention. In contrast to the 1968 Democratic National Convention in Chicago, which precipitated a full-scale riot in that city's streets, present-day conventions are tame affairs. Speakers are screened to ensure that dissent or strident partisanship (which may throw off independents) is minimized.

The 1992 Republican National Convention, generally considered a poorly managed affair, violated the basic rule of projecting an image of party unity when it included prime-time speeches by dissident voices. Pat Buchanan, who had challenged Bush in the Republican primaries, described the Clinton–Gore campaign as advocates of "radical feminism" and "the homosexual rights movement." Marilyn Quayle, the vice president's wife, though less strident, commended stay-at-home moms for furthering family values.

The trade-off of scripted conventions is reduced press coverage. Gavel-to-gavel coverage was last provided in 1976. Since then, television coverage of the conventions has been sporadic. In 2004, the three major networks allocated each convention three hours of total coverage on only three of four days (at the least desirable prime-time slot of 10:00 PM).[1] The networks did air an hour of coverage on each of the four days of each convention in both 2008 and 2012, but again chose not to air the coverage during the peak viewing hours (8:00 PM–10:00 PM). The Romney campaign was forced to move Ann Romney's speech from Monday to Tuesday because the three major networks decided to ignore the first day of the convention.

The reduced newsworthiness of the convention has forced campaign strategists to work harder for news coverage. The appearance of celebrities (such as Arnold Schwarzenegger) attracts news, but the overall theme of party unity tends to dampen press interest. In an unusual move designed to stimulate media interest, the Republicans decided to hold their 2004 convention in early September rather than the usual July–August timing. Their choice of New York as the host city was not mere coincidence. President Bush's advisers realized that the third anniversary of the 9/11 attacks would provide them with a convenient photo opportunity immediately after a convention dominated by terrorism and national security as the Bush campaign's signature issues.

The decision to delay the convention is a textbook example of the strategy of *riding the wave*—coordinating the campaign with events of consequence so that the campaign will benefit from the additional coverage elicited by the newsworthy event. In 2008, the collapse of Lehman Brothers in September signaled the onset of the banking crisis. This story became the overriding focus of the news media. Both presidential campaigns attempted to ride the wave of economic news. McCain went so far as to suspend his campaign on the grounds that helping to save the American banking industry took precedence over partisan politics.

Video Archive 6.2
McCain Announcement

REGULATING ACCESS

Providing the press with access to the candidate is an important ingredient of campaign management. On one end of the spectrum, there is the open-door strategy, designed to maximize the candidate's availability. As one might expect, this strategy is favored by candidates who trail in the polls—the ones who typically lack the resources to engage in advertising. When more competitive, or when emerging as the front-runner, the candidate limits access. The

---

◎ IN FOCUS

"Riding the Wave"

Riding the wave refers to the way candidates seek to coordinate their campaigns with external events of consequence so that the campaign will benefit from the additional media coverage elicited by newsworthy events. In the aftermath of the September 11 attacks, for example, the 2002 campaigns featured frequent references to the threat of terrorism and the need for US military preparedness.

campaign's press secretary may be made available for questioning, but the candidate does not appear in person. The most extreme form of attempts to restrict press access is the Rose Garden strategy, named for incumbent presidents who enjoy such substantial leads in the polls (for example, in the 1972, 1984, and 1996 elections) that the candidate prefers to ignore the press altogether. Thus there is an inverse relationship between press access and electoral standing. Candidates throw themselves at the press (such as Senator McCain's "Straight Talk Express" in 2000) when they anticipate that every additional news report may help them gain on their opponents, but they maintain a closed-door posture and ration information more sparingly once they attain a more competitive position in the polls. In an exception that proves the rule, the trailing McCain campaign severely restricted media access to Sarah Palin in 2008. This decision hurt the campaign, as it seemed to confirm analysts' suppositions that she was unprepared for office. (When Palin finally agreed to do news interviews, her comments—and her inability to name a single newspaper that she read—only raised more doubts about her credentials.)

Video Archive 6.3 Palin Interviews

Video Archive 6.4 Advertising Dialogue

Exactly the same ritual is played out in the context of debates. Front-runners are loath to participate in debates at all, but trailing candidates seek to have as many debates as is humanly possible. As the 2008 Democratic primary contest reached its final stages, Hillary Clinton's campaign, trailing Obama in the polls, pushed for more and more debates, while Obama's campaign came up with more and more reasons to avoid debating. Clinton even ran advertisements that stated, "Maybe [Obama would] prefer to give speeches than have to answer questions."

In regulating access, the principle of risk aversion dominates candidate behavior. Candidates who are ahead in the polls know that they represent appropriate targets and that the press will adopt an even more aggressive and skeptical posture when covering them. For the leading candidates, therefore, less press access is better than more.

PLAYING ONE SOURCE AGAINST ANOTHER

The abundance of reporters covering a major campaign provides candidates with the option of awarding access to sources on the basis of the anticipated quality of their coverage. The Bill Clinton campaign emerged from the 1992 primaries with a number of serious character-related liabilities, any one of which could have erupted into a full-scale press crisis. The Whitewater scandal, the Gennifer Flowers affair, the state of the Clinton marriage, and Clinton's draft deferment were all red meat to the national press corps. No serious news organizations would cover Clinton without making reference to these nagging questions.

Rather than subject the candidate to this line of potentially damaging coverage, the Clinton campaign decided to schedule appearances on programs not typically associated with national political news. Clinton played the saxophone on *The Arsenio Hall Show*. His candidacy was the subject of an hour-long special on MTV (during which he was asked about his use of marijuana and responded, "I didn't inhale"). The Clinton team also arranged for the candidate to provide in-person interviews with local TV anchors at every campaign stop. In short, the campaign was able to shield the candidate from the hostile posture of the national press by cultivating less prominent news outlets.

For a local television correspondent, an exclusive interview with a presidential candidate offers significant professional prestige; for candidate Bill Clinton, the naïveté and inexperience of outer-ring reporters allowed him to dominate the interviews, avoid all reference to his troubled past, and stay on message—that is, hammer away on the state of the national economy. What was the end result? A steady stream of favorable news reports that, according to Clinton insiders, allowed the candidate to transform his image from "Slick Willie" to the candidate with a plan to rejuvenate the economy.

The use of local news to spearhead the campaign message not only offers the candidate greater control over the message but also makes for a better fit between the message and the audience. In presidential campaigns, candidates visit states that are up for grabs, not those that are firmly in the grasp of either party. The issues that concern voters are not the same in all battleground states. Disposal of nuclear waste, for instance, is a major concern for residents of New Mexico (the location of a major federal nuclear waste site); when campaigning in Wisconsin, where dairy subsidies are a major source of farmers' income, the candidate must demonstrate expertise on matters of agriculture policy. Local news, which is typically an intrastate medium, allows candidates the ability to switch messages depending on the local context.

DUELING PRESS RELEASES

A final element of press relations takes its cue from advertising. Candidates continually react to each other's statements and actions, mainly in the form of competing press releases. Each campaign maintains a war room to research and uncover weaknesses in the opponent's record. As soon as Romney selected Paul Ryan as his running mate in 2012, Democrats orchestrated a series of press releases attacking Ryan's record in Congress. Senator Harry Reid's release noted, "By picking Representative Paul Ryan, Governor Romney has doubled down on his commitment to gut Social Security and end Medicare as we know it. Romney's choice demonstrates that catering to the Tea Party and the far-right is more important to him than standing up for the middle class" (Fox News, August 8, 2012). The Romney team responded with a quote from former primary opponent Rick Perry who extolled the choice of Ryan as "underscoring the Republican Party's commitment to job creation and fiscal responsibility" (Fox News, August 8, 2012). These dueling press releases were designed to offer the media a coherent story line for the day's coverage. In fact, a significant amount of daily news coverage can be attributed to the candidates' strategists. Both teams maintain a complete roster of so-called analysts to represent them on the talk radio and cable television circuit.

The fact that both campaigns sift through each other's actions and words with an eye on particularly newsworthy items creates a form of objectivity in news reports; when one side successfully plants a story, the other side is typically asked to react. When John McCain commented in an interview that he couldn't remember how many houses he owned, the Obama campaign seized the opportunity to paint him as an out-of-touch fat cat and even aired an ad titled "Seven" (referring to the number of McCain's homes). The day after the Obama ad aired McCain spokesman Brian Rogers responded,

> Does a guy who made more than $4 million last year, who just got back from vacation on a private beach in Hawaii and bought his own million-dollar mansion with the help of a convicted felon really want to get into a debate about houses? Does a guy who worries about the price of arugula and thinks regular people "cling" to guns and religion in the face of economic hardship really want to have a debate about who's in touch with regular Americans? (Martin & Allen, 2008)

As this example illustrates, a first principle of press management is the immediate rebuttal of unflattering stories in the news. Seeking to counter the series of reports about Kerry's combat experiences in Vietnam, the Bush campaign contacted veterans who had witnessed Kerry participate in protests against the Vietnam War. The campaign then made available the dates of the protests and the contact information of eyewitnesses. A more surgical strike was carried out by the Dukakis campaign in the 1988 primaries when they provided a videotape of a plagiarized speech given by Senator Biden, with the intention of aborting his campaign. The existence of the videotape was uncovered not by the press, but by the "opposition research crew" within the Dukakis campaign.

Campaign press releases are designed not only to show the candidate in the most favorable light, but also to help simplify the reporter's task of sorting out the various events, announcements, messages, and retorts that make up the daily news cycle. Campaigns are careful to synchronize their daily activities around a common principle or theme, in the hope that reporters will find it more convenient to organize their coverage around the message of the day. Naturally, the press staffers are well aware of the special needs of the broadcast media and maintain a steady supply of colorful comments from their candidate suitable for inclusion as sound bites in the national newscasts.

In sum, candidates are no longer in a position to manufacture news. Since 1988, the press has become more combative and less willing to recycle the candidates' rhetoric. In response, candidates have taken a series of steps all meant to focus the attention of reporters on subjects that they consider advantageous: from the candidate's plan to revive the economy to misstatements by the opponent, they offer up their version of the message of the day in the hope of providing reporters with a story line they can't resist. When the national press corps proves insufficiently malleable, candidates turn to less prestigious news outlets where they are ensured gentler treatment.

ADVERTISING STRATEGY

Unlike press management, where success requires campaigns to cater to the needs and values of journalists, advertising provides candidates with a much more direct route to the minds of voters. There is a significant trade-off, however: advertising is unmediated, but it is also a much less credible messenger than news reports are.

Effective advertising is not simply a question of designing a persuasive and memorable campaign jingle. The overall game plan is to strengthen the sponsoring candidate's market share. That goal may be accomplished by adjustment in the advertising message to the stage of the campaign and to the specific attributes of the candidates in the race. In addition to synchronizing the advertising message to the context, campaigns must decide on the precise mix of affirmative messages in favor of the candidate (positive advertising) and negative messages designed to increase voter aversion to the opposing candidate. The extensive use of negative appeals is the hallmark of political advertising. Commercial advertising stays positive; automobile companies and department stores rarely criticize their competitors. Political advertising is different: candidates are much more likely to attack their opponents than praise themselves. As Figure 6.1 shows, the

FIGURE 6.1

The Rise of Negative Advertising in Presidential Campaigns

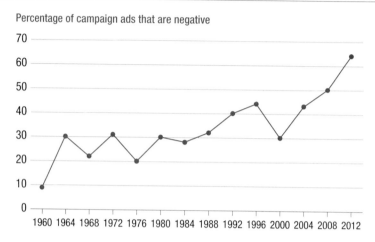

Source: 1960–1996 data from J. Geer. (2010). *Fanning the flames: The news media's role in the rise of negativity in presidential campaigns* (Discussion Paper). Cambridge, MA: Joan Shorenstein Center on the Press, Politics, and Public Policy, Harvard University; 2000–2012 data from Wesleyan Advertising Project (2012). *2012 shatters 2004 and 2008 records for total ads aired*. At http://mediaproject.wesleyan.edu/releases/2012-shatters-2004-and-2008-records-for-total-ads-aired/.

negativity of campaign advertising has increased steadily over time; by 2008, the tone of the presidential ad campaign was predominantly negative.

TARGETING THE AUDIENCE

Television advertising takes different roles over the course of the campaign. Before we spell out the temporal contours of advertising strategy, it is important to understand that advertising is a highly targeted form of communication, no matter what the stage of the campaign. Unlike brand-name product appeals, which air on a national basis, political advertising is much narrower in scope. As the use of local news illustrates, candidates are interested primarily in reaching voters whose preferences may be pivotal to the outcome of the race. Senator Obama had little interest in any of the California media markets in 2008 because he fully expected to win the state by a comfortable margin. Conversely, even the most optimistic Democratic strategist will avoid wasting advertising dollars in Texas, where the probability of a Democratic victory is near zero. By this logic, nearly forty states are off the advertising table. As shown in Figure 6.2, during the 2008 and 2012 presidential races, residents of strongly red (Republican) or blue (Democratic) states saw no presidential ads at all. The remaining battleground states, however, were blanketed with advertising.

The strategy is no different in statewide races. Counties or areas that are heavily Democratic or Republican are bypassed; instead, the candidates invest in markets where a small movement in the numbers can make the difference

FIGURE 6.2

Campaign Advertising from June–November in 2008 and 2012

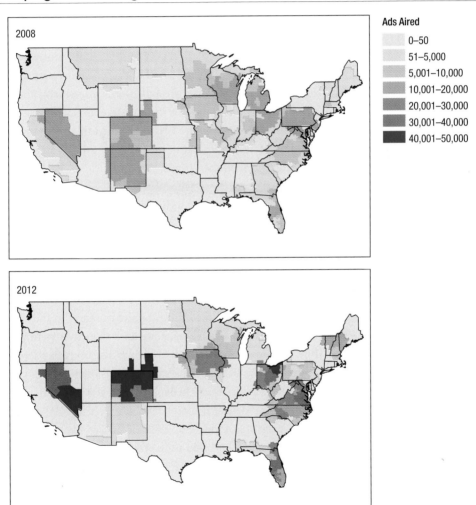

Source: Data from Wesleyan Advertising Project, 2012. *2012 shatters 2004 and 2008 records for total ads aired.* At http://mediaproject.wesleyan.edu/releases/2012-shatters-2004-and-2008-records-for-total-ads-aired/.

between winning and losing. In California, for example, voter preferences in the Bay Area are too one-sided to warrant an ad campaign, so candidates for statewide office concentrate on the Central Valley and the densely populated and more competitive Southern California markets.

In addition to singling out particular locations, campaigns engage in a different form of targeting designed to maximize the impact of advertising. For advertising to work, the audience must include adults who intend to vote. Clearly, advertising during children's programs would be meaningless, and advertising on MTV would be just as irrational, given the low rate of turnout among youth. Ideally, the ad would air during a program that drew likely voters. Local news, a form of programming that has enjoyed steady increases in viewership, provides just such an audience; people sufficiently motivated to watch the news are also likely to vote. The first half of the local newscast is thus a prime-time slot for campaign advertising; the audience is tuning in to the top stories of the day, and their attention has yet to wander. Campaigns also rely heavily on *news adjacencies*—time slots just before or just after a local newscast. In some battleground states, the most desirable advertising slots (during local newscasts in particular) are booked ninety days in advance. Residents of Michigan or Wisconsin—at least those who watch television regularly—are sometimes exposed to the same ad so frequently that they claim they can recite the text in their sleep!

One other overarching factor affects candidates' use of advertising: the state of the campaign budget. Advertising is the single largest expenditure in most major campaigns. A single airing of a thirty-second commercial during a 6:00 PM newscast in the two biggest television markets (New York City and Los Angeles) costs approximately $7,000. In contrast, candidates can run the ad ten different times for that amount in Las Vegas, and more than twenty times in South Dakota or Montana. Thus, allocating resources into ad campaigns depends not only on geography (targeting battleground states) but also on cost considerations. Residents of smaller media markets are likely to receive greater amounts of advertising simply because candidates get more for their advertising dollar.

Given the cost, campaigns attempt to reach as many likely voters as possible with each of their ads. The basic unit of exposure to advertising is the *gross rating point*, or GRP.[2] GRPs are scored to reflect the percentage of the media market that is exposed to the ad. Buying a hundred GRPs for an ad, for instance, would mean one exposure for each viewer; a thousand GRPs would mean that viewers would see the ad ten times. In recent years, with the increased proliferation of cable and satellite channels, consultants have been forced to ratchet up their ad buys to fight channel and advertising clutter. In the 1990s, for instance, running a single ad five times was considered the norm.

Today, an ad is likely to air ten times. Internet advertising is still in its youth, but, given the significant increase in the size of the online audience, candidates are allocating substantial amounts of their budget to Internet ads. In 2012 the Romney campaign spent slightly more than a third of its conventional advertising budget on online ads. For the Obama campaign, the figure was slightly smaller, amounting to 28 percent.

Ad buying is more art form than science. Depending on the ad, the stage of the campaign, and the scale of the budget, buyers might opt for the same level of GRPs throughout the campaign or, more likely, vary their buys to synchronize exposure to the ad campaign with the level of news coverage. The expectation is that candidates get more bang for their advertising buck when the campaign is in the news. This logic also influences the content of advertising. When a particular issue or event grabs the headlines, the candidates tend to incorporate that issue into their ads. In the 2001 and 2002 election cycles, for example, it was no surprise—given the exposure following 9/11—that the most popular spokesperson for Republican candidates across the country was the New York City mayor, Rudy Giuliani.

PLANTING THE SEED: EARLY ADVERTISING

Early in the campaign, advertising introduces the candidate to the electorate. Biographical spots focus on the candidate's personal background and record of public service. Military service is especially noteworthy as an indicator of fitness for office. For candidates who cannot claim to have risked their lives for the nation, alternative qualifications include humble beginnings, the ability to overcome adversity, strong family ties, adherence to a core set of political principles, or a demonstrated commitment to public service. By focusing on personal virtues, campaigns attempt to instill confidence in the candidate's suitability for public office. Barack Obama's first ad of the general election, titled "Country I Love," spoke to his relatively poor upbringing and the "values straight from the Kansas heartland" that were taught to him by his mother and grandparents.

Video Archive 6.5 Introducing the Candidate

In nonpresidential races, in which candidates might be unknown to voters, the first goal of the ad campaign is more mundane—namely, to deliver a boost in the candidate's name recognition. In some cases, biographical spots focus specifically on the candidate's name. Ed Zschau and Wyche Fowler, both little-known candidates for the US Senate, opened their campaigns with ads that simply explained the correct pronunciation of their names. In politics, familiarity is a necessary condition of electability; voters are disinclined to vote for a name they do not recognize.

IMAGE VERSUS ISSUE SPOTS

Once they have provided voters with a snapshot of their lives, candidates move on to their credentials. *Image ads* maintain thematic continuity with the biographical message by presenting the candidate as a likable human being with a strong sense of public service. *Issue ads* are more substantive and either focus on the candidate's past experience and record in public life, or outline the candidate's positions on major policy issues.

The relative importance of image and issue advertising depends on the electoral context. By 1984, the international tensions associated with the Cold War had eased and voters felt secure on the economic front. This atmosphere of political tranquility was captured by the Reagan campaign in what is generally considered the classic image ad. Labeled "Morning in America," the ad listed President Reagan's accomplishments against a background of idyllic rural landscapes and smiling children. Four years later, Vice President George H. W. Bush aired a textbook example of an issue ad, calling into question Governor Dukakis's credentials on the issue of national defense. When voters are concerned about the state of the country, both incumbents and challengers turn to issue ads. As President George H. W. Bush found out in 1992, voters who were worried about losing their jobs were relatively forgiving of a challenger with questionable personal attributes; they made their choices based more on questions of performance. The "Slick Willie" nickname applied to Bill Clinton was not as relevant as "It's the economy, stupid."

Video Archive 6.6
Image and Issue Appeals

From the beginning of campaign advertising, image ads have inevitably portrayed the candidate as a man of the people. American voters do not take kindly to millionaire candidates from privileged backgrounds, especially when they make disparaging remarks about ordinary people (as Mitt Romney learned in 2012). The focus on the common touch is ironic; most presidential candidates are in fact members of a distinctly elite group with appropriate prep school and Ivy League credentials. One of President George H. W. Bush's greatest liabilities during the 1992 campaign was that he personified the gulf between well-to-do and middle-class America. In a well-circulated story, the president was said to have expressed his delight with the advanced technology of price scanners at a local supermarket, thus revealing his utter unfamiliarity with grocery-store shopping.[3] This story line reappeared in the 2008 presidential elections as both candidates sought to paint the other as out of touch with the average American. In addition to the question of McCain's many homes, Obama's comment about bitter working-class voters gave his opponents (both Hillary Clinton and McCain) ample opportunity to depict Obama as an elitist. More recently, Hillary Clinton attempted to forestall questions about her

Video Archive 6.7
"Bitter Voters"

own wealth (and credibility on the issue of income inequality) by claiming that the Clintons "pay ordinary income tax, unlike a lot of people who are truly well off . . . and we've done it through dint of hard work" (*Washington Post*, June 22, 2014). This statement generated abundant news coverage and critical commentary since the Clintons have earned substantial fees from speaking engagements and book royalties.

Issue ads fall into two broad classes: performance messages touting the sponsoring candidate's experience and proven accomplishments as a public servant, and policy messages summarizing the candidate's preferences on public policy. Campaigns featuring an incumbent invariably gravitate to performance themes, with the challenger habitually framing the choice as a referendum on the performance of the incumbent. Challengers might broadcast ads suggesting that the incumbent has weakened the economy or that the administration has done nothing to make the world more secure from terrorism. In 2012, lingering concerns over the speed of the economic recovery prompted the Romney campaign to fixate on economic themes. More than 80 percent of their ads discussed unemployment. Conversely, incumbents are quick to take credit for economic growth, balanced budgets, reductions in crime, or other such indicators of effective governance.

ISSUE OWNERSHIP

Policy advertising follows a simple formula: highlight the candidate's positions but focus only on issues for which your candidate is favored. This directive has two specific implications: First, do not publicize your support for unpopular or controversial positions (that task will be taken up by your opponent). Second, single out issues on which you and, more important, your party are seen as more likely to provide relief. In sum, parties and candidates often *own* certain issues, and these owned issues are featured in campaign advertising.

Issue ownership is a by-product of American political culture. Long before they reach voting age, most Americans are socialized to associate each party with a set of interests and, by inference, with a set of issues or problems on which they will deliver. In general, Republican-owned issues include national security, taxes, government spending, and crime. That is, the public typically assumes that Republicans are better able to deal with these issues than Democrats are. Conversely, voters favor Democrats on most quality-of-life issues, including job and income security, healthcare, and issues affecting women (see Figure 6.3). The public rates the two parties evenly on certain other issues, such as gun control and foreign policy.

IN FOCUS

Issue Ownership

Issue ownership refers to the fact that the public considers each party to be more capable on different issues—for example, Republicans are thought to perform better in the area of military and defense policy, and Democrats are viewed more favorably on issues such as education and Social Security. Candidates tend to campaign on issues that their party owns because their message is more credible when consistent with the stereotype of the party.

How do voters rate the parties on the salient issues today? Recent polling data (see Figure 6.3) indicates that Democrats own the environment, issues important to women, and the government's role in helping the middle class, whereas Republicans are favored on government spending, national security and the war on terror, as well as taxes.

FIGURE 6.3

Perceptions of the Parties on Major Issues

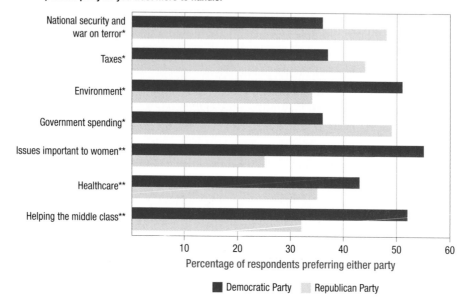

Which political party do you trust more to handle:

*Rasmussen poll—November 2013.
**Washington Post poll—April 2014.
Source: Data from Rasmussen and Washington Post polls.

166   Chapter 6 | Campaigning through the Media

Issue ownership was central to the Bush administration's reelection campaign of 2004. The strategy was to make the war on terrorism the centerpiece of the campaign and capitalize on the Republican Party's reputation on the issue. The first round of Republican ads, released on March 5, 2004, made frequent references to 9/11 and terrorist threats. Later in the campaign, the Bush team produced "Wolves," an ad that attacked Senator Kerry as being weak on defense. It is interesting that this ad borrowed heavily from "Bear in the Woods," President Reagan's 1984 ad promoting a strong military posture vis-à-vis the Soviet Union. For its part, the Kerry campaign followed the standard Democratic script and promoted Kerry's positions on job loss and healthcare while attacking Bush as a stooge of the wealthy.

Video Archive 6.9
Advertising on Owned Issues

The principle of issue ownership extends to attributes of the candidate other than party affiliation. Gender is an especially visible attribute, and American culture provides ample cues about the traits of males and females. Given these widely held gender stereotypes, male and female candidates have reason to project their masculinity and femininity, respectively. Masculine issues, such as defense, terrorism, and crime, resonate well for a male candidate; child care and matters of educational policy confirm voters' beliefs about the credentials of a female candidate. Hillary Clinton may well have suffered during the 2008 Democratic primaries because of a lack of perceived credibility on the issue of the war in Iraq. Moreover, she positioned herself as the candidate more capable of keeping America safe, as evidenced by the "3 AM" advertisement in which she claimed an edge over Obama on matters of national defense. Clinton's recent experience as Secretary of State, however, gives her considerable credibility on foreign relations and diplomacy, issues generally seen as favoring men.

Video Archive 6.10
Running as a Woman

Between owned issues are policy areas in which neither party enjoys a decisive advantage. These can be seen as leased issues on which parties can claim short-term occupancy, depending on the nature of the times or the track record of particular candidates. The two ongoing wars in Iraq and Afghanistan that were largely seen as failures under the Bush administration provided Obama and the Democrats the opportunity to challenge McCain and the Republicans on issues of national security and foreign policy. A poll taken shortly before the 2008 presidential election asked respondents which candidate would do a better job dealing with the situation in Iraq. Even though McCain had significant military experience and had served on the Armed Services Committee in the Senate, more people thought Obama would handle Iraq better.

Beliefs about party performance also fluctuate in the short term, driven by events and evidence of incumbents' performance. The massive intelligence failure on which the invasion of Iraq rested provided Kerry with the opportunity to challenge Bush on the issue of national security. Similarly, the subprime mortgage crisis of 2007, which precipitated a collapse of the housing market and massive losses at major banks, allowed Democrats to exploit lax regulation of financial institutions as a campaign issue in 2008. On the other side, the less than smooth rollout of the Affordable Care Act together with the Obama administration's misrepresentations of the impact of the law on consumer choice allowed Republicans to narrow the gap on the issue of healthcare in several 2013 and 2014 polls.

Although leased issues attract ads from both candidates, the principle of playing to one's strengths creates few opportunities for candidates to engage in an exchange on issues. Advertising campaigns generally do not resemble a dialogue between the competing candidates. Instead, they typically offer two essentially unrelated streams of messages. Candidates prefer to talk past each other in the hope of promoting their comparative advantages.

There is one notable exception to this pattern. The frequent use of negative advertising means that the attack–counterattack spiral is a typical outcome of ad campaigns. Before we discuss negative advertising, however, let's look at another strategy of agenda control.

WEDGE APPEALS: US VERSUS THEM

Consider the following scenario. As the traditional kickoff of the 2004 fall campaign approached, the economy remained stagnant, the federal budget deficit had ballooned, and American troops were dying every day in Iraq. Obviously this state of affairs represented a serious liability for President Bush. Boxed in by the war on one side and the domestic economy on the other, the only recourse seemed to be to introduce so-called wedge issues into campaign discourse. *Wedge issues* are designed to pit groups against each other, to appeal to voters' sense of group identity. (As we'll discuss, gay marriage became the wedge issue of the day in the 2004 election.) When candidates turn to wedge appeals, it is generally a tacit acknowledgment that they are losing the debate on other issues.

As noted in Chapter 1, President Obama handed the Republicans a wedge issue in 2010 when he waded into the controversy surrounding the proposed construction of a mosque in Lower Manhattan, two blocks from Ground Zero. At a White House dinner, the president stated that in keeping with the Constitution, Muslims had a right to build a place of worship. Obama's comments ignited a series of partisan retorts from Republicans, who scented an opportunity to score points with the voting public, many of whom have strong anti-Muslim sentiments. Former Speaker Newt Gingrich compared the construction of the mosque to placing Nazi swastikas near the Holocaust memorial, while to Senator John Cornyn, Obama's comments suggested that "the White House, the administration, the president himself seems to be disconnected from the mainstream of America" (CBS News, August 16, 2010).

Video Archive 6.11 Ground Zero Mosque Controversy

The mosque controversy addressed questions of religious tolerance. Most wedge issues, however, represent issues of race and ethnicity. From the Civil War through the passage of landmark civil rights legislation in the 1960s to current debates over affirmative action and reparations, Americans have been consistently divided by race. One set of wedge appeals seeks to capitalize on this racial division. Typically, the strategy is used by Republican candidates, who hope to attract white Democrats and independents on the basis of their opposition to race-based policies such as affirmative action in employment and diversity credits in college admissions.[4]

In recent years, the emergence of immigration-related issues has injected a parallel Latino–Anglo divide into campaigns. In this case, the strategy is for candidates to position themselves as opponents of immigration or immigrants' rights. When California governor Pete Wilson ran an ad in 1994 that began with the line "They keep coming," most Californians immediately understood what he meant. (We will say more about the immigration issue later.) In short, wedge appeals based on race or ethnicity are aimed at capturing white votes by depicting the candidate as taking a stand against the threatening demands of blacks or Hispanics. The appeal is either explicit—as in the case of immigration or affirmative action—or implicit, as in the case of law and order.

Cultural identity (or "family values"), provides an alternative basis for dividing voters. Initially introduced by President Nixon in 1968 as an appeal to conservative southern Democrats, based on Republican opposition to school busing, the family values slogan has since broadened into a code word for general conservatism and opposition to nonmainstream lifestyles. A call for family values is generally interpreted as opposition to abortion, feminism, gay rights, and sex education in the public schools.

For President George W. Bush, the family values theme represented a clear advantage in 2004. In February of that year, the decision by the mayor of San Francisco to issue same-sex marriage licenses attracted considerable media attention across the country. It was not coincidental that the Republican-controlled Senate took up the proposed constitutional amendment banning same-sex marriage (framed by Republicans as the amendment to "save traditional marriage") two weeks before the Democratic convention. They hoped to elevate family values as a criterion for differentiating between Kerry and Bush. Conservative groups placed measures banning same-sex marriage on the November ballot in eleven states (including the key battleground states of Ohio and Oregon).[5] Moral issues became a battle cry for conservative Republicans, many of them evangelical Christians. In fact, the response "moral issues" was checked as the "most important issue" in the 2004 exit poll by over 20 percent of voters. This group voted for President Bush by a 4-to-1 margin.

Explicit appeals to wedge issues were made in both the 1988 and 1996 presidential campaigns, in which crime and illegal immigration, respectively, were major issues. Given the one-sided nature of the 1996 election, it is unlikely that Senator Robert Dole's attempts to run on the immigration issue had any role in the outcome. In August 1988, however, the airing of the notorious "Willie Horton" ad attacking Michael Dukakis for his support of prison furlough programs was thought to have played a major role in the Bush campaign's ability to overcome what was then a double-digit deficit in the polls. It is surprising, given the historic nomination of the first African American candidate for president, that wedge issues were of little consequence during the 2008 campaign. Although there were indirect references to race during the Democratic primaries (for example, Hillary Clinton's claim that she championed the interests of "white working-class voters" and her harsh criticism of Obama's pastor, the Reverend Jeremiah Wright), after the conventions, issues of race and ethnicity disappeared from the campaign radar entirely because of the overwhelming magnitude of the economic crisis.

Wedge appeals are not limited to presidential contests. In 1990, conservative Republican senator Jesse Helms was locked in a close race with African American Democrat Harvey Gantt (the mayor of Charlotte, North Carolina). During the closing days of the race, Helms released an ad opposing the use of affirmative action in employment decisions. This "White Hands" ad is credited with producing a significant surge in white support for Helms. Eight years later the tables were turned. Opponents of Proposition 209, a measure to end affirmative action in California, aired an ad featuring David Duke, a well-known member of the Ku Klux Klan, in the hope that the negative imagery of hooded Klansmen and cross burnings would weaken moderate whites' support for the measure. The strategy failed, however, and Proposition 209 passed easily.

In recent campaign cycles, immigration has emerged as a hot wedge issue in many states. Some candidates contesting House seats in 2008 supported construction of a wall along the US–Mexico border. In 2009, Representative Lamar Smith (Republican–Texas) introduced the Birthright Citizenship Act, which would deny citizenship to children of illegal immigrants. In 2010, the Arizona legislature enacted a law granting law enforcement officers broad discretion to detain individuals on the grounds they were undocumented

Video Archive 6.12
Dividing by Race and Ethnicity

immigrants. The next year Alabama passed an even tougher bill; police officers were required to arrest individuals without valid documentation. In the first implementation of the law, a German national was pulled over for driving a rental car with expired registration tags. The individual turned out to be an important executive with Mercedes Benz, a major employer in Alabama. After a similar episode involving a Honda executive—and an outcry from the business community—the state legislature backtracked; police were no longer required to arrest people without appropriate identification papers.

Given that California has a Hispanic population amounting to nearly 40 percent of its population, and considering the state's proximity to Mexico, it is not surprising that California has been in the thick of the battle to limit immigration. To illustrate how immigration has affected California political campaigns we will compare the 1994 race for governor of California between incumbent Republican Pete Wilson and Democratic challenger Kathleen Brown with the 2010 campaign between Republican Meg Whitman and Democrat Jerry Brown.

The 1994 Campaign: "They Keep Coming"

As governor of California, Pete Wilson faced a challenging reelection campaign in 1994. The state was in the throes of a severe recession, with an accompanying exodus of companies and jobs. Wilson, a Republican, faced a popular and well-known Democrat, State Treasurer Kathleen Brown. Naturally, Brown's ads emphasized the recession, Wilson's inability to bring relief to the state, and her own economic expertise. With this theme, she established a substantial lead over Wilson.

Video Archive 6.13 1994 Immigration Ads

Recognizing that a debate over the state of the economy was a hopeless cause, Wilson campaigned as a crime fighter and an opponent of illegal immigration. He linked his candidacy to two well-known statewide propositions: 184 and 187. Proposition 184, known as the "three-strikes measure" for its tough stance on law breakers, won approval by an impressive 72-to-28 percent margin. Proposition 187, which proposed limiting or eliminating illegal immigrants' eligibility for a variety of government services, also passed with majority support.

Wilson's efforts to shift the agenda were aided by the Brown campaign, which engaged Wilson on the issue of crime despite Brown's opposition to the death penalty. As a result, the California electorate was exposed to a genuine dialogue on the issue of crime and punishment. Voters' impressions of the candidates became increasingly linked to their positions on crime. On this issue, most voters (including many Democrats) favored Wilson over Brown. Brown's support eroded and Wilson was reelected by a comfortable margin.

The 2010 Campaign: Flip-Flopping on Immigration

In the race to succeed Arnold Schwarzenegger as governor, Meg Whitman faced Steve Poizner in the Republican primary. (The Democratic candidate, Jerry Brown, who had previously served as governor and was attorney general at the time, had no primary challenger.) Whitman, a multimillionaire, outspent Poizner by more than 10 to 1 and opened up a large lead in the polls. The Poizner campaign decided to attack Whitman on the grounds that she was soft on undocumented immigrants and favored a "path to citizenship." As Poizner began to cut into Whitman's lead, she backed off her earlier statements on legalization, ran ads in which she claimed to be "tough as nails" in cracking down on illegals, and enlisted former governor Pete Wilson, the iconic anti-immigration candidate, as one of her major supporters.

Whitman eventually won the primary quite easily, but then did an abrupt about-face on immigration for the general election. She ran ads on Spanish-language television asserting that she opposed Proposition 187 and the Arizona immigration law. She described her views on immigration as no different from the views of her Democratic opponent. (In the middle of the campaign, Whitman had to deal with the revelation that she had unknowingly employed an illegal immigrant as her housekeeper.) Of course, conservative groups and commentators were enraged by Whitman's new centrist rhetoric and threatened to withhold their support. Latino voters were unpersuaded by Whitman, voting Democratic by a 3-to-1 margin and contributing to Brown's comfortable victory.

The differing trajectories of the Wilson and Whitman strategies on immigration indicate that while ethnicity is still a potent divider in California politics, the sheer size of the Latino electorate has changed the candidates' political calculus. Republicans' efforts to attract white voters by representing themselves as being opposed to immigration now runs the risk of alienating a sizeable Latino electorate. In 1994, Wilson could do so with impunity since whites outnumbered Latinos by a wide margin. In 2010, however, Whitman had to reverse course on immigration once the primary campaign was over for fear of losing Latino votes. More generally, as Latinos are mobilized and their turnout increases, Republican candidates in California will be forced to take more nuanced positions on the issue.

As American society becomes more diverse, the costs of taking an overtly hostile position on immigration will increasingly affect national campaigns, not just those occurring in California or Texas. The 2012 presidential election provides a case in point. Mitt Romney famously declared his support for "self-deportation" during the Republican primaries. On election day, 10 percent of the electorate was made up of Latinos, less than 1 in 4 of whom supported Romney.

NEGATIVE ADVERTISING

In recent years, research on the subject of negative campaign advertising has become a growth industry. As we have noted, a striking attribute of political advertising campaigns is the heavy reliance (at least in comparison with product advertising campaigns) on so-called negative or attack advertising. Although the number and ratio of positive to negative ads varies across campaigns, there can be no denying that political advertising is a relatively hostile and impolite form of discourse. In contrast to normal discourse, which is characterized by a positivity bias (we normally greet others with a smile and a cheery hello), candidates tend to dwell on the flaws—either personal or substantive—of their opponents. In the case of so-called issue ads—advertisements aired by groups not directly affiliated with a candidate—almost the entire advertising budget is devoted to attack advertising. In the 2012 election, for example, 90 percent of the airtime purchased by Republican-leaning groups went to messages questioning President Obama's fitness for office. It has reached the point at which candidates routinely air ads attacking their opponents for running negative campaigns.

Certainly criticism, counterargument, and rebuttal are legitimate and essential ingredients of fair political debate. In the context of political advertising, however, it is possible for a candidate to focus exclusively on defining the opponent while remaining silent about his own suitability for office. Gray Davis was reelected governor of California in 2002 using just this strategy. Davis spent millions attacking his Republican opponent (Bill Simon) as a wealthy and corrupt businessman with no political experience. But even before Simon won the Republican nomination, Davis spent millions on ads attacking Simon's Republican rival, Richard Riordan. As the mayor of Los Angeles, Riordan had accumulated an impressive record in office, was well known, and could appeal to moderate voters. Realizing that Riordan would be a more dangerous direct opponent, Davis broadcast ads attacking Riordan for his frequent policy reversals on abortion (a charge likely to resonate with conservative Republican voters). Subject to attacks from both Davis and Simon, Riordan's poll numbers dropped and Simon won the primary.

In the end, though, did the Davis strategy really work? It can't be disputed that Simon defeated Riordan in the primary and Davis easily defeated Simon in November. However, having campaigned against both Riordan and Simon without giving voters a single affirmative reason to reelect him, Davis was vulnerable to a rising tide of political discontent that was orchestrated by Republican activists into a full-scale recall campaign. Lacking public support, Davis was ousted from office less than a year after his reelection.

NEGATIVE THEMES

Negative campaigns run the gamut from direct attacks on the personal attributes of a candidate to ads linking the candidate with unsavory groups or causes. Typically, consultants differentiate between character assassination in which the opponent is depicted as an immoral human being and performance critiques that focus on the candidate's record. Personal attacks are standard fare in lower-level races. As one moves up the political ladder, attack ads become more performance oriented. In 2000, for instance, the Gore campaign lampooned Governor Bush's credentials on education by pointing out that Texas schools ranked forty-ninth on basic indicators of school achievement.

The most common genre of political attack is the flip-flop ad. For example, given Mitt Romney's moderate record as Governor of Massachusetts (where he supported abortion rights), he has consistently attracted the flip-flopper label. A 2008 primary ad by John McCain—"A Tale of Two Mitts"—became the template for a series of attack ads targeting Romney aired by his more conservative Republican primary rivals. As another example, in the 2010 California gubernatorial race, Jerry Brown was quick to attack Meg Whitman for her dramatic change of heart on immigration. In 2004, the Bush campaign repeatedly juxtaposed Kerry's criticisms of the Iraq War with his Senate vote authorizing the war (using the punch line "John Kerry: whichever way the wind blows"). This line of attack is thought to be especially effective because it resonates with voters' stereotypes of politicians as insincere and willing to say anything to get elected.

An especially effective attack on a candidate's record is the guilt by association spot. Criticizing a candidate for having voted to weaken the Patriot Act is unlikely to have much impact because most voters are not very familiar with that act. Linking the candidate with Osama bin Laden, however, would make it crystal clear that the candidate is soft on terrorism. In 1996, the Clinton campaign repeatedly portrayed Senator Dole as out of touch with majority opinion by depicting him side-by-side with House Speaker Newt Gingrich. A similar advertising ploy by Democrats in 2008 showed Republican candidates side-by-side with outgoing President George Bush, who was extremely unpopular at the time. Obama aired an ad showing McCain hugging Bush. McCain retaliated by linking Obama with one-time domestic terrorist William Ayers.

Video Archive 6.14
Guilt by Association

REACTIVITY: ATTACKS PROVOKE COUNTERATTACKS

The prominence of negative appeals in campaign advertising can be attributed to several factors. Politics is seen as a dirty business, and the public is cynical about the motives and behaviors of candidates for office. In this context, an attack is more credible than a message promoting a candidate's virtues. Equally important, bad news and conflict are far more newsworthy than good news and civility. The ripple effect of negative advertising can be considerable. That is, attacks are especially effective in attracting press coverage; in fact, campaigns often schedule a press conference to announce their latest attack ad.

Video Archive 6.15 Newsworthy Attacks

Sometimes the ad is merely a ruse designed to titillate the press, and no airtime is purchased. The Republican National Committee (RNC) announced the hard-hitting anti-Clinton "Soldiers and Sailors" ad to the press in 1996, and the attack was summarized and critiqued in all the leading outlets, but the ad was never actually aired. From the perspective of the Dole campaign, putting Clinton's penchant for sex scandals on the front pages was well worth the criticism of releasing "misleading" information. During the 2004 campaign, a group funded by Republican donors (Swift Vets and POWs for Truth, a group of veterans who served in Vietnam on US Navy swift boats) aired an ad accusing Senator John Kerry of lying about his military record in Vietnam. Although the amount of money invested in both of these ads was trivial, the sponsors attracted a torrent of news reports across the country simply because their message was so controversial. The Swift Boat ad not only generated an avalanche of newspaper reports within the United States but also attracted considerable attention in the international press. For the media, personal attacks are big stories. According to one study, the press devoted more attention to the Swift Boat ad than to the Iraq War in the 2004 campaigns. As Figure 6.4 shows, the press has increasingly devoted more attention to political ads. Oftentimes, more people hear about the controversial ads from the news than see the actual ads. The added newsworthiness of negative ads gives campaigns a clear incentive to produce ads that will spark controversy.

The most compelling explanation of negative campaigning is that one attack invites a counterattack, thus setting in motion a spiral of negativity. Among campaign professionals, a fundamental principle is that the attacked candidate must punch back, and the sooner the better. In this sense, at least, negative campaigns amount to a debate.

There is limited scientific evidence available that supports the efficacy of counterattacks, but the anecdotal evidence is consistent with the view that these ads work. In the 1988 presidential election, Michael Dukakis enjoyed a substantial lead over Vice President Bush after the Democratic nomination. The Bush campaign then released a series of negative ads attacking Dukakis on crime (including a version of the "Willie Horton" ad) and the polluted state of Boston's harbor. Inexplicably, the Dukakis campaign ignored these attacks,

FIGURE 6.4

News Media Attention to Advertising, 1960–2008

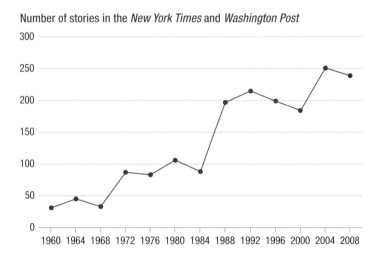

Number of stories in the *New York Times* and *Washington Post*

Source: Data from J. Geer. (2010). *Fanning the flames: The news media's role in the rise of negativity in presidential campaigns* (Discussion Paper). Cambridge, MA: Joan Shorenstein Center on the Press, Politics, and Public Policy, Harvard University.

even though the ads were highly controversial and the subject of interminable news coverage across the country. Eventually Bush was able to catch Dukakis in the polls, and he went on to win the election.

Since 1988, campaign strategists have become convinced of the necessity to mount counterattacks. Mindful of the Dukakis experience, Clinton's advisers saw to it that every attack in 1992 was rebutted, in some cases even before the Republican ad hit the airwaves. Rapid response became the hallmark of advertising strategy, thus accelerating the pace at which ad campaigns arrived at the negative–negative endgame. One of the major themes in postmortems of the 2004 campaign concerned the Kerry campaign's unwillingness to rebut the Swift Boat allegations. According to Kerry pollster Mark Mellman, the campaign was hesitant to counter the attacks, for fear of adding credibility to the charges.[6]

In one of the few controlled studies to examine the value of counterattacks, Ansolabehere and Iyengar (1995) compared the vote shares of candidates who responded to an opponent's attack either by running a positive ad or by attacking the attacker. Respondents in these studies watched the initial attack and the attacked candidate's response. Applying this method to two statewide campaigns, the authors showed that the attacked candidate was significantly better off to counterattack. Moreover, they also demonstrated that support for the attacked candidate who responded with a positive ad dropped substantially among voters who shared the attacked candidate's party. That is, Democrats were less enthusiastic about voting Democratic when the Republican attacked and the Democrat countered with a positive message. Overall, Ansolabehere and Iyengar's results show clearly that rational candidates should counterattack.

The extensive use of negative campaigning raises serious questions about accountability in campaign discourse. Journalists can be sued for knowingly printing inaccurate information about public figures with intent to harm. The victims of negative advertising campaigns, on the other hand, have recourse only to the dictum of more speech—in this context, counterattacks. The lack of accountability for the use of misleading or inaccurate attacks is compounded by the frequent use of surrogates rather than the candidate as the messenger. In general, the more personal or controversial the attack, the less likely it is that the sponsoring candidate will appear in person. In the 2004 campaign, the most hard-hitting attacks on President Bush were delivered not by John Kerry, but by liberal interest groups such as MoveOn.org. In the 2010 race for governor of California, when the news broke that Republican Meg Whitman had employed an undocumented immigrant as her housekeeper for nine years, union-backed groups immediately aired an ad contrasting Whitman's rhetoric and behavior: "Whitman attacks undocumented workers to win votes, but an undocumented woman worked in her home for nine years" (CNN PoliticalTicker, September 30, 2010).

Video Archive 6.16 Third Party Attacks

As a means of making candidates more responsible for their advertisements, reform-minded groups have been urging the passage of legislation that makes the connection between specific ads and the sponsoring candidate more transparent. Their efforts succeeded in 2003 when Congress adopted a provision requiring presidential candidates to appear on-screen in their ads while stating "I'm Candidate X, and I approved this message." Because candidates can no longer rely on surrogates among their supporters willing to do their dirty work for them, we may anticipate that the negativity quotient in campaign advertising will fall. At the very least, the in-person rule is likely to deter campaigns from engaging in character-related attacks. Of course, these provisions do little to dissuade the political party committees or other groups involved in campaigns to refrain from attacking. As noted earlier, data from the 2008 and 2012 campaigns shows that group-sponsored ads are invariably negative.

IN FOCUS

Campaign Advertising Strategies

- Target voters who may be pivotal to the outcome of the race—that is, voters in states or regions considered competitive.
- Advertise during programs watched by those likely to vote (such as during local news shows).
- Ride the wave by connecting advertising to issues or events in the headlines.
- Use biographical spots early in the campaign to introduce the candidate; then move on to image and issue ads.
- Take advantage of issue ownership.
- Use wedge appeals when necessary.
- Go negative to generate media coverage and be credible to voters, and use surrogates to deliver the most controversial claims.
- When attacked, mount a counterattack.

DIRECT MAIL AS AN ALTERNATIVE TO TELEVISED ADVERTISING

For nonpresidential candidates, especially those running in geographically compact districts, televised advertising is an inefficient medium. The Los Angeles media market includes all or part of seventeen congressional districts. New York City provides even less overlap between the media market and political district boundaries. The audience for New York City television includes voters in three different states (New York, New Jersey, and Connecticut). A congressional candidate who advertises on Los Angeles TV, or a candidate for governor of New York who buys time on New York City stations is paying top dollar (New York and Los Angeles are the two most expensive markets in the country) to reach people who cannot vote for her.

In congested markets, such as Los Angeles and New York, candidates rely on a more precise method of reaching voters: direct mail. Mail is the most extensive form of advertising in congressional and other localized campaigns. Direct mail is big business; total expenditures on mail during the 2008 campaign amounted to over $1 billion, and in California alone, there are some seventy-five registered mail consultants. As in the case of television advertising, mail consultants are affiliated by party; they work exclusively for Republicans or Democrats.

Direct mail is used by all candidates, from the top of the ticket to the bottom. In some cases, mailers may focus on an individual candidate, but more commonly they urge the voter to support an entire slate. So-called slate mailers are typically financed by state party organizations, but they are also published by private campaign consultants, some of whom mail millions of pieces per election.

Slate mail is the most economical form of political advertising. Not only does it maximize the ability of the candidate to target the message to voters (as opposed to nonvoters), slate mail also allows several candidates to share in the cost of advertising. For candidates whose budgets do not run into several millions of dollars (which includes virtually every candidate for county or local office), slate mail is the only advertising medium.

Because slate mailers usually feature candidates for several offices, lesser-known candidates benefit from their association with more-visible candidates and causes. For instance, in the midst of the impeachment proceedings against President Clinton, a 1998 mailer sent to California Democrats featured the slogan "end the Washington witch hunt."

One final advantage of direct mail, at least from the candidate's perspective, is that the message is generally ignored by the news media. Candidates often resort to using misleading, unsubstantiated, and personal attacks against opponents. In one mailer sent to Los Angeles voters, a candidate for the state assembly attacked his opponent using the slogan "Sex, Booze and Strippers . . ." During the 2012 primaries, the Romney campaign sent out a mailer to Florida voters that described Newt Gingrich as a "well of sleaze." In comparison with direct mail, negative television advertising is rated PG.

In the final analysis, despite widespread concern that political ads trivialize democracy and transform campaigns into shouting matches, they remain an essential form of campaign communication. In the era of interpretive journalism, ads represent the only unmediated form of communicating with voters. It is not surprising that candidates use the opportunity to extol their own virtues and denigrate their opponents. If voters seem more responsive to a particular form of advertising, rational candidates converge on that form.

Attempts to regulate the content and form of campaign advertising are exercises in futility. As an ingredient of political speech, advertising is fully protected by the First Amendment. In races with evenly matched candidates, voters encounter countervailing and retaliatory messages—that is, the campaign creates a free flow of information. As for the notion that voters need protection from ad campaigns, it suffices to note that voters are not fools. Recognizing the nature of the medium, they discount ads appropriately. The evidence on the effects of exposure to advertising presented in Chapter 9 demonstrates that the principal effect of advertising is to make fellow partisans more enthusiastic about the sponsoring candidate. Seen in this light (preaching to the choir), efforts to police campaign advertising and monitor the accuracy of the charges and countercharges seem both elitist and excessive. Not only do ad watchers have the potential to recycle the message in the guise of a news report, but they are just as lacking in accountability as the ads themselves. And who watches the ad watchers?

Campaign advertising is expensive. Except for presidential candidates, whose campaigns are paid for by public funding (unless, like Obama and Romney in 2012, they opt out of public financing), all candidates must raise large sums of money if they are to engage in advertising. Since 1972, the total amount of money expended on campaigns has increased exponentially, reaching $6 billion in 2012. The huge sums of money involved and the resulting preoccupation with fund-raising have provoked considerable discussion about the role of money in politics. Should candidates who accept money from contributors return the favor by voting for legislation supported by the donors? Does the high cost of campaigning create the appearance that candidates are bought by powerful interests, thus compromising the political process? These and other questions have propelled campaign finance reform to the forefront of the policy agenda.

CAMPAIGN FINANCE REFORM: A BRIEF OVERVIEW

The present era of campaign finance reform began in 1971 with the passage of the Federal Election Campaign Act (FECA), whose stricter requirements concerning the disclosure of sources of campaign funding played a role in the Watergate scandal. The remaining provisions of the 1971 FECA never took effect, because Watergate prompted their replacement by the 1974 FECA amendments. Those amendments remain the backbone of federal campaign finance regulation.

Aside from disclosure, the 1974 amendments contained three broad categories of regulation: limits on the size of contributions, limits on the amount of spending, and limits on public financing. The limits on how much a campaign could spend were supplemented by limits on how much candidates could spend of their own money on their campaigns and on how much outsiders could spend independently to help the candidate. The contribution and spending limits applied to all federal candidates, but the public financing was available only for presidential elections. Public funds matched private contributions in presidential primaries, and the public funds were supposed to pay all the costs of the national nominating conventions and of the presidential general-election campaigns. The Federal Election Commission (FEC), with members appointed by the president and by party leaders in the House and Senate, was created to administer the new law.

BUCKLEY V. VALEO

The first challenge to campaign finance regulations was considered by the US Supreme Court in 1976 in *Buckley v. Valeo*. The Court ruled that all three forms of spending limits were violations of the First Amendment guarantee of freedom of speech. In an oft-quoted passage, the Court said, "The concept that government may restrict the speech of some elements of our society in order to enhance the relative voice of others is wholly foreign to the First Amendment" (*Buckley v. Valeo*, 1976, pp. 48–49). Although the Court thus rejected promotion of equality as a justification for speech restrictions, it gave more credence to the goal of preventing corruption (such as the buying of influence) and the appearance of corruption. That goal justified the limits on the size of contributions by individuals, political action committees (PACs), and other entities.

The Court rejected challenges to most other parts of the law, including the disclosure and public financing provisions. Furthermore, even spending limits could be constitutional, if they were conditions attached to the voluntary acceptance of benefits received from the state, such as public financing. However, the Court found that the ability of congressional leaders to appoint members of the FEC violated the separation of powers required by the Constitution. Congress quickly amended the law in 1976 to allow the president to appoint all the members. By custom ever since, the president has deferred to the leadership of the other party on half the FEC appointments.

An additional set of FECA amendments was enacted in 1979. In an attempt to strengthen the role of party organizations, Congress excluded party-building activities, such as get-out-the-vote efforts and administrative upkeep, from regulation. This provision became significant in later years as parties took advantage of the party-building exclusion to raise unlimited amounts of contributions known as *soft money*.

Federal campaign law then remained stable for nearly a quarter of a century. Campaign practices evolved, however, usually to the discomfort of reform activists, who tended to be Democrats. The first major development was the rise of business-oriented PACs during the 1970s. As is often the case with political reform, this development contained some irony, in that it had been labor unions, not corporations, that had pressed Congress to make clear the legality of PACs in the 1974 amendments. But business took the most advantage. Four major types of organizations sponsored PACs in the 1970s: unions, corporations, trade groups, and ideological groups. All were significant, but it was the corporate PACs that grew the fastest and raised the most money.

Nevertheless, the PAC situation eventually stabilized, and in the meantime, activists became preoccupied with a new development: independent spending. Because the Supreme Court had upheld limits on the size of contributions but protected the right to independently spend unlimited amounts for a candidate, some organizations found that to have a noticeable effect on elections, they had to turn to independent spending. In particular, certain conservative PACs had considerable success in 1978 and 1980 using independent spending to defeat incumbent Democratic senators. Reformers who were Democrats clamored for control of independent spending for both partisan and ideological reasons. But by 1982, Democratic senators had learned how to defend themselves against attacks driven by independent spending. Reformers' attention turned to the issue of soft money and, later, to the related issue of issue advocacy.

SOFT MONEY AND ISSUE ADVOCACY

Soft money has been defined in various ways. Its original meaning was money that political parties could raise and spend that was exempt from the disclosure requirements and, especially, the contribution limits imposed by FECA. Now the term often denotes campaign money that is exempt from limitation, whether or not it is spent by a party. Concern over soft money began to be expressed in the 1980s and grew steadily through the mid-1990s. Despite the reformers' concern, however, soft money does not appear to have played a major role until the 1996 election.

To understand *issue advocacy*, which also emerged as a major issue in 1996, we must go back to the Supreme Court's decision in *Buckley v. Valeo*. The FECA definition of campaign expenditures turned on whether money was spent for a *political purpose*, a term that the Court regarded as unduly vague. To avoid that vagueness, the Court in *Buckley* interpreted FECA to cover only expenditures for speech that expressly urged the election or defeat of a clearly identified candidate. Phrases like "vote for Smith," "defeat Lopez," or "reelect the president" would qualify. Ads referring to candidates but not containing express advocacy were referred to as *issue ads* or *issue advocacy*, and they were not covered by FECA.

The Court itself admitted in *Buckley* that the narrow definition of what was included as a campaign expenditure would allow evasion of the campaign law. Nevertheless, and perhaps surprising, for about two decades very little advertising took advantage of this loophole. But the new possibilities of both soft money and issue advocacy exploded in 1996.

In that year, parties began raising soft money in much larger amounts than in the past, much of it in contributions of six or seven figures. Furthermore, much of the soft money was more directly related to particular federal campaigns than it had been before. The clearest and most important example was issue advertising that targeted particular candidates but that evaded regulation because it did not use words such as *vote for* or *defeat*.

In addition to the explosion of soft money raised by parties, the 1996 election saw a new large-scale use of issue advertising by nonparty groups. Unions paid for ads attacking Republican candidates, and business funded ads attacking Democrats. Unlike the use of soft money by the parties, nonparty issue advertising evaded not only the contribution limitations and prohibitions but also the disclosure requirements.

Soft money and issue advocacy expanded dramatically in 1996 and grew even more in subsequent elections. Reformers, who in the early and mid-1990s had been proposing broad new campaign regulations that were going nowhere in Congress, began focusing on soft money and issue advocacy. They enjoyed widespread support from the press, but the passage of legislation might not have been possible if not for a political boost from scandals that erupted early in 2002 regarding fraudulent accounting practices of Enron and other large corporations.

BIPARTISAN CAMPAIGN REFORM ACT

The legislation, passed by Congress in 2002 and signed by President George W. Bush, was known as the McCain–Feingold bill in the Senate and the Shays–Meehan bill in the House. Its official name is the Bipartisan Campaign Reform Act (BCRA), which is a misnomer because, despite support from a few prominent Republicans, such as Senator John McCain, it relied primarily on Democratic support.

Although BCRA doubled the limit on contributions from individuals to federal candidates from $1,000 to $2,000, virtually all the remaining provisions consisted of new or tightened regulations. These regulations cover a wide variety of subjects, but the most important provisions are aimed at parties (and therefore at soft money) and at issue advocacy.

The BCRA method of dealing with soft money is rather severe. All money raised by parties at the national level has to be *hard money*—specifically, money raised within the federal contribution limits and subject to federal prohibitions, such as those relating to corporate and union contributions. This restriction applies even to money raised for purposes far removed from campaigns, such as building party headquarters. Furthermore, restrictions on state and local parties are greatly tightened. Suppose, for example, that a state party spends $100,000 on get-out-the-vote activities. Before BCRA, a formula would be applied to determine the portion of the expenditure attributable to federal races. If that portion were 40 percent, then $40,000 of the state party's expenditure would have to be paid for out of contributions raised within the federal limits and prohibitions, but the remaining $60,000 would be subject only to whatever limits were imposed by state law. Under BCRA, all the funds must come from hard money if the ballot contains any federal candidate at all.

BCRA's approach to issue advocacy is equally broad, but also surprisingly incomplete. To deal with the vagueness that caused problems in *Buckley*, BCRA creates a new category called *electioneering communications*, consisting of any broadcast advertising that identifies a federal candidate and is run within thirty days before a primary or sixty days before a general election. Electioneering communications must be disclosed and must be paid for out of hard money. The concept sweeps broadly because it includes not only ads clearly targeted at the campaign, but other ads that mention, say, the president or a senator while debating a particular legislative or policy controversy having no direct relation to the campaign. On the other hand, all nonbroadcast advertising and all advertising airing more than a month or two before the election are excluded.

Despite BCRA's early success in court, it had little impact on the money chase in the 2004–2008 election cycle. To the surprise of some, parties were able to make up for the loss of large contributions by raising increased amounts of hard money, partly with the aid of relatively small donations raised through the Internet. But the large donors, blocked from giving to the parties, found a new vehicle in the so-called 527 groups (named after the section of the Internal Revenue Code under which they are organized). George Soros and other wealthy Democrats announced that they would be contributing millions to 527s in their efforts to defeat President Bush, and the Republicans were quick to follow suit, claiming they would raise an equivalent sum to support the president's campaign. Most analysts agree that the 527 groups are evidence of the perverse consequences of campaign finance regulation. By eliminating soft money raised by political parties—whose role in the electoral process is essential and legitimate—reformers have encouraged the development of a class of groups with no electoral accountability whatsoever.

In addition to the rise of the 527s, tighter campaign finance restrictions may be a cause of increased incumbency advantage in congressional elections. Incumbents are reelected more than 90 percent of the time, primarily because they are more well known to voters than their challengers are. Incumbents receive regular media exposure and various other perks (free use of television studios to produce videos, multiple trips to their district, all costs of mailings to their constituents being covered by taxpayers, and so on) that contribute to their greater visibility. Placing equal limits on challengers' and incumbents' fund-raising inevitably has unequal consequences because challengers need to spend more money to overcome the incumbent's considerable recognizability advantage.

Another drawback of BCRA is its incredible complexity. It used to be said that if you wanted to run for office, the first thing you had to do was hire a lawyer. In this post-BCRA era, it is likely that your lawyer will have to hire a lawyer, because only a few specialists have a firm grasp on the ins and outs of the law. Although the effects are hard to quantify, campaign finance regulations of this order of magnitude may tend to discourage some people from becoming active in politics as candidates, party officials, or activists.

CITIZENS UNITED AND McCUTCHEON

In the most recent developments, the Supreme Court ruled, in *Citizens United v. Federal Election Commission*), that corporations and labor unions have the same First Amendment right to make unlimited independent expenditures in election campaigns that individual citizens and other kinds of organizations have. In the aftermath of the decision, public attention has focused on the possible unleashing of corporate political power, although whatever increases there may be in corporate and union expenditures are likely to offset each other. Three years later, in *McCutcheon v. Federal Election Commission*, the Court decided that the cap on the total amount individuals could donate to multiple campaigns (which was $123,000) was an unconstitutional impediment to freedom of speech. The Court did leave intact the cap on donations to individual candidates ($2,600 across primary and general-election races). The practical impact of the decision, therefore, is that wealthy individuals can make contributions to as many candidates and causes as they like. Most observers expect that the new rules will make for significantly higher levels of campaign fund-raising in 2014 and 2016.

CANDIDATE DEBATES

Video Archive 6.17 Nixon/JFK Debate

The final element of campaign strategy in the post-television era concerns debates. On September 26, 1960, an audience of 70 million gathered around their television sets to watch the first of four debates between John Kennedy and Richard Nixon. Nixon was in poor health and appeared without makeup (thus revealing that he had not shaved). Kennedy, in contrast, appeared tanned, fit, and youthful. Audience reaction to the historic debate was remarkably one-sided; a significant majority gave the nod to Kennedy (see Chapter 9). In future debates, candidates would be more attentive to matters of appearance and imagery.

Oddly enough, debates occur more frequently in primary than in general-election campaigns. In the 2007–2008 Democratic primary and preprimary seasons, there were so many debates (twenty-six in all) and joint appearances on the schedule that the candidates found it difficult to carry on with their normal activities (such as fund-raising). More importantly, the opportunity to participate in multiple debates gives candidates who do not have the backing of the party establishment an incentive to prolong their campaign by attacking the front-runner. The Republicans held more than twenty primary debates in 2012, allowing the candidates to "slice and dice" each other for months on end. Following the election, the Republican National Committee decided that there would be fewer than ten debates in 2016. The idea is to make the primary process less divisive and thus boost the general-election prospects of the nominee.

In fact, the term *debate* is something of a misnomer when applied to campaigns. It is true that the audience observes the candidates answering questions and offering summary introductory and closing statements, but these resemblances to conventional debates are superficial. In fact, debates—at least those occurring in the fall of election years—are closely managed by the candidates so as to maximize their ability to score points with the relevant judges—namely, the viewing audience. From the subject matter of the questions, to the identity of the questioners, the dates, and even the details of the shape of the stage and the podiums, campaigns control the protocol. The Bill Clinton campaign, for instance, pushed hard for adoption of a town hall format in the 1992 campaign; the Bush campaign, knowing that its candidate was more reserved and less apt to connect with ordinary people, argued in favor of the more conventional panel of questioners. In the end, the town hall format was used for one debate and the other two debates relied on the conventional panel of questioners.

A recurring issue with televised candidate debates concerns eligibility. Major party candidates may participate, but all minor party candidates are excluded. In fact, the reason for the suspension of debates between 1964 and 1976 was that the television networks (who were then the principal sponsors) were legally bound to include minor party candidates under the provisions of the FCC's Fairness Doctrine. If one candidate was offered ninety minutes of prime-time exposure, then all other candidates for the same position were entitled to similar treatment. In 1976, the rule was evaded, and the debates resumed by use of third-party sponsor the League of Women Voters. The league invited only the major party candidates, giving the networks the freedom to televise the debates as a newsworthy event. Today, organization of the debates is in the hands of a nonpartisan commission on presidential debates. The commission has formulated a set of criteria for eligibility, the most notable of which is that a candidate must demonstrate a level of public support (in reputable polls) of at last 15 percent. By this standard, virtually all third-party candidates are excluded.

With the advent of cable television and the greater freedom afforded the viewing audience, presidential debates no longer attract the majority of those people watching television at the time. As Figure 6.5 shows, the size of the debate audience has declined substantially from its peak in 1960. If we translate the Nielsen ratings into the percent of households watching, the decline amounts to 22 percentage points between 1960 and 2012. The debates held in 1960, 1976, and 1980 attracted well over half the total viewing audience. Since 1984, however, only once has the debate audience amounted to one half of the total audience and that was in 2008 with the historic candidacy of Barack Obama. Clearly, the television audience has deserted the debates in favor of more entertaining fare. The declining trend in audience size also applies to entertainment programming, including such high-profile events as the Major League Baseball's World Series and the Academy Awards, suggesting a generalized fragmentation of the national television audience. Even with

FIGURE 6.5

The Shrinking Audience for Presidential Debates

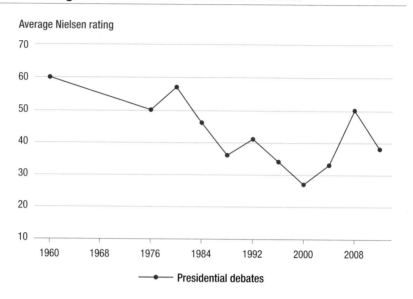

Average Nielsen rating

—•— Presidential debates

Source: Unpublished data from Nielsen Media Research.

their diminished share of the audience, debates reach a much larger number of voters than any single advertisement or news report can. For the candidates, the benefits (and risks) of performing before 50 million viewers mere weeks in advance of the election are huge. Campaigns understandably go to great lengths to prepare their candidates. They suspend the travel schedule, hold no other events, and devote several days to preparation, even to the extent of holding full-scale dress rehearsals.

The fact that the debates are far from spontaneous exchanges does not seem to have reduced their credibility with the public. In comparison with television ads and news reports, debates are easily the most favorably evaluated form of campaigning. Nearly one-third of the electorate reported that they took debates into account in 2008. Surveys also indicate that, unlike advertising and news coverage, which the public dismisses as unhelpful to the task of voting, large majorities rate the debates as either "very helpful" or "somewhat helpful." In 2012, while two-thirds of the electorate judged the debates as helpful, more than three-fourths considered the political ads unhelpful.[7]

From the candidate's perspective, the benefits of debates include an opportunity to demonstrate their fitness for office: their command over the issues, their demeanor under duress, their sense of humor, and their ability to deal with conflict. The principal risk is that they will say or do something that makes them look less than presidential. Their first priority, accordingly, is to avoid committing a *gaffe*—a major misstatement of fact. The best example of such a misstatement occurred in the 1976 foreign policy debate between incumbent Republican Gerald Ford and Democrat Jimmy Carter. President Ford incorrectly asserted that the countries of Eastern Europe were generally free of Soviet domination—a statement that he made not once, but twice. Remarkably, as we will discuss in Chapter 9, this blunder had no immediate impact on viewers' evaluations of Ford and Carter.

Scoring points with undecided voters sometimes calls for more than verbal fluency or command over the subject matter. Candidates must also convey cues concerning their personality, emotions, and people skills. When Michael Dukakis was asked in 1988 if his position on the death penalty (he was opposed) would change if his wife, Kitty, were raped and then murdered, his relatively calm response led many commentators to suggest that he was a cold fish, incapable of expressing emotion. Newt Gingrich adopted precisely the opposite approach in 2012 when asked by John King of CNN about his alleged extramarital affairs. Gingrich turned the tables on King by condemning the question as an attempt by the "liberal media" to sabotage any discussion of political issues. In fact, Gingrich made media bias toward his candidacy a major theme of his debate rhetoric (see Video Archive 6.18).

Video Archive 6.18
Gingrich Attacks the Media

Sometimes candidates send the wrong signal not by what they say, but rather their demeanor. In the first debate of the 2000 campaign, Vice President Al Gore repeatedly cut off Governor Bush's answers, generally coming across as an arrogant know-it-all. President George H. W. Bush committed a nonverbal gaffe in the town hall debate of 1992; obviously uncomfortable with the format and the proceedings, the president was seen studying his watch, thus conveying the impression that he found the discussion, which concerned mostly middle-class worries, of little interest.

The gold medal for debate gaffes clearly goes to Texas Governor Rick Perry who, in an early 2012 campaign debate, repeated his campaign pledge to eliminate three major federal agencies. He identified two—the Departments of Commerce and Education—but was unable to remember the third (the Department of Energy). Perry responded to questions about his debate performance by noting that "everybody makes mistakes," but his poll numbers stayed low and a few weeks later he withdrew from the race.

Video Archive 6.19
Debate Gaffes

In nonpresidential campaigns, debates contribute little. It's not that candidates for statewide office do not debate. They do, and frequently. But voters have little opportunity to view these debates because they are rarely televised in prime time. In a study of statewide campaigns in ten states, the Committee for the Study of the American Electorate found that two-thirds of the debates were televised, but only half were shown on network affiliates with large shares of the audience. Debates between candidates for the US House were even less newsworthy—only 30 percent were televised.

CONCLUSION

The basic objective of any campaign strategy is simple: maximize the number of positive messages about yourself and the number of negative messages about your opponent. Given the role of the press, candidates can no longer expect reporters to do their bidding. As a result, the campaigns have taken to more-subtle forms of spin, from staging events to uncovering newsworthy information concerning opponents. On the advertising front, candidates attempt to promote their candidacies with personal and performance-based appeals. More often than not, advertising campaigns do not address the same issues; instead candidates talk past one another, each emphasizing their respective strengths. In the case of negative campaigns, the candidates engage in a debate of sorts, not concerning the strengths of their policy proposals but over the veracity and fairness of the charges and countercharges they hurl at each other. Finally, debates provide candidates with opportunities to close the deal—to demonstrate to voters that what they see in the ad campaign is what they get for real.

SUMMARY

1. Media-based campaigns take place on two stages: *free media* (news coverage) and *paid media* (candidate advertisements). Presidential races enjoy virtually unlimited news coverage, making the ad campaign only a small trickle in the cumulative message stream; advertising strategy is still extremely important to presidential candidates, however, because it represents their only opportunity to present their case unfiltered by journalists. In the case of nonpresidential races (congressional, gubernatorial, and so on), paid media dominate because news coverage is sparse.
2. Although advertising provides candidates with much greater control over their message than news coverage does, there is a significant trade-off; advertising is a much less credible messenger than news reports.

3. Candidates take numerous steps to focus news coverage on subjects that they consider advantageous:
   - Candidates try to avoid the media feeding frenzies that arise whenever they demonstrate a personal or character flaw.
   - Candidates can gain an advantage in coverage if the opponent makes a major misstatement of fact or reverses course on a matter of public policy.
   - Campaigns often attempt to set low expectations about their candidates' prospects or standing—especially during the primary season—so that any level of achievement above this low baseline will be more surprising to journalists, and hence be covered more extensively and favorably.
   - The nuts and bolts of press management is the strategic handling of events, which are scheduled in such a way as to maximize press coverage.
   - Campaigns regulate media access to candidates on the basis of the candidate's standing in the polls; candidates who are trailing may follow an open-door strategy with the press; candidates who are ahead tend to severely limit media access.
   - Candidates can limit the access of journalists who are more likely to be critical, while devoting time to outlets more likely to provide favorable coverage. Campaigns dogged by critical coverage may try to shield the candidate from the national press by cultivating less prominent outlets, such as local news and talk-show formats.
   - Candidates react to each other's statements and actions on a continuous basis, mainly in the form of competing press releases. Campaigns research the opponent's record and monitor the opponent's actions and words, with the aim of pouncing on any particularly newsworthy item.
4. Candidates follow several strategies in designing their advertising campaigns:
   - Campaigns aim their advertisements at voters whose preferences may be pivotal to the outcome of the race—that is, voters in states or areas considered competitive.
   - Candidates change the content and tone of their advertisements over the course of the campaign, from biographical spots early in the campaign to image and issue ads later.
   - In their advertising campaigns, candidates emphasize issues on which they enjoy an advantage over their opponent. A particularly important aspect of this strategy is issue ownership.
   - Candidates may also use wedge appeals in their advertising, particularly if they are losing the debate on generic issues. Wedge issues are designed to pit groups against each other, to appeal to voters' sense of group identity.

- A striking attribute of political advertising campaigns is the heavy reliance on negative or attack advertising.
- Negative ads dominate campaign advertising both because they tend to be more newsworthy than civil discourse and because the public's low opinion of politicians makes attacks on opposing candidates more credible than promoting one's own virtues. Furthermore, among campaign professionals a fundamental principle is that a candidate must punch back when attacked.
- Candidates often use direct mail to target voters more effectively. Direct mail is especially important in lower-level races, where TV advertising is inefficient,

5. Advertising is expensive and necessitates the raising of huge sums of money for political campaigns. In recent decades, concern about the role of money in politics has led to several attempts at campaign finance reform. In most cases, however, these attempts have merely encouraged campaigns to find loopholes and new, creative financing techniques.

6. Another important element of campaigns is the candidate debates. Campaigns closely manage debates to maximize their candidates' ability to score points with the viewing audience.

FURTHER READINGS

Ansolabehere, S., & Iyengar, S. (1995). *Going negative: How attack ads shrink and polarize the electorate.* New York: Free Press.

Bartels, L. M. (1988). *Presidential primaries and the dynamics of public choice.* Princeton, NJ: Princeton University Press.

Diamond, E., & Bates, S. (1992). *The spot: The rise of political advertising on television.* Cambridge, MA: MIT Press.

Geer, J. (2010). *Fanning the flames: The news media's role in the rise of negativity in presidential campaigns* (Discussion Paper). Cambridge, MA: Joan Shorenstein Center on the Press, Politics, and Public Policy, Harvard University.

Jacobson, G. C. (1997). *The politics of congressional elections* (4th ed.). New York: Longman.

Lau, R. R., Sigelman, L., Heldman, C., & Babbitt, P. (1999). The effects of negative political advertisements: A meta-analytic assessment. *American Political Science Review, 93,* 851–875.

Petrocik, J. R. (1996). Issue ownership in presidential elections, with a 1980 case study. *American Journal of Political Science, 40,* 825–850.

Popkin, S. L. (1994). *The reasoning voter: Communication and persuasion in presidential campaigns* (2nd ed.). Chicago: University of Chicago Press.

Shaw, D. R. (2006). *The race to 270: The electoral college and the campaign strategies of 2000 and 2004.* Chicago: University of Chicago Press.

Vavreck, L. (2008). *The message matters: The economy and presidential campaigns.* Princeton, NJ: Princeton University Press.

NOTES

1. The networks were quick to point out that this limited coverage did not amount to an abdication of their civic responsibility, stating that they intended to provide gavel-to-gavel coverage on their online subsidiaries.

2. A GRP is defined as the sum of all Nielsen rating points (one Nielsen point is approximately 1 percent of the media market in which the ad airs) for the programs in which the ad was placed.

3. After the campaign, the story was exposed as Democratic spin; no such event occurred.

4. Because there are more Democrats than Republicans in the national electorate and the Democrats have traditionally enjoyed near-unanimous backing from the African American community, the incentive to use wedge appeals based on race is especially enticing for Republican candidates.

5. It is unclear whether these ballot measures had any impact on the presidential vote. All eleven measures passed, however, suggesting that the median voter is to the right of the center on issues involving gay rights.

6. Mellman made his comments at a conference on the 2004 election held at Stanford University on November 9, 2004.

7. The debate audience is drawn disproportionately from the ranks of the politically engaged— partisans, the educated, and people over the age of forty.

7

Going Public

Governing through the Media

It used to be that when an election was over, the winning candidates took office, put away their campaign paraphernalia and rhetoric, and got down to the serious business of governing. For a US president, this meant cultivating majority support in Congress for the key provisions of the presidential platform. The White House became the center of serious behind-the-scenes negotiations. The end result was the passage of legislation that reflected and accommodated competing interests. In the pre-media era, an essential element of presidential leadership was the ability to create winning coalitions from across the party or ideological divides.

Amassing support for the president's proposals typically required both patience and a horse-trader's knack for compromise. Presidents with extensive personal networks on Capitol Hill (Lyndon Johnson, for example), were in the best position to readily elicit bipartisan support. In the Johnson era, conservative southern Democrats supported civil rights legislation in return for increased defense spending directed to southern states. This bargaining model of policy making rested on face-to-face communications among a relatively small group of elites who felt a common sense of obligation to place the interests of the nation ahead of the narrow confines of party or ideology.

Of course, bargaining among the elites did not guarantee sound policy. "Pork barrel" considerations typically trumped cost–benefit analysis of political problems as the basis for compromise. Powerful committee or subcommittee chairs could see to it that a significant share of federal spending was deposited into the pockets of their constituents. Despite these flaws, however, the bargaining model did, for the most part, result in smoothly functioning governance. The federal budget, for instance, was routinely enacted into law in advance of the fiscal-year deadline.

As elections became more media-centric, the president's increasingly important role as direct spokesman to the public began to alter the policy-making process. Rather than dealing directly with congressional leaders, presidents preferred to influence them indirectly by making them respond to "the people." As political scientist Samuel Kernell (1986) defined the new approach, "It is a strategy whereby a president promotes himself and his policies in Washington by appealing to the American public for support" (p. 2).

The increased reliance on the modern bully pulpit of television intensified partisan conflict and ill will, making it more difficult for rival elites to engage in good-faith bargaining. The more confrontational atmosphere in Washington led to the shutdown of the federal government on seventeen occasions between 1977 and 1995 because of irreconcilable policy differences between the president and Congress over the federal budget. In most cases, federal offices were closed for only a day or two. In 1995, however, in the longest shutdown in history, involving 800,000 federal employees, essential government services were unavailable for 22 days because President Clinton and the Republican-led Congress could not reach agreement on lifting the federal debt ceiling as a precondition for passage of the budget. Gridlock rather than compromise had become the order of the day. A further impasse occurred in 2013 when Republicans in Congress refused to support an increase in the debt ceiling without extracting concessions from Democrats in the form of changes to the Affordable Care Act (Obamacare). When the Democrats refused, the government shut down for 16 days before the Republicans—in response to poll results showing that the public held them responsible—capitulated and voted to raise the borrowing limit.

The deterioration in the relationship between competing elites can be attributed in significant part to media-based electoral campaigns. When hard-edged rhetoric and, often, personal attacks are directed at opponents during the campaign, it becomes difficult for elected leaders to extend the olive branch once the election is over. Incumbents must look over their shoulders constantly, for fear of offending potential donors to their next campaign, or of casting a vote that might become the focus of the next round of attack ads. A vote on the debt ceiling is no longer a routine legislative duty, but rather, an opportunity to go on the record as opposing "big government." More generally, the very same tools and strategies that are used to win the election are now applied for purposes of policy making. Going public has gradually superseded give-and-take bargaining as the preferred approach to governance.

The central ingredient of going public as a strategy of leadership is the cultivation of public approval. Given the overriding importance of reelection to the

IN FOCUS

Going Public

Going public is a strategy used by presidents and other politicians to promote their policies by appealing to the American public for support. If a president enjoys strong public support, that popularity creates an important bargaining advantage. A president with a high level of public approval can often count on being able to persuade a few members of the opposition who may fear that they will not be reelected if they take a stand against a well-liked president.

strategic calculations of elected officials, the most basic consideration is to avoid offending the voters. A president's popularity creates an important bargaining advantage; a president who enjoys a high level of public approval can count on being able to persuade a few members of the opposition. When the public backs the president, the president's credibility is enhanced; members of Congress are more likely to defer to the president's legislative proposals because they fear that the potential costs of opposition are too high. As Brody (1991) puts it, popularity enables the president to "achieve his program, keep challengers at bay, and guide his and other political leaders' expectations about the president's party's prospects in presidential and congressional elections" (p. 4).

The effects of a president's popularity on the ability to garner legislative support are most evident when the president's proposals address issues that are salient to the public but concern subject matters about which the public possesses little information. For example, the public is unanimously in favor of policies that reduce terrorism but has little ability to discriminate between the pros and cons of military intervention versus economic development as possible solutions. In such circumstances, presidential rhetoric has a double-barreled effect: it makes the targeted issues more prominent for the public, and it makes Congress more responsive to the president's proposals.

Conversely, a president buffeted by allegations of illegal or immoral behavior will be much less effective at pushing through a legislative program. Nixon's credibility with Congress was minimal once the Watergate allegations began to hold the public's attention.

Overall, the evidence suggests that going public is an indispensable ingredient of presidential influence with Congress. According to Canes-Wrone (2001), "modern presidents systematically achieve policy goals by promoting issues to the public" (p. 326).

Ronald Reagan's presidency provided a number of illustrations of a popular president's power to persuade. Reagan had defeated incumbent president Jimmy Carter on a platform of smaller government and tax cuts. Reagan's first budget proposal (1981) called for unprecedented cuts in social welfare programs, coupled with significant increases in defense spending. On both counts, the budget was an abomination to congressional Democrats, who still controlled the House. Undeterred, Reagan embarked on a systematic media campaign to promote the budget. The president gave several speeches across the country urging citizens to convey their support for his budget to their congressional representatives. The speeches were carefully designed (with catchy sound bites) to attract coverage from local and network newscasts. Reagan also made it plain that he would personally campaign against any Democrats who voted against his budget. Here's how David Gergen (Reagan's director of communications) described the closing stages of the campaign:

> We learned about it [the impending congressional vote on the budget resolution] the next day . . . Reagan was flying off to Texas. I was back at the White House, and we worked it out by sending statements to the plane for Reagan to make a planeside statement in time to get it on the evening news. We wanted to give it hype, to elevate the issue on the evening news so that the nation was getting a message. We were calling the press and doing whatever we could to build the issue. At the same time, the political office went to work, notifying all their allies around the country, bringing the calls and pressure onto Congress as quickly as possible. (Hertsgaard, 1988, p. 120)

Reagan's strategy paid off. Despite the radical nature of his proposals and the deep hostility of congressional Democrats to the Reagan agenda, the budget was passed. Recognizing President Reagan's considerable appeal to the voting public, a sufficient number of Democrats voted against their party. Fear of angering voters rather than some form of political inducement had become the basis for creating policy coalitions in government. Directly appealing to the public had replaced negotiations among elites as the basis for governance.

President Barack Obama has been quick to take advantage of the multiple media opportunities afforded the chief executive. In the beginning of 2009, Obama held his first prime-time press conference to shore up support for the Economic Recovery and Reinvestment Plan. He then brought his message to the *Tonight Show with Jay Leno*, and made history by being the first sitting president to appear on such a venue. Six months later, with the fate of his healthcare bill in the balance, Obama undertook a media blitz. In one day, he

Case Study:
A TALE OF TWO DISASTERS

The contrasting ways in which Presidents George W. Bush and Barack Obama dealt with Hurricane Katrina in 2005 and the Gulf oil spill in 2010, respectively, illustrate the overriding importance of news media coverage to the president's ability to govern effectively. In the case of Katrina, the Bush administration failed to recognize the urgency of the situation and allowed the continuous stream of vivid images depicting "an environmental disaster of biblical proportions" to dominate the news. When the president finally traveled to New Orleans to deliver a televised speech to the American people, he was forced to admit that "the system at every level of government was not well-coordinated, and was overwhelmed." In the weeks after Katrina, Bush's public approval plummeted.

In the case of the Gulf spill, the Obama administration immediately orchestrated a series of events suggesting that the president was in control of the situation. Secretary of the Interior Ken Salazar was dispatched to BP's command center to review their procedures. Admiral Thad Allen of the Coast Guard was appointed to head the Unified Command Center, the group overseeing BP's efforts to cap the well. In a nationally televised address, President Obama announced that BP would establish a victims' compensation fund. The president made multiple trips to Louisiana to express his solidarity with the residents of the affected region. As the oil spill dragged on, Obama's public approval remained stable.

appeared on CBS's *Face the Nation*, ABC's *This Week*, NBC's *Meet the Press*, CNN's *State of the Union*, and Univision's *Al Punto, con Jorge Ramos*. Over the next ten days, he did *60 Minutes*, Bloomberg Television, CNBC, and the *Late Show with David Letterman*. Clearly, Obama has elevated going public to new heights.

The transition from a style of governance based on negotiations among elites to one based on media imagery can be attributed in part to the growing prominence of media professionals in the electoral process. Increasingly, political appointments have come to be distributed among the members of the winning campaign team, rather than among party supporters. Key campaign professionals have taken up positions in the executive branch with the principal agenda of ensuring the president's reelection. At the other end of Pennsylvania Avenue, members of Congress have behaved in similar fashion, recruiting political operatives for their office staffs whose major responsibility is to prepare for the next campaign.

Once appointed to office, media professionals have continued to serve by exploiting their expertise in dealing with the media and the public, and they have focused less on building coalitions among elites or on developing substantive policy initiatives. Hamilton Jordan, President Carter's campaign manager and White House chief of staff, was a stark example of this type. Because Jordan had no contacts in Congress and engaged in little outreach, and because the president's popularity with the public eventually suffered under the pressure of the Iran hostage crisis, most of President Carter's legislative proposals were ignored or defeated. Despite the mixed track record of media professionals appointed to government positions, presidents have continued the revolving door between the campaign and White House staff. David Axelrod, President Obama's senior political adviser (until he left to work on the 2012 reelection campaign) and closest confidant, had limited policy experience, as he previously had been a political campaign consultant (including chief strategist for the Obama presidential campaign).

The many repercussions of going public as a way of governing are taken up in detail in Chapter 10. In brief, the consequences include a preoccupation with media relations and public popularity. In the case of the president, close control over news coverage, especially symbolism—pomp and ceremony, images of the president at work tackling the issues of the hour—is the order of the day, and few resources remain for developing and pushing through policy proposals.

The remainder of this chapter will discuss the role of public communication by the president today. Why is communication with the public so essential? What are the key forms of presidential communication and why?

PRESIDENTIAL COMMUNICATION

The conventional wisdom in Washington is that going public is indeed essential to political success. As explained by President George W. Bush's political guru Karl Rove:

> I think in the post-1980 era we all owe it to [Michael] Deaver who said turn off the sound of the television and that's how people are going to decide whether you won the day or lost the day, the quality of the picture. That's what they're going to get the message by, with the sound entirely off. I think that's simplistic, but I think it's an important insight. There's a reason why the old saw, a picture is worth a thousand words, how we look, how we sound and how we project is important. So winning the picture is important. (Kumar, 2003, p. 385)

Validating Rove's analysis, recent presidents have all adapted their behavior to harness the power of television. Exercising control over the media message rather than cultivating good relations with Congress has become an absolutely essential element of presidential leadership. Herbert Hoover's media staff consisted of a single assistant for press relations. In the 1950s the White House media operation expanded to include the press secretary, the press secretary's deputy, and five secretarial employees. Today, the vast White House media complex (see Figure 7.1) has sixty-nine full-time employees and five distinct organizational branches within the White House counselor's office. Clearly, the strategy of going public has magnified the function of press management in the contemporary presidency.

THE PRESIDENT'S MEDIA MANAGERS

The nerve center of the executive branch's communication efforts is the Office of the Press Secretary, commonly referred to as the *press office*. The office has five distinct branches, of which press and communications are the most significant. These are headed by the press secretary and communications director, respectively, both of whom play a pivotal role within the administration. The Press Office issues all press releases and responds to inquiries from the

FIGURE 7.1

Media Operations in the White House

Source: Data from M. J. Kumar. (2003). The White House and the press: News organizations as a presidential resource and as a source of pressure. *Presidential Studies Quarterly, 33,* 669–683.

national media. The Office of Communications is responsible for planning the president's media appearances, including press conferences and other public events. The communications director is also responsible for coordinating the message of the various spokespersons throughout the administration. The Office of Media Affairs provides the same services as the Office of Communications, but for the benefit of local and regional news outlets. Finally, the Office of Global Communications provides "strategic direction and themes" to government agencies (such as the Voice of America) that produce information and media content for overseas audiences.[1] The newly created Office of New Media ensures that the president's message is made widely available through the White House website, YouTube channel, the White House live channel on Facebook, Twitter, and other online sources.

The communications director is responsible for overseeing the production and release of information throughout the administration. Given the number of agencies and offices that deal with the media, message coordination is often impossible. Getting the federal government to speak with one voice is the goal, but more often than not, there are inconsistencies and misstatements that must be explained. On some occasions, advisers within the White House might leak information about internal debates to the press. In a recent case, the Obama administration went to great lengths to mount a sting operation to reveal the identity of a staffer who issued several tweets criticizing administration foreign policy (Nakamura, Gearan, & Wilson, 2013).

Unlike the press secretary, who acts mainly as a conduit between the press and the White House, the communications director is more of an ideas person, a strategist who seeks to define and market the president's image. Gerald Rafshoon, Jimmy Carter's communications director, instructed the president to carry his own bags when disembarking from Air Force One. This advice was meant to help Carter project a man-of-the-people image.[2] Fearing Ronald Reagan's penchant for off-the-cuff remarks, his communications director, Michael Deaver, prohibited the press from asking questions during photo ops.

The press secretary, the president's point person for dealing with the national media, is much more likely to occupy the spotlight. The press secretary (or the secretary's deputy) conducts two daily press briefings for the White House press corps. On occasion, the press office also arranges special background briefings (usually by a policy specialist) for reporters. In addition, there are more informal off-the-record sessions between reporters and administration officials. Behind the scenes, the press office regulates journalists' access to the White House (by issuing credentials) and maintains the elaborate on-site facilities necessary for journalists to transmit their news reports.

The position of press secretary imposes difficult demands on the incumbent, who often has to walk a fine line between meeting the political objectives of the White House staff ("spin and more spin") on the one hand and maintaining journalistic credibility on the other. As a member of the president's inner circle, the press secretary is expected to do as much as possible to score points for the administration. Some press secretaries engage in so much spinning, however, that they find themselves facing an increasingly disbelieving press corps. During the closing stages of the Watergate scandal, relations between Nixon's press secretary, Ron Ziegler, and the press corps became so strained that Deputy Press Secretary Gerald Warren was frequently asked to stand in at the daily press briefing.

Other press secretaries lose the confidence of the press because it is widely known that they are not part of the president's inner circle. As media management becomes critical to the effectiveness of the presidency, reporters have adapted by more aggressively challenging the press secretary at the daily briefings and other appearances. According to Ari Fleischer (President George W. Bush's first press secretary), the resulting pressures are so intense that no press secretary can hope to serve out a full four-year term (Auletta, 2004). Validating this assertion, Robert Gibbs, Obama's press secretary, announced that he would leave the post in February 2011 to work on the reelection campaign. He was succeeded by Jay Carney, who lasted three years, four months.

Oftentimes the press secretary does not even know whether the information that is being channeled from the White House is true or false. Naturally, the press secretary's credibility suffers when he or she delivers, knowingly or unknowingly, disinformation. Scott McClellan (2008), George W. Bush's press secretary, described the fallout from his repeated denials of any White House involvement in the CIA leak scandal (in which Valerie Plame was identified as a covert CIA agent): "I had allowed myself to be deceived into unknowingly passing a falsehood. It would ultimately prove fatal to my ability to serve the president effectively. I didn't learn that what I'd said was untrue until the media began to figure it out almost two years later" (p. 3).

The more effective press secretaries, while enjoying the trust and confidence of the White House political operatives and the president, have maintained an "objective" posture with the press. Mike McCurry, press secretary to President Clinton, was able to draw on his reputation as a straight shooter to weather the storms of the Monica Lewinsky scandal, when all too often he was forced to claim ignorance in response to reporters' questioning. In the text on pages 206–207, McCurry describes his daily routine as press secretary.[3]

As the complexity of the White House media apparatus suggests, managing the press has become a key function within the administration. Going public requires that the administration orchestrate the news media to present a consistently positive image of the president. At the same time, as outlined below, the president must be protected against being put on the defensive by aggressive or unexpected questioning of actions the administration has taken.

GETTING THE MESSAGE OUT

There are three distinct media opportunities that presidents may pursue. In each case, the amount of resources invested varies with the payoffs, namely, the number of people who can be reached and the degree of control over the message. In the ideal scenario (from the president's perspective), the president would command a nationwide news audience and be granted free rein to influence public opinion, unimpeded by skeptical reporters or critical commentary from opposing elites. Over the years, as media audiences have changed and the national press corps has adopted a more critical perspective, presidents have taken to travel and speechmaking as their principal communication strategies. The presidential press conference, once prized as an opportunity to demonstrate the president's leadership before a captive audience, has all but fallen into disuse.

News Coverage

As Mike McCurry points out in the speech excerpted on pages 206–207, the president is the focal point of the national government. Given reporters' reliance on official sources, the president can count on regular and sustained news coverage from all forms of news media. Studies of national news repeatedly demonstrate the visibility of the White House. In the case of *New York Times* coverage between 1948 and 2005 (see Figure 7.2), the share of front-page news accorded to the president was initially below the level of coverage accorded to Congress. Beginning with the election of John Kennedy, however, presidential coverage increased and reached the level of congressional news reporting. By the late 1970s, the president was clearly the principal source of news; averaging across the presidencies from Carter to Clinton, presidential coverage exceeded congressional coverage by a significant margin ($p < .01$).[4]

Executive power is especially pronounced in the arena of foreign policy. By virtue of the president's constitutional prerogatives as commander in chief, the president is unquestionably the principal source of news on American foreign policy. When we examine news reports about foreign policy (see Figure 7.3), the dominance of the president is apparent: since Reagan,

FIGURE 7.2

Coverage of Congress and the President, 1948–2005

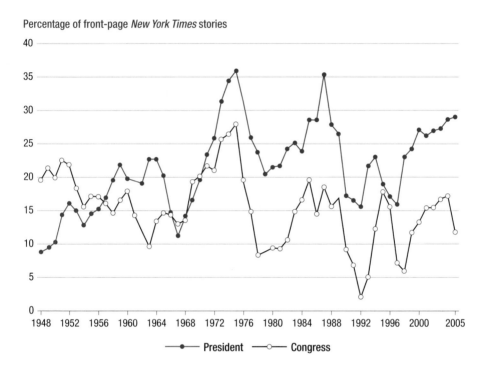

Percentage of front-page *New York Times* stories

President Congress

Source: Data from Policy Agendas Project. (2010). University of Texas. Retrieved January 2011, from www.policyagendas .org.

Note: These observations represent a moving average of three consecutive observations. A moving average has the effect of smoothing a data series.

the president's share of foreign affairs news coverage has been three times the level of congressional coverage. Foreign policy news, for all practical purposes, is presidential news.

Unfortunately, there is no comparable database for broadcast news coverage of the president (archived videotape recordings of network news began only in 1968). In tracking CBS News coverage between 1968 and 1978, Grossman and Kumar (1981) found that the network devoted substantial attention to the executive branch, even more so than print news did. On average, CBS aired four news reports each day on the president, amounting to approximately 20 percent of the newscast.[5]

Clearly, the president can command the attention of the national media at will. But does the president also influence the story line? Studies of news content suggest that news coverage of incumbent presidents follows the same

FIGURE 7.3

Coverage of Congress and the President, Foreign Affairs, 1948–2005

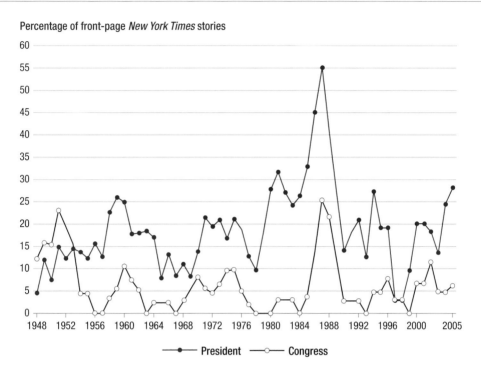

Percentage of front-page *New York Times* stories

Source: Data from Policy Agendas Project. (2010). University of Texas. Retrieved January 2011, from www.policyagendas
.org.

Note: These observations represent a moving average of five consecutive observations. A moving average has the effect
of smoothing a data series.

pattern as coverage of presidential candidates—evolving from generally positive
coverage in the 1960s and 1970s to more interpretive and critical coverage in the
1990s. In Grossman and Kumar's 1968–1978 comparative study of *Time*, the
New York Times, and CBS News, favorable coverage of the president exceeded
unfavorable coverage by a wide margin in both print outlets. Only in the case of
CBS was the assessment mixed: the network aired an equal number of positive
and negative reports (Grossman & Kumar, 1981, p. 256). Although the content of
the CBS News reports was mixed, the accompanying visual imagery was invariably flattering: 40 percent of the pictures used in the newscasts were positive, and
only 8 percent were negative (p. 258). Thus the evidence suggests that, during this
period at least, the efforts of the White House media apparatus paid rich dividends.

Over time, as journalists learned to resist the persuasiveness of media consultants and press secretaries alike, news reports began to take on a sharper

Case Study:
A DAY IN THE LIFE OF THE PRESIDENTIAL PRESS SECRETARY

The hardest part of the job is to just get on top of the flow of information that is crushing, all-consuming, surrounding you every waking moment of the day with some new plotline that you have to think about. Because part of the problem is that the White House has become, for most of the US press corps, the prism through which every story anywhere can sometimes be seen. I don't know if, when Princess Diana died, what was that, a Saturday night? It was like a Saturday night that she died in Paris. And it was awful and tragic but I was watching a ball game or something. And I suddenly got this flood of calls at home from angry network executives saying "Your people said they won't open up the White House press office so we can go live from the White House." And I said, "Well, what does the White House have to do with Princess Diana dying in this car accident?" But the immediate thought was that this big, significant, huge moment had to be reflected through this stage that most Americans associate with big events. If it's a big event, clearly the White House has something to do with it. . . . But anyhow, the reality is that every single day everything happening in the world is going to at least be a possible source of questions in the White House.

I'd get to work about 7, 7:30 and then start a process by which the White House would decide, well, what's the news we want to make today versus what's the news that's coming at us because that's going to be the agenda of the press corps that day and how do you reconcile the two and how do you make some guess over which is going to top the other? Because a successful day for the White House was a day in which the story that we put out there and wanted to drive made the network news that night and was the dominant focus of the press corps that day versus some other storyline that presented us with more risk and less advantageous coverage of our own point of view. . . .

tone. Presidents Bill Clinton and George W. Bush both elicited news coverage that proved more critical than complimentary. Even though it is acknowledged that the press and the political opposition generally defer to the president's proposals during the first few months of an incoming administration (the so-called honeymoon period), Clinton and Bush were not treated kindly by the press during their first hundred days in office. According to a study by the Pew Project for Excellence in Journalism (2009), network news coverage of Bush was more negative than positive by a margin of 6 percent (28 percent negative,

But the press corps would then come into my office in the West Wing and we would sit and go through our schedule, and they would want me to try to react to any breaking news or anything that had happened overnight or if some big news organization had a big story on the front page that day they would want an initial reaction to that story. This was the working briefing. It was off-camera and we did not make a transcript of it. At that first briefing of the day, it was perfectly legitimate for me to say, "I'll do that question at 1 o'clock," because that would then give me time to research what the right answer was.

At some point every morning I would either see Clinton or swing by the Oval Office and kind of walk through my briefing book and say, "Here's what we are going to say about this, that or the other," and he would kind of like dial me one way or the other. If he wanted me to be sharper or more provocative on one point, or usually he would dial me in the other direction and want me to tone it down and not be as pithy or as partisan as probably my own instinct would have had me be. But he kind of got me where he wanted me to be as I articulated an answer. And then

Mike McCurry

when I would give the briefing for the press at 1 o'clock, I would then spend the next hour cleaning up whatever messes I had created or get more information or trying to deal with the immediate aftermath of the briefing, and then just a lot of one-on-one work with reporters to get additional information for them. . . .

And then everybody would kind of watch the news collectively at 6:30 and 7, and that was your report card at the end of the day because either your story made it and you got that out there, or something else came in to dominate the storyline about the White House that day.

Source: From a speech at Stanford University on May 8, 2001. Photo courtesy of Cynthia Johnson/Time Life Pictures/Getty Images.

22 percent positive, 50 percent neutral); and for Clinton, positive and negative reports aired with equal frequency (28 percent negative, 27 percent positive, 45 percent neutral). However, President Obama's news coverage over this same period was more positive than negative by a ratio of 2 to 1 (42 percent positive, 20 percent negative, 38 percent neutral).

The advent of cable outlets with a tendency to slant the news (for example, Fox News), has made it more difficult for partisan leaders with opposing views to get their message out. In 2009, President Obama described Fox News as biased in a CNBC interview with reporter John Harwood, stating, "I've got one television station that is entirely devoted to attacking my administration. . . . That's a pretty big megaphone. You'd be hard-pressed if you watched the entire day to find a positive story about me on that front" (CNBC, 2009). The president's comments were only slightly exaggerated; during his first year in office—a time when most news organizations provided favorable coverage— the ratio of negative to positive reporting on Fox News was 3 to 1. As Obama's communication director, Anita Dunn, pointed out (in an Interview with the *New York Times*), "As they are undertaking a war against Barack Obama and the White House, we don't need to pretend that this is the way that legitimate news organizations behave" (Stelter, 2009).

While media are clearly willing to run critical coverage of the president, overt conflict with the White House is a risky strategy for news organizations because presidents have considerable means at their disposal to retaliate. They may, for instance, refuse to take questions from reporters representing the offending source, provide exclusive interviews with competitors, or deny the offending reporter a front-row seat at major campaign events. The Obama administration punished Fox News, for instance, by excluding *Fox News Sunday* with Chris Wallace from a round of Sunday presidential appearances in September 2009.

The increasingly negative tone of press reports is symptomatic of decreased presidential control over the national press. In response, presidents and their media advisers have pursued alternative media strategies. President Obama, facing a more hostile press corps during his second term, has turned to off-the-record interviews in Washington and frequent speaking trips where he attracts more sympathetic coverage from local and regional news outlets.

Speechmaking

Speechmaking is a relatively recent form of presidential leadership. The framers of the Constitution did not expect the president to interact with the public. They preferred that the president spend the time in office deliberating with Congress and other leaders. During the early days of the republic, presidential speechmaking was limited to formal presentations to Congress.[6]

With the rapid development of radio in the twentieth century and the gradual enfranchisement of adult voters, presidents took to communicating with the public on a regular basis. The use of presidential rhetoric to rally public opinion was pioneered by Teddy Roosevelt, whose frequent appeals for public support proved instrumental in his efforts to persuade Congress to enact significant trustbusting legislation. A few years later, Franklin Roosevelt introduced his *fireside chats*, held before a nationwide radio audience. These were occasions for Roosevelt to explain what his administration intended to do to combat the Depression. He used these addresses to mobilize support for key provisions of his New Deal.[7]

With the advent of television, the audience at the president's command climbed still further. A prime-time speech carried by all three of the networks might reach as many as 60 percent of all American households (see Figure 7.4). The period of the late 1960s—when network television was the dominant media source—is referred to as the "golden age of presidential television" because presidents could count on a massive captive audience for their speeches. Of course, presidents were quick to exploit this opportunity; in 1970 alone, Nixon delivered nine major policy speeches in prime time.

The ability to reach a majority of the American public through prime-time appearances proves especially useful when presidents become embroiled in controversy (see Video Archive 7.1). In the aftermath of revelations that members of his staff had arranged for arms to be sold to Iran and had then diverted the proceeds of the sales to the right-wing Contra rebels in Nicaragua,

Video Archive 7.1
Presidential Speech-making as a Form of Damage Control

FIGURE 7.4

TV Audience for Presidential Addresses, 1971–2014

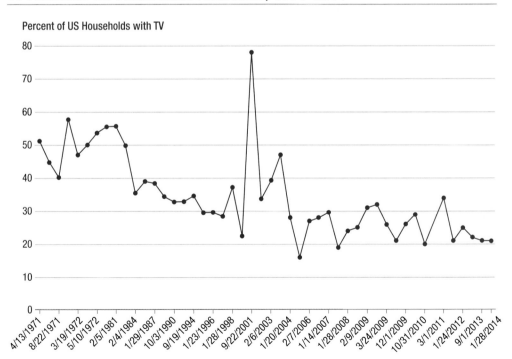

Source: Data from S. Kernell & L. R. Rice, 2011; nielsen.com.

Ronald Reagan delivered a prime-time address assuring the public that he was indeed awake at the steering wheel. Earlier in his term of office, on the day the *Challenger* exploded, causing the deaths of all seven crew members, Reagan both consoled and inspired the nation.

> For the families of the seven, we cannot bear, as you do, the full impact of this tragedy. But we feel the loss, and we're thinking about you so very much. Your loved ones were daring and brave, and they had that special grace, that special spirit that says, "Give me a challenge and I'll meet it with joy." They had a hunger to explore the universe and discover its truths. They wished to serve, and they did. They served all of us. . . . We don't hide our space program. We don't keep secrets and cover things up. We do it all up front and in public. That's the way freedom is, and we wouldn't change it for a minute.

Of course, the golden age of television proved short-lived. With the growth of cable networks, not only did people have the ability to tune out the president, but the commercial pressures on the major networks were sufficient to deter the regular provision of free airtime. Since the advent of cable television, the president's prime-time opportunities are limited to the annual State of the Union address and, on occasion, prepared remarks on a topic of unusual importance (such as President Clinton's apology to the nation for his behavior related to his affair with Monica Lewinsky; the most watched speech given by President Obama concerned the killing of Osama bin Laden in 2011). It is not surprising that the audience for these prime-time addresses is considerably smaller in the post-cable era, averaging around 25 percent of the total television audience. Research by Kernell and Rice (2011) shows that the only people who tune in to televised presidential speeches in the post-cable era are those who support the president. Thus, presidential speechmaking today is equivalent to preaching to the choir. There is very little possibility of the president reaching out to his opponents.

The declining audience for presidential addresses has obvious implications for the television networks. Giving the president free time means they have less opportunity to air profitable entertainment programs. In 2013, facing widespread public criticism over the incompetent rollout of Obamacare and the inability of Americans to sign up at the official website, the president sought to deliver a prime-time address announcing that the problems had been fixed and that 7 million people had signed up for health insurance. The networks declined, claiming that the announcement was insufficiently newsworthy.

Deprived of the captive nationwide audience, presidents have turned to other media venues. Local and regional audiences, particularly those living in critical battleground states, are the new targets of presidential rhetoric. This "narrowcasting" approach to going public is designed to attract favorable coverage in areas that could prove pivotal in the next election.

The behavior of recent presidents reveals the new look of going public. The incumbent increasingly synchronizes his official travel with the reelection campaign. Presidents Bush and Clinton both visited competitive or battleground states more frequently than noncompetitive states during their first terms in office. Clinton made about 75 more trips to competitive states, whereas Bush made about 225. Obama has continued this trend; in his first term, more than half of his domestic travel targeted the thirteen battleground states.

Presidents are especially prone to travel in election years, and they increasingly choose to speak about the state of the economy. Given the importance of economic conditions to voter decision making, the president's election-year speeches typically sound an optimistic note concerning the economy. The frequency of presidential speechmaking also responds to the state of the economy. During periods of economic distress, presidents typically turn up the volume of their economic message.

In sum, speechmaking remains the major form of presidential communication, but presidents have substituted local for national audiences. In the golden age of network television, presidents could count on unmediated access to the whole country, thanks to the programming monopoly enjoyed by the three television networks. Today, with the proliferation of television channels and programming choices, the president is no longer a major draw on national television. In response, presidents have taken to playing local and regional venues. Unlike the more aggressive and skeptical national press corps, local reporters are typically more malleable and willing to accept the tone of the president's rhetoric.

The Press Conference

Like speechmaking, presidents' use of the press conference has evolved in response to the risks and rewards of the medium. When the prime-time audience was there for the taking, the benefits of reaching the entire nation outweighed the risks of appearing before a group of seasoned reporters who were all bent on asking the toughest question. With the loss of the national audience, however, the risks of committing a gaffe or appearing uninformed have deterred modern presidents from holding frequent press conferences.

Before the development of the press conference, presidents generally granted interviews to reporters and editors on an ad hoc basis. Teddy Roosevelt attempted to systematize the process by increasing reporters' access to the White House while maintaining tight control over their stories. Calvin

Coolidge flatly refused to take questions from reporters. Warren G. Harding was willing to take questions, but only if they were submitted in advance.

A more open posture toward the press was the hallmark of the first Franklin Roosevelt (FDR) administration. Under FDR, the press conference became the principal source of news; in fact, FDR still holds the record for the number of scheduled press conferences—more than the combined total of all his successors!

Holding press conferences during prime time was the brainchild of the Kennedy administration. Kennedy's advisers were well aware that Kennedy's telegenic characteristics would impress the audience. When Pierre Salinger (Kennedy's press secretary) first announced the plan, it was met with uniform derision from the press establishment (which was dominated at the time by newspaper reporters). Still, the first-ever televised press conference attracted more than four hundred reporters, and the president's remarks were watched by an audience in excess of 60 million.

Despite the 1960s transformation of the press conference into a television spectacle, the institution has since fallen out of favor. Reporters' interests in catching the president in a moment of spontaneity clash with White House objectives of scripting the president in the best light possible. At press conferences, the risks are high that the president might misspeak or be put on the defensive by a tough line of questioning. Even as accomplished a public speaker as President Reagan stumbled on several occasions, demonstrating that he did not know the answers to important questions, and that his command of the facts was, at best, limited.[8] To be revealed as ignorant on national television, of course, is not likely to impress voters.

To reduce the risks of appearing inept, presidential staff personnel have attempted to choreograph presidents' appearances. Presidents Ford, Carter, and Reagan all staged elaborate dress rehearsals, attempting to fine-tune their answers to anticipated questions. The press office is intimately familiar with most White House reporters and, on the basis of the daily press briefings, can reliably predict what individual reporters might ask. Larry Speakes, press secretary to Reagan, claimed that "out of 30 questions and follow-ups the press would ask, we might fail to anticipate one. And often, we could even predict which reporters were going to ask which questions" (Ansolabehere, Behr, & Iyengar, 1993, p. 114).

The press office often takes advantage of journalistic competition by planting questions. The term *planting* refers to the practice of getting a pliable reporter to ask a softball question provided by the White House. In exchange, the reporter might be awarded a significant journalistic coup (such as an exclusive interview with the First Lady). Although it is difficult to demonstrate the frequency of planted questions, it is generally accepted that all administrations engage in the practice. Planting questions was fairly common during the Eisenhower and Johnson administrations; Eisenhower's press secretary often received questions in advance from reporters, allowing the president to call on a specific reporter and deliver a prepared answer. President Johnson is said to have instructed his staff to arrange a press conference in which all the questions were planted.

A clearer case of planted questions, though not in a national press conference, occurred in December 1990 during a telephone question-and-answer session between President George H. W. Bush and newspaper reporters in Southern California. Not realizing that his microphone was live, the president complained aloud that one of the questions was not "in the right order." In another instance illustrating White House influence over press conferences, President George W. Bush recognized a relatively unknown Web journalist (Jeff Gannon) in the first national press conference after his reelection in 2004. The question Mr. Gannon put to President Bush was not exactly objective:

> Senate Democratic leaders have painted a very bleak picture of the U.S. economy. Harry Reid was talking about soup lines and Hillary Clinton was talking about the economy being on the verge of collapse. Yet, in the same breath, they say that Social Security is rock solid and there's no crisis there. You've said you're going to reach out to these people. How are you going to work with people who seem to have divorced themselves from reality? (CNN, 2005)

Even with all the preparation, however, press conferences can prove damaging to the president's image. Perhaps the most extreme case of presidential blundering occurred during a Reagan press conference held in early 1987 after disclosure of the Iran–Contra scandal. The president's answers to the questions were so frequently confused and inaccurate (for example, he indicated that Israel had not been involved in the transaction) that the press office took the unprecedented step of issuing a news release immediately after the conference—even before the networks had concluded their coverage—clarifying the president's remarks.

Recent presidents have adopted several routines to help bolster their performance at press conferences. They typically make an opening statement in the hope of setting the agenda for reporters' questions. They may also schedule the event on short notice. The most extreme case of this tactic was one occasion in which President Johnson held a press conference without notice to reporters, addressing only those who happened to be present in the White House press room at the time. Presidents have also taken to sharing the spotlight by holding joint press conferences (usually with a visiting foreign leader). This approach not only shifts the burden of performance from the president, but it also permits the administration to present the image of a unified front.

Despite their considerable ability to stage-manage the event that is afforded them by their position, presidents have concluded that the risks of frequent press conferences outweigh the benefits. As noted in Chapter 3, reporters have become savvier about officials' efforts to spin the news and have reacted by adopting a more adversarial approach. This applies to press conferences as well; the number of hostile questions asked during televised press conferences has increased significantly over time (Clayman, Elliot, Heritage, & Beckett, 2010; Clayman, Elliot, Heritage, & McDonald, 2007). The overall trend is one of fewer press conferences per month. Although Bush Sr. held more conferences than any of his predecessors while in office, most of the occasions were reserved for discussion of foreign affairs, a subject on which Bush was especially authoritative. Naturally, the press office sought to minimize Bush's exposure to tough questions on domestic issues; between 1989 and 1991 Bush answered a total of four questions on AIDS and two questions on the widespread bankruptcy of savings and loan institutions.

When we compare the frequency of solo press conferences with joint appearances (usually with a visiting head of state), the aversion of recent presidents to the media spotlight is quite clear (see Figure 7.5). Since the first President Bush, all presidents have taken to sharing the stage. The average number of solo press conferences has declined precipitously. President Obama, in his first term, went seven months without holding a press conference, the longest interval in ten years.

In short, the recent history of the presidential press conference illustrates the fundamental tension in the relationship between the national press and the president. Reporters crave information, particularly information that is objective and free of political spin or distortion. Presidents demand control over the story. Today, in the era of interpretive reporting, the risks of critical news coverage have come to outweigh the benefits of television exposure, especially in the era of consumer choice when presidents no longer command vast audiences. As a result, the frequency of the presidential press conference has decreased dramatically.

Alternatives to the Press Conference

Instead of subjecting themselves to the entire White House press corps, presidents often negotiate appearances on individual television programs or grant interviews to small groups of reporters. President Reagan granted more than two hundred private interviews to reporters during his first term.

FIGURE 7.5

Solo and Joint Presidential Press Conferences

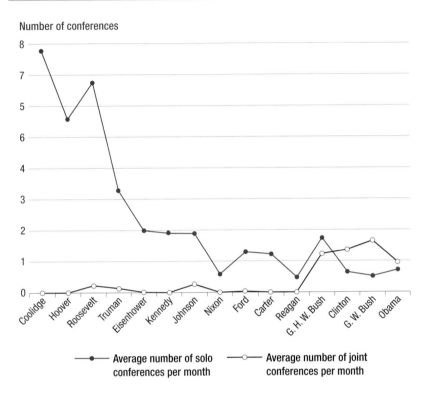

Number of conferences

Legend:
— Average number of solo conferences per month
— Average number of joint conferences per month

Source: Based on data compiled by Professor Martha Kumar.

Question-and-answer sessions with local reporters (sometimes referred to as end runs) are particularly rewarding from the administration's perspective because local reporters are more easily impressed than their Washington counterparts are.

As in the case of the press conference, presidents have increasingly reduced their availability for press questioning. One occasion on which presidents are expected to take questions is when a pool of journalists is brought to the White House to cover some official event such as the president meeting with a foreign leader. These *pool sprays*, provide reporters with a rare opportunity to catch the president off script, but in recent years, their questions have been increasingly ignored. During his first year in office, President Obama answered only 47 questions during these sessions. His predecessor responded to 147 questions during his first year. Bush and Obama were both less accessible than President Clinton, who answered 252 impromptu questions in his first year.[9]

When the White House loses control over the message, as is the case during major scandals (such as the affair between Clinton and Monica Lewinsky) or policy debacles (such as the Enron collapse and the failed rollout of Obamacare), the president may be forced to engage in a variety of fire-extinguishing maneuvers. Such measures might include scheduling newsworthy events on diversionary issues (for example, inviting injured servicemen to the White House for an awards ceremony) or enlisting popular celebrities to promote an unpopular program. In the aftermath of widespread press ridicule over the inability of the Department of Health and Human Services to host a website capable of enrolling Americans seeking health insurance, the White House asked NBA superstar LeBron James to appear in a YouTube public service announcement encouraging people to enroll. Two other basketball legends—Earvin "Magic" Johnson and Alonzo Mourning—appeared in infomercials produced by the government. Simultaneously, a number of other celebrities promoted the law on Twitter, urging their followers to enroll (#GetCovered). On other occasions, the president may attempt to seize the initiative by making a solo appearance on a highly rated news program. In the aftermath of the invasion of Iraq and the failure to discover Iraqi weapons of mass destruction, for example, President Bush decided to appear on *Meet the Press* to defend the administration's actions and explain the many inconsistencies between his prewar and postwar rhetoric.

Sometimes the White House responds to press criticism more combatively, by attempting to repudiate particular reports or questioning the motives of the reporter or outlet. We have already described the back and forth between the Obama White House and Fox News. The second Bush White House responded to a CBS News report on the president's National Guard service by calling into question Dan Rather's objectivity (Rather had once spoken at a Democratic fund-raiser) and journalistic competence. In the face of these attacks on Rather's objectivity—as well as a firestorm of criticism for its sloppy reporting—CBS decided to postpone until after the 2004 election a *60 Minutes* segment investigating the Bush administration's claims concerning Iraqi weapons of mass destruction.

At other times, the president enlists members of the press to deliver the message on his behalf. The George W. Bush administration paid at least three conservative syndicated columnists to promote their policy agenda. Armstrong Williams, a syndicated columnist and cable television pundit, was paid $240,000 to write columns and make speeches extolling the virtues of No Child Left Behind, the administration's signature education policy. Maggie Gallagher and Michael McManus, both syndicated columnists, were paid

IN FOCUS

Three Principal Forms of Presidential Communication

- Attracting news coverage.
- Making speeches.
- Holding press conferences.

$41,500 and $53,000, respectively, to promote Bush's marriage policies, which included redirecting welfare money to pay for abstinence education and an initiative that limited marriage to unions between a man and a woman only.

Another layer of covert presidential public relations agents are retired military officers. The *New York Times* revealed that during the run-up to the invasion of Iraq in 2002, the Pentagon recruited several former high-ranking military officials to serve as *message force multipliers* who could be counted on to repeat the administration's story line on television news programs where these officials served as paid analysts. They were given special access to Pentagon information in exchange for their efforts to provide commentary in favor of the war.

Overall, there can be no denying the inherent newsworthiness of the presidency. Presidents are not so much subjects of news coverage as they are sources of news about the actions of the federal government. Presidential media management is essentially a process of spoon-feeding: the president gives a speech or holds a press conference, and reporters write stories about what the president had to say. The president stages a photo opportunity with a visiting foreign dignitary, and images of the two leaders appear on the evening news. Of course, as we will demonstrate in Chapter 8, the power to shape the news is tantamount to shaping the public's perceptions of the president.

THE PUBLIC CONGRESSPERSON

The president is not alone in seeking to use the media for political gain. Everyone else in Washington plays the same game. However, members of Congress find it more difficult to achieve media leverage because there are so many of them, each promoting a different story or angle. Reporters are much more likely to gravitate to a story that can be personalized and that offers a clean story line. Reports on parliamentary procedures or legislative protocol typically do not meet the requirements of appropriateness, making it difficult for journalists to put the legislative branch in the spotlight.

COMMITTEE HEARINGS

Committee hearings provide the best opportunity for congressional media coverage. The subject matter is timely, the number of congressional participants is relatively small, and in many cases the witnesses who appear have considerable star power. As early as the 1950s, congressional hearings attracted national television coverage. The first televised hearings were organized by Senator Estes Kefauver's special Senate committee investigating the influence of organized crime. Shortly thereafter, Senator Joseph McCarthy's hearings on security lapses at military installations (the Army–McCarthy hearings) became big news and led eventually to the end of McCarthy's crusade to root out American communists. In the 1970s, the spotlight was directed at the House Judiciary Committee proceedings to consider the impeachment of President Nixon. By the late 1970s, it was clear that regular television coverage of Congress would facilitate the policy and electoral interests of members and also enable the public to monitor the actions of their representatives. C-SPAN coverage of the House began in 1977, followed by Senate coverage in 1986.

Even though hearings provide committee members much-needed national exposure, the fact that legislative committees represent a wide range of political preferences makes it difficult for Congress to compete with the president. Whereas the White House provides a solo speaker, congressional committees represent a chorus. The famous Hill–Thomas hearings provide a striking case of the more confused nature of the congressional message.

In 1991, President George H. W. Bush nominated Clarence Thomas for the US Supreme Court. Senate Democrats had challenged the nomination on a number of grounds, including Thomas's weak judicial credentials, his stance on abortion, and his record as head of the Equal Employment Opportunity Commission (EEOC). When a young African American college professor (Anita Hill) publicly accused Thomas of sexual harassment, the possibility of lukewarm support from within the black community appeared to doom the nomination. The confrontation, featuring sexually explicit material, made for dramatic television (see Video Archive 7.2). On the first day (a Friday) the television audience numbered 30 million viewers. Over the following weekend, the networks cut away to their regularly scheduled sports programming, leaving PBS to cover the hearings. The interest in the controversy was so intense that PBS

Video Archive 7.2
The 1991 Hill–Thomas Hearings

achieved its largest audience ever; more people watched the hearings than watched college football, the baseball playoffs, or the NFL.

Despite the intense and potentially damaging media coverage, Thomas was confirmed. Opponents of the nomination had no common argument. Some Democrats took issue with his pro-life stance; others singled out his handling of age discrimination cases at the EEOC, the ambiguity of his testimony, or his lack of judicial experience. On the other hand, the president offered a succinct defense of his nominee as a deserving minority candidate who had acquired his credentials through effort and hard work. Against this simple theme of mainstream American individualism, the Democratic message—"Some of us think he's not qualified. Some of us don't like him because he may not be pro-choice. Some of us think he lied to us. And some of us think he's just fine."—was no match (Ansolabehere, Behr, & Iyengar, 1991, p. 119).

A textbook case of a legislative leader's exercise of going public was provided by Republican congressman Newt Gingrich in 1994. Realizing the importance of a unified and defining message for Republican candidates, Gingrich drafted a ten-point "Contract with America" representing the conservative legislative agenda of House Republicans. Each agenda item was given an appropriately catchy label ("Fiscal Responsibility Act," "American Dream Restoration Act," etc.). The contract was signed by 433 of the 435 Republican candidates running for the House in 1994. In effect, Gingrich nationalized the 1994 elections by providing each Republican candidate with a common theme.

Although it is hard to know just how much the contract influenced voters, the results of the 1994 election were spectacular: the Republicans picked up more than 50 seats and became the majority party in the House for the first time since 1954. Gingrich himself became the House Speaker, but his efforts to implement the provisions of the contract met with mixed success. President Clinton vetoed most of the bills, others became the basis of protracted budget disputes (some of which shut down the federal government), and still others were watered down before being passed. Nevertheless, in a testament to the perceived effectiveness of the Republicans' 1994 strategy, House Democrats in 2004 considered a similar statement of intent, designed to help them reclaim their majority status. As one Democratic leadership aide put it, "We're recognizing that in a world of sound bites we really are far behind and we're playing catch-up. We're trying to come up with a very succinct way of explaining who we are and what we stand for" (Billings, 2004).

Congress can generate substantial media attention when it subpoenas athletes and celebrities to committee hearings. In March 2005, an all-star roster of baseball players were grilled over steroid use in Major League Baseball. Later, one of the star witnesses, pitcher Roger Clemens, was indicted on charges of

Video Archive 7.3
MLB Steroid Hearings

lying to Congress. Dr. Phil, the well-known television host, testified on cyber-bullying in 2010.

In the era of divided government, congressional hearings are increasingly used to highlight the deficiencies of presidential leadership. The IRS's attempt to audit the tax returns of conservative groups and the attack on the US consulate in Benghazi were both exploited to the fullest extent by congressional Republicans eager to depict the Obama administration as either incompetent or unprincipled.

Finally, hearings also give congresspersons the opportunity to vent collective anger at individuals or government agencies and hence to portray themselves as on the side of their constituents. Although Congress had in fact failed to exercise oversight of the Mineral Management Service, and therefore bore considerable responsibility for the 2010 Gulf oil spill, the subsequent congressional hearings gave incumbents ample opportunity to ignore their own lack of oversight at the expense of BP CEO Tony Hayward.

Despite the media opportunities provided by hearings, the fact remains that Congress is much less newsworthy than the presidency. In fact, the vast majority of congressional hearings are treated as routine events and ignored by the media. It requires unusual circumstances and high-profile witnesses for these events to warrant media attention.

POLICY VERSUS ELECTORAL GOALS

Political scientists generally assume that the overriding aspiration of all legislators is political survival or reelection. A secondary aspiration is moving up the legislative hierarchy and becoming known as an effective legislator with high-profile committee memberships or leadership assignments. In the premedia days, congressional representatives worked their way up the career ladder by acquiring seniority, and by currying favor with party and committee leaders (which meant obediently voting the party line). Today the road to legislative success is much more likely to include maintaining a media profile. Congressional press secretaries are now ubiquitous; their principal role is to flood the media with daily press releases claiming credit for Congressperson X's legislative accomplishments.

In line with their career objectives, legislators typically seek out two forms of press coverage. First, they hope to attract attention for their legislative performance: sponsoring important legislation, shepherding bills through the intricacies of the legislative process, eventually getting bills enacted into law, and—most importantly—their success in obtaining federal funds for local projects (typically referred to as "pork"). Recent research demonstrates that the ability to deliver federal funds is an important electoral asset for legislators and that voters are especially likely to approve of incumbents who deliver multiple projects (Grimmer, Messing, & Westwood, 2012).

Policy or performance coverage is more likely to come from the national press or from regional outlets with full-time Washington correspondents. We noted earlier that Congress was on a par with the presidency in the pages of the *New York Times* until the 1970s; most of this coverage focused on substantive issues (civil rights legislation, the Great Society programs, the War on Poverty, etc.). National media recognition is likely to boost a congressperson's reputation and leads to increased influence with party leaders.

National reports dealing with matters of public policy are unlikely to reach a congressperson's home district or state, however. The goal of reelection can best be served by local news. Most local television stations do not have full-time Washington correspondents. Instead, they subscribe to a video wire service that feeds cookie-cutter reports to multiple stations across the country. Wire services have a strong economic incentive to provide congressional news with a local angle because they are paid by the report. Members of Congress can take advantage of this system by creating an appropriate local angle—by inviting local VIPs to testify at committee hearings or by holding a press conference to announce the funding of local programs.

Of course, members of Congress with legislative influence are better able to attract local coverage. In Arnold's 2004 study of newspaper coverage, members of Congress holding leadership positions were assigned substantially more print coverage than were rank-and-file members. Newspapers also assigned greater coverage to more-senior legislators.

Which of the two branches of Congress is better able to generate news? The smaller size of the Senate, coupled with the greater prestige of the office, grants senators a distinct advantage. In Tim Cook's (1998) comparative study, almost all senators (90 percent) were interviewed on network news at least once; for House members, only one-third were given similar treatment.

One form of notoriety that members of Congress would do well to avoid is involvement in scandal or being the target of ethics-related investigations. To be the subject of an investigation is to be featured in the news. In the past four years, US Representatives Thad Viers, David Wu, Mark Souder, Chris Lee, Anthony Weiner, and Eric Massa all resigned their seats following revelations that they had engaged in inappropriate behavior with women. Moreover, reporters seem inclined to test the hypothesis that congresspersons implicated in ethics violations are vulnerable at the polls; coverage of the allegations therefore usually continues well into the campaign (Arnold, 2004, p. 47). For instance, the 2006 Republican primary for the House seat held by

Texas Congressman Tom DeLay attracted significant press coverage because of his resignation from his position as House majority leader in the aftermath of allegations that he had violated campaign finance regulations.

The ability to attract news depends not only on the degree to which members of Congress "make news," but also on the nature of the media market in the areas that they represent. In Los Angeles or New York, an individual representative rarely makes the news, simply because the competition for coverage is too intense; to give one of the seventeen Los Angeles–area House members a story in the *Los Angeles Times* is bound to generate complaints of favoritism from the remaining sixteen. When the *Times* has provided such coverage, it has generally been buried in the metro rather than the national section (Arnold, 2004, p. 67).

The problem is especially acute in broadcast news. Local newscasts in the Los Angeles area rarely mention a congressperson by name, because then they would be obliged to provide coverage of all the others in their viewing area. In Vinson's 2003 study of Los Angeles local news, not a single congressional representative or senator appeared in the news over a four-week period. Thus, *incongruent media markets*—areas where a media outlet is shared by multiple elected officials (the classic case is New York City, where media serve residents of three different states)—generate fewer local reports on incumbent legislators.

Members of Congress who attract media attention by virtue of their constituency service or their legislative accomplishments can be said to have earned their publicity. In other cases, however, a congressional representative can elicit news coverage on nonsubstantive grounds, either by staging an event with considerable human interest (such as Ohio Congressman Tony Hall's twenty-two-day hunger fast in 1993, aimed at drawing attention to the problem of hunger in the United States) or by exploiting the media's penchant for covering stories involving sex, sleaze, or scandal. Former Senator Arlen Specter (of Pennsylvania) earned a justifiable reputation as the tabloid king of Congress. In 1985, while presiding over a subcommittee investigating the effects of pornography on women, Specter called Linda Lovelace, Veronica Vera, and Seka—all famous pornographic movie actresses—as key witnesses. Of course, the hearings attracted more reporters than any other Washington event that day.

In sum, elected officials' ability to lead depends increasingly on their public image. Presidents and members of Congress invest heavily in efforts to attract media coverage and to shape the media message. Favorable coverage is seen as contributing to public approval, and public approval is thought to strengthen the official's hand in Washington. In comparison with Congress, the president enjoys significant media advantages: the presidential office is the classic authoritative source, and the president is one person rather than an impersonal institution. Legislators can also generate news, but their multiple messages often amount to a confusing jumble, making it difficult for them to compete with the executive branch's message of the day.

When reporters prove less than malleable, the White House often resorts to old-fashioned public relations. In several recent instances, federal agencies provided video news releases having the appearance of a news report, distributing them as news items to local television stations across the country. In the case of one such news release plugging the 2004 Medicare prescription drug plan, the announcer signed off as "Karen Ryan reporting from Washington."[10] This particular video appeared in more than fifty different local newscasts. In the effort to promote No Child Left Behind, the federal government retained Ketchum Communications, a leading public relations firm, to produce video material and recruited Armstrong Williams, a conservative commentator, as the spokesperson for the legislative initiative.[11]

THE RISE OF ISSUE ADVERTISING

The president and members of Congress are not the only media players. The identical strategy of making and shaping the news is pursued by the vast army of interest groups intent on influencing public policy. During policy debates, it is not unusual for organized interests on either side to take to the airwaves in an effort to signal their position. The "Harry and Louise" ad campaign successfully mobilized opposition to the Clinton healthcare reform package in 1993 (the American Health Security Act). The ads featured a middle-class couple who spoke out against the Clinton plan on the grounds that it would create a massive bureaucracy. At the time the ads appeared (September 1993), Americans supported the Clinton plan by a 2-to-1 margin. After approximately $15 million worth of exposure to Harry and Louise (concentrated in Washington, DC, and a few other markets), the Clinton proposals suffered a substantial erosion of public support.

The passage of the Affordable Care Act in early 2010 sparked the onset of a second major advertising campaign focusing on healthcare. The ads were exclusively negative in tone and aired by conservative groups hoping to persuade Congress to roll back the legislation. Between May 2010 and June 2013, interest groups such as the Chamber of Commerce spent $475 million worth of advertising on ads attacking the law.[12]

Interest groups air ads not because they think the advertising will persuade decision makers. Rather, they hope to get the attention of the news media and frame the policy debate in terms of their own choosing. In the case of the "Harry and Louise" campaign, the story line in each ad—the creation of a bloated healthcare bureaucracy—became the story line in the press and the rallying cry of the Republican opponents. The ads became even more newsworthy when President Clinton and the First Lady attempted to rebut them. In the end, the reform bill was voted down, sending First Lady Hillary Clinton into involuntary retirement as the administration's point person for healthcare reform.

The effectiveness of the original "Harry and Louise" campaign in 1993 has prompted multiple repeat appearances by the couple. In an ironic role reversal, Harry and Louise reappeared in 1998 and in 2009, but this time on behalf of people without health insurance. In 1998, the couple lamented the epidemic of uninsured families and lent their support to a plan that offered government health insurance vouchers for low-income groups. In 2009, they urged Congress to pass the Affordable Care Act.[13]

Issue advertising has also played a major role in the ongoing efforts to regulate the tobacco industry. In 1998 the US Senate defeated a bill that would have raised the tax on a pack of cigarettes by more than a dollar and granted the federal Food and Drug Administration wide regulatory authority over all tobacco products. The bill also would have imposed restrictions on cigarette advertising. Manufacturers would have been subject to stiff financial penalties if youth smoking rates did not decrease to specified levels over the coming years. The tobacco companies launched a major advertising offensive against the bill. Invoking a familiar Republican theme, the ads suggested that the cigarette tax was just another case of Washington's tax-and-spend appetite. The convenience store industry (which derives most of its revenue from cigarette sales) also weighed in, claiming that the bill would amount to a "devastating disaster" for family-owned convenience stores. Framing the bill as a tax increase and harmful to small business not only had the effect of weakening public support for the legislation but also helped create a defensible cover story for Republicans voting against the bill.

As the healthcare reform and tobacco legislation cases both illustrate, issue advertising is the modern version of old-fashioned lobbying. Interest groups in favor of and opposed to policy legislation relay their preferences to policy makers in the form of television ads. As soon as the gun-control advocacy group funded by former New York City Mayor Michael Bloomberg began airing ads during the 2014 election calling for stricter gun-control legislation (featuring the testimony of several parents who had lost a child in the Sandy Hook Elementary School killings), the National Rifle Association responded in kind with ads featuring survivors of violent crime who argued in favor of their right to carry concealed weapons so as not to be "defenseless." (These and other recent cases of issue advertising are illustrated in Video Archives 7.5 and 7.6.)

Unlike conventional lobbying, which is aimed exclusively at public officials, issue advertising is designed to influence both elite and mass opinion. By framing the Clinton healthcare proposals as attempts to create healthcare by bureaucracy, the 1993 Republican ad campaign stirred up public opposition to the bills, thus providing wavering or undecided members of Congress the impetus to join the opposition. In the debate over Social Security, supporters of President Bush's private retirement accounts hoped to persuade Republican-leaning members of AARP[14] to desert, thus weakening AARP's influence with Democratic legislators.

Video Archive 7.5
Issue Ads For and Against Gun Control

Video Archive 7.6
Issue Ads For and Against Supreme Court Nominees

CONCLUSION

The power of elected officials to govern depends increasingly on their public image. The number of people who support the president is a key barometer of the president's persuasiveness in Washington, and maintaining a high level of popularity requires close attention to the media. Presidents and their advisers strive to capitalize on the inherent newsworthiness of presidential events, speeches, and press conferences to focus the media spotlight on success stories, while avoiding reference to issues or outcomes that cast aspersions on the president's leadership. In recent years, speeches have replaced press conferences as the president's principal media opportunity because they provide the president with more control over the message and minimize his exposure to difficult questions from reporters intent on scrutinizing the president's claims. In general, cost-benefit media management has become central to effective governing.

The focus on using media relations to maintain a high level of public approval is not without cost. At the very least, the time and effort devoted to working the press detracts from elected leaders' ability to develop and implement policy initiatives. Moreover, the fear of alienating public opinion may be additional disincentive for leaders to tackle difficult problems that may require the prescription of bitter medicine (such as higher taxes). These and other ways in which going public affects the policy process are described in Chapter 10.

SUMMARY

1. Going public is a strategy used by presidents and other political actors to promote their policies by appealing to the American public for support. Given the overriding importance of reelection to the strategic calculations of elected officials, a president's popularity creates an important bargaining advantage; a president who enjoys a high level of public approval can often count on being able to persuade a few members of the opposition.

2. The effects of a president's popularity on the ability to garner legislative support are most evident when the president's proposals address issues that are salient to the public but concern subject matter about which the public possesses little information (such as the best way to combat terrorism).

3. The White House media complex has become a vast operation, with sixty-nine full-time employees and five distinct organizational branches. Two of the main players are the communications director and the press secretary:
   - The communications director, who seeks to define and market the president's image, is responsible for overseeing the production and release of information throughout the administration.
   - The press secretary, who conducts daily press briefings for the White House press corps, must walk a fine line between meeting the political objectives of the White House staff (spin and more spin) and maintaining personal credibility with the media.

4. Presidents have three distinct media opportunities: attracting news coverage, making speeches, and holding press conferences.
   - Given reporters' reliance on official sources, the president can count on regular and sustained news coverage from all forms of news media.
   - In response to the increased negativity of news coverage and the decrease in the size of the audience for national television appearances, presidential speeches around the country have become more common as presidents hope to attract more sympathetic coverage from local and regional news outlets.
   - With the decrease in size of the national audience, presidents have lost the incentive to make themselves available for tough questioning by the press; the risks of holding press conferences—committing a gaffe or appearing uninformed—have led presidents to increasingly abandon this form of public communication.

5. As alternatives to the three main approaches to gaining exposure in the media, presidents often negotiate appearances on individual television programs or grant interviews to small groups of reporters (preferably local reporters, who are more easily impressed and controlled than their Washington colleagues are). These strategies are particularly useful and common when the White House has lost control over the message, as is the case during major scandals.

6. Like the president, members of Congress seek to use the media for political gain, with two particular goals: reelection and moving up within the legislative hierarchy. Members of Congress (particularly in the House of Representatives) find it much more difficult to garner media attention than the president does, however, because there are so many of them and each is promoting a different story or angle, and because legislative dynamics do not make for clean, easily explicated story lines.

7. Legislators typically seek out two forms of press coverage. First, with the aim of boosting their reputation and increasing influence with party leaders, they hope to attract attention from national and important regional news outlets. Second, with the goal of reelection in mind, they target local news in their home districts.

8. Interest groups intent on influencing public policy pursue the same strategies that elected officials use for making and shaping the news. During policy debates, organized interests on either side often take their case to the airwaves, with the aim of framing the policy debate in terms of their own choosing and garnering public support for their position.

FURTHER READINGS

Arnold, R. D. (2004). *Congress, the press, and political accountability*. Princeton, NJ: Princeton University Press.

Auletta, K. (2004, January 19). Fortress Bush: How the White House keeps the press under control. *The New Yorker*. Retrieved March 28, 2006, from www.newyorker.com/fact/content/?040119fa_fact2.

Baum, M. A., & Kernell, S. (1999). Has cable ended the golden age of presidential television? *American Political Science Review, 93*, 99–114.

Canes-Wrone, B., & de Marchi, S. (2002). Presidential approval and legislative success. *Journal of Politics, 64*, 491–509.

Charnock, J. E., McCann, J. A., & Tenpas, K. D. (2009). Presidential travel from Eisenhower to George W. Bush: An electoral college strategy. *Political Science Quarterly, 124*, 323–339.

Cook, T. E. (1998). *Governing with the news: The news media as a political institution*. Chicago: University of Chicago Press.

Grimmer, J., Messing, S., & Westwood, S. J. (2012). How words and money cultivate a personal vote: The effect of legislator credit claiming on constituent credit allocation. *American Political Science Review, 106*, 703–719.

Kernell, S. (1986). *Going public: New strategies of presidential leadership*. Washington, DC: Congressional Quarterly Press.

Kumar, M. J. (2003). The White House and the press: News organizations as a presidential resource and as a source of pressure. *Presidential Studies Quarterly, 33*, 669–683.

McClellan, S. (2008). *What happened inside the Bush White House and Washington's culture of deception*. New York: Public Affairs.

Tulis, J. K. (1987). *The rhetorical presidency*. Chatham, NJ: Chatham House.

Wildavsky, A. (1991). The two presidencies. In S. Shull (Ed.), *The two presidencies: A quarter century assessment* (pp. 11–25). Chicago: Nelson-Hall.

NOTES

1. The fifth office (Speechwriting) is entrusted with drafting the president's speeches and public remarks.

2. According to the *New York Times* columnist William Safire, the bags were in fact empty.

3. Mike McCurry served as President Clinton's press secretary from 1995 to 1998. Before that, he served as spokesperson for the Department of State from 1993 to 1995, and as director of communications for the Democratic National Committee from 1988 to 1990.

4. The *New York Times* data quoted throughout this discussion come from the Policy Agendas Project (2010) at the University of Texas. The data were originally collected by Frank R. Baumgartner and Bryan D. Jones, with the support of National Science Foundation (NSF) grant number SBR 9320922, and were distributed through the Center for American Politics and Public Policy at the University of Washington and/or the Department of Political Science at Pennsylvania State University. Neither NSF nor the original collectors of the data bear any responsibility for the analysis reported here.

5. The 20 percent figure is based on the assumption that a typical network newscast includes between twenty and twenty-five reports.

6. In fact, one of the articles of impeachment brought against President Andrew Johnson alleged excessive use of rhetoric. Specifically, he was accused of "intemperate, inflammatory and scandalous harangues ... [and of being] unmindful of the high duties of his office and the dignities and proprieties thereof" (Tulis, 1987, p. 91).

7. Roosevelt broadcast thirty fireside chats between 1933 and 1944.

8. As we noted earlier, President Reagan's fondness for off-the-cuff remarks led the White House to implement the Deaver rule (named for Michael Deaver, the president's communications director), which stipulated that no reporter was permitted to ask Reagan questions during photo opportunities. The networks initially threatened to boycott these sessions if the rule was enforced, but NBC capitulated immediately and within two days the rule was in force.

9. These statistics were compiled by Professor Martha Kumar.

10. Ms. Ryan was a public relations specialist on contract to the Department of Health and Human Services.

11. The political fallout from the Armstrong Williams and fake news release episodes included a warning from the Government Accountability Office (the investigative arm of Congress) that federal agencies must clearly disclose that they paid their spokespersons or "reporters." The warning went on to state, "While agencies generally have the right to disseminate information about their policies and activities, agencies may not use appropriated funds to produce or distribute prepackaged news stories intended to be viewed by television audiences that conceal or do not clearly identify to the audience that the agency was the source of these materials" (Kornblut, 2005).

12. Source: Kantar Media, June 5, 2013.

13. Not content with their work in the health field, the couple has also starred in ad campaigns addressing other issues. In 1998, they appeared in ads that opposed government restrictions on the export of US encryption technology (on behalf of US technology companies). Later, in a 2002 ad campaign aired in Utah and Washington State, the couple spoke out in favor of human cloning (and in opposition to the Bush administration's efforts to ban cloning).

14. Originally called the American Association of Retired Persons, this organization now goes by just its initials: AARP.

8

News and Public Opinion

Despite politicians' fixation on their public image as presented by the media, the conventional wisdom in academic circles until quite recently has been that the media's influence on public opinion is somewhere between weak and nonexistent. Communication scholars have long bought into the doctrine of *minimal consequences*.

What can explain the astounding divergence between the observed behavior of practitioners and the judgment of scholars? The paradox of so much media campaigning with so little apparent effect is, in part, a question of definition. Communication scholars initially conceptualized media effects simply as changes in voter preference; no other outcomes were recognized as evidence of media influence. Against this standard, evidence that campaigns reinforced rather than altered voters' preexisting partisan sentiments was taken as a symptom of minimal effects.

Over time, researchers began to incorporate other measures of influence instead of relying simply on evidence of change in voter preference. When additional indicators were included in research studies—for example, changes in the prominence of particular political issues and in the weight ascribed to particular issues in evaluations of candidates—the effects of media campaigns quickly became more apparent.

The earlier verdict that mass media exerted minimal consequences on public opinion was a result not only of a limited definition of *effects*, but also of a methodological artifact. As in all social scientific fields, there is more than one possible approach to studying a phenomenon of interest (in this case the political effects of media on citizens). The doctrine of minimal consequences was predicated on decades of survey research. Unfortunately, survey research simply lacks the power to detect evidence of influence, because it cannot assess causation. More recent scholarship has increasingly turned to experimental methods, which, unlike survey research, provide unequivocal evidence of causal impact.

To illustrate the difference between the powers of survey and experimental methods, consider, for example, a scholar who wants to find out whether watching a negative campaign advertisement has any influence on voter turnout. In this case, intention to vote is the *dependent variable*, the variable that the researcher believes might hinge on or be influenced by some other, *independent variable*, such as watching the negative campaign ad. The researcher can use either surveys or experiments to investigate whether the independent variable (watching the negative campaign ad) has any effect on the dependent variable (intention to vote). For a survey, the researcher might select a representative sample of citizens and ask them whether they saw the negative campaign ad and whether they intended to vote. For an experiment, the researcher might select a group of citizens, show half of them—selected at random—the ad while showing no ad (or a positive ad) to the other half, and afterward ask the citizens in both groups whether they intend to vote.

Both research methods (surveys and experiments) have strengths and weaknesses, which we will discuss in detail. In short, though, experiments are especially powerful for detecting causation. By contrast, surveys lack the ability to detect causation, but their results can be generalized more easily to larger populations.

Unlike other areas of mass communication, such as marketing, the field of political communication (particularly in its earlier years) relied predominantly on survey research. For reasons that we will discuss, surveys are notoriously imprecise instruments for detecting media or campaign effects. As soon as scholars increased the power of their methodology by turning to experimentation and more elaborate survey designs, the balance of evidence turned in the direction of maximal rather than minimal consequences. Thus any account of the development of research on media effects must cover both changing conceptualizations of media influence and advances in the methodologies employed in mass communication research.

CONCEPTUALIZATIONS OF MEDIA INFLUENCE

Serious research into the effects of mass communication can be dated to about the 1930s, following the large-scale spread of radio. Political events in Europe, most notably the rapid development of extremist political parties in Germany and Italy, prompted widespread speculation that public opinion could easily be swayed by demagoguery or xenophobic appeals. To horrified observers in the

United States, Hitler and Mussolini appeared to be the products of effective propaganda. If the Nazis and Fascists could move public opinion so successfully, might the American public be equally susceptible to extremist appeals? Answers to these questions were of considerable interest to senior administrators in the US Department of Defense (DOD), who in the late 1940s commissioned a series of studies to understand the dynamics of propaganda campaigns.

The DOD-sponsored research was carried out by a group of social psychologists at Yale University. The leader of the group, Carl Hovland, was one of the founding fathers of the field of media effects. Hovland's team designed a series of experiments to identify the conditions under which people might be persuaded to change their positions on social and personal issues (Hovland, Janis, & Kelley, 1953; Hovland, Lumsdaine, & Sheffield, 1949). Their research program, which remains a backbone of the literature on media effects, was guided by an overarching analytic framework known as *message learning theory*. Attitude change, according to this theory, depends on source (who), message (what), and receiver (whom) factors (which will be discussed in more detail later in this chapter).

While developing the essential ingredients of message learning theory, Hovland's team was especially interested in DOD movies that were meant either to encourage young men to enlist or to boost civilian morale. Through experimental research they found that although the films were informative, they generally failed to shift attitudes toward the war or willingness to volunteer for military service. Thus, the team concluded that concerns over the power of propaganda seemed unfounded.

After World War II, scholars turned their attention to the persuasive effects of political campaigns. Social scientists at Columbia University and the University of Michigan undertook large-scale survey studies of attitude change over the course of several presidential campaigns, expecting to find widespread political conversion (Republicans deciding to vote Democratic or vice versa) resulting from campaign messages. The survey evidence, however, showed no traces of last-minute shifts in opinion. In fact, voters who followed campaigns the most closely were the least likely to be influenced.

The 1948 results proved to be no fluke. A series of election studies—carried out between 1948 and 1960—all reached the conclusion that political campaigns persuaded almost no one (for a summary of the evidence, see Klapper, 1960). People who intended to vote Democratic or Republican at the start of the campaign generally became all the more convinced of their preference. Only a handful of voters switched from one candidate to the other.

Thus, any concept of an all-powerful media gave way to the idea of minimal media effects.

Naturally, these results eventually caused scholars to question whether persuasion was, or should be regarded as, the only indicator or criterion of media influence. Researchers began to change their approach. Rather than asking, "What do people think?" researchers focused on asking, "What do people think *about*?" Changes in the political agenda became the operative definition of media influence. The media were thought to act as gatekeepers—selecting some issues for presentation and ignoring others—rather than as marketers of specific points of view.

As scholars began to test and refine the idea of agenda setting by the media, they discovered that the process of defining the political agenda did, in fact, contribute to attitude change or persuasion. Consider the case of the 2008 election. The economic crisis reached a peak in mid-September of that year with the collapse of Lehman Brothers and the imminent bankruptcy of several other prominent banks with major investments in housing mortgages. In response to the banks' troubles, the stock market lost 20 percent of its value in the first 10 days of October. Given the scale of these events, it is no wonder that voters were subjected to saturation-level news reporting on the state of the economy. In response, the public deemed the economy to be the single most important problem facing the nation. Because the economy was the paramount concern, voters focused on Obama's and McCain's relative ability to cope with the crisis. In other words, the doctrine of agenda control holds that the more news coverage is assigned to an issue, the more weight voters will accord that issue when evaluating the candidates. This extension of the agenda-setting logic (which we will take up later in this chapter) is called the *priming effect* of news coverage.

The gradual extension of the agenda-setting argument to the determination of voter choice in effect delineated a process of indirect persuasion. If, by increasing the visibility of a particular issue, campaigns also make voters more attached to that issue as a basis for voting, for all practical purposes the effect is equivalent to persuasion. Substitution of the criteria on which candidates are evaluated produces a different bottom-line choice. Thus the theoretical orientation of research on media effects turned full circle. In the early days of mass media, researchers set out with a notion of powerful media capable of altering all manner of social and political attitudes. In the aftermath of repeated failures to document widespread persuasion during campaigns, scholars assigned media a more limited agenda-setting function. Eventually, studies showed that agenda setting and priming could generate effects that were similar to persuasion.

THE CHOICE OF METHODS

Just as the concept of media influence has waxed and waned, so, too, has the debate over the appropriate tool kit for measuring the effects of the news media. Within the field of mass communication are two distinct methodological traditions: experimentation and survey research. Each tradition is associated with a set of distinctive results. The discovery of agenda-setting and priming effects resulted primarily from the extensive use of experimental methods; the earlier period of minimal consequences, on the other hand, was marked by exclusive reliance on surveys. This pattern suggests a general effect caused by the methodology itself—namely, that experimental and survey studies lead to diametrically opposing conclusions about the effects of mass communication.

The impact of methodological choices on research findings was first identified by Hovland (1959). After enumerating the complementary strengths and weaknesses of experiments and surveys, Hovland warned that exclusive use of one or the other would inevitably lead to biased results. Accordingly, the optimal research strategy was a combination of survey and experimental methods. Here we retrace and update Hovland's classic analysis.

Identifying Causes: The Advantage of Experiments

The major advantage of the experiment over the survey—and the focus of the discussion that follows—is its ability to isolate the effects of specific components of political messages. Consider the case of political campaigns. At the aggregate level, campaigns encompass a set of messages, channels, and sources, all of which may influence the audience, often in inconsistent directions. The researcher's task is to identify specific causal factors and specify the range of their relevant attributes.

What was it about the infamous "Willie Horton" ad that is thought to have moved so many American voters in 1988? Was it, as widely alleged, the race (African American) of Willie Horton, whose crimes the ad highlighted? Alternatively, was it the violent and brutal nature of his behavior, the fact that he was a convict, the dramatic voice-over used in the ad, or another factor? By manipulating the possible causal attributes, experiments make it possible to isolate the explanation. Surveys, on the other hand, can provide evidence only on self-reported exposure to the causal variable in question; respondents are unlikely to remember even whether they saw a particular campaign commercial, let alone its unique features. (In fact, as we will discuss, many people do not even accurately report whether they have seen an ad, watched the news, or voted.)

Experimentation is the method of choice in every scientific discipline, therefore, because the researcher can tightly control the phenomenon under investigation. Potential causal factors can be switched on and off. Consider the key phenomenon of media exposure. The experimenter can measure exposure with almost total precision because she creates it. Using random assignment, she can ensure that the treatment group (those exposed to the message) and control group (those not exposed to the message) will be similar on average; for example, the two groups will have approximately the same proportion of Democrats and Republicans.[1] Thus, any observed difference between the treatment and control groups after the experiment will have been caused by the manipulation of the message.

For example, using the context of the 1990 gubernatorial campaign between Republican Pete Wilson and Democrat Dianne Feinstein, Ansolabehere and Iyengar (1995) manipulated the negativity of the candidates' advertising on the environment and examined the effect of this manipulation on intention to vote. In the positive-ad condition, the sponsoring candidate was depicted as being opposed to offshore oil drilling; in the negative-ad condition, the sponsor's opponent was said to be in favor of offshore drilling. This difference in the candidate's position was accomplished by the substitution of three words into the soundtrack of a thirty-second commercial—*yes* for *no*, and *will destroy* for *will preserve* (see Video Archive 8.1). Because this was the sole difference between the positive- and negative-ad conditions and because study participants were randomly assigned to either condition, the researchers could attribute any observed difference between the conditions to negativity. The experiment showed that participants who watched the negative version of the ad were less likely to report that they intended to vote in the election.

Video Archive 8.1
Experimental Manipulation of Advertising Tone

Experimental studies, of course, do have their own limitations. Long considered the Achilles' heel of experiments, the problem of generalizability—that is, being able to generalize the results observed in an experiment to the population as a whole—manifests itself at three levels: mundane realism, sampling bias, and the nonrandom basis of media exposure in the real world. In the sections that follow, we'll look at each of these.

Mundane Realism Because of the need for tightly controlled stimuli, the setting in which the typical laboratory experiment is conducted is often quite different from the setting in which individuals ordinarily experience the target phenomenon. Although asking participants to report to a location on a university campus may be convenient for the researcher, it is also a highly unnatural environment for watching television or for other types of activities that are of interest to political-communication researchers. The artificial properties of laboratory experiments are likely to influence the behavior of participants. To avoid the reactivity of the laboratory setting, researchers have increasingly turned to so-called field experiments, in which the procedures and settings more closely reflect ordinary life (providing participants with a milieu that better matches the setting of their living room or den, for example).

In general, building realism into experimental designs necessitates some loss of experimental control. Watching treatments in a mock living room means that some respondents may not pay attention to the stimulus, for example, just as many people zone out when watching TV at home.

Sampling Bias The most widely cited limitation of experiments concerns the composition of the participant pool. Typically, laboratory experiments are conducted on "captive" populations—for example, college students who often serve as guinea pigs to gain course credit. College sophomores may be a convenient subject population, but they are hardly representative of the general population; they have been found, for example, to have less resolute attitudes and a stronger tendency to comply with authority than do older adults. College sophomores might be persuaded by a stimulus, but what about likely voters?

One solution to the sampling problem is to transport the experiment to public locations and recruit participants from nonstudent populations. Ansolabehere and Iyengar, for instance, administered their experiments on campaign advertising at three different shopping malls in and around Los Angeles, and they offered a financial incentive to attract participants.

Fortunately, technology has both enlarged the pool of potential experimental participants and reduced the per capita cost of administering subjects. Today, it is possible to use traditional experimental methods online. Advantages of using the Internet as the experimental site include the ability to reach diverse populations without geographic limitations, since respondents can easily self-administer experimental manipulations in their own homes. The rapid diffusion of the Internet has made it possible for market research companies to assemble large online panels, consisting of individuals willing to participate in research studies for a token incentive (such as the chance to win an iPod). YouGov, a firm founded in Silicon Valley, maintains an online research panel of 1.5 million adult Americans and millions more in 30 other nations. Because of the size of their panel, YouGov is able to deliver samples that match the population on key attributes including party affiliation, gender, and education. In the 2010 US elections, the accuracy of YouGov preelection online polls equaled or exceeded that of conventional telephone-based polls.

Self-Selection An especially important difference between experimental and real-world contexts concerns the nature of exposure to media messages. The defining advantage of the experiment is that exposure is made equivalent to a lottery, thus guaranteeing equivalence between the experimental and control groups. In the real world, however, exposure to political messages is far from a lottery. Some people receive the message, others do not; and the distinction is based on self-selection. The audience for news consists disproportionately of relatively attentive voters, and the increased level of consumer choice only makes it easier for less-interested voters to tune out. Thus, the challenge facing experimental researchers is to design communication-related manipulations that more closely reflect processes of self-selection by the audience.

One approach is to give participants some control or choice over their exposure to the experimental treatment. In one study, for example, researchers had participants watch video clips of talking heads on cable shows arguing with each other to test the proposition that watching uncivil and rude behavior decreases political trust (Arceneaux & Johnson, 2013). Previous research had detected this effect, but by using a design that forced participants to watch either program in question (Mutz & Reeves, 2005). When participants were given the choice to watch some other program, however, the effect of argumentative talk shows on those who chose to watch them disappeared.

In summary, the experiment is unsurpassed in its ability to isolate cause from effect. By physically manipulating the causal factor and holding all other factors constant, the researcher provides unequivocal evidence of causation. At the same time, by maximizing control, the researcher necessarily sacrifices realism, often casting doubts on the generalizability of experimental results to the real world.

Generalizability: The Advantage of Surveys

Surveys are almost the exact complement of experiments: they yield evidence that is ambiguous with respect to causation, but which may be confidently generalized. For communication scholars, the most fundamental weakness of the survey is that it provides little control over the key phenomenon of media exposure. In the experimental context, exposure is turned on or off; in the survey context, it is approximated by the request that participants reconstruct their past behavior. In the closing days of a campaign, for instance, respondents might be asked to recall which political commercials they watched on television. Survey researchers treat respondents' self-reported exposure to campaign communication as a substitute for actual exposure. Accordingly, the standard test for campaign or media effects is to compare voting choice or candidate preference across respondents who self-report high or low levels of exposure to the campaign. If those with higher levels of self-reported exposure are more likely to prefer one candidate over another (all other factors being equal), the researcher concludes that this preference was due to exposure to the campaign.

The assumption that self-reported exposure is an accurate approximation of actual exposure is problematic on several grounds. People have notoriously weak memories for past events, especially when the event in question concerns an encounter with a political campaign or media message. In the experiments conducted by Ansolabehere and Iyengar (1998), over 50 percent of the participants who were actually exposed to an advertisement were unable—a mere thirty minutes later—to recall having seen the advertisement. On the other side of the coin, survey respondents tend to err in the opposite direction, often overreporting exposure, possibly because they feel that these affirmative responses speak well of their civic virtue. For example, although ratings data showed that only 6 percent of adults listened to NPR at least once per week, fully 35 percent of respondents in a 1989 National Election Studies pilot study reported that they did so (Price & Zaller, 1993). In a comparison of self-reported network news exposure with actual exposure, one study found that the former provided estimates of audience size that were, on average, three times higher than the actual size. Overreporting also differs between subgroups, with younger people overreporting their exposure to TV news by a factor of nine (Prior, 2009; see also Vavreck, 2007). The gross inaccuracy in self-reports necessarily weakens the ability of survey researchers to detect media effects.

Fortunately, technology provides researchers with the tools to monitor actual rather than self-reported exposure to news. As people increasingly turn to their cell phones and tablets for news reports, it is possible to track what they read quite precisely. In a recent study, participants' cell-phone records were examined to assess which news sources they accessed most frequently. Not surprisingly, the results showed that local news attracted the most attention (LaCour & Vavreck, 2014).

Even more problematic for the survey researcher is the fact that self-reported media use is typically a by-product of the very same political attitudes that are considered effects of media consumption. Those who remember encountering political messages (candidate ads, for example)—and therefore are likely to report having seen them when asked about it in a survey—are likely to be those who are already highly politically engaged. People who are not already interested in politics are less likely to pay attention to campaign ads that appear when they are watching television, and therefore are unlikely to remember—and report—having seen them.

The fact that those who are highly politically engaged are more likely to report exposure to political messages has predictable consequences for research on media effects. In experiments that manipulated the tone of campaign advertising, researchers found that exposure to negative messages discouraged turnout (Ansolabehere & Iyengar, 1995). On the basis of self-reports, however, survey researchers concluded the opposite—that exposure to negative campaign advertising stimulated turnout (Wattenberg & Brians, 1999). But was it recalled exposure to negative advertising that prompted turnout, or the greater interest in campaigns among likely voters that prompted higher recall? When statistical techniques were used to control this problem, the sign of the coefficient for recall was reversed, indicating that those who recalled negative advertisements were less likely to intend to vote (see Ansolabehere, Iyengar, & Simon, 1999). Unfortunately, most survey-based analyses fail to disentangle the reciprocal effects of self-reported exposure to the campaign and partisan attitudes/behaviors.

Over the years, survey design has improved, survey measures of media exposure have become more finely calibrated, and scholars have become more adept at data analysis. Panels (before and after surveys) and aggregate time-series designs make causal inferences from the results much more reliable. During the 2004 election, for instance, the National Annenberg Election Study interviewed a large number of respondents on a daily basis to yield evidence that spanned the entire life of the campaign (Johnston, Hagen, & Jamieson, 2004). Because respondents were interviewed more or less continuously from the earliest stages of the campaign, the researchers could aggregate respondents into precise temporal groupings corresponding to before and after major events. It is not surprising that work based on longitudinal surveys replicates several experimental findings of significant campaign effects. All told, these significant methodological advances have strengthened survey researchers' ability to detect media effects.

Surveys do have their advantages. A relatively small sample yields evidence that reflects a much larger population because the respondents can be a microcosm of the entire population rather than a sample limited to college students. Estimates based on probability samples come very close to approximating the true value of a particular population parameter. In addition to providing generalizable evidence, surveys are less intrusive than experiments. Answering the phone is a routine task for most people, compared with visiting the local college campus, as participants still must do in the case of many experiments.[2] Survey responses are less likely to be contaminated by the novelty of the situation.

IN FOCUS

Methodological Trade-Offs

Surveys and experiments each have strengths and weaknesses as methods of establishing the nature of relationships between independent and dependent variables. By giving the researcher greater control, *experiments* provide the most unambiguous evidence of causation. Because of issues of mundane realism, sampling bias, and self-selection, however, the results from experimental studies often cannot be generalized to the real world.

Surveys do not have such generalizability problems. Because they rely on self-reported data (which are often inaccurate because of errors of memory and self-presentation biases), however, they often fail to reveal the true relationships between cause and effect.

Combining Experimental and Survey Approaches

Given the complementary strengths and weaknesses of experiments and surveys, the least-biased methodology for the study of communication effects is to combine the two. Using experiments in tandem with surveys, as Hovland (1959) put it, amounts to "the royal road to wisdom." Over the years researchers have come to heed Hovland's advice. Their tool kit now includes experiments, quasi experiments, telephone surveys, in-person surveys, survey experiments, and, as noted, Web-based surveys and experiments.

Methodological advances and the adoption of multimethod research strategies have gradually eroded the minimal consequences verdict in the scholarly literature. Today, it is generally acknowledged that media presentations leave their mark on the audience and that media campaigns can affect the outcome of an election. We will summarize the evidence regarding the effects of news presentations on public opinion in the next section of this chapter. Then, in Chapter 9, we'll turn to the effects of campaigns.

VARIETIES OF MEDIA EFFECTS

Ordinary people encounter the political world only through what they see and read about in the media. This dependence has motivated political elites to invest heavily in efforts to shape the content of the news. As we'll describe in this section, this strategy is not irrational; what appears in the news does influence the state of public opinion.

LEARNING

The dissemination of public affairs information is considered a basic responsibility of the news media in democratic societies. By tuning in to the news, Americans can acquire factual information about the course of events—for example, that the number of American soldiers killed in Iraq has passed the 3,000 mark, or that President Obama has nominated a new Supreme Court justice. However, as we will note shortly, the media do not write on a blank slate. Voters' partisan beliefs affect their willingness to learn.

One of the most striking characteristics of American public opinion is that it does not appear to rest on a command of political facts. Americans offer opinions about candidates or issues even when they possess minimal amounts of information. Examples abound: one month after the Republican sweep of the 1994 congressional elections, 57 percent of the electorate could not identify Newt Gingrich and a majority had never heard of the "Contract with America" (which we discussed in Chapter 7). In August 2010, nearly two years after he assumed the presidency, 20 percent of the public believed Obama was a Muslim. That same month, a majority of the public expressed disapproval of the proposed Islamic Center in New York City even though 25 percent admitted to "knowing nothing at all" about Islam.

There are several explanations for the unusually high level of political ignorance in the most media-rich society on earth. Americans' relative affluence is thought to contribute to their inattentiveness to politics. For most citizens, decisions made in Congress or the state legislature are seen to have little impact on their daily lives. The benefits of knowing who does what in government are minimal. Hence, voters may consider it unnecessary—even irrational—to accumulate large amounts of political information.

A variation on the rational–ignorance theme is that people do not need facts to express informed opinions. The public is able to arrive at reasonable approximations of informed political decisions using shortcuts, or *heuristics*, such as voting on the basis of their liking or disliking the groups that support a particular candidate or cause, or supporting a candidate because of that candidate's standing in the polls. Although not all scholars agree that the public's use of heuristics produces opinions equivalent to opinions that are based on hard factual information,[3] opinions and voting behavior are undeniably much less affected by information per se than by relevant cues.

In recent years, as American politics has become polarized across party lines (a development discussed in greater detail later in this chapter), what people claim to know about politics and current events increasingly depends on their partisan affiliation, making it difficult to distinguish information from misinformation. In the months following the invasion of Iraq in 2003, for instance, Republicans believed (incorrectly) that the United States had uncovered evidence of weapons of mass destruction, while Democrats answered, correctly, that no such evidence had been found (Kull, Ramsey, & Lewis, 2003). This partisan knowledge gap is attributable not only to "wishful thinking"—believing in facts that make one's party and party leaders look good—but also to differential reliance on partisan sources of information which provide biased accounts of the events in question. In the case of the invasion of Iraq, people who relied on Fox News were the most likely to be misinformed (Kull, Ramsey, & Lewis, 2003).

Other scholars believe that the explanation for Americans' low level of information about current events is that people use relevant information items to make appropriate changes in their opinions and attitudes, but then discard the information. On hearing that Candidate X voted against tax cuts, a conservative voter may shift her opinion of Candidate X in a more critical direction. Later, the voter can remember that she does not like the candidate, but not the information on which the evaluation rests.

A further explanation for widespread civic ignorance concerns the performance of the media in delivering public affairs information. One reason that Europeans are significantly more informed about politics than Americans may have to do with the quality of news programming (see Curran, Iyengar, Lund, & Salovaara-Moring, 2009; Iyengar, Curran, Lund, Salovaara-Moring, Hahn, & Coen, 2010) that they encounter on a daily basis. According to this view of the situation, Americans are less informed because they are exposed to less substantive news programming. Europeans know considerably more about hard news because their media are more likely to deliver hard news. Americans, however, can match the Europeans on knowledge of soft news because their media supply vast amounts of soft news.

The question of whether broadcast or print sources are more informative has attracted considerable research. The conventional wisdom is that print journalism—because it allows greater depth of coverage—conveys more information than TV, which provides only an abbreviated version of the news. This expectation was confirmed in a recent cross-national study of political knowledge in several European nations (Fraile & Iyengar, 2014); individuals dependent on a newspaper were substantially more informed than were those who regularly watched broadcast news.

Most research on civic information has focused on mainstream news sources. In recent years, however, soft news and infotainment programs—such as the late-night talk shows and Comedy Central's *The Daily Show*—have become increasingly important as sources of political information, particularly for young people. In a 2012 survey of media use by the Pew Research Center for the People and the Press, about 1 in 10 Americans said they regularly get their news from these sources, and people under the age of thirty made up 40 percent of the audience for *The Colbert Report* and *The Daily Show*.

Evidence concerning the extent to which people acquire information from nontraditional news media is just as mixed as the evidence from mainstream media studies. Some researchers suggest that soft news programs, by presenting political issues in a more entertaining format, also inform their audience. According to Baum (2002), the growing popularity of soft news outlets means that "many otherwise politically inattentive individuals are exposed to information about high-profile political issues, most prominently foreign policy crises, as an incidental by-product of seeking entertainment" (p. 91). Other studies, however, have found little evidence of "incidental learning" from soft news sources.

Overall, the jury is still out on whether exposure to the news contributes significantly to factual information about politics. The American public's low level of knowledge can be attributed not only to the increasingly nonsubstantive content of news programming but also to the lack of incentives for becoming informed, and to the easy availability of psychological cues that allow individuals to form opinions despite their lack of information.

AGENDA CONTROL

As casual observers of the political scene, most Americans notice only those issues that are in the news; events, issues, and personalities not covered by the media might as well not exist. What the public notices becomes the principal basis for their beliefs about the state of the country. Thus, the relative prominence of issues in the news is the major determinant of the public's perceptions of the problems facing the nation (see, for example, Dearing & Rogers, 1996; McCombs & Shaw, 1972). The media's issue agenda becomes the public's agenda. This is particularly true in the case of national and international issues, about which the public has almost no opportunity to learn from firsthand experience.

The famine that devastated Ethiopia in the early 1980s provides a clear example of the public's responsiveness to the media agenda. Although the famine had persisted for many months with loss of life in the thousands, most Americans were completely unaware of the issue until it finally attracted attention from the news media in October 1984. Once the spotlight was turned on,

IN FOCUS

Agenda Setting and Priming

The central idea of *agenda setting* is that, by giving differential attention to certain issues, the media set the agenda of public discourse. That is to say, by covering some issues and ignoring others, the media influence which issues people view as important and which they view as unimportant.

An extension of agenda setting, *priming* refers to the way in which the media affect the criteria by which political leaders are judged. The more prominent an issue becomes in the public consciousness, the more it will influence people's assessments of politicians.

there was an outpouring of relief efforts. As the executive producer of NBC's *Today* show commented, "This famine has been going on for a long time and nobody cared. Now it's on TV and everybody cares. I guess a picture is worth many words" (Boyer, 1986, p. 293).

The relationship between news coverage and public concern has come to be known as the *agenda-setting effect*. An early statement of the hypothesis was formulated by B. E. Cohen (1963): the media, Cohen said, "may not be successful most of the time in telling people what to think, but it is stunningly successful in telling its readers what to think *about*" (p. 13). The first study to test for the effect was conducted by McCombs and Shaw (1972) in the context of the 1968 presidential campaign. They surveyed a random sample of Chapel Hill, North Carolina, voters, asking them to identify the key campaign issues. Simultaneously, they monitored the news media used by residents of the Chapel Hill area to track the level of news coverage given to different issues. They found almost a one-to-one correspondence between the rankings of issues based on amount of news coverage and the number of survey respondents who mentioned the issue as important.

Although evidence of agenda-setting effects of media coverage is plentiful, some scholars have suggested that the convergence of the public and the news media on the same issue agenda may result simply because both respond to the same real-world events, and *not* because the media is influencing the public. This explanation is unlikely to be correct, however, because most political issues can be experienced only through exposure to the news. How would ordinary voters know about global warming, for example, without encountering any discussion of the problem in the news?

The case of crime provides a striking example of public concern and real-world indicators moving in opposite directions. As Figure 8.1 shows, the FBI nationwide violent crime index has declined significantly since the early 1990s. Despite the substantial reduction in crime, the percentage of the public that viewed crime as among the three most important national problems remained at a high level (averaging 25 percent in the 1990s), and peaking in 1999. Not coincidentally, the decade of the 1990s witnessed a dramatic increase in the availability of local television news, which is likely to feature stories on crime. Figure 8.1 suggests, at least in the case of crime, that public opinion is more responsive to what appears on the television screen than to the state of the real world. It is not until the September 11 terrorist attacks that public concern for crime falls as terrorism and national security become the focal points of media coverage.

Survey-based studies of agenda setting have difficulty establishing the direction of causality. That is, some scholars suggest that the correlation between the media and the public agenda reflect editors' decisions to run stories on issues

FIGURE 8.1

Violent Crime Rate and Public Concern about Crime, 1994–2012

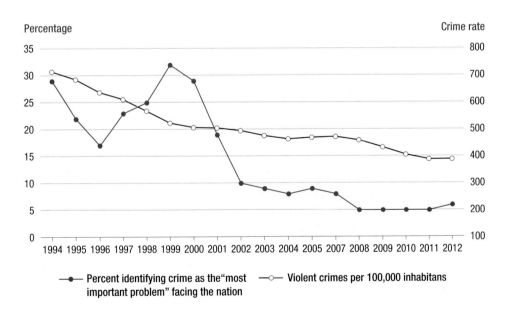

Source: Data from the Gallup "most important problem" series (taken from the Policy Agendas Project website: www .policyagendas.org/datasets/index.html); FBI violent crime index (available at http://www.fbi.gov/about-us/cjis /ucr/crime-in-the-u.s/2013/crime-in-the-u.s.-2013/tables/1tabledatadecoverviewpdf/).

deemed important by the public, rather than the other way around. Researchers have attempted to tease out the direction of causality by tracking changes in public opinion and news coverage over time, thus establishing whether it is the media that leads public concern or vice versa. In one such study—the first to test for feedback from the level of public concern to news coverage—the authors found no traces of shifts in the amount of news devoted to the economy induced by changes in public concern for economic issues (Behr & Iyengar, 1985). The authors thus effectively dismissed the possibility that news panders to the concerns of the audience. The same study, however, also showed that television news coverage of economic issues predicted the level of public concern for these issues independent of real-world economic conditions. The researchers concluded that correspondence between the media and public agendas was not a result of the fact that both were responding to the same real-world conditions.

Experiments provide the most compelling evidence concerning the direction of causality in agenda setting by the media. By manipulating the issue content of news programs, researchers have shown that even small amounts of coverage are enough to significantly shift people's perceptions of the importance of various issues. In the early 1980s, for example, Iyengar and Kinder (1987) administered a series of experiments that varied the level of news coverage accorded to several target issues. They found that participants who watched one story every day for a week on a particular issue came to see that issue as one of the three most important problems facing the country (see Table 8.1).

Overall, the evidence in support of the agenda-setting effect is overwhelming. One-shot surveys, time-series analysis of public opinion, and laboratory experiments all agree on the finding that issues in the news *are* the issues that people care about.

Setting the Elite Agenda

The effects of news coverage on the perception of which issues are important extend beyond the mass public. The fact that ordinary citizens care about an issue is of considerable interest to policy makers, who view public opinion as a strategic resource. Policy makers know that when the media spotlight is aimed at a particular issue, they are likely to have greater success in proposing or moving along legislation on that issue, because it is more difficult for those who might normally try to block such efforts to do so when the public is clamoring for action. Legislators interested in regulating the tobacco industry, for instance, are more likely to propose policy initiatives designed to curb smoking when health issues are moving up the public agenda. In fact, as Baumgartner and Jones (1993) have demonstrated, congressional hearings

TABLE 8.1

Agenda Setting by Network News: Changes in the Public's Perception of the Importance of a Problem

Problem	Percentage of Viewers Naming the Problem as One of the Country's Most Serious		
	Before the Experiment	After the Experiment	Change
Defense	33	53	+20[a]
Inflation	100	100	0
Pollution	0	14	+14[a]
Arms control	35	65	+30[a]
Civil rights	0	10	10[a]
Unemployment (experiment 8)	43	71	+28[a]
Unemployment (experiment 9)	50	86	+36[a]

Source: Data from S. Iyengar & D. R. Kinder. (1987). *News that matters: Television and American opinion.* Chicago: University of Chicago Press.
[a]The reported change is statistically significant.

on the public health consequences of smoking were preceded by periods of relatively heavy media coverage of the issue. Across a variety of policy issues, Baumgartner and Jones found that the frequency of congressional committee hearings on particular issues over time corresponded to the level of news coverage. As Figure 8.2 shows, hearings on environmental issues were scheduled more frequently when the state of the environment attracted more attention in the pages of the *New York Times*.

Several researchers (e.g., Edwards & Wood, 1999; Eshbaugh-Soha & Peake, 2005, 2008) have found that the relationship between media attention and elite attention to issues differs across policy areas. On foreign policy issues, as well as some domestic issues (such as crime and education), presidential attention follows the level of media attention. In other domestic policy areas, however, the relationship is reciprocal, with the level of media attention also responding to the level of presidential attention. On issues that are already high on the public agenda, presidents are especially responsive to news coverage. For other less visible issues, however, it is the media that responds to presidential actions (Eshbaugh-Soha & Peake, 2011).

Thus, media coverage not only moves public concern but also motivates policy makers to take action. And because political elites (most notably the president) are the primary generators of news stories, they are in an especially

FIGURE 8.2

Attention Trends in Congress and the Media on Environmental Issues, 1946–2010

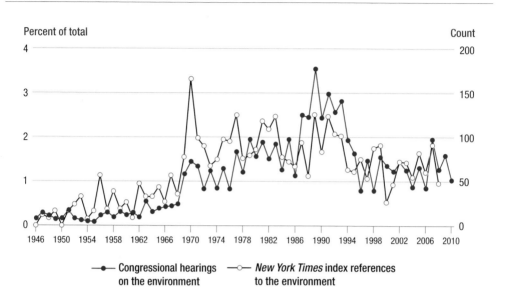

Source: Data from coverage of environmental issues in Policy Agendas Project.

Note: Nonreferred hearings may be of an investigative or oversight nature and signify general committee interest in the issue.

advantageous position to simultaneously influence the media and public agendas.

Psychological Accounts of Agenda Setting

Scholars have identified at least two psychological mechanisms that influence agenda setting. First, people may respond to news coverage because the issues receiving attention in the news are more likely to be top-of-the-head—that is, coming to mind more quickly and easily—and are therefore more likely to be cited when respondents are asked to name important national issues. If every newspaper headline and every TV news report you saw prominently featured a story on Iraq, it would not be surprising if that were the first thing that sprang to mind if somebody asked you to name the problems facing the country today.

An alternative perspective treats agenda setting as a more thoughtful process. In this view, people treat journalists as credible sources for judging the importance of issues. When a particular issue receives regular and high-profile coverage, citizens surmise that it must be an important issue for the nation.

Researchers studying agenda setting have also looked at the conditions that underlie the media's ability to shape the public's priorities. Such factors include the personal relevance of the issue and the visibility of the coverage. In general, the more prominent the coverage given an issue, the more likely it is that that issue will move up the public agenda. Front-page news, newspaper stories accompanied by photographs, and lead stories in television newscasts tend to be particularly influential. This could be taken as evidence in favor of the thoughtful account of agenda setting. On the other hand, the greater impact of front-page and lead-story coverage might indicate that the public's attention to news is so limited that they notice only glaring headlines or lead-story coverage.

Some individuals are more responsive to the media agenda than are others. In general, the further removed an issue or event is from direct personal experience, the weaker the agenda-setting effects of news coverage are. In other words, when an issue is in the news, people personally affected by it are the first to have their agendas set by that issue. Iyengar and Kinder (1987) found, for example, that after being exposed to broadcast news reports detailing the financial difficulties of the Social Security fund, elderly viewers were much more likely than their younger counterparts to name Social Security as one of the most important problems facing the country.

PRIMING EFFECTS

Beyond merely affecting the perceived importance of issues, news coverage influences the criteria that the public uses to evaluate political candidates and institutions—a phenomenon known as *priming*. An extension of agenda setting, priming is a process by which news coverage influences the weights that individuals assign to their opinions on particular issues when they make summary political evaluations, such as which candidate deserves their vote. As Ansolabehere, Behr, and Iyengar (1993) put it, "Priming refers to the capacity of the media to isolate particular issues, events, or themes in the news as criteria for evaluating politicians" (p. 148).

In general, the evidence indicates that when asked to appraise politicians and public figures, voters weight their opinions on particular policy issues in proportion to the perceived importance of those issues: the more prominent the issue, the greater the impact of opinions about that issue on the appraisal (for reviews of priming research, see Krosnick & Kinder, 1990; and Miller & Krosnick, 2000). If crime is the issue receiving the most attention in the news, for example, people will be more likely to support the candidate or public official who they think is best able to deal with crime.

Priming effects can be especially important during election campaigns. The closing days of the 1980 presidential campaign provide an especially dramatic example of priming. With less than a week to go before the election, the polls showed Jimmy Carter and Ronald Reagan to be dead even. Suddenly, the Iranian government offered President Carter a last-minute proposal for releasing the Americans whom they had held hostage for over a year. Carter suspended his campaign to devote full attention to these negotiations. The hostage issue and the progress of the negotiations became the major news story of the day. The media's preoccupation with the hostage story caused voters to seize on the candidates' ability to control terrorism as a basis for their vote choice. Given his record in office, this logic proved disadvantageous to President Carter.

Similar volatility in the public agenda bedeviled President George H. W. Bush in the 1992 election. In the previous year, as he presided over the successful liberation of Kuwait from Iraqi occupation, his popularity ratings had soared to 90 percent. Following the end of the Gulf War, news coverage of the economy drowned out news about military and international issues; on economic issues, voters preferred Clinton over Bush by a wide margin. Had the media played up military or security issues, of course, it's likely that the tables would have been turned.

A recent instance of priming comes from the post-9/11 era. Prior to the terrorist attacks, President George W. Bush's overall popularity was closely tied to perceptions of his performance on economic issues (see Figure 8.3). After September 11, 2001, and extending through 2003, Bush's popularity moved more closely in tandem with public assessments of his performance on terrorism. Terrorism and national security had replaced the economy as the yardstick for judging Bush's performance. Only in 2004, after the onset of the presidential campaign, were economic performance and overall performance again linked. Our analysis of presidential popularity in Chapter 10 reinforces this finding. There we show that, following the 9/11 attacks, news coverage of terrorism became the single most important determinant of Bush's public approval.

As already noted in Chapter 6, voters' tendency to focus on highly visible issues creates strong incentives for candidates to introduce issues on which they enjoy an advantage. September 11 gave George Bush a significant advantage over John Kerry on national security. Among the exit-poll respondents who cited terrorism as the most important issue facing the country, 86 percent said they voted for Bush. Among voters concerned about the economy, however, 80 percent said they voted for John Kerry. As these data suggest, elections often turn on the issue that voters find most important. Had the state of the economy been more prominent, Kerry would likely have been elected. Conversely, if voters had been even more preoccupied with terrorism, Bush would have won by a landslide.

FIGURE 8.3

Terrorism versus the Economy as Criteria for Evaluating President Bush

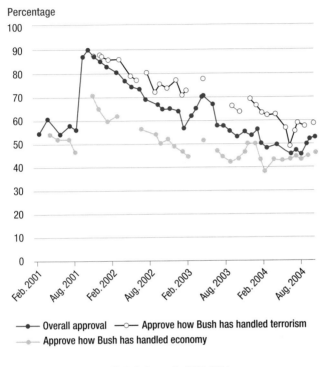

Percentage

— Overall approval   —○— Approve how Bush has handled terrorism
— Approve how Bush has handled economy

Source: Data from Gallup CBS News polls & Gallup polls, 2001–2004.

The economic crisis of 2008 provides a classic case of priming. Before the onset of the crisis, Americans were concerned about a variety of issues, including the war on terror, illegal immigration, education, and the economy. In June 2007, for instance, 15 percent of the public named immigration as one of the most important problems facing the nation, while another 15 percent named corruption and dishonesty in government. In the aftermath of the economic crisis, however, the economy became the overriding concern and previously hot issues such as immigration disappeared entirely from the public's agenda. In early 2009, the number of those surveyed who named immigration as an important problem was barely 1 percent. The emergence of the economy as the national concern is shown when we compare the public's overall evaluation of President Obama with their ratings of his performance on the economy and immigration (as shown in Figure 8.4). Clearly, for this period, ratings of Obama's performance on the economy show closer correspondence with ratings of his overall performance, suggesting that it is the economy

FIGURE 8.4

The Economy versus Illegal Immigration as Criteria for Evaluating President Obama

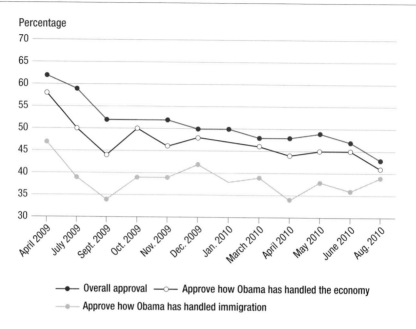

Source: Overall performance numbers are from Gallup. Economy and immigration performance data are from AP-GFK Polls.

rather than immigration that explains the downward trend in his overall popularity. Had people evaluated Obama more in terms of immigration, his popularity would have been considerably lower. (We will provide more evidence on the relationship between economic conditions and President Obama's popularity in Chapter 9.)

It is important to distinguish the concept of priming from other psychological mechanisms that might induce the same observed outcome, such as a greater impact of salient issues on evaluations of elected officials. One such mechanism is projection—the tendency of voters to attribute favorable qualities to leaders they like. For example, a voter who has a generally favorable impression of President Obama may evaluate his performance on healthcare favorably even though the voter lacks meaningful information about actual performance. Projection and priming support opposite inferences concerning the direction of causality; in the case of the former the general evaluation drives the performance evaluation with the opposite holding for priming. To date, most studies of priming fail to consider projection.[4] However, the authors of a recent study set out to investigate both possibilities with respect to President Obama's performance on education and the environment. They found that the effects of priming surpassed the effects of projection (Hart & Middleton, 2014).

Media priming effects have been documented in a series of experiments and surveys targeting evaluations of presidents and lesser officials and covering a variety of attitudes, including assessments of incumbents' performance in office and ratings of their personal attributes. Overall, news coverage of issues elicits stronger priming effects in the area of performance assessments than in the area of personality assessments.

A special case of priming concerns the phenomenon of momentum in primary elections. News coverage during the early primaries tends to focus exclusively on the state of the horse race. Because horse-race coverage is so pervasive (as explained in Chapter 3), primary voters are likely to rely heavily on information about the candidates' electoral viability when making their choices. In a study of the 2004 primary campaign, researchers found that the single most important determinant of Democrats' primary-vote preference between Senators John Kerry and John Edwards was perception of the two candidates' personalities (Luskin, Iyengar, & Fishkin, 2005). The second most powerful predictor of vote choice was the candidates' electoral viability. Viability was more important to voters than the candidates' positions on major issues, including the war in Iraq and outsourcing of American jobs. But among voters who were given ample information about the candidates' positions on the issues, policy agreement (defined as the extent to which a voter's own opinion on major issues matched the voter's perception of where the candidates stood on these issues) proved more important than viability as a determinant of candidate preference.

Priming can also lead citizens to give greater weight to other evaluative criteria, such as character traits. Druckman and Holmes (2004) found that President Bush successfully used his 2002 State of the Union address for image priming, increasing the influence of trait evaluations (strong leadership, integrity) on his approval rating. Similarly, Mendelsohn (1996) found that voters (in the 1988 Canadian election) who were heavily exposed to media reports were more likely to base their vote choice on candidate character evaluations and less likely to base them on issues.

Just as the influence of news coverage on the state of the public agenda is conditioned both by properties of news stories and by characteristics of individual members of the audience, the ability of the news to prime political evaluations is similarly tempered. It is not surprising that priming effects peak when news reports explicitly suggest that politicians are responsible for the state of national affairs or when they clearly link politicians' actions with national problems. Thus evaluations of President Reagan's performance were more strongly influenced by news stories when the coverage suggested that Reaganomics was responsible for rising American unemployment than when the coverage directed attention to alternative causes of unemployment.

In another parallel with research on agenda setting, individuals differ in their susceptibility to media priming effects. Miller and Krosnick (2000) found that priming effects occurred only among people who were both highly knowledgeable about political affairs and highly trusting of the media. Iyengar and Kinder (1987) found that partisanship affected the issues on which people could be primed: Democrats tended to be most susceptible to priming when the news focused on issues that favor Democrats, such as unemployment and civil rights; and Republicans were influenced most when the news focused on traditional Republican issues, such as national defense.

In sum, people use patterns of news coverage as an indicator of the state of the nation. Issues and events in the news are deemed important and weigh heavily in evaluations of incumbent officials and political candidates. As is clear from the way in which President George H. W. Bush benefited from media coverage of the 1991 Gulf War and then suffered from coverage of the economy, priming results equally from news of political successes or news of political failures. Priming is a double-edged sword.

FRAMING EFFECTS

The term *framing* refers to the way in which opinions about an issue can be altered by emphasizing or de-emphasizing particular facets of that issue. Framing theory was developed by the psychologists Amos Tversky and Daniel Kahneman, who showed that choices could be reversed if outcomes were simply defined as potential gains or losses. A program that would certainly save two hundred out of six hundred people from an outbreak of a rare disease, for example, was chosen by a majority of subjects over an alternative with the identical outcome that was couched in terms that made it seem more risky ("a one-third probability of six hundred people saved"). But when the choice was presented in terms of loss (four hundred deaths for sure, or a two-thirds probability of six hundred deaths), the majority now preferred the riskier-seeming alternative (see Tversky & Kahneman, 1981). Similar presentation effects occur in surveys. Trivial changes in the wording of survey questions can bring about large shifts in public opinion—for example, people respond far less charitably when asked about the desirable level of government aid for "people on welfare" than when asked about aid for "poor people."

Media researchers have identified two distinct types of framing effects: equivalency framing effects and emphasis framing effects. *Equivalency framing effects* involve "the use of different, but logically equivalent, words or phrases" to describe the same possible event or issue; *emphasis framing effects* involve highlighting different "subset(s) of potentially relevant considerations" of an issue (Druckman, 2001, pp. 228, 230).

The previous example—"people on welfare" versus "poor people"—belongs more in the category of *emphasis* framing because the two phrases emphasize different aspects of poverty (referring to poor people puts the focus on the plight of the less fortunate, whereas referring to welfare brings up the question of whether government has the responsibility to take care of them, as well as the negative stereotype that Americans have of people "on the dole"). Other examples of documented emphasis framing effects include presenting a Ku Klux Klan rally as either a free-speech issue or a public-safety issue (respondents reported higher levels of support for allowing such a rally when it was framed as a free-speech issue) and presenting gun control as either an individual rights issue or a public-safety issue. Because equivalency framing is rarely possible in real-world political contexts, emphasis framing effects are most relevant to our purposes here—and the issue of who is responsible for national problems is a particularly important case, as we will now discuss.

News coverage of political issues comes in two distinct genres of presentation corresponding to thematic and episodic news frames. A *thematic* news frame places a public issue in a general context and usually takes the form of an in-depth background report. An example of thematic framing would be a story about a war that addressed the historical context of the relations between the two sides, the factors that contributed to the current conflict, and so on. *Episodic* framing, on the other hand, depicts issues in terms of individual instances or specific events—the carnage resulting from a particular terrorist bombing, for example. Episodic coverage typically features dramatic visual footage and pictures; thematic reports tend to be more sedate, consisting primarily of talking heads.

In the United States, episodic framing is by far the predominant mode of presentation in news stories, largely as a result of market pressures. The preponderance of episodically framed news has serious political repercussions, for it affects viewers' attributions of responsibility for political issues. Most political issues are capable of being viewed either as the creations of societal and/or governmental forces or as the result of private actions of individuals. Rising unemployment, for instance, might be attributed to the changing nature of the job market or to government economic policies (societal responsibility).

◎ IN FOCUS

Framing

Framing refers to the way in which the media, by highlighting some aspects of an event or issue and ignoring others, can influence how people think about that event or issue. Changing the manner of presentation of a news story can result in a very different audience perception of that story.

Alternatively, unemployment might be attributed to the unwillingness of the unemployed to work for low wages (individual responsibility). The tendency of people to attribute responsibility to societal or individual factors depends, in part, on how television frames political issues.

In a series of experimental studies (see Iyengar, 1991), viewers exposed to thematic framing attributed responsibility for issues to government and society. Following exposure to news reports about increases in malnutrition among the US poor, participants in the study discussed poverty in terms of inadequate social welfare programs; confronted with news accounts of the shrinking demand for unskilled labor, participants described unemployment as a result of inadequate economic policies or insensitive public officials; and provided with news reports on increasing rates of crime in the inner cities, participants cited improved economic opportunities for the underprivileged as the appropriate remedy for crime. Thus, when television news coverage presented an analytic frame of reference, attributions of responsibility—both for causing and curing national problems—were societal in focus.

When provided with episodic news, however, viewers attributed responsibility not to societal or political forces but to the actions of particular individuals or groups. For example, when poverty, crime, and terrorism were depicted in episodic terms, viewers attributed causal and treatment responsibility primarily to poor people, criminals, and terrorists. In response to news stories describing particular illustrations of national issues, viewers focused on individual and group characteristics rather than on historical, social, political, or other general forces.

The importance of episodic and thematic news frames extends beyond viewers' attributions of responsibility. In each of the framing experiments (and in replications with national survey data), individuals who attributed responsibility for national issues to general societal factors were found to be significantly more critical of the performance of elected officials than were individuals who attributed responsibility to nonsocietal factors. Thus, television news is generally a significant asset for incumbent officials; the predominance of event-oriented and case-study news coverage tends to insulate them from any rising tide of disenchantment over unemployment, poverty, corporate corruption, or other such problems. In contrast, when television casts its coverage in thematic terms, issues are more likely to become campaign ammunition with which to attack incumbents.

More recent work has extended analysis of the episodic frame to local news coverage of crime (see Video Archive 8.2). Typically, local crime reports provide a physical description—and perhaps a police sketch, or even security camera footage or an old mug shot—of the suspect. The visual emphasis of television, and the focus of crime reports on particular offenders, means that, as depicted in the news, the principal determining factor of criminal behavior appears to be race (since race is something that is clearly evident in a news report, whereas poverty and other social factors obviously are not). Episodic framing thus necessarily introduces racial stereotypes into the public's understanding of crime. Viewers are compelled to evaluate their racial beliefs in light of what seem to be empirical realities. Lacking the focus on an individual suspect or perpetrator, by contrast, thematic framing directs the viewers' attention to alternative and more contextual accounts of crime.

Video Archive 8.2 Episodic versus Thematic Framing of Crime

Experiments by Gilliam and Iyengar (2000) further demonstrated that the race of the suspect in episodic crime reports is a meaningful cue. The researchers presented the *same* individual as either a white or an African American male suspect (see Video Archive 8.3). Their results showed that when the suspect depicted in the news was African American, the number of viewers who endorsed punitive criminal justice policies increased significantly. In addition, exposure to the black suspect strengthened viewers' racial stereotypes (ratings of blacks as lazy and unintelligent) and their hostility to black leaders such as Jesse Jackson. Interestingly, in the case of crime, episodic and thematic framing have the same effects. In a recent study, participants who were given statistical information about racial disparities in the US prison population (a significant overrepresentation of African Americans) expressed greater fear of crime and more support for punitive crime policies (Hetey & Eberhardt, 2014).

Video Archive 8.3 Race Manipulation in Crime News Study

Racial stereotypes, particularly those associating crime and race, are also exploited by politicians (hence the rise of wedge appeals, as discussed in Chapter 6). Not only does exposure to information about crime influence viewers' attitudes toward crime and race, but it can also prime racial stereotypes as a basis for judging the performance of elected officials or for choosing between candidates for elective office. A study by Mendelberg (1997) found that among voters who watched the infamous 1988 "Willie Horton" ad, racial prejudice was more closely linked to their attitudes about civil rights and social welfare policies than among voters who did not view the ad. Similarly, Nelson and Kinder (1996) found that frames which focused attention on the perceived beneficiaries of a policy (such as homosexuals in the case of AIDS spending) increased the importance of attitudes toward that group in determining attitudes toward the policy.

Some news frames originate with the media themselves (as by-products of news production processes). Episodic coverage is one such media-generated frame, since in most cases it results from the organizational and commercial pressures on news organizations. Other frames are inserted into the news by politicians and candidates in pursuit of political advantage (as in the case of the "Willie Horton" ad used by the George H. W. Bush campaign). If politicians can increase their support by using appeals—either explicit or coded—to racial prejudice, it is only to be expected that such appeals will become even more frequent during political campaigns.

Frames can occur on a number of levels as well. Political elites generate frames both on the level of individual issues (for example, is spending on social welfare an equality issue or an economic issue?) and on the level of elections. Campaigns often amount to framing battles between parties, each fighting to define the election in terms of the issues or concerns on which they enjoy a strategic advantage. (Republicans have been very successful, for example, in framing elections in terms of values.)

A candidate might also be framed as an in-group member on the basis of race, gender, age, or other physical attributes. Evolutionary psychologists argue that physical similarity is a kinship cue and that humans are motivated to treat their kin preferentially. In an attempt to appeal to swing voters in Ohio, John Kerry dressed in camouflaged attire and went duck hunting. A recent study tested the idea that voters would be more likely to vote for the candidate whose face more closely resembled their own (see Bailenson, Iyengar, Yee, & Collins, 2009). Participants were asked to provide their photographs in advance of the 2004 presidential election. One week before the election, these same participants participated in an online survey of political attitudes that included a variety of questions about the presidential candidates (President George W. Bush and Senator John Kerry). In some cases, the photograph of Bush had been morphed with the face of the participant, in other cases it was the photograph of Kerry. Figure 8.5 shows two of the morphs used in this study. The results of the face-morphing study showed that weak partisans and independents moved in the direction of the more similar candidate (see Bailenson, Iyengar, Yee, & Collins, 2009). Thus this study demonstrates that nonverbal frames can

FIGURE 8.5

Facial Morphing

subject — George Bush — 60:40 Blend

subject — John Kerry — 60:40 Blend

Courtesy of Shanto Iyengar

Source: Data from J. Bailenson, S. Iyengar, N. Yee, & N. Collins. (2009). Facial similarity between voters and candidates causes influence. *Public Opinion Quarterly, 72,* 935–961.

influence voting, even in the most visible and contested of political campaigns. More generally, candidates whose looks convey group membership (as in the case of skin complexion or feminine facial features) are likely to be evaluated through the lens of the voter's own sense of group identity. Candidates with typical Afrocentric features will lose support among whites and gain support among African Americans.

Frames that originate with the media also occur on a number of different levels. On one level, what the media tend to cover and not cover over the long term amounts to a frame; in campaign coverage, the heavy emphasis on candidates' strategy and poll standings overwhelms coverage of their issue positions, thus framing elections—and politics more generally—in terms of superficial rather than substantive matters (Cappella & Jamieson, 1997). Indeed, in some ways a specific medium could itself be considered a frame—for example, television—as a visual medium—tends to focus attention on superficial aspects of political presentations, such as candidate appearance or demeanor. The media generate frames on the within-story level, too, as can be seen in the case of the distinction between thematic and episodic coverage.

Like agenda setting and priming, framing effects are conditioned by individual and contextual factors. Source credibility (believing a source to be knowledgeable and/or trustworthy) has been shown to be necessary for framing effects to occur. Researchers have also demonstrated that, when given an opportunity to deliberate on issues, people are less susceptible to framing. People are more likely to accept frames that are congruent with their political predispositions. This conclusion is consistent with the finding, mentioned earlier, that Republicans and Democrats are each more easily primed by issues traditionally associated with their own parties. Findings concerning the role of political knowledge are more ambiguous, with some studies showing the less-informed to be more open to framing effects, and others finding them to be less so.

In summary, despite mediating factors on both contextual and individual levels, the manner in which the news media frame issues and events affects the public in a number of important ways. Politicians fight to frame issues and elections in terms that are advantageous to themselves. The news media assist them in their task, focusing on nonsubstantive facets of elections and presenting individualistic rather than contextualized accounts of political issues that discourage citizens from holding politicians accountable for national problems.

PERSUASION EFFECTS

Persuasion is typically defined as attitude change. As discussed at the outset of this chapter, early political-communication researchers, looking for evidence of reversals in voter preference, found little evidence of persuasion effects. However, attitude change does not necessarily mean converting from one candidate or one side of an issue to the other. For example, persuasion can involve switching from having no opinion at all to having an opinion, or from having a weak opinion to having a strong opinion, or from not intending to act on an opinion to intending to act. Television news coverage of the abortion issue might encourage viewers to alter their position from uncommitted or slightly pro-choice to strongly pro-choice. A political advertisement might induce some undecided citizens to vote for a particular candidate. News reports on business activity might increase consumer confidence in the economy. And under certain circumstances, people may reverse their preferences or opinions.

Communication theorists typically analyze persuasion situations from the perspective of "who says what to whom." Thus the major determinants of attitude change are source, message, and receiver characteristics. Applied to politics, the sources are either the news media in general, particular news organizations, or candidates and political parties. Message-related factors might include the particular subject matter of a news report (crime versus the economy), the content of news reports (such as accounts suggesting that Iraq was involved in the 9/11 attacks versus reports suggesting that it wasn't), or the tone of a candidate advertisement (positive versus negative appeals). Receiver factors include a wide variety of political predispositions (is the voter Republican or Democrat?) and general background characteristics (is the voter young or old, more educated or less?). As we will describe, the evidence suggests that political persuasion, like persuasion in other contexts, requires a set of joint contingencies among message, source, and receiver factors.

Receiver-Related Contingencies

In his classic paper on persuasion effects in campaigns, Converse (1962) demonstrated that the most- and the least-attentive strata of the electorate remained equally stable (unpersuaded) over the course of political campaigns. The former group encounters a host of campaign messages, in the form of either news reports or candidate advertisements, but rejects most of them. This is because attentiveness is associated with partisanship: those most likely to tune in to campaigns are strongly Republican or Democratic in affiliation. The less attentive, on the other hand, are drawn disproportionately from the ranks of nonpartisans. Although willing to consider any campaign message, they encounter none.

Political campaigns thus typify the golden-mean maxim of attitude change theorists: voters at the upper end of the attentiveness curve cannot be persuaded because they already have strong preferences; those at the bottom cannot be persuaded because they are never exposed to political messages. Therefore, the middle strata of political engagement—citizens who are moderately interested or informed—are the most influenced by campaigns. Those who paid no attention to news during the 2004 presidential campaign, for instance, would have had no exposure to the "Swift Boats" ads attacking John Kerry's veracity (discussed in Chapter 6) and could not possibly have been persuaded by them. Strong Democrats and Republicans, two groups that were especially likely to have heard about the ads, would have been equally unpersuaded—the former because they rejected the ads as just another Republican attack on their candidate, the latter because they were already staunchly anti-Kerry. However, weak Democrats and Republicans who were only mildly interested in the campaign but who saw the ads could have been swayed to vote against Kerry.

The opposing effects of exposure and acceptance on susceptibility to persuasion help explain why reinforcement rather than persuasion is the typical outcome of political campaigns. Voters' partisan loyalties provide a filter for interpreting campaign messages: messages that oppose viewers' attitudes are actively resisted; those that agree with viewers' attitudes are accepted. Of course, nonpartisans are far less attentive to campaigns than partisans are; nonpartisans' attitudes remain unaffected because they are unaware of what the candidates are saying. Thus, as we will demonstrate in greater detail in

Chapter 9, the principal effect of campaigns is to push Republicans and Democrats further into their respective camps.

The importance of the party filter has increased dramatically in the last two decades as the two major parties have moved apart on the issues, leaving very few elected officials in the political center (McCarty, Poole, & Rosenthal, 2006). As the party leaders have gravitated to the ideological extremes, rank-and-file partisans have aligned their positions on the liberal–conservative continuum with their party affiliation, which means that there are very few liberal Republicans or conservative Democrats. This phenomenon is known as "sorting"—the opposing political camps are now based on both party and ideological affiliation (Levendusky, 2009; Mason, 2014).

As the electorate has become more sorted, the level of animosity expressed by partisans toward each other has steadily increased. Since the early 1970s, the American National Election Studies (ANES) has included a "feeling thermometer" question measuring positive or negative feelings about several groups including the two parties. Thermometer scores of zero indicate an extreme negative evaluation, while a score of 100 represents the opposite. Beginning in the late 1970s, the thermometer score given by partisans to the "out" party—the party they do not affiliate with—has declined significantly from a high point of around 60 to the mid-30s, whereas the rating of the "in" party has remained enthusiastic (thermometer scores in the mid-70s). In the 2008 ANES survey, the average thermometer rating of the "out" party was around 30, making the out party the most disliked of all the groups included in the survey, even more so than Muslims and atheists (for details on the thermometer data, see Iyengar, Sood, & Lelkes, 2012). Defined in terms of affect, there is no doubt that the electorate is polarized.

The ANES thermometer data represents but the tip of an iceberg of evidence showing animus and ill will across party lines. A 2014 Pew Poll found that 27 percent of Democrats and 36 percent of Republicans believed that the policies of the opposing party actually threatened the well-being of the country. Around 40 percent of the partisans in this survey (those who said they identified as Democrat or Republican) viewed the out party in very unfavorable terms, a level of animosity more than double that expressed in 1994 (see Figure 8.6). Politics may not be contact sport, but Democrats and Republicans harbor generally hard feelings toward their opponents. The sense of partisan identity is increasingly associated with a Manichean, "us against them," view of the political world.

The harshly critical image of the opposition party suggests that political divisions run deep for Americans, so much so that party affiliation has become

FIGURE 8.6

A Rising Tide of Mutual Antipathy

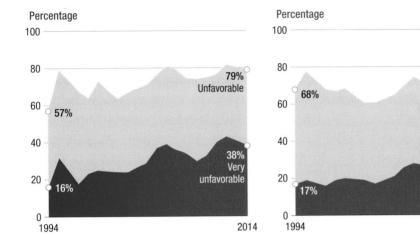

Source: 2014 Polarization in the American Public. Pew Research Center. (2014).
Note: Republicans include Republican-leaning independents; Democrats include Democrat-leaning independents.

an important cue for the initiation and conduct of interpersonal relationships. We increasingly socialize with and develop close personal ties with people whose political views we find congenial. Fifty years ago, in their classic study of political culture, Almond and Verba asked a national sample of Americans how they would feel if their son or daughter were to marry someone from the party they did not favor. Barely 5 percent of the partisans in the sample expressed any concern at the prospect of their progeny entering into an interparty marriage (Almond & Verba, 1963). But when a similar version of the question was asked in 2010, nearly half the Republicans and a third of the Democrats responded that they would feel somewhat or very unhappy at the prospect of their son or daughter marrying across party lines. The startling increase in partisans' unease over a family member crossing party lines cannot be dismissed as survey respondents simply conforming to what they believe is expected of them. Examination of the actual party registration of male and female adults residing at the same address (using both national and California voter registration files) reveals a level of spousal agreement that is close to 90 percent.

Perhaps the most startling evidence of affective polarization comes from a recent study that examined the applicability of party cues to entirely nonpolitical settings. Study participants were asked to indicate which of two high school students was more deserving of an academic scholarship. The resumes of the two students were manipulated so that in all cases, one student's grade average was higher than the other's. The resumes also revealed a difference in the students' extracurricular interests; one was active in the student wing of the Republican Party while the other was described as similarly active for the Democratic Party. Rather than nominating the student with the better grades, partisans on both sides overwhelmingly preferred the student whose political affiliation matched their own (Iyengar & Westwood, in press). Thus, it appears that the party cue is now all-encompassing and just as likely to influence non-political as political choices.

There is no shortage of explanations for increased party polarization—both ideological and affective. Primary elections may be implicated, since those at the far ends of the ideology scale far outnumber moderates among primary voters. The fact that the groups who donate large sums of money to candidates hold extreme views is another contributing factor. Because the parties diverge not only on traditional economic issues such as government spending and taxation, but also on "hot button" cultural and moral questions related to religion and other deeply held values (e.g., the issues of abortion and same-sex marriage), policy debates have become more intense and personal. Candidates' reliance on negative appeals during campaigns, as documented in Chapter 6, makes the liabilities and flaws of opposition party candidates especially salient. Finally, the nonstop rhetoric offered by partisan commentators and bloggers only serves to inflame partisan disagreements.

The fact that partisan animus has increased during a period of increased consumer choice has led many scholars to suggest that the two parallel trends are not coincidental. The ability of partisans to self-select into segregated news audiences, each encountering news and analysis reinforcing their point of view is an especially plausible account of polarization. However, as discussed in Chapter 5, at the present time partisan news sources command only a tiny slice of the media audience and the people sufficiently motivated to seek out partisan sources are those whose views of the opposing party are especially critical (see Lelkes, Sood, & Iyengar, 2014). If there is a causal relationship between news consumption and polarized attitudes, it more likely goes from polarization to media choices than in the opposite direction.

The heightened state of polarization has important implications for research on persuasion and attitude change. Given their strong views, partisans can be persuaded by party cues, but little else. They will resist information and arguments damaging to their cause. They even go so far as to deny established facts. For example, despite the noticeable improvement in the economy during the Reagan presidency, many Democrats incorrectly claimed that unemployment and inflation had increased (Bartels, 2002).[5] As we document in Chapter 10, no matter how effective the president in managing the economy or foreign affairs, he is evaluated unfavorably by supporters of the opposing party. Conversely, evidence of mismanagement and scandal does little to reduce the president's support from members of his own party.

Source- and Message-Related Contingencies

While exposure to and acceptance of persuasive messages are both conditioned by the political predispositions of receivers, some scholars have uncovered a different family of interactions—this time between message and source factors. Their argument is that persuasion effects also depend on the degree of fit between the *what* and *who* factors. Readers should recognize this argument as none other than the strategy of issue ownership. That is, Republican candidates are more persuasive when they (the source) discuss issues on which Republicans are generally preferred (the message), and the same is true for Democrats and their preferred issues.

Ansolabehere and Iyengar (1995) experimentally tested for the interaction of source and message factors. The identical advertisement (one on unemployment and one on crime) was attributed to either the Democratic or the Republican candidate running for US Senate in California. Whereas exposure to the unemployment ad elicited greater gains for the Democratic candidate, exposure to the crime ad did the same for the Republican candidate. In a related study, voters rated campaign ads aired by presidential candidates Dole and Clinton during the 1996 presidential campaign. Republicans were more likely to rate Dole's ads as informative (and less likely to rate them as misleading) when the ads addressed Republican issues (Iyengar & Valentino, 2000). Conversely, Democrats were more impressed by Clinton's ads dealing with Democratic issues. Thus the parties' policy reputations are tantamount to assessments of source credibility.

The logic of differential source credibility extends easily to attributes of the candidates beyond their party affiliation. Gender is an especially visible attribute, and the popular culture provides several cues about the traits of males and females—cues that are amply reinforced by the media's depiction of female candidates (Kahn, 1994). Given the availability of gender stereotypes, certain issue messages might be expected to have differential effects across male and female candidates. In fact, the evidence reveals that masculine issues such as defense or crime are especially persuasive as campaign material for male candidates, whereas preschool funding and other matters of educational policy work well for female candidates. Not surprisingly, given their ownership of issues of

⊚ IN FOCUS

A New Era of Minimal Effects?

Changes in the media environment and increased party polarization may weaken the media's influence over the audience. In a recent article, Bennett and Iyengar (2008) suggest that the increased availability of partisan news sources makes it more likely that many consumers will find themselves in the audience for programs they already agree with (for example, Republicans watching Sean Hannity and Democrats watching Rachel Maddow). Eventually, increasing partisan motivation and opportunities to self-select into partisan audiences may lead to a new era of minimal effects, wherein the primary effect of the media is reinforcement. The more interesting question becomes not how exposure to news programs influences the audience's attitudes but the exact opposite—how attitudes influence the selection of particular news sources.

social welfare, Democratic politicians are deemed more compassionate than Republicans (Hayes, 2005).

In short, persuasive messages are not encountered in a vacuum and must blend in with voters' partisan motives and attitudes. Persuasion effects are thus inherently interactive—involving interactions between the message and the source, interactions between the message and the partisan values of the receiver, or higher-order interactions that also capture individual differences in exposure to campaign messages.

CONCLUSION

Writing eighty years ago with remarkable foresight, Walter Lippmann (1922, 1925) offered a series of comments about the nature of American democracy. First, he warned that the great majority of American citizens were too apathetic and uninformed to govern themselves. Lacking firsthand knowledge, the public had no recourse but to rely on the "pictures in their heads" when attempting to make sense of political issues and events. Second, he warned that opportunistic political elites could take advantage of citizens' apathy and dependence on the media to manipulate public opinion to their advantage.

The evidence summarized in this chapter matches the first part of Lippmann's argument quite closely. Ordinary citizens are preoccupied with their personal lives and pay little attention to public affairs. Among the advanced industrialized democracies, the United States exhibits an unusually low level of civic literacy. Unable to weigh the pros and cons of policy debates, citizens make do with what they have: the images and sound bites transmitted by the media. They follow the lead of news programming when asked to identify the important issues of the day. Those who influence the media agenda also hold a great deal of power to mold public opinion because issues in the news become the principal yardsticks for evaluating public officials. The impact of media messages on political attitudes, however, is limited by the audience's partisan predispositions.

Another lingering question in media effects research concerns the duration or persistence of media effects on public opinion. Most experiments expose subjects to a single message and then measure the effects of the message immediately afterward. There is very little evidence concerning the long-term implications of agenda-setting, priming, or framing effects.

Taken cumulatively, the evidence indicates that media presentations achieve considerable influence over public opinion. When journalists parrot the views of political elites—as is the case during periods of military conflict—they allow elites to bolster their popularity and gain an important strategic advantage in the policy arena. In Chapter 10, we will demonstrate that fluctuations in presidential popularity have become less dependent on the state of the American economy and more dependent on media coverage—a finding we take as suggestive of Lippmann's manufactured-consent hypothesis. First, however, in Chapter 9 we'll consider the impact of political campaigns on election outcomes.

SUMMARY

1. As a result of a limited conceptualization of media effects (defining them only in terms of persuasion) and a reliance on survey methodology (which tends to underestimate media effects), political-communication researchers have long held that media effects were minimal. Methodological advances (including wider use of experiments), along with a broadened definition of media effects, have since led scholars to acknowledge that media presentations can make a difference in politics.

2. Surveys and experiments, the two methods used to study media effects, each have strengths and weaknesses. Experiments give researchers control over the stimuli to which study participants are exposed, allowing them to isolate causality, but the results from experiments cannot be easily generalized. Surveys,

on the other hand, are highly generalizable, but inaccuracy in participants' self-reports weakens the ability of survey researchers to detect media effects.

3. A variety of media effects on citizens have been examined by researchers:

- *Learning.* By tuning in to the news, Americans can acquire factual information about events. However, many studies have shown Americans to be severely lacking in political information.

- *Agenda setting.* The term *agenda setting* describes the way in which the media set the agenda for public opinion by highlighting certain issues and ignoring others.

- *Priming.* An extension of agenda setting, priming is the way in which the media affect the criteria by which political leaders are judged. The more prominent an issue becomes in the public consciousness, the more that issue will influence people's assessments of politicians, candidates, and other public figures.

- *Framing.* By highlighting some aspects of an event or issue and ignoring others, the media can influence how people think about that event or issue.

- *Persuasion.* Although most early studies on media effects failed to find evidence of persuasion, the media do have some persuasive influence—especially when the definition of persuasion is not limited to conversion from one candidate or one side of an issue to the other.

FURTHER READINGS

Abadie, A., & Imbens, G. (2002). *Simple and bias-corrected matching estimators* (NBER Technical Working Paper No. 283). Cambridge, MA: National Bureau of Economic Research.

Bartels, L. M. (1997). *How campaigns matter.* Unpublished manuscript, Princeton University, Princeton, NJ.

Bennett, W. L., & Iyengar, S. (2008). A new era of minimal effects? The changing foundations of political communication. *Journal of Communication, 58,* 707–731.

Berelson, B., Lazarsfeld, P. F., & McPhee, W. (1954). *Voting.* Chicago: University of Chicago Press.

Cohen, B. E. (1963). *The press and foreign policy.* Princeton, NJ: Princeton University Press.

Gilliam, F. D., Jr., & Iyengar, S. (2000). Prime suspects: The influence of local television news on the viewing public. *American Journal of Political Science, 44,* 560–573.

Hovland, C. L. (1959). Reconciling conflicting results derived from experimental and survey studies of attitude change. *The American Psychologist, 14,* 8–17.

Iyengar, S. (1991). *Is anyone responsible?* Chicago: University of Chicago Press.

Iyengar, S., & Kinder, D. R. (1987). *News that matters: Television and American opinion*. Chicago: University of Chicago Press.

LaCour, M. J., & Vavreck, L. (2014). Improving media measurement: Evidence from the field. *Political Communication, 31*, 408–420.

Lenz, G. S. (2012). *Follow the leader: How voters respond to politicians' performance and policies*. Chicago: University of Chicago Press.

Mutz, D. C., & Reeves, B. (2005). The new videomalaise: Effects of televised incivility on political trust. *American Political Science Review, 99*, 1–15.

Popkin, S. L. (1994). *The reasoning voter: Communication and persuasion in presidential campaigns* (2nd ed.). Chicago: University of Chicago Press.

Price, V., & Zaller, J. (1993). Who gets the news? Alternative measures of news reception and their implications for research. *Public Opinion Quarterly, 57*, 133–164.

Zaller, J. R. (1992). *The nature and origins of mass opinion*. New York: Cambridge University Press.

NOTES

1. Of course, as in any probabilistic outcome, there is some chance (typically small) that the two groups might not be equivalent.

2. Perhaps the imposition of answering the phone is not so trivial. The response rate in most major surveys has dropped in recent years and now approaches 30 percent.

3. Critics of the "heuristics as equivalent to information" argument cite evidence showing that when voters are made to acquire factual information, they express opinions that are often significantly different from the opinions they held previously. We will discuss this evidence in Chapter 11.

4. An exception is the work by Lenz (2012) which documents significant projection effects.

5. Interestingly, recent research indicates that "biased" answers to factual questions in surveys can be reduced, but only when partisans are given economic incentives to provide the correct answer (Bullock, Gerber, Hill, & Huber, 2013).

9

Campaigns That Matter

Candidates spend millions of dollars on political campaigns and deploy small armies of professional consultants in hopes of gaining a competitive edge. But in the end, would they be any worse off without this investment? Do campaigns really make a difference?

This chapter begins by providing an overview of two competing perspectives on this question and suggesting how these disparate perspectives may be reconciled. We then turn to the dynamics influencing voter behavior, the role of campaigns in providing civic education, and factors influencing voter turnout.

POLITICAL CONTEXT VERSUS CAMPAIGN EFFECTS

There are two competing perspectives on the question of how much campaigns matter. In the minimalist view typically advanced by academics, political campaigns represent "sound and fury signifying nothing." The evidence shows that, at least in the case of presidential elections, the results can be predicted with a high degree of accuracy from indicators of economic growth and public approval of the incumbent administration. In this account, changes in gross national product (GNP) during the preceding twelve months and the level of public approval of the incumbent president four months before the election are relevant to election outcomes; day-to-day tactics of the candidates in October, seemingly, are not. At the very least, this evidence suggests that the general political and economic context in which elections occur is just as important as anything the candidates themselves might do or say over the course of the campaign.

The view from the trenches is quite different. Campaign consultants claim considerable prowess in improving their clients' electoral prospects. By their account, well-executed campaign maneuvers can produce a significant increase in the candidate's level of support. They claim that the level of political advertising and the candidates' travel schedules, verbal dexterity, and demeanor in the debates make all the difference to voters. The theory is that image matters; therefore, image is what campaigns seek to project, using creative and intensive interventions.

Mounting evidence supports the existence of short-term campaign effects. Typically a presidential candidate's visit to a state generates considerable media publicity and increases that candidate's support statewide. But an opposing candidate who arrives the very next day creates an equally powerful ripple in the opposite direction. It seems that day-to-day tactics can significantly move public opinion; however, if campaigns have similar levels of resources (in terms of both funding and professional expertise), any campaign-induced shifts in voter support will cancel each other out over the course of the campaign.

Between the strictly context-driven and engineered explanations of electoral outcomes is a more realistic middle ground. Every election occurs within a distinct political context to which the candidates adapt their messages. During the recession of 1992, Americans' general sense of economic insecurity led the Clinton campaign to adopt "It's the economy, stupid" as its core message and mantra. In 2004, in the aftermath of the 9/11 attacks and the first stages of the war in Iraq, President Bush ran for reelection on the grounds that he had made the country more secure from terrorist attacks. In 2012, President Obama's case for reelection rested on his stewardship of the country's return from the brink of economic collapse. Each campaign was seeking to position itself advantageously within the current political context to which the candidates had to respond. Economic messages were profoundly relevant in 1992 and 2012, but less so in 2004, when national security concerns were paramount.

No matter what the nature of the current political context is, a perennial element of campaigns is the track record of the candidate or party in power. Voters tend to rely on their assessments of the incumbent's performance as a guide for choosing between the candidates. In their eyes, the state of the country reflects either favorably or unfavorably on the incumbent. Ronald Reagan understood the intuitive appeal of this psychological barometer when he asked voters, "Are you better off today than you were four years ago?"

However, well-entrenched perceptions of the state of the nation and the qualities of the incumbent administration do not make campaign strategies irrelevant. To the contrary, campaign professionals know full well that voters care about the current political context, and they therefore design their messages accordingly. They position their clients to capitalize on what voters deem important. Thus, in any given campaign, exposure to the candidates' messages makes voters even more reliant on the underlying fundamental or contextual forces.

VOTER DYNAMICS: FORECASTING PRESIDENTIAL ELECTIONS

Political scientists have devised a variety of statistical models for forecasting the results of presidential elections. In most cases, the forecasts combine the incumbent's popularity with the state of the economy. The dynamic underlying the forecasting models is exactly as implied by Reagan's rhetorical ploy—namely, the logic of reward or punishment based on the incumbent's stewardship of the country. Voters are expected to reelect the incumbent during times of economic growth but opt for change during times of distress.

Forecasters capture this logic by incorporating some measure of public support for the incumbent (typically the incumbent's standing in trial heat polls on Labor Day or the percentage of the public who approve of the president's job performance) with standard indicators of economic performance. The economic indicators are generally recorded considerably in advance of the campaign; examples include change in real gross domestic product (GDP) during the second quarter of the election year, consumer satisfaction with personal finances in the second quarter, or the percentage change in gross national product between the fourth quarter of the preceding year and the second quarter of the election year.

Basing their predictions on a combination of incumbent approval and the past state of the economy, the forecasting models have accumulated an impressive track record: with the exception of the 2000 election (which was the closest on record), the models have accurately predicted the winner in elections from 1948 to 2012 with only a small spread between the predicted and actual results. Recent elections have proven especially predictable. For the 2008 and 2012 elections, the average forecast proved accurate to within a half of a percentage point of the actual outcome.

Figure 9.1 shows the overall correspondence between the state of the economy in the months preceding the election and the fate of the incumbent party's presidential candidate. Clearly, favorable economic conditions benefit incumbents. On the basis of this particular model (devised by political scientists John Zaller and Larry Bartels), President Obama won in 2008 and was reelected in

FIGURE 9.1

The Economy and the Vote for President, 1948–2012

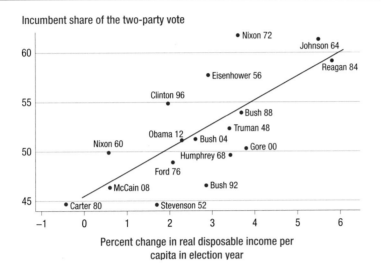

Source: Data from Bureau of Economic Analysis, compiled by John Zaller.

2012 by almost exactly the expected margin, given the state of the economy (Bartels & Zaller, 2001).

The data in Figure 9.1 show that Al Gore was—as widely asserted in the media—an underachieving candidate. Gore's share of the 2000 vote was some five points below his expected share. Some scholars suggest that Gore's decision to distance himself from his predecessor (Clinton), under whose leadership the economy had boomed, was what hindered his candidacy. Others who fared worse than they should have include President George H. W. Bush in 1992, Gerald Ford in 1976, Hubert Humphrey in 1968, and Adlai Stevenson in 1952. On the positive side, Presidents Nixon (1972), Clinton (1996), and Eisenhower (1956) all beat the forecast. Overall, Figure 9.1 suggests that, at the margin, campaigns produce relatively small deviations from the outcome one would see if voters cared only about the state of the economy.

THE INFLUENCE OF CAMPAIGNS

The fact that presidential elections generally follow the reward–punish rule is not, in and of itself, an argument against the influence of campaigns. First, when the contest is competitive and the candidates are separated by only a few points in the polls, the efforts of campaign strategists may make all the difference between winning and losing. Trailing in the key battleground states in the closing weeks of the 2000 campaign, the Bush campaign outspent the Gore campaign on the airwaves and narrowed the gap. Second, as we will discuss, considerable evidence suggests that exposure to campaign messages encourages voters, especially those with lower levels of political interest and motivation, to behave in ways that are exactly as anticipated by the forecasting models.

Contrary to the conventional wisdom, the evidence suggests that campaigns do not manipulate voters into supporting the candidate with the most attractive appearance or compelling advertisements. Instead, one of the principal effects of campaigns is to bring candidate preferences into line with the voter's sense of party identification. By the end of the campaign, very few partisans contemplate voting for the out-party candidate.

In the rest of this chapter we will look at the ways in which campaigns influence voters. After presenting the evidence concerning the reinforcing effects of campaigns, we will turn to the ways in which campaigns attract so-called swing, or undecided, voters. Typically lacking an attachment to a party, these voters are susceptible to image- and issue-oriented appeals. They might vote for the candidate deemed more trustworthy or the candidate who stands for policies that more closely approximate their own preferences.

Next we will take up the educational or civic impact of campaigns. Presumably the onslaught of advertising, news coverage, and partisan rhetoric adds something to voters' store of knowledge about the candidates and the issues. The evidence suggests that voters do indeed learn from campaigns, but they find it easier to learn about image than about issues. In the case of primary elections, voters are especially likely to gain information about the question of *viability*—a candidate's ability to win. The proliferation of early primaries and the fact that primary voters cannot fall back on their party affiliation creates the possibility of significant bandwagon effects by which voters flock to candidates who demonstrate vote-getting prowess in the early primaries.

Finally, we will address the role of campaigns in influencing the level of voter turnout. In recent cycles, both parties have invested significant resources in the ground game—contacting their potential supporters and getting them to the polls. For voters who may be less than enthusiastic about politics, get-out-the-vote efforts can be especially effective. While striving to increase turnout among their supporters, campaigns may simultaneously take steps to discourage would-be opponents from voting. One of the objectives of negative campaigning is to make undecided voters cynical about both candidates, thus weakening their incentive to vote.

VOTING AS AN EXPRESSION OF PARTISANSHIP

Decades of research into why individuals vote the way they do has made it abundantly clear that party affiliation is the single most important determinant of vote choice. Most Americans are socialized into identifying with one of the two major political parties even before they enter kindergarten. This basic sense of loyalty to the party sticks with individuals through their entire lives. In the jargon of voting research, party identification is the *long-term* influence on elections; year in and year out, Americans vote according to their standing commitment.[1] Contrary to popular accounts, party identification is alive and well within the electorate; if anything, party-line voting is on the increase.

Of course, not all Americans claim to identify with a political party. As Figure 9.2 shows, more than a third of the electorate rejected partisan labels in 2012, preferring to call themselves *independents*.[2] For this pivotal group, the voting decision varies from election to election—hence their designation as *swing voters*. Swing voters might choose candidates on the basis of their positions on the issues or according to their assessments of incumbent performance. More likely, swing voters are attracted to a candidate on personality

FIGURE 9.2

Party Identification in the Electorate

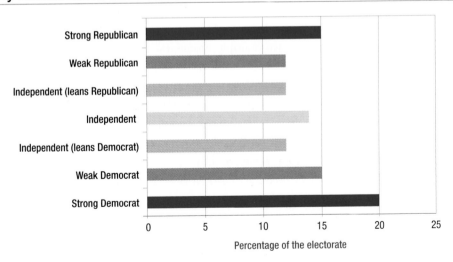

Percentage of the electorate

Source: American National Election Studies, 2012. Retrieved January 9, 2015, from http://www.electionstudies.org /studypages/cdf/cdf.htm.

grounds; they are willing to vote for someone they believe is a strong leader, with the necessary experience or, alternatively, a person of impeccable character. In short, swing voters choose on the basis of candidate and not party considerations. We will consider the evidence concerning candidate-based voting shortly.

Going into the campaign, Democrats and Republicans have a strong predisposition to support their nominee. Except when the party nominates a candidate who is largely unrepresentative of rank-and-file voters (such as Goldwater in 1964, McGovern in 1972), the great majority of partisans can be counted on to vote correctly. Rather than responding objectively or "on the merits," partisans interpret campaign events and messages in ways that confirm rather than contradict their sense of political identity. For Democrats, candidate Mitt Romney was a billionaire businessman who took advantage of loopholes to avoid paying income tax; for Republicans he was an able chief executive with a proven track record in both business and government. Over the course of the campaign, the pressure to maintain consistency between party affiliation and beliefs about the candidates makes partisans increasingly likely to vote for their nominee. Exposure to the campaign thus reinforces party loyalty.

Unlike partisans, independents enter the campaign with an open mind. As the campaign progresses, they encounter information and form impressions of the candidates. When the information flow is relatively balanced (an equal number of favorable and unfavorable encounters with both candidates), non-partisans may remain undecided until the very last moment. In other cases, when one candidate generates more favorable messages than the opponent, independents are persuaded accordingly.

Thus, campaigns have multiple objectives. The first is to ensure that their partisans remain steadfast (holding the base). The second is to attract a sufficient number of independents to win them a plurality. Implicit to both of these goals is the task of informing voters about the personal characteristics, political credentials, and policy visions of the candidates. Finally, campaigns seek to optimize turnout by encouraging supporters and discouraging opponents and would-be opponents from voting.

HOLDING THE BASE

Beginning in the 1940s, large-scale sample surveys noted that campaigns induced very few voters to cross party lines. Instead of converting partisans, campaigns made Republicans even more enthusiastic about voting Republican, and Democrats all the more inclined to vote Democratic. The reinforcement effect means that campaigns typically polarize the electorate along partisan lines.

As the campaign progresses and more voters encounter the candidates' messages, voters increasingly come to align with their party affiliation, their evaluations of the incumbent administration, or their assessments of the state of the country.

In the 1988 presidential campaign, for instance, Republican candidate George H. W. Bush trailed Michael Dukakis by double digits in June and July. Once the campaign began in earnest, more and more Americans reacted in a partisan manner; those whose standing connections were predominantly Republican became more likely to declare their intention to vote for Bush. As a result, the gap between Bush's expected support (based on voters' partisan pre- dispositions) and his actual support narrowed. Of course, Bush went on to win the election. In the 2008 campaign, there was the opposite trend. Early in the campaign (July–August) McCain and Obama were locked in a close contest even though the forecasts indicated a comfortable victory for Obama. While McCain's early numbers were close to his forecast, Obama was underachiev- ing among Democrats, in part due to some voters' concerns over his race and lack of political experience. The onset of the economic crisis on September 18, however, fundamentally altered the trajectory of voter preference. McCain's support dropped from a high of 48 percent in early September to 43 percent in mid-October. Over the same period, Obama's support increased from 45 to 52 percent. Over the final weeks of the campaign, both candidates' levels of support converged with the forecast models.

A simpler barometer of partisan reinforcement in campaigns is to track the number of voters who say they intend to vote for their party candidate. Using national surveys conducted over the entire period of the 1988, 1992, and 1996 presidential campaigns, researchers found that the level of party voting increased steadily with time, generally peaking by October (see Figure 9.3). A few weeks before the election, strong partisans (those who claim they are strongly affiliated with their party) were almost unanimously behind their candidate (with levels of party voting in excess of 90 percent). Note that the reinforcing effect of the campaign proved much stronger among voters whose sense of party loyalty was ambivalent (people who said that they were only weak Republicans or Democrats). Weak partisans registered larger increases in support for their nominee; over time they tended to catch up with their more intense copartisans. By October, the gap between strong and weak partisans was significantly narrowed. As the election approached, more than 70 percent of the weak partisans were prepared to vote for their candidate.

The pattern shown in Figure 9.4 suggests that voters' sense of partisanship is activated or strengthened through exposure to specific partisan messages or events. Both campaign advertisements and televised debates contribute to reinforcement. In the case of the former, exposure to a single advertisement is

FIGURE 9.3

Party Allegiance in Voting Patterns

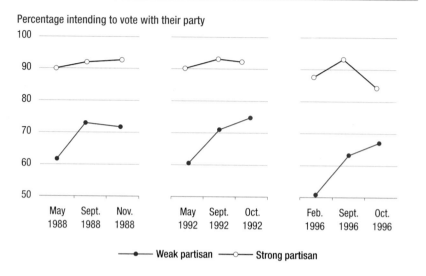

Percentage intending to vote with their party

Source: Data from S. Iyengar & J. R. Petrocik. (2000). Basic rule voting: The impact of campaigns on party- and approval-based voting. In J. Thurber, C. J. Nelson, & D. A. Dulio (Eds.), *Crowded airwaves: Campaign advertising in elections* (pp. 113–148). Washington, DC: Brookings Institution Press.

sufficient. During the 1990 and 1992 campaigns, Ansolabehere and Iyengar (1995) conducted several experiments in which they inserted a campaign ad into a fifteen-minute local newscast. Residents of Southern California watched the newscast and then completed a survey of their political attitudes. Overall, exposure to the political ad proved persuasive—the percentage of the sample reporting that they would vote for the candidate featured in the ad increased by 7 percent. However, almost all of the effect occurred among viewers who shared the party affiliation of the sponsoring candidate. When the ad was from a Democratic candidate, the Democrats in the study responded favorably, but independents and Republicans were unmoved. Similarly, when the sponsor was Republican, the ad produced significant gains primarily among Republican voters. Averaged across studies, the effect of watching an ad among in-party viewers was a 14 percent increase in support for the sponsoring candidate. Thus the benefits of advertising were concentrated among partisans. Over time, as more and more voters encounter ads, members of the electorate are increasingly pushed into their respective partisan camps.

What is especially revealing about the experimental studies is the relationship between the reinforcing effects of advertising and voters' level of political

FIGURE 9.4

Reinforcing Effects of Campaign Advertising on Voter Choice

Effects of exposure to a political ad are concentrated among viewers who share the party affiliation of the sponsoring candidate.

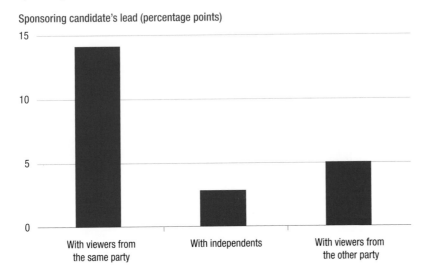

Sponsoring candidate's lead (percentage points)

Source: Data from S. Ansolabehere & S. Iyengar. (1995). *Going negative: How attack ads shrink and polarize the electorate.* New York: Free Press.

interest (see Figure 9.5). Consider an intense Republican who follows the campaign religiously. She is so enthusiastic that her preferences need no reinforcing. On the other hand, a more lukewarm partisan may not be particularly familiar with the candidates or the issues. For this voter, a television advertisement may provide the necessary spark to fire up partisan sentiments. The reinforcing effects of campaigns, accordingly, should be especially pronounced among the less motivated and attentive partisans.

This graded pattern of reinforcement effects by level of interest is precisely what occurred in the advertising experiments. As Figure 9.5 shows, the persuasive effects of exposure to a television commercial were concentrated among the less interested partisans. For Democrats with a relatively high level of political interest, encountering an ad from a Democratic candidate represents overkill: they are already committed to the Democratic candidate. For the less motivated partisan, however, advertising provides a necessary wake-up call; among this group, candidates can increase their level of support by up to 20 percent.[3]

Over the years, the reinforcing effects of campaigns have steadily increased as the level of party conflict over issues has risen and party identifiers have

FIGURE 9.5

Reinforcing Effects of Campaign Advertising by Level of Political Interest

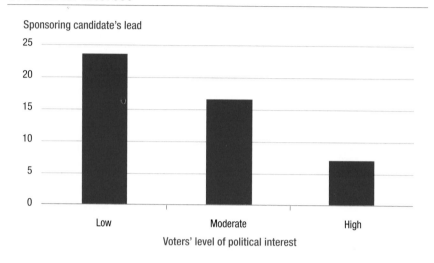

Source: Data from S. Ansolabehere & S. Iyengar. (1995). *Going negative: How attack ads shrink and polarize the electorate*. New York: Free Press.

sorted themselves into liberal and conservative camps. As noted in Chapter 8, the party label has become more important to an individual's sense of group identity, making it even less likely that a partisan will defect and support a candidate from the out-party. In the case of presidential campaigns, the candidates can count on getting close to 95 percent of the vote from their respective camps.

As in the case of advertising, the evidence suggests that voters react to televised debates not as objective judges but rather as partisan fans. No matter how poorly their candidate might perform, that candidate is deemed to have outdebated the opponent. Perceptions of who won the debate (in a general election), for all practical purposes, are proxies for voters' party affiliation.

The most extreme case of selective perception occurred in 1976 in a debate between Gerald Ford and Jimmy Carter (see Video Archive 9.1). During the debate, as noted in Chapter 6, Ford was asked a question about American policy concerning the Soviet-controlled nations of Eastern Europe. He replied that the United States did not tolerate Soviet interference in the affairs of sovereign states and that the countries of Eastern Europe were free of Soviet control.[4]

By any standard, Ford's statement represented a major gaffe. The Soviets exercised tight control over Eastern European governments at the time and, as the Czechs learned in 1968 (and the Hungarians before them in 1956), any attempts at autonomy would be crushed by Soviet military might. President

Video Archive 9.1

Ford/Carter Debate, 1976

Ford seemed blissfully unaware of recent history. But despite this blunder, polls conducted immediately after the debate showed that voters' support for the candidates remained unchanged. Democrats felt that Carter had won the debate, and by equally wide margins, Republicans gave the nod to Ford. It was not until several days later, in the aftermath of extensive press coverage of Ford's debate misstatement, that Carter eked out a small lead over Ford in the polls.

Although neither candidate committed a major gaffe, the first debate between Romney and Obama in 2012 was generally interpreted as a significant victory for the former. Romney repeatedly highlighted the weakness of the national economy while Obama was listless and unwilling to challenge Romney's critical characterization of his economic record. Following the debate, Republicans' support for their candidate surged, especially their views of Romney as effective, bold, inspiring, and intelligent. However, despite Obama's lackluster performance in the debate, Democrats continued to rate him highly. Eighty-six percent of Democrats viewed Obama as intelligent before the debate and this number slipped by only two points in the aftermath of the debate. (The only rating on which Obama lost some support from Democrats was for effectiveness, and even here a majority of Democrats supported him following the debate.) Thus, the main effect of the debate was to solidify Republicans' support for Romney. Overall, partisans became even more polarized in their ratings of the candidates after the debate despite the one-sided outcome (see Figure 9.6).

In general, viewers evaluate what the candidates say depending on their party. Even when candidates commit a major faux pas, or demonstrate considerable ignorance about the state of the world, they manage to hold on to the support

🎯 IN FOCUS

The Reinforcement Effect

- One of the primary effects of campaigns is *reinforcement*, bringing voters' candidate preferences in line with their party identification. As a campaign progresses and more voters encounter the candidates' messages, they are increasingly inclined to vote for their party's candidate. By the end of the campaign, very few partisans contemplate voting for another party's candidate. Thus, the reinforcement effect means that campaigns typically polarize the electorate along partisan lines.

- Overall, the evidence on reinforcement indicates that, contrary to conventional wisdom, media-based campaigns do not manipulate voters. Instead, campaigns steer voters in the direction of their respective parties, encouraging them to vote in accordance with their core political loyalties. Reinforcement of partisanship is a far cry from manipulation.

FIGURE 9.6

Changes in Partisans' Ratings of the Candidates' Traits after the First 2012 Presidential Debate

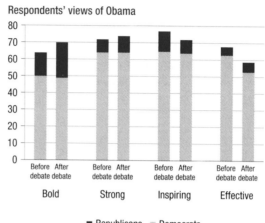

Respondents' views of Obama

■ Republicans ▨ Democrats

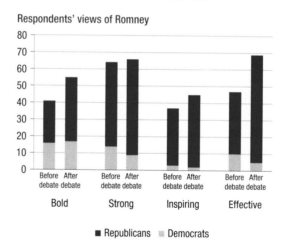

Respondents' views of Romney

■ Republicans ▨ Democrats

Source: Data from YouGov polls conducted September 29–October 1 and October 6–8. Graph by John Sides.

of their partisans. It takes a significant mistake, and one that generates considerable buzz in the media, before debates make a dent in the candidate's support.

ATTRACTING SWING VOTERS

For partisans, their candidate can do little wrong. Independents, however, are more open minded and, depending on the course of a campaign, can be moved in either direction. Once candidates have secured their base, they direct their overtures at this group.

The most important clue to the behavior of independent voters concerns their impressions of the candidates' personalities, especially the traits of competence and integrity. To be seen as intelligent, decisive, and knowledgeable is a prerequisite for attracting voter support. The candidate's moral bearings are also relevant; Senator Edward Kennedy was unable to mount a successful run for the presidency in 1980 because large numbers of the public questioned his integrity in the wake of the notorious Chappaquiddick incident.[5]

As we noted in Chapter 6, advertising early in a campaign tends to portray the candidate as a pleasant, upstanding, experienced problem solver. A favorable personal image can go a long way among independent voters. Independents were drawn to John F. Kennedy's youthful charisma, Jimmy Carter's image as a hardworking and honest public servant, Reagan's charm and strong values, and Obama's appeal for change. Conversely, they were turned off by Michael Dukakis's lack of personal warmth, by President George H. W. Bush's apparent lack of concern for the welfare of working people, and by Al Gore's arrogance and inconsiderate behavior in the first debate of the 2000 campaign. In all these instances, images of the candidates' personal traits were one-sided. Most recently, in the case of the 2012 debate between Romney and Obama, which was dominated by Romney, independents reacted as dispassionate judges. Their ratings of Obama as intelligent and effective fell by more than 10 percentage points, while their views of Romney became more favorable by the same margin.

In general, voters do not care equally about all facets of a candidate's character. Depending on the circumstances, they seize on particular traits. In 1992, President George H. W. Bush was a decorated war hero with an unblemished personal life. His opponent, Bill Clinton, had not only managed to avoid military service but was also dogged by allegations of womanizing and marital infidelity. During the debates President Bush repeatedly reminded voters of Clinton's history, but to no effect. For most voters, even though Bush was apparently the more trust-worthy candidate, Clinton was perceived as the more able manager, who would turn around the economy. Because voters assigned higher priority to competence over integrity, Clinton won despite his unfavorable image on the latter.

A similar focusing effect, although of a different variety, occurred in the first debate of the 2000 campaign. In addition to continually interrupting Governor Bush and making clear his irritation with Bush's answers, Vice President Gore casually stated that he had accompanied Federal Emergency Management Agency (FEMA) Director James Witt on a tour of Parker County, Texas—an area devastated by wildfires. The vice president had misspoken; he had not accompanied the FEMA director on that particular tour.[6] The Republicans seized on this error and other misstatements (including one concerning his grandmother's out-of-pocket expenses for prescription drugs) as further evidence of Gore's penchant for exaggeration and bravado. Fanned by Bush campaign press releases, a secondary debate over Gore's veracity burst out in the media, especially on talk radio. Gradually a significant number of swing voters came over to Bush on the grounds that Gore played fast and loose with the facts.

In addition to responding to their impressions of the candidates' personalities, swing voters may base their choices on a more substantive evaluation that focuses on the candidates' policy platforms. In the idealized case, an *issue voter* is one who holds preferences on policy issues and who is aware of both of the major candidates' positions on these issues. Assume that voter Smith is pro-choice and supports affirmative action and government-subsidized healthcare. In the 2012 election, Smith would have concluded that Obama was the closer candidate on all three issues and cast his vote accordingly.

Voting on the issues requires relatively well-informed and opinionated voters. As we will note in the next section, however, relatively few Americans are capable of casting strictly issue-based votes. Many voters do not have a clear preference on any given issue, and even more are unaware of the candidates' positions. The media's penchant for covering the horse race does not make the task any easier. And when voters have the opportunity to watch the candidates debate the issues, they are drawn to evidence of personality rather than ideology. The 1960 debates between Kennedy and Nixon were thought to have given Kennedy an advantage because viewers were drawn to the visual contrast between the youthful-looking and tanned Kennedy and the pale, sickly looking Nixon. Among people who listened to the debate on the radio, however, it was Nixon's debating skills that made an impression.[7]

In a recent experimental re-creation of the first Kennedy–Nixon debate (Druckman, 2003), one group watched on television, while another was given

Video Archive 9.2
Bush/Clinton and Bush/Gore Debate

Video Archive 9.3
Kennedy/Nixon Debate, 1960

only the audio track. As expected, the television group was more likely to rely on image factors (such as integrity) when considering the candidates' performance in the debate. The radio group, on the other hand, took into account both image and the candidates' positions on the issues. This study confirms that the visual imagery provided by candidate debates encourages voters to focus on personality-related rather than issue-related considerations when evaluating the candidates.

An additional set of candidate attributes can come into play, especially during nonpresidential campaigns, in which news coverage and other forms of campaign communication tend to be less prevalent. In state and local races, clearly visible physical attributes, such as the candidate's gender, ethnicity, or physical attractiveness, may influence their level of support. Female candidates, for instance, run well among women, as do black candidates in districts with large numbers of African American voters. Because the decibel level of the campaign is lower, voters lack information about the candidates' personal attributes or policy positions. They make do by inferring these attributes from the candidate's gender or ethnicity. Extrapolating from cultural stereotypes, for instance, they may view a female candidate as caring and compassionate, and more willing to support government funding for child-care and nutrition programs. Conversely, male candidates tend to be seen as strong leaders who are more likely to support a tough stance on issues of national security.

EDUCATING VOTERS

Partisan voters have a convenient basis for voting, even without the benefit of specific information concerning the candidates and the issues. Independents, however, are not similarly equipped. For independents to express a vote preference, they must first acquire a basic impression of the candidates. Campaigns facilitate this task by delivering information about their candidate's personal background and positions on major issues. Gradually, voters develop differentiated, though not necessarily accurate, images of the candidates.

There are three levels of relevant candidate information. At the most basic level, voters must recognize the candidates' names. Voters are unlikely to select a candidate whose name they encounter for the first time on the ballot. In presidential campaigns, the candidates typically achieve universal name recognition (either through news coverage of their candidacies or by using biographical advertisements) by the time they are officially nominated in late summer. In lower-level races, however, candidates tend to be less visible and must expend more effort to achieve public familiarity. The fact that incumbents have much higher levels of name recognition than their challengers, as we noted in Chapter 6, makes for an inherently unequal contest. Incumbents attempt to preserve their tactical advantage by limiting their participation in debates, thus denying their lesser-known opponents much-needed opportunities to catch up.

Although it helps to be recognized, candidates cannot count on mere familiarity as a basis for voter support. They must flesh out their candidacies by telling voters about their experience and qualifications (competence), moral values, and concern for the needs of ordinary people (trustworthiness). As demonstrated in Chapter 6, early advertising is designed to provide voters with an image of the candidate as a likable person capable of political leadership.

The final layer of campaign information concerns the candidates' positions on the issues. Given the penchant of the news media to downplay issues at the expense of the horse race and character-related stories, it is not surprising that acquiring information about the candidates' stances on major issues is the most difficult task confronting voters. Not only do they infrequently encounter issue information but they also lack the sophistication and motivation to know where to find this information (such as at the candidates' websites). Compounding the problem, the candidates are often deliberately ambiguous in their messages, hoping to attract votes from both sides of a contested issue.

Unlike the case with issues, voters have little difficulty forming impressions of the candidates' personal qualities. The percentage of voters who can offer an opinion about presidential candidates' intelligence, sincerity, honesty, or other related attributes generally rises dramatically during the initial stages of the campaign. Of course, the learning trajectory varies, depending on the visibility of the candidate and the attentiveness of the voter. Household names such as Ronald Reagan, George H. W. Bush, and Hillary Clinton all entered the race with universal name recognition. Others, such as Jimmy Carter (initially referred to as "Jimmy Who?"), Bill Clinton, and Barack Obama had to build up voter familiarity through early primary successes. Once again, incumbents enjoy a substantial advantage. At the outset of the 2004 campaign, for instance, almost all Americans could rate President George W. Bush's personal attributes, but only a bare majority could do the same for Senator Kerry and the rest of the Democratic field. Unlike Senator Kerry, who had to invest substantially in biographical ads, President Bush could proceed directly to discussing the issues.

In the 2008 campaign, many candidates entered with historically high levels of name recognition. When asked if they could name *any* candidate running in the 2008 Democratic presidential primary, 78 percent of survey respondents named Hillary Clinton, 68 percent named Barack Obama, and 81 percent were able to name at least one candidate. Four years earlier, only 41 percent could name any candidate contesting the Democratic primaries (Pew Research

FIGURE 9.7

Increases in Familiarity with McCain and Obama during the 2008 Campaign

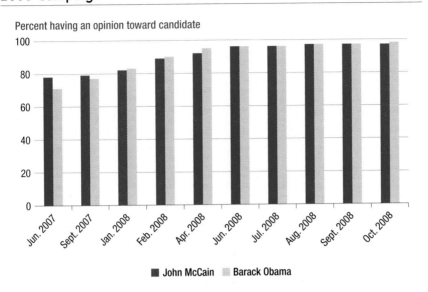

Percent having an opinion toward candidate

■ John McCain　▨ Barack Obama

Source: Data from Gallup Poll. Available at http://www.gallup.com/poll/27673/Despite-Campaign
-Familiarity-Candidates-Has-Changed-Substantially.aspx.

Center, 2007). As Figure 9.7 shows, while 70 percent of voters could offer an opinion of John McCain and Barack Obama sixteen months before the election, by April 2008 the number exceeded 90 percent.

The ability to learn about the candidates' traits also depends on just who is tuning in to the campaign. Voters with higher levels of interest and stronger partisan preferences are more likely to acquire opinions about the candidates and at a relatively earlier stage. In general, campaigns only widen the knowledge gap between the haves and the have-nots.

Figure 9.8 shows the percentage of voters identifying as Republican (including leaners) who could recognize some of their party's 2012 presidential candidates in mid-2011. Clearly, for well-known candidates such as Gingrich and Romney, the benefits of being in the spotlight were minimal since relatively few people hadn't heard of them. For the candidates who started out as relative unknowns, such as former Utah Governor Jon Huntsman and Herman Cain, media attention produced very large gains in their visibility; the percent of Republicans recognizing them doubled between May and July.

One reason that voters find it generally easier to acquire personality impressions than policy impressions of the candidates is that the former task is

FIGURE 9.8

Increases in Familiarity with Republican Candidates (2012)

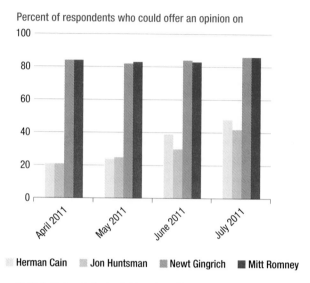

Percent of respondents who could offer an opinion on

Herman Cain   Jon Huntsman   Newt Gingrich   Mitt Romney

Source: Data from Multiple Gallup Polls. Available at http://www.gallup.com/topic/election_2012.aspx.

equivalent to the everyday process of forming impressions of friends, neighbors, or colleagues. Small and colorful snippets of information, telltale incidents or events, and the candidate's demeanor at an interview or debate all fuel inferences about personality (a phenomenon psychologists call the *fundamental attribution error*). In 1976, President Gerald Ford's unfamiliarity with Mexican cuisine (Ford neglected to remove the husk from a tamale before biting into it at a televised rally in San Antonio) was interpreted by Hispanic voters as revealing insensitivity to their needs. In 1980, Ronald Reagan insisted that a New Hampshire Republican primary debate be open to all the candidates (breaking his earlier pledge to debate only George Bush). Bush, who had agreed only to a one-on-one debate with Reagan, refused to participate. When the moderator of the debate asked the uninvited candidates to leave, Mr. Reagan strode over to the podium, grabbed the microphone, and proclaimed, "I paid for this microphone, Mr. Green." To voters, his actions conveyed an image of decisiveness and conviction. In 1996, when Republican candidate Bob Dole stumbled and fell off a speaker's platform at a campaign event, the incident immediately raised alarm about Dole's age and fitness.

In contrast with matters of personality, voters generally take much longer to become aware of the candidates' positions on policy issues. By normal standards, issues are considered the most appropriate criteria for evaluating candidates.

Against this standard, American campaigns are woefully inadequate; voters tend to be poorly informed at the start of the campaign, and their ignorance persists.

Voters remain ignorant of the candidates' positions even when the candidates address particular issues at length. In the 2004 primary campaign, American intervention in Iraq and the outsourcing of American jobs were central issues. Howard Dean catapulted to the top of the Democratic field in advance of the primaries because he was the first to come out against American intervention in Iraq. Later, John Edwards mounted a strong challenge to John Kerry using the outsourcing of American jobs as his signature issue. As Figure 9.9 shows, however, the level of public awareness of the candidates' positions on these two issues was slight.

With the solitary exception of President Bush's position on unilateral military intervention, only a minority of the public could accurately identify candidates' positions on the issues. Perhaps because of the stridency of his message, Dean's position was initially more widely recognized than the position of either

FIGURE 9.9

Changes in Awareness of Candidates' Issue Positions

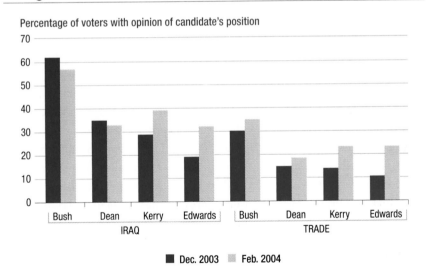

Source: Data from S. Iyengar, R. Luskin, & J. Fishkin, 2004. *Deliberative public opinion in presidential primaries: Evidence from the online deliberative poll.* Paper presented at the Voice and Citizenship: Rethinking Theory and Practice in Political Communication Conference, University of Washington, Department of Communication, Seattle.
Note: These data are based on a representative sample of approximately 500 adult Americans who were interviewed in December 2003 and February 2004. The sample was drawn from the Knowledge Networks panel and comprised the control group in a study designed to assess the effects of online deliberation on voter information.

Kerry or Edwards. Two months later, the number of voters able to identify Kerry's position had increased significantly (by 10 points), making Kerry the most recognized Democrat. Edwards's position on the issue also had become significantly more visible. In comparison with President Bush, however, Kerry and all the Democrats trailed by substantial margins.

Relative to the question of military intervention, the issue of free trade versus protectionism remained invisible. In December, the proportion of voters able to identify the Democrats as protectionists was about 10 percent. President Bush's well-publicized support for free trade was recognized by a mere 30 percent of the public. Two months later, as a result of the Democratic primary campaign, the gap between Bush and the two leading Democrats had narrowed. Overall, however, fewer than 1 in 3 Americans could identify the views of the major candidates on this issue. Despite the amount of rhetoric devoted to the trade issue during the early primary campaign, information about the candidates' positions had not trickled down to the level of the ordinary voter.

Voter unfamiliarity with the issues at the outset of the campaign changes little as an election draws near. A study of the 1988 presidential campaign (Buchanan, 1991) compared the number of voters who became reasonably informed about issues that received either extensive press coverage (such as taxes and capital punishment) or minimal coverage (such as the line-item veto and federal tax credits for day care). Between September and October, voters became more informed (on average) about where Vice President Bush and Governor Dukakis stood on the high-visibility issues by a margin of 10 percent. For low-visibility issues, the comparable level of learning was only 3 percent. A mere two weeks before the election, only 29 percent of the public had heard of Bush's pledge to be the "education president." Similar levels of ignorance applied to the Dukakis position on defense: only 30 percent were familiar with his proposals to strengthen US conventional forces.

Despite everything we've said up to this point, the public's unfamiliarity with the candidates' policy positions should not be overstated. Although voters may be unfamiliar with the details of the party platforms, they can compensate through their familiarity with the groups and interests that stand to gain from Democratic or Republican policies—for example, blue-collar workers and senior citizens in the case of Democrats, business interests and fundamentalist Christians in the case of Republicans. They are also aware of the broad policy emphases of the political parties. A majority, for instance, correctly recognize that Democrats are more sensitive to unemployment than Republicans are, and Republicans are seen as more likely to adopt policies that minimize inflation.

Thus, although information about specific pledges may be missing, voters do have a gut sense of the candidates' ideology and general policy orientation.

In summary, campaigns seek to flesh out voters' impressions of the candidates. The task is generally easier in the case of personality because voters infer or form impressions from casual incidents and isolated pieces of information. In the case of issue positions, voters tend to be aware of the candidates' overall vision of government, but most people remain uninformed about candidates' specific policy positions.

LEARNING AND MOMENTUM IN PRIMARY CAMPAIGNS

Primary elections represent a special case of campaign effects. The principal determinant of vote choice—party identification—is no longer applicable. With a relatively large field of sometimes unfamiliar candidates, the task of voting is made more difficult. Moreover, candidates in primaries often deliberately state their positions ambiguously, not wishing to alienate voters with opposing views or to unnecessarily constrain their messages later in the campaign. Instead of highlighting issues, they often campaign on the basis of background and personality, seeking to present themselves as likable, competent leaders and the best bet to win in November.

As we noted in Chapter 6, press coverage of the early primaries can play a key role in determining candidate trajectories. Candidates who win the expectations game (who do better than expected in Iowa and New Hampshire) are labeled serious contenders, while the rest of the field is left to gradually wither away. In recent years, the importance of early primary successes has been amplified because the Iowa and New Hampshire contests are no longer isolated events. Instead, a host of states have moved up their primaries to follow closely on the heels of New Hampshire. Thus the primary process has become front loaded. In 2004, a candidate could accumulate the number of delegates required to win the Democratic nomination as early as "Super Tuesday," which fell on March 2. The process was further complicated in 2008. Iowa and New Hampshire moved up their contests to January 3 and 8, respectively, and "Super Tuesday" (when twenty-one states held primaries) occurred on February 5.

The major consequence of front loading is a serious reduction in the flow of information between candidates and voters. In a context of rapid-fire primary elections occurring in far-flung locations, it is virtually impossible for the candidates—no matter how well financed they might be—to reach a majority of primary voters. There is simply not enough time to mount an adequate advertising campaign or to schedule multiple visits to primary states. Time and resource constraints make it inevitable that voters in early primaries will lack information when they go to the polls.

When they don't have much information, voters must fall back on available cues. Given the media's penchant for horse-race coverage of primaries, voters are likely to know which candidates are doing well and which ones are faring poorly. As primaries occur and the media seize on the latest results to handicap the race further, voters encounter an abundance of information that they can use to assess the relative viability of the candidates. As Brady and Johnston (1987) put it: "Citizens . . . learn too slowly about every aspect of the candidates except their viability. And, one of the major reasons that citizens learn quickly about viability is the enormous emphasis placed on the horse race by the media, especially right after the Iowa caucuses and the New Hampshire primary" (p. 184).

Because viability is all that most voters have to go on, a candidate who comes to dominate the early races benefits from momentum, standing to reap a whirlwind of public support in the upcoming primaries. Thus, early results and media coverage of these results reward candidates who perform especially well.

In primaries, voting on the basis of viability is far from irrational. After all, it is in the voters' interest to select a candidate who can unify the party and defeat the opposition in November. In fact, some primary voters consciously vote for the candidate who may be only their second or third choice in terms of personal attributes and the issues but whom they view as the candidate with the best prospects of winning the White House. In 2004, nearly 30 percent of those who voted in the 2004 Iowa caucuses rated "can beat Bush" as the most important attribute they were looking for in the candidates.

The 2004 Democratic primary campaign provides a textbook example of electoral momentum, both positive and negative. Over the space of a few weeks, beginning with the Iowa Democratic caucuses, Senator John Kerry rose from a self-financed, underachieving candidate to the presumptive nominee, while Howard Dean fell from front-runner to underdog to certain loser.

Figure 9.10 traces the emergence of the Kerry candidacy in nationwide opinion polls between December 2003 and February 2004. For comparative purposes we also show the level of support for candidates Howard Dean, John Edwards, and Wesley Clark.

In mid-December, Kerry was at the bottom of the group, with less than 5 percent backing from Democrats and independents. Fearing elimination, the Kerry campaign decided to go all out in Iowa. They closed their field offices in

FIGURE 9.10

Trends in Candidate Support Nationwide during the 2004 Campaign

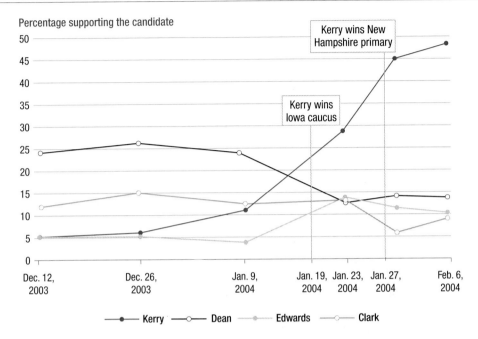

Source: Data from Polling Report, Inc. (n.d.). *White House 2004: Democratic nomination.* Retrieved August 5, 2005, from the Polling Report website: www.pollingreport.com/wh04dem.htm.

other states and devoted all their resources to Iowa. Senator Kerry campaigned continuously in the state during the ten days before the caucuses.

The Kerry campaign's investment in Iowa clearly paid rich dividends. On January 9, ten days before the caucuses, Kerry's support nationwide was at 10 percent. Two weeks later, after his unexpected victory in Iowa, his poll numbers had climbed to 30 percent. Between the Iowa victory and his win in New Hampshire, Kerry's national support climbed to 45 percent. Following his victories in Missouri, South Carolina, and four other states on February 6, he climbed still further, to 48 percent. Thus, in a matter of just four weeks (January 9 to February 6), Kerry had registered a meteoric rise in the national polls.

While Kerry's candidacy was booming, Howard Dean's support was collapsing. Dean went into Iowa with a double-digit lead over his closest competitor (at that time, General Wesley Clark). Two weeks later, after his loss in Iowa and the "scream heard around the country," his support was cut in half (from 25 to 12 percent). Dean was unable to halt this reverse momentum; for all practical purposes the loss in Iowa was the death knell of his campaign.

Such dramatic fluctuations in candidate support are unusual. Since the large-scale adoption of primaries, initial front-runners have typically maintained their advantage and locked up the nomination at a relatively early stage. Vice President Gore, for example, had relatively little difficulty overtaking Senator Bradley in 2000. On the Republican side that year, even though Senator McCain scored a major upset win over the front-running George Bush in New Hampshire, McCain's momentum was short lived. He was defeated in the next primary (South Carolina) and was out of the race soon after. In other cases, two evenly matched candidates are unable to deliver a knock-out punch and the primary contest is prolonged. Hillary Clinton entered the 2008 Democratic primaries as the clear front-runner, but Obama's win in Iowa and his strong showing in New Hampshire (where he lost to Clinton by only 2 points) allowed him to catch Clinton in the national polls. For the next two months the candidates remained tied until Obama pulled ahead for good in April. Clinton eventually conceded the race and endorsed Obama in June.

Apart from 2004, the only other cases of dark-horse candidates emerging from early primary successes include Jimmy Carter, who was catapulted from relative obscurity to win the 1976 Iowa caucuses and New Hampshire primary and, eventually, the presidency. Eight years later, in a particularly dramatic case of momentum, the little-known senator Gary Hart finished third in the Iowa caucuses behind the odds-on favorite Walter Mondale and 1972 nominee George McGovern. His third-place showing was surprise enough to provide a surge in media attention. Hart went on to score a remarkable upset in New Hampshire, where he defeated former Vice President Mondale by nearly ten thousand votes. At that moment, national polls showed Mondale with only a slight lead over Hart. The Mondale campaign was forced to invest in a major advertising campaign questioning Senator Hart's credentials (including a famous commercial modeled on the Wendy's "Where's the beef?" query). Mondale eventually hung on to win the nomination, but as Senator Hart himself acknowledged, "You can get awful famous in this country in seven days." (Four years later he might have added that you can become equally infamous just as fast.)

CAMPAIGNS AND TURNOUT

Campaigns have a clear interest in getting out the vote, but only among voters who support them. Among partisans of the other side, or swing voters who are leaning toward voting against them, campaigns would prefer that as few of them vote as possible. The ideal outcome is maximum turnout among supporters, minimum turnout among opponents.

Unlike most other nations, the United States makes voting a relatively difficult task. Despite a series of reforms aimed at increasing the number of eligible voters (such as eliminating literacy requirements and the poll tax, and lowering the voting age to eighteen), Americans still must register before they can cast votes. In most states, voters must register at least a month in advance of the election. Only ten states and the District of Columbia have adopted same-day registration. The two-step process, coupled with high rates of mobility (each time you move, you need to reregister), is a significant impediment to voting.

In comparison with most other affluent, industrialized societies, American voter turnout is low. Figure 9.11 graphs two different indicators of turnout in national elections: the percentages of the population that are eligible to vote and of the registered population that cast ballots.[8] Clearly, registered voters are regular voters; turnout in this group approximates turnout in the European democracies. Among the *eligible* population, however, turnout is much lower— in most off-year elections, less than a majority.

The sawtooth pattern of eligible-voter turnout suggests that the decibel level of the campaign stimulates people to vote. When the candidates and their activities are more visible, more people vote. In presidential elections, the media buzz and the level of advertising (at least in the battleground states) generate a

FIGURE 9.11

Trends in Voter Turnout, 1976–2012

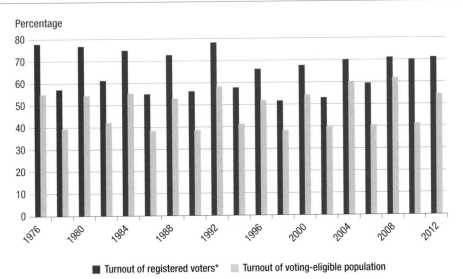

Source: Data for registered voters from the Federal Election Commission. Data for voting-eligible population from Michael McDonald, available at: http://elections.gmu.edu/Election_of_a_Century.html.

*Because the registered-voter turnout figures are based on self-reports, they are likely to be inflated.

sufficient level of interest and information; turnout increases to two-thirds of registered voters and a slight majority of all adults eligible to vote. In off-year elections, as media coverage drops off, the campaigns generate less excitement, voters find it too burdensome to acquire information, and turnout drops considerably. Thus, turnout depends on the level of voter *stimulation*.

The most effective form of stimulation is personal contact. Campaigns often send volunteers door to door, make reminder telephone calls (often with recorded voice messages from VIPs about the importance of voting), provide absentee ballots for those unable to make it to the polls, and generally urge their supporters to vote. These get-out-the-vote efforts are likely to be concentrated in areas where the election is hotly contested. In the case of the 2000 presidential election in Florida, an increased turnout of only 500 voters on the Democratic side would have swung the election to Al Gore.

Voter mobilization efforts are effective. As we noted in Chapter 5, journalists covering the 2012 election attributed Obama's victory, in part, to the superior "ground game" deployed by the Democrats. In fact, a systematic examination of voters contacted by either campaign in 2012 (Enos & Fowler, 2014) demonstrates that there was no Democratic advantage and that both campaigns mobilized their supporters effectively. The presidential campaigns raised the turnout level among their targeted voters by more than 10 percent.

Yale researchers Alan Gerber and Donald Green (2008) have conducted numerous experiments designed to assess the conditions under which voter mobilization efforts succeed or fail. Their work demonstrates that the method of contacting voters makes a big difference; telephone calls have no effect at all (since most people screen incoming calls), but in-person contacts are highly effective. Contacting voters by direct mail also stimulates higher turnout, but only by a slight margin. Gerber and Green also assessed the effects of different get-out-the-vote appeals. Messages that conveyed implicit social pressure to vote (by suggesting that the turnout rate in the targeted household would be publicized to neighboring households) had the strongest impact on actual turnout.

Two groups that are the most likely to require campaign outreach if they are to vote at all are young people and members of ethnic minorities. Eighteen-year-olds are busy with their personal affairs—transitioning to college or getting a job. They are less likely to be connected to a network of politically attentive friends or acquaintances. Youth culture includes a healthy dose of cynicism, which makes young people view the act of voting with disdain. For these reasons and more, the turnout rate of eighteen- to twenty-one-year-olds has never exceeded 30 percent. In the 1998 congressional elections, youth voters numbered 13 percent of the voting-age population, and a mere 5 percent of those who voted. When we look at actual (as opposed to self-reported) turnout, the level of abstention among younger voters is remarkable. In the 2002 gubernatorial election in California, for instance, a mere 11 percent of eighteen-year-olds voted.[9]

The consequences of age-related imbalances in political participation for the policy process are obvious. Elected officials respond to the preferences of voters, not to nonvoters. As rational actors, candidates and parties tend to ignore the young, thereby contributing to the disillusionment of young voters and perpetuating a vicious circle that discourages young voters from participating in the electoral process.

The second group of voters who suffer from electoral underrepresentation are racial and ethnic minorities. In the case of African Americans, the gap can be attributed to lower socioeconomic status. In the case of Hispanics, language and unfamiliarity with voting procedures may be key barriers. Whatever the explanation, the underrepresentation of minorities in the electorate has significant consequences for the conduct of campaigns. The wedge appeals discussed in Chapter 6 are successful only because whites remain the dominant voting bloc. When an influx of Latino immigrants alters the ethnic composition of the state population quite dramatically (as has occurred in California), the incentives to engage in appeals based on ethnicity are weakened. Whereas whites accounted for 60 percent of the adult population of the state in 1992, they numbered only 42 percent in 2009. The Latino share of the population, on the other hand, increased from 24 to 37 percent. Among registered voters in the state, the share of Latinos increased from less than 10 percent to 21 percent. The candidate who attempts to use immigration as a wedge issue in California, therefore, risks alienating a significant number of voters.

What holds true in California today is increasingly applicable to the nation at large. In the 2012 election, the white share of the national electorate dropped to 72 percent (from 80 percent in 2004). On average, Democratic presidential candidates receive only 41 percent of the white vote, meaning that the party's electoral success is based on high levels of support among African American and Latino voters. Among Obama voters in 2012, 62 percent were white and 38 percent were nonwhite. Romney voters, in contrast, were 91 percent white.

Voter mobilization drives can be especially effective if they reach groups that lack the motivation to vote. The Yale studies demonstrate that canvassing young people significantly increased their probability of turning out to vote (Gerber, Green, & Nickerson, 2002). In a different study, Stanford University researchers attempted to raise youth turnout by providing a free interactive election CD featuring youth-oriented diversions such as politically oriented arcade games and interactive quizzes. Although the great majority of the eighteen- to twenty-five-year-olds who were mailed the CD ignored it, those who chose to use it voted at a higher rate in the 2002 California election than did a control group that did not receive the CD (Iyengar & Jackman, 2003). Unfortunately, the reality is that get-out-the-vote efforts typically reach only the relatively motivated strata of the electorate. A recent *meta-analysis* (an analysis that combines several studies) of the turnout experiments conducted in the United States suggests that the effects of campaign mobilization are significantly stronger among groups that are more inclined to vote (Enos, Fowler, & Vavreck, 2014).

Campaigns are not only interested in boosting turnout but, at times, may also attempt to achieve the opposite result by discouraging would-be opponents from voting. The incentives to demobilize are considerable. In the first place, as virtually every study of campaign effects demonstrates, very few partisans can be converted. Running ads that attempt to persuade Democrats to vote Republican is not a good use of scarce resources. Persuading Democrats that the Democratic candidate may have undesirable attributes, however, may be easier to accomplish. If some Democrats become sufficiently unenthusiastic about their candidate, they may decide not to bother with the election. Rather than casting a vote for the other party, these Democrats may prefer not to vote.

Thus, negative campaigning can have a negative impact on turnout. In the experiments conducted by Ansolabehere and Iyengar (1995), exposure to negative rather than positive campaign ads reduced participants' interest in voting by nearly 5 percent. Among viewers who considered themselves independents (who tend to find political campaigns far from interesting to begin with), the demobilizing effects of negative advertising were doubled: independents who watched negative rather than positive ads were nearly 10 percent less likely to say that they intended to vote. For nonpartisans, negative campaigning not only diminishes their opinion of the candidates but also engenders cynicism about the process.[10]

Campaign managers and candidates are well aware of the effects of negative campaigning on turnout. Why else would negative campaigning prove so popular? They are more diplomatic, however, in their public accounts of the strategy. Fearing the controversy that accompanies discussion of intentional vote suppression, practitioners are not inclined to acknowledge their efforts publicly. In the immediate aftermath of the New Jersey gubernatorial election of 1993, Republican consultant Ed Rollins openly admitted (in a C-SPAN broadcast) that the winning Republican strategy included systematic efforts to reduce African American turnout. Once Rollins's comments had made the news, civic groups threatened litigation to overturn the election result on the grounds that minority voters had been disenfranchised. Rollins immediately recanted, claiming that he had exaggerated the role of campaign tactics. In an op-ed piece for the *Washington Post*, Rollins explained, "I spun myself out of control."

A number of states, particularly those with Republican-controlled legislatures, have recently passed strict voter identification requirements. These requirements, typically involving presentation of an official photo ID or birth certificate, may have the effect of vote suppression when applied to the poor or racial minorities. Historically, such identification requirements had frequently been overturned by federal courts as violating the 1965 Voting Rights Act (which mandated federal oversight of voter eligibility requirements in states with a history of racial discrimination). In 2013, however, the United States Supreme Court ruled, in a case involving an Alabama statute, that these provisions of the Voting Rights Act were unconstitutional. Accordingly, Southern states, and indeed all states, are now empowered to enforce strict voter identification requirements (Liptak, 2013).

Republican support for voter identification is motivated at least in part by the possibility of reducing Democratic turnout. Whether these laws in fact reduce voter turnout, and whether any such effect is concentrated among the underprivileged, is as yet unclear. Some studies report minimal effects (Ansolabehere, 2009; Mycoff et al., 2009; Pastor, Santos, Prevost, & Stoilov, 2010); these authors attribute their results to the possibility that most voters have valid identification and that individuals without the necessary IDs are less likely to vote in any event—without regard to the specific eligibility requirements applied at the polling place. Other scholars have found that voter ID requirements do decrease turnout in states with the most restrictive statutes and that this effect is concentrated among groups lacking economic resources (Dropp, 2014; Government Accountability Office, 2014). For example, Dropp (2014) found significant demobilizing effects among young adults, renters, the poor, and African Americans. This study also found stronger demobilizing effects in midterm than in presidential elections, suggesting that the impact of these laws is felt most strongly where motivation levels are lowest.

CONCLUSION

Campaigns do not occur in a vacuum. Candidates design their messages to fit the political environment. During times of international tension, candidates run as advocates of a strong military; during times of recession, they propose policies to stimulate economic expansion. Individually and cumulatively, the effect of campaign messages is either to activate or to reinforce viewers' long-term political predispositions (their party identification) as well as their assessments of the performance of the incumbent administration. The most frequent instance of the reinforcement effect is the shepherding of wayward partisans back into the fold. Thus the contradiction between the ability to forecast elections on the basis of structural indicators that have little to do with day-to-day campaign activities and the candidates' substantial investments in media campaigning is more apparent than real.

A common criticism of modern campaigns is that they are light on substance (issues). Sound bites and 30-second commercials, the critics suggest, are inherently superficial forms of political discourse. The news media are equally responsible, given their unwillingness to elevate issues to the same level of newsworthiness as campaign strategy and the horse race. Voters have to look harder to become informed about the issues, and in most cases they don't. At the level of the candidates' personal qualities, however, campaigns do prove informative. By election day, most voters can compare the candidates on questions of competence, experience, or integrity.

A second criticism of media-based campaigns is that they intend to deceive and manipulate. Advertisements that deal in symbols and slogans rather than careful and well-documented analysis are thought to deflect voters from the real issues of the day. Here the evidence suggests that the critics have underestimated the intelligence of the electorate. When voters change their minds during campaigns (something they don't do often), it is invariably in the direction of the "correct" partisan or retrospective vote. Thus the cumulative effect of the campaign is at least as likely to enlighten as to manipulate.

SUMMARY

1. There are two competing perspectives on the question of how much campaigns influence voter behavior:
    - In the minimalist view, the general political and economic context in which elections occur is just as important as anything the candidates themselves might do or say during the campaign. Evidence shows that, at least in the case of presidential elections, the results can be predicted with a high degree of accuracy from indicators of economic growth and public approval of the incumbent administration.
    - The booming campaign industry suggests a different conclusion. Campaign consultants claim that well-executed campaigns can produce a significant increase in the candidate's level of support. Growing evidence supports the existence of campaign effects.

2. Between these two positions is a more realistic middle ground: Every election occurs within a distinct political context to which the candidates adapt their messages. Campaign professionals are aware of the political context and design their messages accordingly, positioning their clients to capitalize on what voters deem important.

3. Political scientists have devised a variety of statistical models—most of which combine the incumbent's popularity with the state of the economy—for forecasting the results of presidential elections. Voters are expected to reelect the incumbent during times of economic growth but to opt for change during times of economic distress.

4. One of the primary effects of campaigns is reinforcement, bringing voters' candidate preferences in line with their party identification. As a campaign progresses and more voters encounter the candidates' messages, they are increasingly inclined to vote for their party's candidate.

5. Another task of campaigns is to attract swing (undecided) voters, who lack strong attachment to a party and thus are susceptible to image- and issue-oriented appeals. The behavior of independent voters is most clearly linked to their impressions of the candidates' personalities. Swing voters may also base their choice on candidates' policy platforms, siding with the candidate whose positions most closely match their own.

6. Campaigns also have an educational impact. This is especially important for independent or swing voters, who must figure out how to decide between candidates during the campaign. Campaigns deliver information about their candidate's personal background and positions on major issues.

7. Primaries represent a special case of campaign effects because the principal determinant of vote choice—party identification—is no longer applicable. With a relatively large field of sometimes unfamiliar candidates, voters must fall back on cues such as the relative viability of the candidates.

8. Campaigns can also significantly affect the level of voter turnout. While striving to increase turnout among their supporters, campaigns may simultaneously take steps to discourage would-be opponents from voting.

FURTHER READINGS

Ansolabehere, S., & Iyengar, S. (1995). *Going negative: How attack ads shrink and polarize the electorate*. New York: Free Press.

Bartels, L. M., & Zaller, J. (2001). Presidential vote models: A recount. *PS: Political Science and Politics, 33,* 9–20.

Brady, H. E., & Johnston, R. (1987). What's the primary message: Horse race or issue journalism? In G. R. Orren & N. W. Polsby (Eds.), *Media and momentum:*

The New Hampshire primary and nomination politics (pp. 127–186). Chatham, NJ: Chatham House.

Campbell, A. (1960). Surge and decline: A study of electoral change. *Public Opinion Quarterly, 24,* 397–418.

Campbell, J. E. (2004). Introduction: The 2004 presidential election forecasts. *PS: Political Science and Politics, 37,* 733–735.

Fiorina, M. P. (1981). *Retrospective voting in American national elections.* New Haven, CT: Yale University Press.

Gelman, A., & King, G. (1993). Why are American presidential election polls so variable when votes are so predictable? *British Journal of Political Science, 23,* 409–451.

Gerber, A. S., & Green, D. P. (2008). *Get out the vote.* Washington, DC: Brookings Institution Press.

Green, D., Palmquist, B., & Schickler, E. (2002). *Partisan hearts and minds: Political parties and the social identities of voters.* New Haven, CT: Yale University Press.

Iyengar, S., & Petrocik, J. R. (2000). Basic rule voting: The impact of campaigns on party- and approval-based voting. In J. Thurber, C. J. Nelson, & D. A. Dulio (Eds.), *Crowded airwaves: Campaign advertising in elections* (pp. 113–148). Washington, DC: Brookings Institution Press.

Johnston, R., Hagen, M. G., & Jamieson, K. H. (2004). *The 2000 presidential election and the foundations of party politics.* New York: Cambridge University Press.

Lazarsfeld, P. F., Berelson, B. R., & Gaudet, H. (1948). *The people's choice.* New York: Columbia University Press.

Mayer, W. G. (2003). The basic dynamics of the contemporary nomination process: An expanded view. In W. G. Mayer (Ed.), *The making of the presidential candidates 2004* (pp. 83–132). Lanham, MD: Rowman & Littlefield.

McDonald, M. P., & Popkin, S. L. (2001). The myth of the vanishing voter. *American Political Science Review, 95,* 963–974.

Niemi, R. G., & Jennings, M. K. (1991). Issues and inheritance in the study of party identification. *American Journal of Political Science, 35,* 970–988.

Shaw, D. R. (2005). *The race to 270: The electoral college campaign strategies of 2000 and 2004.* Chicago: University of Chicago Press.

NOTES

1. Although partisan attachments are considered stable dispositions, there is evidence that some voters change their identification to make it consistent with their opinions on the issues and the candidates.

2. Since the label *independent* speaks well of the respondent's civic virtue, the designation is likely to include many closet partisans. Note that most tabulations of the number of independents include respondents who indicate they lean toward one of the parties.

3. It is important to note that the effects of exposure to particular ads are momentary rather than persistent. The successive "waves" of ads from the opposing candidates serve to neutralize or counteract any lingering effects of ads encountered earlier.

4. Much later, after he had retired from public life, former president Ford joked that he had merely been fifteen years ahead of his time!

5. A young woman, Mary Jo Kopechne, had accompanied Senator Kennedy to a party. She drowned after the senator lost control of his car while driving across a bridge. Senator Kennedy did not report the accident until the next day.

6. Vice President Gore subsequently issued a press release noting that he had accompanied Witt on numerous tours, including one in neighboring New Mexico.

7. It is difficult to make strong causal claims about these media differences because television viewers and radio listeners at the time differed in several ways, including their predebate feelings about Kennedy and Nixon.

8. The voting-eligible population is a more appropriate definition of the electorate than the voting-age population because it excludes two groups that are deprived of voting rights: noncitizens and convicted felons.

9. We computed this result from the California secretary of state's turnout database (available on CD from the California secretary of state).

10. It is important to note that evidence of demobilization is limited to a handful of experimental studies in which the tone of the ad campaign was manipulated while all other factors were held constant. Survey-based studies, which lack any semblance of control over the content of the advertising message, have found no connection between advertising tone and turnout. Some survey-based studies even suggest that negative campaigning boosts turnout. A compilation of all published studies on the subject (both experimental and survey based) thus concluded that there was no relationship between negative campaigning and turnout (Lau, Sigelman, Heldman, & Babbitt, 1999).

10

The Consequences of Going Public

Once elected, public officials face a conundrum. Elected officials are usually in a better position than ordinary voters to analyze the merits of policy proposals. But because the public is generally uninformed about the intricacies of policy debates, decisions that result in good policy are not necessarily popular. However, to succeed in office officials must remain well liked by the public.

How do incumbents reconcile the need to maintain their popularity with doing what's best for the nation? This chapter focuses on the implications of going public for the exercise of leadership. We begin by tracing the ups and downs of presidential popularity over the past four decades in an attempt to assess whether the public responds more to real-world events or to news media coverage of these events. The evidence shows that voters are sensitive to events; they reward or penalize presidents running for reelection depending on the state of the economy. Our analysis also indicates that in the national security arena, where news is powerfully shaped by government officials, the president's popularity depends more on news coverage than on events; for instance, the more media coverage there is of terrorism, the more popular the president becomes. Media management matters.

In Chapter 7 we discussed the ability of presidents to leverage their popularity into enhanced bargaining power with rival elites. Here we will address the implications of going public for the exercise of political leadership. On the surface at least, the use of popularity as a bargaining chip to persuade rival elites means that presidents and the policies they pursue will be responsive to public opinion. At the same time, though, a system predicated on personal popularity creates strong disincentives for officials to lead; presidents may pursue policy initiatives that are not in the best interests of the nation but that voters find popular.

THEORIES OF PRESIDENTIAL POPULARITY

In October 1983, a suicide bomber rammed a truck filled with explosives into the barracks used by American marines on peacekeeping duty in Lebanon. Nearly 300 marines died. By any measure, the event represented a military disaster. That evening, President Reagan addressed the nation on prime-time television. It is surprising that his popularity actually increased in the immediate aftermath, leading some to label Reagan the "Teflon president." The Beirut tragedy suggests that presidents can use symbolic appeals or staged rhetoric to maintain high approval ratings even in the face of events that signify obvious policy or performance failures.

Research suggests that three principal factors influence presidential popularity: length of time in office, the course of events, and public relations.[1] Let's look at each of these.

INEVITABLE DECLINE?

Some theorists have suggested that a president's support inevitably declines over the length of his term in office. Given sufficient time, even the most popular president will eventually decline in popularity. This systematic erosion in public approval is attributed to presidential decision making: over the course of the term, as presidents make decisions and take positions, they accumulate opponents. According to this view, there is nothing the president can do to forestall the effects of time. The downward trend in popularity has led some scholars to propose the idea of the *throwaway presidency*, which suggests that "the probability of failure is always tending toward 100 percent" (Lowi, 1981, p. 11).

However, several presidencies have not conformed to the general theory of inevitable decline. As Figure 10.1 indicates, President Reagan experienced two major drops in popularity, and on both occasions he recovered. During the prolonged 1981–1982 recession, his approval dropped 20 points, but by the summer of 1984, his approval rating had rebounded, and he was reelected in a landslide. During his second term, Reagan's standing fell in early 1985 after allegations of corruption in the Department of Labor. A more serious scandal erupted in November 1986, when it was revealed that the administration had secretly sold arms to Iran and illegally channeled the proceeds to the Nicaraguan Contras. The observations immediately before and after the news of the Iran–Contra scandal show that Reagan's approval rating fell from 63 to 47 percent. Once again, however, Reagan proved buoyant. By the end of

FIGURE 10.1

Reagan Approval Ratings, 1981–1988

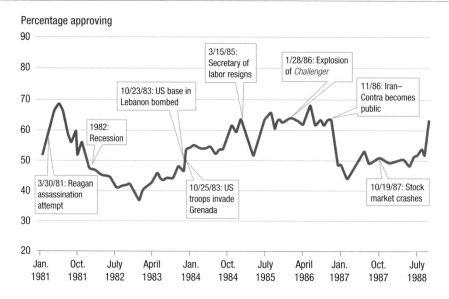

Percentage approving

- 3/30/81: Reagan assassination attempt
- 1982: Recession
- 10/23/83: US base in Lebanon bombed
- 10/25/83: US troops invade Grenada
- 3/15/85: Secretary of labor resigns
- 1/28/86: Explosion of *Challenger*
- 11/86: Iran–Contra becomes public
- 10/19/87: Stock market crashes

Source: Data from Gallup, Presidential Job Approval Center. Retrieved January 5, 2015, from the Gallup website: http://www.gallup.com/poll/124922/Presidential-Job-Approval-Center.aspx.

his second term, his popularity stood at 63 percent, higher than when he first entered office.

The case of Bill Clinton provides an even more convincing rebuttal of the theory of inevitable decline (see Figure 10.2). President Clinton's popularity suffered a series of early setbacks associated with controversies surrounding some of his cabinet nominees, his position on gays in the military, and somewhat later, the resounding congressional defeat of his healthcare-reform proposal. In between, Clinton's ratings got a boost when he sent American troops into Somalia to oversee relief operations. By 1996, Clinton was well positioned in the polls and went on to defeat Senator Dole easily in the 1996 election.

The Monica Lewinsky scandal erupted early in President Clinton's second term, creating a firestorm of controversy that eventually developed into a full-scale effort to remove him from office. Yet in the immediate aftermath of the allegations, Clinton's job approval actually increased! When the president appeared on television to deny the affair with Lewinsky, a White House intern, with the First Lady at his side, one poll showed an 8-point increase in popularity from the previous day. The rebound in his popularity continued during the period leading up to the House vote on impeachment. Ultimately, Clinton's approval ratings stabilized in the 60 to 65 percent range. Maintaining

FIGURE 10.2

Clinton Approval Ratings, 1993–2000

Percentage approving

90

80

10/17/93:
Troops sent
to Somalia

5/6/94: Paula
Jones files
lawsuit

4/19/95:
Oklahoma
City bombing

1/21/98:
Clinton
publicly denies
affair with
Lewinsky

12/19/98:
House votes
to impeach

2/19/99: Senate
acquits Clinton

70

60

50

8/6/98:
Lewinsky
testifies to
grand jury

3/24/99:
Air strikes in
Yugoslavia

40

7/19/93:
"Don't ask, don't
tell" policy announced

9/26/94:
Clinton health
plan fails

11/5/96:
Clinton
wins
reelection

8/17/98:
Clinton testifies
and publicly
admits affair
with Lewinsky

8/14/00:
Clinton
addresses
Democratic
convention

30

20

| Jan. | Oct. | July | April | Jan. | Oct. | July | April | Jan. | Oct. | July |
| 1993 | 1993 | 1994 | 1995 | 1996 | 1996 | 1997 | 1998 | 1999 | 1999 | 2000 |

Source: Data from Gallup, Presidential Job Approval Center. Retrieved January 5, 2015, from the Gallup website: http://www.gallup.com/poll/124922/Presidential-Job-Approval-Center.aspx.

this level of public approval in the midst of extreme political adversity was an important signal to moderate Senate Republicans. When it came time to vote on Clinton's impeachment, a sufficient number of them deserted their party to acquit him.[2]

The case of President George W. Bush, on the surface at least, supports the theory of inevitable decline. After his controversial victory over Al Gore in 2000, he took office with an unusually low level of popularity for an incoming president (46 percent). The September 11 attacks unified the nation behind the president, and in October Bush's popularity peaked at 87 percent. Seven years later, when he left office, his popularity had been cut by more than half.

The substantial decline in Bush's popularity (see Figure 10.3) had more to do with the course of events than with the calendar. As American casualties mounted in Iraq and the media broke stories of abuse and torture of Iraqis at the Abu Ghraib prison, more Americans came to oppose the Iraq War. The federal government's inept response to the Hurricane Katrina disaster further contributed to disillusionment with Bush's leadership. The most important drag on Bush's approval, however, was the steady deterioration of the economy, which culminated in the historic collapse of the American banking industry. When Bush left office, his popularity stood at 30 percent.

FIGURE 10.3

Bush Approval Ratings, 2001–2008

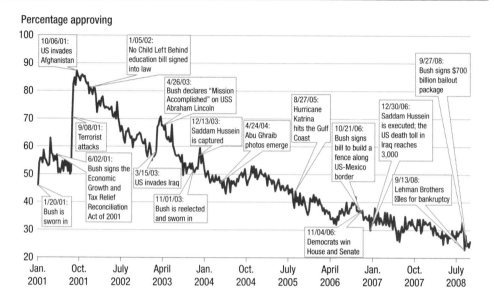

Source: Data from Gallup, Presidential Job Approval Center. Retrieved January 5, 2015, from the Gallup website: http://www.gallup.com/poll/124922/Presidential-Job-Approval-Center.aspx.

The case of President Obama (shown in Figure 10.4) bears the closest resemblance to Lowi's notion of the throwaway presidency. Taking office with more than two-thirds of the country behind him, his popularity has declined steadily as of the time of this writing (mid-2014), when the number of people disapproving of his performance easily exceeds those who approve. On only a handful of occasions has he benefited from events: his popularity improved in 2009 after he signed the massive economic stimulus bill committing $787 billion toward the economic recovery, following his announcement of the end of United States military involvement in Iraq, and in the immediate aftermath of the attacks on the American consulate in Benghazi. Surprisingly, news of the death of Osama bin Laden prompted only a small and short-lived boost to Obama's popularity in 2011.

Obama's signature policy accomplishment—the passage of the Affordable Care Act in 2010—only accelerated the decline in his standing as government-funded healthcare was anathema to the great majority of Republicans and many independents. But as in the case of Bush, the steady decline in Obama's numbers in his first term was driven mainly by the sluggish state of the economy.

What is especially interesting about Obama's popularity is the gulf dividing the views of Democrats and Republicans. As discussed in Chapter 8, the

FIGURE 10.4

Obama Approval Ratings, 2009–2014

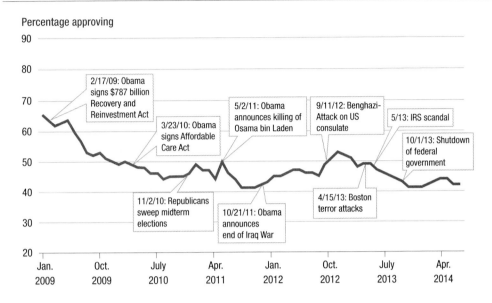

Source: Data from Gallup, Presidential Job Approval Center. Retrieved January 5, 2015, from the Gallup website: http://www.gallup.com/poll/124922/Presidential-Job-Approval-Center.aspx.

president's performance is increasingly viewed through a partisan lens (for evidence, see Jacobson, 2008). The partisans from the president's party serve as cheerleaders, while those from the other side remain critics from beginning to end. As shown in Figure 10.5, President Obama's support from Democrats has never fallen below 75 percent, but his approval from Republicans averages only 15 percent. Independents' views were closer to Democrats when the president took office; by his second term, however, their enthusiasm had cooled considerably and they generally disapproved of the president.

REAL-WORLD CUES

The ebbs and flows in presidential popularity suggest that presidents are not necessarily doomed to end their terms with low approval ratings from the public. Instead, changes in presidential popularity reflect the unfolding of events and issues. Peace and prosperity generally produce high approval ratings and assured reelection; recessions, military defeats, policy debacles, and allegations of official misconduct do the opposite. According to this *environmental connection* account, the American public holds the president responsible for the state

FIGURE 10.5

Polarized Evaluations of President Obama

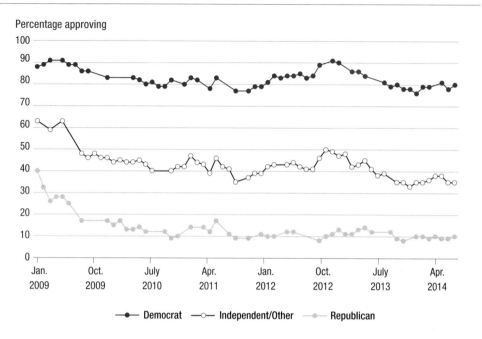

Source: Data for approval are from Gallup. Available at the Gallup Daily website: www.gallup.com/poll/113980/gallup
-daily-obama-job-approval.aspx.

of the nation. When events signify that the country is doing well (for example, the unemployment rate drops or the Saddam Hussein regime is toppled with minimal loss of American life), the president is rewarded with an approval bonus. Conversely, when events imply less satisfactory outcomes for the country (for example, the number of American troop casualties overseas continues to increase, with no end in sight, or the federal government leaves the victims of a natural disaster to fend for themselves), the president is punished.

The frequency and duration of these approval-enhancing and approval-diminishing events are the major determinants of presidential popularity. During the Lewinsky scandal—which, other things being equal, should have been an approval-diminishing event for President Clinton—the American economy expanded significantly; personal income grew by more than 2 percent, a rate of growth higher than at any other time during Clinton's term in office. The net change in Clinton's popularity during this period was therefore positive: the booming state of the economy more than neutralized the Lewinsky revelations.

The impact of events on popularity raises important questions about the real significance of rhetorical leadership and going public. Is it simply that popular

◎ IN FOCUS

Theories of Presidential Popularity

Research suggests that three principal factors influence presidential popularity:

- **Length of time in office.** Over the course of the term, as presidents make decisions and take positions, they accumulate opponents and thus lose popularity.
- **The course of real-world events.** The American public holds the president responsible for the state of the nation. When events suggest that the United States is doing well, the president's popularity increases, but it drops when events imply less-satisfactory outcomes for the country.
- **Public relations efforts.** By influencing the way in which events are defined and framed in news accounts, the president is able to exert substantial influence over his standing with the public.

presidents are those who happen to be lucky enough to hold office during prolonged periods of peace and prosperity? Or does prowess as a communicator, an appealing persona, the ability to capitalize on the symbolism and trappings of high office, and skill in cultivating and framing news coverage produce varying images of effective leadership? Is "merchandising no match for history" (Neustadt, 1960, p. 73)? Or is the interpretation of history sometimes subject to shrewd public relations? Perhaps President Clinton would not have survived the Lewinsky scandal had he remained silent and simply counted on the state of the economy to protect him from his opponents.

The Role of Presidential Rhetoric

Scholars have tried to trace the connection between presidential rhetoric and shifts in popularity, but with inconsistent results. Some studies show that major presidential speeches boost public approval and that the effects of speechmaking on popularity are stronger than the corresponding effects of events. Other studies show precisely the opposite—namely, that once the effects of events and the state of the economy are taken into account, the frequency of presidential speechmaking and international travel add little to approval ratings. This view implies that President Clinton owed his surprising buoyancy during the Lewinsky scandal not to any media tour de force, but to the public's satisfaction with the state of the nation. Collectively, the studies suggest that practitioners' beliefs about the importance of spin and public relations may be exaggerated. Perhaps presidential rhetoric falls on deaf ears. Had Ronald

Reagan—the "great communicator"—held office during the energy crisis or prolonged periods of inflation, he, too, probably would have suffered significant declines in popularity.

We concede that real-world events, especially those concerning the state of the economy, are important cues for the public, although the overwhelming importance of the party connection means that events are primarily important for voters who are not affiliated with either party. For these voters, responsibility for national events is blamed or credited to the president, rather than to members of Congress; it is well known that people overattribute responsibility for national events to the chief executive. The influence of the media on voter assessment of the president's performance, however, is mediated by the type of news. Media coverage of the economy might not have much impact because voters experience economic conditions themselves. During periods of rising unemployment, for instance, people hear about layoffs either through word of mouth or by observing activity in the workplace. For economic issues, accordingly, news coverage may be redundant; people hold the president responsible because of their own experiences. However, as we discuss below, the president's ability to influence interpretations of events in the arena of national security proves to be a significant political asset. Television news coverage, which typically features government officials promoting their efforts to combat terrorism, has the effect of making people significantly more inclined to support their president.

WHY MEDIA MANAGEMENT MATTERS

There are several reasons to believe that media management has an impact on presidential popularity. In the first place, the real-world events surrounding national security and international affairs can be just as important as the state of the American economy. These are classic mediated events, and ones over which the president exercises especially strong leverage. For instance, for much of the country, the 9/11 attacks were encountered only through news coverage and not through direct experience. Indeed, an analysis of presidential popularity post-9/11 reveals that changes in the level of television news coverage of terrorism proved to be a more powerful predictor of presidential popularity than changes in the actual incidence of terrorism (Hahn & Iyengar, 2007).

Moreover, although it is true that the national audience for presidential speeches has shrunk (fewer people watch the State of the Union address today than did twenty years ago), presidents still exercise opinion leadership over more narrowly defined audiences. A presidential speech on tax cuts in

Cleveland, for example, will likely elicit prime local news coverage on Ohio television stations. Even the president's national media appearances, such as his opening statement in a press conference, trickle down into the local news (Eshbaugh-Soha, 2013). At bottom, the key difficulty with the argument that history trumps media management is that events do not speak for themselves but require interpretation and explanation. Thus, the distinction between an approval-enhancing and an approval-diminishing event is typically blurred, and contingent on media treatment.

The case of the American invasion of Grenada, which proved to be a significant approval-enhancing event for the Reagan administration, is revealing. As we noted in Chapter 4, the administration prevented the press from directly covering the invasion and then fed reporters a steady stream of stories and images that portrayed the invasion in the most favorable light possible. Thus, the public's understanding of the invasion reflected the administration's framing of the event rather than any independent reading of conditions in Grenada. Had the media treated the invasion of Grenada as a public relations exercise or another case of US domination in the Americas, public reaction might have been less than enthusiastic.

Unlike the invasion of Grenada and all subsequent US military actions, the media were granted relatively free rein to cover events in the case of "Operation Restore Hope"—the use of American troops to oversee humanitarian relief efforts in Somalia in December 1992. The very fact that media access was granted suggests that the Bush administration saw the operation as an approval-enhancing event. After all, American troops were on a mission of mercy. Media coverage of the operation, however, turned out to be less than charitable. In fact, as Zaller and Chiu (2000) demonstrated, news coverage of the Somalia operation was the most negative of any major foreign policy event of the 1990s.

The coverage was more critical in tone because American reporters, no longer confined to Washington and solely reliant on official sources, could turn to field representatives of international relief organizations or foreign diplomats stationed in Somalia for competing and equally authoritative accounts of the situation. Zaller and Chiu concluded their examination of the Somalia episode by noting,

> There is little evidence that reporters are indexing their Somalia coverage to the views of the American government or, still less, to the views of Congress or the president. The views of the president are certainly reported . . . but they do not frame or dominate the account. Rather, the bulk of coverage seems to reflect the opinions of a range of expert sources, many of them non-Americans. (p. 78)

In a final case illustrating the importance of the media's interpretation of events, consider a more recent example. Had President George W. Bush gone before Congress in 2003 and justified the invasion of Iraq as an exercise in "spreading freedom around the world," he would most likely have been ridiculed. But by invoking the threat of weapons of mass destruction and Iraqi collusion with terrorists, he was able to elicit near-unanimous congressional support for going to war.

In short, events do not speak for themselves. The public interprets events through the filter of news coverage especially in the case of events concerning national security or foreign affairs. History may trump merchandising in the case of the economy, but for issues with no direct "observables," news coverage is pivotal. The amount of news coverage devoted to terrorism was the paramount influence on President Bush's popularity. The legacy of the 9/11 attacks included two major US military interventions and occupations. The steady drumbeat of terrorism-related news helped make the 9/11 rally on President Bush's approval ratings the longest on record. On September 1, 2001, President Bush's approval stood at 54 percent. The immediate impact of the terrorist attacks was to raise his approval level to 87 percent. It was nearly two years later (August 2003) before Bush's popularity returned to the pre-9/11 baseline.

In summary, popularity is not driven entirely by media management or by history, but by a combination of the two. In the case of unemployment, an issue with several visible indicators (such as friends and neighbors who have lost their jobs), the state of the economy is a key determinant of the president's popularity. As unemployment rises, the president's approval level falls. In the case of national security issues, however, the tables are turned. Events have less significance than media representations of the events. Because the Oval Office exercises considerable influence over the content of national security news, presidents can more easily maintain their popularity independent of the course of events.

The Rally Effect

The importance of media management to presidential popularity comes into sharp relief in the case of the so-called rally phenomenon. In the aftermath of major foreign policy actions undertaken by the US government, people rally behind the president. George H. W. Bush achieved a new high in the history of the Gallup poll when his approval rating soared to 85 percent in the immediate aftermath of Operation Desert Storm. After the 9/11 attacks, his son's popularity increased even further, to 87 percent (see Figure 10.6). In both instances, Americans were nearly unanimous in evaluating their president favorably. Generally, whenever the president acts as the nation's commander in

FIGURE 10.6

Operation Desert Storm and 9/11 as Rally Points

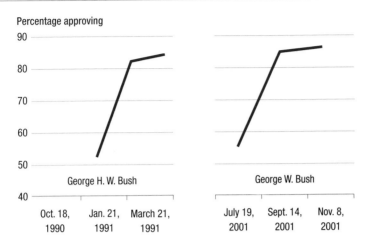

Note: Operation Desert Storm was launched on January 17, 1991.

chief, Americans are more inclined to bury their partisan differences and rally to the side of their leader. Although President Obama's tenure in office has not coincided with a major national security crisis, he was able to raise his approval among Republicans (albeit to a mere 25 percent) following his announcement of the killing of bin Laden.

What is intriguing about rally effects is that they frequently occur when the triggering event represents a failure of American policy and leadership. President Kennedy's popularity increased after the attempted invasion of Cuba, even though it proved to be a spectacular failure.[3] President Carter actually benefited when Iranian militants stormed the American embassy in Tehran, taking all the occupants hostage in a brazen violation of international law. Reagan's popularity improved in the immediate aftermath of the *Challenger* disaster (as documented in Figure 10.1), and George H. W. Bush gained significantly in the polls when Iraq annexed Kuwait in August 1990, a major US ally (and oil supplier) in the Middle East.

The importance of rally events to presidential popularity is obvious when we examine the ten largest month-to-month changes in presidential popularity (see Figure 10.7). In six of the ten cases, the change in approval was positive, and five of the six rallies were stimulated by foreign policy or national security events. Three of the four instances of widespread withdrawal of public approval occurred in the aftermath of domestic political controversy: the Iran–Contra

FIGURE 10.7

Top Ten Month-to-Month Changes in Presidential Popularity

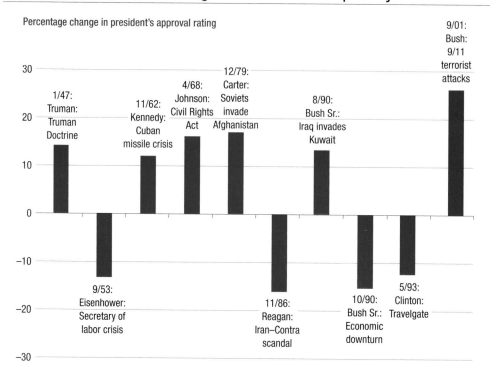

Percentage change in president's approval rating

Source: Data from Gallup, Presidential Job Approval Center. Retrieved January 5, 2015, from the Gallup website: http://www.gallup.com/poll/124922/Presidential-Job-Approval-Center.aspx.

scandal under Reagan, the so-called Travelgate affair early in President Clinton's first term, and the resignation of Eisenhower's secretary of labor over the administration's lax enforcement of the Taft–Hartley Act of 1947.

The most plausible explanation of rally events is the indexing process described in Chapter 4. Foreign policy and national security events are easier to frame in a manner that supports administration policy. During times of international tension, the president's spin is less subject to challenge, and the public responds accordingly. But when opposition leaders openly contest the president's interpretation of events (as is typical during a political scandal), the media messages become one-sided in the opposite direction, and the public turns against the president.

The 1990 Iraqi invasion of Kuwait provides a clear example of the ebb and flow of elite discourse. Initially the event was a significant rally point because of the silence of congressional Democrats. Congress happened not to be in

IN FOCUS

The Rally Effect

The term *rally effect* describes how, in the aftermath of major foreign policy actions undertaken by the US government, people rally behind the president. Generally, whenever the president acts as commander in chief, Americans bury their partisan differences and throw their support behind their leader.

session during the first month of the Iraqi occupation, and the administration's accounts of its various "successes" (such as the creation of a worldwide coalition in opposition to Saddam Hussein) went unchallenged. After Congress reconvened in September, some prominent Democrats expressed skepticism about the timetable proposed by President Bush, suggesting that economic sanctions against Iraq should be given more time. On September 20, 1990, the *New York Times* noted, "Congressional criticism of the Bush Administration's position on the Persian Gulf, nonexistent in the first days after Iraq's invasion of Kuwait, then muted, is growing louder on both sides of the aisle as lawmakers openly attack the President on several major points" (Apple, 1990). As Americans began to encounter more critical news reports, President Bush's popularity fell from 71 percent in August to 55 percent in November. In general, then, the public's evaluations of the incumbent president rise and fall in accordance with elite cues provided by the media: the louder the criticism of the president's actions, the lower the probability that the public will rally around the president.

In sum, the sensitivity of presidential popularity to ongoing issues and events depends on the ability of the White House to portray events as either good news or bad news and its ability to silence would-be critics. The president's level of influence over the news is thus the critical mediator between the onset of events and the ensuing changes in the public's evaluations of the president.

GOING PUBLIC AND PUBLIC POLICY: POWER TO THE PEOPLE?

Presidents use their leverage over the news to score points with the public. Popularity increases the president's influence in Washington. Some have suggested that the popularity game not only strengthens the president's ability to get things done but also makes the policy process more responsive to public opinion. Because elected officials seek to remain popular, they are also motivated to enact policies supported by the public. In this sense, going public approximates government by referendum.

Our position concerning the impact of going public on the policy process is less optimistic, primarily because the need to maintain high levels of public approval often deters the president from exercising policy leadership. In addition, as we'll outline, catering to public opinion comes with high opportunity costs and increases the risks of governmental stalemate and gridlock.

At the very least, the widespread belief that popularity translates into power has increased the allocation of staff resources to media management at the expense of policy research and development. As we noted in Chapter 7, managing the press has mushroomed into a major organizational objective within both the executive and legislative branches. In the case of the former, key presidential advisers spend more time crafting media strategies than developing policy initiatives. As early as 1978, the media imperative was clear to Lloyd Cutler, President Carter's special counsel for domestic policy:

> I was surprised by how much the substantive decisions in the White House are affected by press deadlines, and, in particular by the evening television news. So that if something happened, let us say, on a Monday, or somebody strongly criticized the President or one of his programs, everything stopped! Whatever you'd been working on as the great priority of the next morning you had to put aside in order to reach a decision about how the President would respond in time for the evening television news. (Quoted in Ansolabehere, Behr, & Iyengar, 1993, p. 202)

The more ominous concern about the increasing use of vocal leadership is the strong possibility that elected officials will be compelled to follow public opinion, without having offered any issue leadership along the way. Going public rests on the assumption that public approval is necessary for the president to govern. To remain popular, presidents must aim to deliver popular policies. However, the mere fact that they pursue policies favored by majority opinion tells us little about the substantive or programmatic rationale underlying policy decisions. The decision might be driven by beliefs about the substantive merits of the policy and its effectiveness in meeting the problem at hand or, alternatively, by the desire to maintain public approval and gain reelection. Thus evaluating the system of going public requires that we decipher some of the programmatic and strategic reasons underlying policy making.

By the usual standards, elected leaders are expected to use their expertise and sense of what is best for the nation to make independent policy choices. Leaders should not slavishly follow public opinion. Ordinary citizens, who cannot be bothered to keep up with the technical complexities of policy debates, entrust the responsibility of choosing policies to elected officials. Under media politics, however, officials face strong incentives to cater to public opinion. Rather than formulating policy on the basis of a coherent theory or systematic cost–benefit analysis and then attempting to bring voters on board, public officials may be guided primarily by their reading of polls. When the results of theory, cost–benefit analysis, and public opinion polling all point in the same direction, elected officials have an easy choice: they select the optimal and most popular policy. But their task becomes more difficult when the public prefers a policy that officials believe to be ineffective or even counterproductive. Should they deliberately pander to the views of the public and risk making the country worse off, or should they support the less popular but more effective alternative and risk voter incomprehension or wrath (no doubt to be accompanied by a barrage of negative advertisements in the next campaign)?

There is little hard evidence bearing on how elected officials resolve the conflict between maintaining public approval, on the one hand, and making sound policy decisions on the other. Canes-Wrone, Herron, and Shotts (2001) have developed a formal model that identifies the range of possible outcomes. Assume that policies are either popular or unpopular with the public and judged as either effective or ineffective from the perspective of the policy maker. The pairing of *popular* and *effective* is of little interest because in this case public opinion is enlightened and the decision maker enjoys the luxury of doing good while simultaneously scoring points with voters. The remaining combinations, however, are more revealing.

True leadership occurs when the decision maker proposes an unpopular but effective policy. In such instances, elected officials are prepared to sacrifice their own political interests for the public good. One example (working on the assumption that NAFTA was an effective policy) was Bill Clinton's support for the North American Free Trade Agreement (NAFTA) during the 1992 presidential campaign, despite only lukewarm support from the public and intense opposition from labor unions and environmentalists—both of which were key Democratic constituencies (to say nothing of the criticism voiced by third-party candidate Ross Perot). As a more recent example, President Obama increased the US military presence in Afghanistan despite vocal opposition from the liberal wing of his party.

Over the years, the issue of taxes has provided a litmus test of true leadership in Washington. The public instinctively opposes higher taxes but insists that government continue to deliver benefits and services. Efforts to persuade voters that it's impossible to have their cake and eat it too are risky. At the outset of the 1984 presidential campaign, Democratic nominee Walter Mondale announced on national television that the size of the federal budget deficit left him no choice but to raise taxes if elected. In November, Mondale carried only his home state of Minnesota. His resounding defeat is still cited by campaign consultants as a textbook example of how not to campaign.

Six years later, President George H. W. Bush faced a similar dilemma. When accepting his party's nomination in 1988, he had coined the slogan "Read my lips: No new taxes" as a means of cementing the Republican conservative base to his generally moderate candidacy. When Bush took office, the budget deficit amounted to about 3 percent of the gross domestic product (GDP). As the economy slowed, however, the deficit ballooned. By the summer of 1990 it was clear that unless Congress and the president took action, red ink could reach $160 billion.

In June 1990, after weeks of negotiations with the Democratic-controlled Congress, the president announced that he would support "tax revenue increases." The compromise budget package increased the marginal tax rate and phased out exemptions for high-income taxpayers. Bush was also forced to renege on his pledge to reduce the capital gains tax. The budget deal had severe consequences for Bush's political fortunes. Conservatives bashed him for breaking his promise on taxes and encouraged Patrick Buchanan to challenge Bush in the 1992 primaries. Bush's popularity never fully recovered; in November he was defeated by the relatively unknown Bill Clinton.

As the Mondale and Bush cases suggest, politicians who advocate or preside over the raising of taxes suffer at the polls. More generally, the successful exercise of leadership requires a highly restricted set of circumstances. First, the policy debate must occur some time before the election, giving voters enough time to observe the beneficial consequences of the unpopular policy and the elected official enough time to persuade voters of the merits of the decision. Second, the policy maker must enjoy a high level of popularity to begin with, thus providing a measure of protection from candidates who might strategically seek to run in opposition. In effect, leadership is more likely when there is a longer time horizon and the incumbent is not subject to a serious reelection threat. Canes-Wrone and Shotts (2004) show that incumbents with unusually high or low levels of public approval are more likely to lead on the merits—the former because of their security blanket, the latter because they have nothing to lose and everything to gain. But when the election is likely to be close, as it has been in most recent presidential races, candidates refuse to lead.

A revealing instance of the pressures against true leadership occurred in 1996 during the campaign to pass Proposition 209 in California. This measure, which won handily, sought to end affirmative action in all state programs. Opponents of Proposition 209, who were drawn disproportionately from California Democrats, appealed to President Clinton for help. At the time, Clinton's national popularity stood at nearly 60 percent, and Clinton led his Republican opponent by more than 20 points in California polls. Thus the conditions were ripe for Clinton to go public with his opposition to the measure. Despite repeated requests to campaign against Proposition 209, however, the president maintained a "deafening silence" until the closing days of the campaign.

The campaign over Proposition 209 demonstrates that high levels of popularity and weak electoral opposition are insufficient conditions for overcoming the fear of offending voters. When given the opportunity to lead, elected officials either pander or remain silent. In the words of the conservative columnist Arianna Huffington (2000), "As we march into the next century, the motto of every politician seems to be: 'I am their leader; I shall follow them'" (p. 77).

During election campaigns, the pressure to pander is especially intense. Facing an uphill battle to secure the Democratic nomination in 2008, Hillary Clinton proposed a holiday from the federal gasoline tax. (John McCain made a similar proposal.) Her campaign did not explain how a short-term reduction in the price of gas would reduce the nation's dependence on foreign oil nor did she explain how people would be affected by the decline in federal revenue. Economists—both liberal and conservative—were quick to dismiss Clinton's plan as political gimmickry. Writing in the *New York Times*, columnist Thomas L. Friedman (2008) labeled the proposal "so ridiculous . . . it takes your breath away."

An especially dangerous form of pandering is making decisions solely on the basis of image building. In some situations, presidents need to appear tough and willing to take decisive action. After several months of failed diplomatic efforts to secure the release of the American hostages in Iran, President Carter came under intense political pressure. His ratings were falling, and he faced a serious challenger from his own party for the 1980 presidential nomination (Senator Edward Kennedy). Even though intelligence reports indicated that the American hostages had been scattered throughout Tehran, Carter authorized a helicopter rescue mission. The mission was aborted when two of the helicopters developed engine trouble en route and a third crashed into an accompanying transport plane. Why did the president approve such a high-risk mission? In Lowi's (1985) words, "A peace-loving, religious man like Jimmy Carter did not take the risk of the Iranian rescue mission merely to give himself a convenient level to move American public opinion. The leverage worked the other way: public opinion had forced upon the president an act of the sheerest adventurism" (p. 173).

In other cases, presidents may be pressured into taking actions that they believe will neutralize or counteract building public opposition. President Clinton's (false) pronouncement "I did not have sexual relations with that woman" on national television was almost certainly motivated by the expectation that an emphatic denial would limit the damage to his standing in the polls.

This same fire-extinguisher logic led the Obama administration to ask for the resignation of Department of Agriculture official Shirley Sherrod less than twenty-four hours after a conservative blogger posted a misleading excerpt from a speech given by Sherrod. The excerpt suggested that Sherrod, then an official with the Georgia Department of Agriculture, had refused to help a farmer in need of economic assistance because he was white. Fox News and other conservative bloggers seized on the Sherrod story. On CNN, Agriculture Secretary Tom Vilsack stated that "there is zero tolerance for discrimination in USDA."

The next day, it became clear that Sherrod had in fact intervened to save the white farmer from bankruptcy. The farmer and his wife both appeared on television to praise Sherrod's efforts. Liberal bloggers and cable outlets weighed in, and the *New York Times* editorialized that the Obama administration "has been shamed by its rush to judgment after it forced the resignation of a black midlevel official in the Agriculture Department who was wrongly accused of racism by the right-wing blogosphere." White House Press Secretary Robert Gibbs issued an apology to Sherrod, and the next day President Obama telephoned her to express his personal regrets.

The Sherrod resignation illustrates the pivotal importance of perception and imagery in modern American politics. Anticipating an all-out attack from conservative media, the Obama administration decided to terminate Sherrod without even considering the possibility that the allegations of racism were false. The pressure of the twenty-four-hour news cycle had forced them to act. As President Obama acknowledged in an interview on *Good Morning America*, his secretary of agriculture had "jumped the gun" because "we now live in this media culture where something goes up on YouTube or a blog and everybody scrambles."

In practice, the distinction between policy making on the merits and pandering to maintain popularity is never clear. For one thing, public opinion is not uniform and simple; elected officials face multiple layers of opinion. Responding to each layer comes with different benefits and costs. Most voters pay little attention to day-to-day government actions, but small groups of voters (the issue publics identified in Chapter 5) have strong preferences and carefully monitor the actions of their leaders. These activists are the lifeblood of campaigns. For elected officials to alienate their key supporters would be tantamount to political suicide. In some cases, therefore, leaders pursue policies that, although unpopular with the general public, have intense support among activists. The fact that activists have the ability to instantaneously voice their disapproval in the blogosphere only intensifies the pressure to appease them.

Politicians resolve the dilemma of responding to vocal minorities without alienating the silent majority in a variety of ways. First, they increasingly resort to what Shapiro and Jacobs (2000) term "crafted rhetoric." On controversial issues, they explain their decisions in ways that allow them to maintain support in both camps. For example, in the face of ardent support from their evangelical base but majority opposition to a ban on same-sex marriage, Republican senators explained their proposed constitutional amendment—called the Marriage Protection Amendment—as an effort to "save traditional marriage." Second, incumbents adjust their priorities to the electoral timetable. The period immediately after the election is devoted to satisfying their activists. As the next election draws near, policy makers shift their emphasis to satisfying the ideological center. In 2004, for example, President George W. Bush persuaded Congress to add a prescription drug coverage plan to Medicare. The program, which would benefit millions of seniors, was estimated to cost approximately $500 billion. Shortly after the election, the cost estimate ballooned to $1.3 trillion.

Another liability of going public is that it raises the level of conflict between the executive and legislative branches, making compromise and accommodation more difficult. As the president increasingly turns to rhetorical leadership, opponents in Congress and their backers have every reason to respond in kind. The ongoing battle between the White House and Republicans in the Congress over Obamacare is typical. President Obama has made numerous public appearances across the country including two nationally televised speeches promoting the law. Through April 2014, the president had referred to the law in more than thirty of his weekly radio addresses. Not to be outdone, the Republican responses to the president's radio speeches focused on their opposition to the law on twenty-five separate occasions. And as we noted in Chapter 9, interest groups have a loud voice as well. Since 2010, they have flooded the airwaves with ads arguing for a repeal of Obamacare (for examples, see Video Archive 7.4).

All told, it is difficult to see any differences between the tactics being used to influence the fate of the Affordable Care Act and those used in recent presidential campaigns. While President Obama and the Republicans in Congress engaged in relatively civil debate, other participants including cable television and talk radio hosts delivered more inflammatory rhetoric. Republican operative Dick Morris called for opponents of Obamacare to "terrorize" Democratic legislators. A Tennessee legislator likened the mandatory insurance requirement in the law to the forced deportation of Jews by the Nazis. In response, the liberal commentator Keith Olbermann declared that Republicans' opposition to the law was based on racism. Thus, as the use of campaign techniques in policy debates escalates, the opposing sides become only more antagonistic and entrenched in their respective positions. Under these circumstances, the prospects for cooperation and compromise are slim.

CONCLUSION

In the final analysis, going public represents a catch-22 of sorts. Presidents need to maintain their popularity to be effective in office. Their inherent newsworthiness and influence over the content of news provides them with considerable Teflon. Nonetheless, the pressure to remain popular makes them averse to taking on difficult problems unless quick-fix solutions are available. Proposing tough answers to tough problems costs popular support; without support, the president has insufficient capital with which to address these problems. The less-than-satisfactory result is that popularity becomes an end in itself.

SUMMARY

1. Research suggests that three principal factors influence presidential popularity:
   * *Length of time in office.* Some theorists have suggested that over the course of the term, as presidents make decisions and take positions, they accumulate opponents and lose support. But some presidencies have not conformed to this theory.
   * *The course of real-world events.* The American public holds the president responsible for the state of the nation. When events signify that the United

States is doing well, the president's popularity increases, but it drops when events imply less satisfactory outcomes for the country.

- *Public relation efforts.* By influencing how events are defined and framed in news accounts, presidents can significantly affect their personal standing with the public.

2. In the case of policy arenas (such as foreign policy) that people cannot really experience directly, presidents can more easily maintain popularity independent of the course of events. In the case of issues that the public can experience firsthand (such as the state of the economy), real-world events are key determinants of the president's popularity.

3. In the *rally effect*, the public supports the president in the aftermath of major foreign policy actions—even when those actions may represent a failure of American policy and leadership. During times of international tension, opponents are afraid to speak out against the president—making the president's spin less subject to challenge—and the public responds accordingly.

4. An optimistic perspective on the impact of going public sees it as a strategy that not only strengthens the president's ability to get things done, but also makes the policy process more responsive to public opinion. In this view, because elected officials seek to remain popular, they are motivated to enact policies supported by the public.

5. An alternative perspective, however, suggests that the need to maintain high levels of public approval often deters the president from exercising policy leadership. Instead of using their expertise at making sense of what's best for the nation to make independent policy choices, leaders may defer to public opinion, which is generally uninformed.

FURTHER READINGS

Brody, R. A. (1991). *Assessing the president: The media, elite opinion and public support.* Stanford, CA: Stanford University Press.

Canes-Wrone, B., Herron, M. C., & Shotts, K. W. (2001). Leadership and pandering: A theory of executive policymaking. *American Journal of Political Science, 45*, 532–550.

Edwards, G. C., III. (2003). On deaf ears: The limits of the bully pulpit. New Haven, CT: Yale University Press.

Hetherington, M. J., & Nelson, M. (2003). Anatomy of a rally effect: George W. Bush and the war on terrorism. *PS: Political Science and Politics, 36*, 37–42.

Hibbs, D. A., Rivers, D., & Vasilatos, N. (1982). On the demand for economic outcomes: Macroeconomic performance and mass political support in the United States, Great Britain, and Germany. *Journal of Politics, 43*, 426–462.

Kernell, S. (1978). Explaining presidential popularity. *American Political Science Review, 72,* 506–522.

Kernell, S. (1986). *Going public: New strategies of presidential leadership.* Washington, DC: Congressional Quarterly Press.

Lowi, T. J. (1985). *The personal president: Power invested, promise unfulfilled.* Ithaca, NY: Cornell University Press.

Neustadt, R. (1960). *Presidential power: The politics of leadership.* New York: Wiley.

Shapiro, R. Y., & Jacobs, L. R. (2000). Who leads and who follows? U.S. presidents, public opinion, and foreign policy. In B. L. Nacos, R. Y. Shapiro, & P. Isernia (Eds.), *Decisionmaking in a glass house: Mass media, public opinion, and American and European foreign policy in the 21st century* (pp. 223–245). Lanham, MD: Rowman & Littlefield.

Tulis, J. K. (1987). *The rhetorical presidency.* Chatham, NJ: Chatham House.

Zaller, J. R. (1998). Monica Lewinsky's contribution to political science. *PS: Political Science and Politics, 31,* 182–189.

NOTES

1. At any given moment in time, the president's popularity can be explained by basic partisan predispositions. That is, when the incumbent is Republican, Republicans approve and Democrats disapprove. In recent years, evaluations of presidential performance have become increasingly polarized along partisan lines. However, we are more interested here in explaining short-term or cyclical changes in popularity.

2. On the first count (perjury before the grand jury), ten Republican senators voted not guilty. On the second count (obstruction of justice), five Republicans defected.

3. The invasion force consisted of a loosely organized group of Cuban exiles who were captured with minimal effort by the Cubans and later returned to the United States in exchange for shipments of food and medical supplies.

11

Evaluating Media Politics

From Jon Stewart's appearance on CNN's Crossfire, *October 15, 2004 (in discussion with Paul Begala and Tucker Carlson):*

STEWART: I made a special effort to come on the show today, because I have privately, amongst my friends and also in occasional newspapers and television shows, mentioned this show as being bad.

BEGALA: We have noticed.

STEWART: And I wanted to—I felt that that wasn't fair and I should come here and tell you that I don't—it's not so much that it's bad, as it's hurting America. But I wanted to come here today and say .... Stop, stop, stop, stop hurting America. And come work for us, because we, as the people—

CARLSON: How do you pay?

STEWART: The people? Not well.

* * * * *

David Bartlett, president, Radio–Television News Directors Association (as cited in Barta, 1996):

The job of a journalist is not to simply stand back and let the candidates say their piece. If I'm the public, what I'm buying is the experience, the analysis, the skepticism of a competent journalist. That's what journalism is. The rest is either publicity or reprinting.

Under ideal conditions, the news media would invigorate the democratic process by providing a widely accessible forum, supplying a regular stream of quality news about the issues of the day, and keeping public officials constantly under the microscope. Present-day practice, however, is quite different. David Bartlett's comments and the Stewart–Begala–Carlson exchange on *Crossfire* illustrate the core problem of modern political journalism. Journalists aspire to deliver more than mere descriptions of the candidates' words and deeds on the campaign trail. But by turning to analysis and interpretation, journalists not only leave their audience uninformed but also risk turning them off. In this concluding chapter, we suggest some approaches for addressing what we take to be the two most glaring failures of American media: (1) the absence of a substantive or policy-oriented electoral forum, and (2) the substitution of journalists and analysts for the candidates as the principal voices in the news.

To deal with the problem of inadequate substance, we first suggest a return to the public-service model of broadcast media. In every industrialized democratic nation except the United States, there is a significant commitment to public broadcasting. The presence of a strong public broadcaster contributes to higher levels of quality news programming, and we recommend increased levels of funding for PBS. In addition, commercial broadcasters should be required to provide candidates with free time in the closing days of the campaign.

As a further remedy for the problem of superficial news, we propose a system of monitoring news organizations for the substantive content of their programming, with the goal of generating greater awareness of the problem and improving the quality and content of the news delivered. Television stations and newspapers might be motivated to improve on their civic performance to avoid being identified as among the worst offenders. Finally, in the case of print media, we advocate a more expansive form of candidate endorsements; instead of limiting endorsements to a single editorial column published a few days before the election, we suggest that newspapers publish a series of articles explaining in detail the rationale for preferring one candidate over the other (or offering detailed comparisons of the candidates' positions). Because American newspapers are evenly divided in the partisan direction of their candidate endorsements, collectively these more substantial endorsements would better inform the reading public. On the subject of giving candidates greater voice, we offer a more radical treatment for the trivialization of American politics through sound bites and ads. A technology-driven system of direct, or unmediated, political communication now has the potential to alter the electoral dialogue in a manner as sweeping as the advent of television. Now that tablets, smartphones, and other portable data devices are almost as ubiquitous as the television set, candidates, and political and civic organizations are in a position to bypass the news media and communicate directly with voters—and voters should be better able to make decisions based on the candidates' issue positions. Preliminary research suggests that direct candidate-to-voter communication does, in fact, feature substantive presentations that increase voter interest in the political process.

Let's discuss each of these recommendations in greater detail.

ISSUELESS COVERAGE: A CASE STUDY OF CRIME

Perhaps the most glaring weakness of modern media-based campaigns is the invisibility of policy issues. Above all else, a meaningful electoral contest should present a clash of ideas, allowing voters to select between candidates or parties on the basis of policy proposals and performance. The present circus-like atmosphere in which campaigns are conducted all but precludes serious attention to policy issues. Questions of program impacts, trade-offs, costs, and benefits cannot be discussed in full, or even at all, within the confines of sound bites and paid advertisements.

To illustrate this point in the context of one social problem, consider crime. The overarching issue is prevention. One approach is to beef up enforcement (focusing on retribution); another approach is to deal with the perceived underlying problems of educational access and employment opportunities (focusing on economic mobility). Which model (or combination of models) will work best in practice? Should voters opt for three-strikes laws or similar policies of punishment, or would they benefit more from supporting rehabilitation and job-training programs?

Meaningful evidence on these questions is available. However, the subject is complex, and candidates who argue for nuanced positions risk appearing sympathetic to criminals. Accordingly, most candidates rely on slogans and symbolism in lieu of serious analysis. The news media, preoccupied with the horse race and strategy, do little to encourage informed debate. Under these circumstances, voters have little choice but to align themselves with proposals that they find intuitively plausible or resonant with basic cultural values—no matter how shortsighted or counterproductive these proposals might be in actuality.

The history of the three-strikes legislation in California provides a representative case study (twenty-five other states have three-strikes laws on the books) of the triumph of imagery and symbolism over objective analysis. In 1994, prompted by the abduction and brutal murder of twelve-year-old Polly Klaas, California became the second state (after Washington) to adopt three-strikes legislation. Fanned by media coverage and red-hot public outrage, the California legislature rushed to enact the most stringent of the three-strikes bills that had been introduced. No scheduled public hearings were held; no policy experts were called to testify. As Willie Brown, the longtime speaker of the California Assembly advised his Democratic colleagues, "Better get the hell out of the way" (Domanick, 2004, p. 141).

California's three-strikes law made the number of felony convictions (strikes) rather than the severity of the crime the basis for sentencing. Hundreds of people were sentenced to a minimum of twenty-five years in prison for petty theft or drug use because the offense represented their third conviction. In one of the most glaring cases of strikes-based sentencing, Leandro Andrade was sentenced to two consecutive twenty-five-year terms for stealing $150 worth of videotapes from two stores.[1]

The Andrade case was hardly atypical. About 3,700 prisoners in the state face life sentences for a third strike that was neither violent nor serious. This is more than 40 percent of the total third-strike population of about 8,500. While these offenders are eligible for parole after twenty years, the state parole board rarely releases any prisoner early.

The severity of the sentences imposed on nonviolent offenders has emerged as the focal point of a debate about criminal justice policy. Reform-minded groups have attempted, unsuccessfully, to persuade the California legislature to amend the law to limit the definition of *strikes* to violent offenses. In 2004, with the financial support of a wealthy corporate executive,[2] these groups placed Proposition 66 on the California ballot. The measure would have restricted the definition of the third strike to violent felonies.

Proposition 66 was endorsed by virtually every major newspaper in California and backed by the Democratic, Green, and Libertarian party organizations. Advocates argued that the measure was a long-overdue reform of an irrational, unfair, and cruel policy that equated petty thieves with violent criminals. They pointed out that of the twenty-three states with three-strikes programs, California is a startling exception: it is the only state that fails to distinguish between violent and nonviolent crimes. They also pointed out that the resulting cost to the California taxpayer is substantial—a minimum of $750,000 to house an inmate in prison for twenty-five years. The policy trade-offs were underscored on the editorial page of the *Sacramento Bee*: "California's prison-industrial complex is strangling the state's future. It's soaking up dollars that could go to education, housing, transportation and other basic infrastructure that enhances the state's prosperity and quality of life" (Editorial, Prop. 66 Reform, 2004).

Despite these striking statistics, the overwhelming majority of the state's elected officials declared their opposition to Proposition 66. In addition to Governor Schwarzenegger and Attorney General Bill Lockyer, former governors Pete Wilson (who had signed the original bill into law), George Deukmejian, Gray Davis, and Jerry Brown all spoke out against weakening the three-strikes law. The list of official supporters also included the district attorney of every county, virtually all law enforcement agencies, fourteen state senators, and twenty-nine members of the state assembly. In contrast to this campaign of opposition led by all-stars who apparently feared negative public reaction, the most prominent proponent of the measure was Irvine mayor Larry Agran.

Armed with an infusion of funds from billionaire Henry Nicholas III, the opponents of Proposition 66 subjected the electorate to a last-minute barrage of television advertising. In one of the ads, Schwarzenegger warned that "child molesters, rapists and killers" would be roaming the streets if the measure passed. In another ad, a rape victim tearfully pleaded with voters not to release her assailant (see Video Archive 11.1).

The impact of the "No on Proposition 66" campaign was pivotal. Nearly three-fourths of the California public had expressed support for the measure during the early stages of the campaign. As late as October 13 (a mere two weeks before the election), 65 percent of the Field Poll sample stated that they intended to vote for Proposition 66. (The same poll showed that a substantial majority correctly identified the policy intent of the proposition.) Then, in response to the advertisements and the campaign appearances of the governor, public sentiment shifted dramatically. In the final Field Poll, taken a few days before the election, the level of support had plummeted 10 points (from 65 to 55 percent), while the ranks of the opposition had swelled by 15 points (from 18 to 33 percent). This trajectory continued: on Election Day the measure was defeated by 53 to 47 percent.

What was missing from the debate over Proposition 66? Voters were not told that California practice deviates from the rest of the nation; that California has imprisoned nearly 4 times as many people under its three-strikes law as all the other states combined; or that there is insufficient space in California's prisons, thus forcing the state to export convicts to other states at considerable

Video Archive 11.1

Ads Attacking Proposition 66

cost.[3] Even the most attentive voters would have been hard-pressed to encounter information about the actual impact of the three-strikes law on the crime rate. In fact, the available evidence suggests that the massive effort to incarcerate has had no impact on crime rates.

Not only were voters deprived of evidence concerning the effectiveness of three-strikes laws as a deterrent, but the debate over Proposition 66 also ignored questions of cost effectiveness. Today the California Department of Corrections budget amounts to nearly $10 billion, and the department employs more personnel than any other state government agency. The budget for the department of corrections in New York State (which lacks a three-strikes law, and which has about half the population of California) is 70 percent less ($3 billion). California has the unique distinction of ranking second in the nation in per capita spending on prisons, but forty-fourth on expenditures per pupil.

None of these arguments against Proposition 66 were publicized during the 2004 campaign because the supporters of Proposition 66 were not as well financed as their opponents. News coverage of the proposition was extensive by the standards of local races: during the entire month of October, some ninety articles appeared in major daily newspapers. But the coverage provided readers with much more information about polling and endorsements than about the substantive arguments pro and con. For most voters, therefore, the only source of information was television advertising that attacked Proposition 66 as soft on crime.

What might the election result have been if the California news media had provided a wider range of perspectives both for and against three strikes and the alternative equality-of-opportunity model of crime prevention? And how would people have voted if the coverage had included discussion of economic factors such as the impact of incarceration on the state budget? Fortunately, we are in a position to address the question because the main provisions of Proposition 66 were reinstated on the ballot in 2012 as Proposition 36 (referred to as the Three Strikes Reform Act of 2012). Unlike the case of the 2004 proposition, three-strikes reform in 2012 was framed overwhelmingly in terms of prison overcrowding and the soaring costs of incarceration for California taxpayers. The overcrowding issue was made salient by a 2011 US Supreme Court decision, which ruled that conditions in California's prisons were inhumane and mandated the state to cut its prison population by 30,000 inmates. (In response, the state passed legislation that reassigned nonviolent offenders from state to county prisons.) The Supreme Court decision and the ballooning cost of prisons effectively shifted the terms of debate over the three-strikes law. Many conservatives supported Proposition 36 on the grounds of cost efficiency (even though the measure was opposed by the California Republican Party). The measure passed by more than a 2 to 1 margin.

There are conflicting views on the differences (or lack thereof) between informed and uninformed opinion. According to one stream of research, informed and uninformed voters are more apt to agree than disagree. Proponents of this view suggest that most people can approximate their full-information opinions by combining simple cues with widely available psychological heuristics or shortcuts. Opponents, on the other hand, cite evidence that informed and uninformed opinions are frequently at odds. In a recent analysis, for instance, Bartels (2005) shows that there was a significant difference between more- and less-informed Americans in their position on President Bush's tax cuts: support for the cuts came disproportionately from the less informed, most of whom received no benefits from the policy.

The most convincing evidence of the distinctiveness of informed opinion comes from studies showing that when people are given the arguments on both sides of an issue, they often change their positions, even when the issue represents a matter of pressing national importance. James Fishkin and his collaborators have devised a technique known as *deliberative polling* for assessing the state of informed opinion (see Fishkin, 1995). The method works as follows. A representative sample of voters is first surveyed and then provided with briefing documents that lay out the arguments for and against particular policy alternatives. The participants in the deliberative poll read the briefing materials and discuss the issues in small groups (either face-to-face or online). After the final group discussion, participants complete a second survey, thus permitting observation of changes in their attitudes before and after deliberation. Typically, a control group that does not deliberate answers the same questions at the end of the process. Thus, deliberative polling is a form of quasi-experimentation for shedding light on the effects of substantive information and debate on political attitudes and policy preferences.

The results of more than twenty deliberative polls covering a variety of issues in several countries demonstrate that delivery of information often changes the participants' policy preferences (both individually and in the aggregate). In one deliberative poll conducted in 2002, a year before the US invasion of Iraq, the discussions focused on the general use of military intervention as an instrument of foreign policy. The results showed that deliberation made people significantly more likely to prefer multilateral over unilateral intervention. The same study also showed that the foreign policy priorities of informed citizens were quite different from the priorities of the uninformed; the former were much more likely to support increased American foreign aid, as well as efforts to raise the standard of living in underdeveloped nations. In short, informed opinion favored economic assistance rather than military force as the major instrument of American foreign policy.

In a different deliberative poll, the researchers investigated public opinion on crime in Britain. After exposure to debate on different perspectives concerning the root cause of crime, participants came to favor less harsh and punitive positions on the issue (Luskin, Fishkin, & Jowell, 2002). Extrapolating from these results, it seems plausible to infer that the first attempt to reform the three-strikes law in California (Proposition 66) would likely have passed in a full-information environment. Voters who had been exposed to more than scare tactics might have responded more favorably to the measure (as indicated by the large majorities favoring Proposition 36 in 2012). More generally, a system of reporting that is more hospitable to policy debate can change the behavior of both candidates and voters. If candidates realize that the details of their positions on crime are newsworthy, they will adapt and spend more time developing them. For their part, voters given a steady stream of reports that focus on the candidates' issue positions rather than on the strategy or horse race are likely to become more informed on the issues and, as documented in deliberative polls, may also change their preferences.

To recap, media-based campaigns systematically underproduce information about the issues. Politicians have little incentive to address issues because they know that the media is not inclined to reprint their *white papers* (detailed reports on issues). For their part, the media, hoping to increase their audience share, seek out alternative topics for discussion. The only way out of this vicious circle is for society to develop institutions, policies, and standards that encourage (or mandate) news organizations to take their civic obligations more seriously and to make available space or broadcast time for explicit policy debates.

STRENGTHENING PUBLIC SERVICE BROADCASTING

The concept of public service broadcasting, introduced in Britain and adopted by most other democracies before World War II, treats the broadcast media as a major pillar of the democratic process. Broadcasters are mandated to provide a vibrant public forum in which citizens encounter significant diversity of perspectives on political issues and the voices of all groups, no matter their size or influence. In recommending the creation of public broadcasting in the United States, the Carnegie Commission emphasized the value of providing citizens with media programming that would allow them "to see America whole, in all its diversity" (Carnegie Commission, 1967, p. 14).

A major impetus to congressional adoption of the Carnegie Commission recommendations was the perception that commercial broadcasters could not be relied on to deliver informative content representing the myriad groups and perspectives making up contemporary America. This fear was well-founded. Research demonstrates that two sets of factors significantly influence news media civic performance: first, the establishment and continued support of a government-funded broadcasting network, and second, the enforcement of regulations that require privately owned media to deliver minimum levels of public affairs programming. As demonstrated in Chapter 2, the United States lags behind the rest of the world on both these factors.

First, the federal government has provided minimal funding for public broadcasting. Because they are starved of resources, PBS and NPR have been unable to develop a repertoire of programs that might be of interest to a non-trivial share of the national audience. In Europe, on the other hand, public broadcasters receive generous government subsidies and attract 30 to 40 percent of the television audience. Public broadcasters in Europe achieve a significant market share, despite the higher public-affairs content and cultural diversity of their programs.

Second, the United States has effectively deregulated the broadcast media. Initially, the Federal Communications Commission (FCC) proposed a variety of criteria for assessing whether broadcasters were living up to their public-interest responsibilities. These included the location of the television station within the community, the quality of reception, the amount of programming devoted to public issues, the education of children, and the representation of cultural minorities. In what came to be known as the 5-5-10 rule (long since abandoned), all stations had to provide 5 percent of their programs to issues of local interest, 5 percent to general news or public affairs, and another 10 percent to nonentertainment programming. Since the FCC had the power to renew the license of every television station, it was assumed that station owners would have a sufficient incentive to provide appropriate levels of public affairs programming. In practice, however, the FCC capitulated to the broadcast industry and failed to enforce the public interest provisions. License renewal was, for all practical purposes, guaranteed.

In the 1980s, the rise of cable television made it possible for broadcasters to argue that the expansion of the spectrum (the unlimited number of cable channels) meant that there was no longer a need for regulation. The expanded number of broadcast outlets meant that the market could provide diversity of programming, making government regulations superfluous. Congress passed a series of bills deregulating broadcasters. But, as we showed in Chapter 3, the abandonment of the regulatory regime meant that broadcasters were free to scale back on news programming in favor of "all entertainment, all the time."

Although most other democracies have also moved in the general direction of deregulation, they continue to maintain significant control over the content provided by both public and private broadcasters. Swedish public television, for example, "is obliged to carry cultural and quality programming, and 55 percent of its programming must be produced regionally outside Stockholm" (Department of Culture, 2009, p. 3). Canadian law requires Canadian broadcasters to provide media programming that is "predominantly and distinctly Canadian" (Canadian Film and TV Production Association, 2002, p. 1) and which reflects the multiracial and multilingual nature of Canadian society. Given the strength and extent of the US broadcast industry lobby, it is unlikely that deregulation can be reversed. A more realistic proposal is to increase the level of government funding for public broadcasting so that the audience will have at least one source they can count on for regular coverage of public affairs. At present, the US federal government contribution to the Corporation for Public Broadcasting amounts to $445 million; in Germany the level of support is 14 times greater. In the UK, it is 15 times greater. Considering that Congress appropriates $805 million each year for our national museums (under the umbrella of the Smithsonian Institution), it does not seem unreasonable or excessive to suggest that public broadcasting—an institution with the exact same mission—receive a similar level of support. If the amount expended on public broadcasting matched that allocated to museums, we would be spending less than $2 per adult citizen on public broadcasting compared to around $10 for the national parks.

GIVING CANDIDATES FREE MEDIA TIME

For decades, campaign reformers have urged Congress and the FCC to strengthen the public interest responsibilities of broadcasters. As we noted in Chapter 2, the United States is the only democracy that does not require broadcasters to provide at least specified minimal levels of public affairs coverage in exchange for their use of the public airwaves. During the 2004 election year, a typical political ad aired nearly 2 million times in the top 100 media markets. If stations were required to provide just as much free time to candidates as the advertising time that they sell, the total amount of free time in 2004 would have exceeded 150 hours (for all campaigns) in each media market!

For several years, a coalition of reform groups has pressured Congress to enact legislation that would require television networks and local stations to provide free time for candidates and ballot questions during the last month of the campaign. Their intent is not just to increase the sheer amount of election-related programming but also to improve the quality of programming. Requiring candidates to make their free-time presentations in person increases accountability and makes it more likely that the discussion will focus on policy. As Kathleen Jamieson noted in her testimony before the FCC in 1996:

> My reading of history suggests that when candidates speak in their own voice, rather than in the voice-overs of ads, or in the editing form of sound bites in news, their discourse is more likely to be constructive. And that means to argue rather than assert, to advocate rather than attack, and to be accountable. Their discourse is also, in that form, more likely to be civil. Those are all characteristics I think we ought to be trying to increase in political discourse. (Federal Communications Commission, 1996)

As is true with most policy innovations, the details of implementation often work against the intent of the policy makers. One such practical roadblock concerns the equal-time requirement. Would the networks be required to grant the same amount of free time to the dozens of minor-party presidential candidates? In 1996 the problem was sidestepped when the FCC ruled that free television time for major candidates was exempt from the equal-time provisions under the *bona fide news event doctrine*. A more difficult problem is scheduling the candidate appearances. In the 1996 experiment, all the networks (with the exception of ABC) adopted a proposal promoted by Rupert Murdoch (who owns the Fox network) to allocate brief blocks of time to Democrat Bill Clinton and Republican Bob Dole. The participating networks made available short segments of time ranging from a low of five 90-second segments (NBC) to a high of twelve 2.5-minute segments (PBS, CNN, UPN). In most cases, the two candidates appeared on alternate nights during the same week and spoke on topics of their own choosing.[4]

As predicted by the proponents, the content of the free-time presentations tended to be substantive. The candidates focused on policy advocacy and their records, rather than on slogans or personal attacks. In comparison with broadcast news, the free appearances were 3 times more likely to focus on issues (Jamieson, 1997, p. 8). In effect, the free airtime produced quality substantive content.

Unfortunately, the candidate presentations reached relatively few voters. For one thing, the 1996 contest was unusually one-sided; Clinton maintained a massive lead in the polls throughout, and public interest in the race was low. Moreover, apolitical viewers could simply switch channels to avoid watching Clinton or Dole.[5] Proponents of the experiment had requested that the networks roadblock the appearances (air the appearances at the same time) so as to maximize the viewing audience. However, the networks chose to run the candidate appearances at different times. CBS, for example, aired the segments during the evening network newscast, and NBC aired them during *Dateline*. Surveys conducted after the election showed that the lack of simultaneous programming was a serious liability; less than 25 percent of the public reported that they had watched any of the candidates' presentations. Given the typically inflated nature of self-reports, the true level of exposure is probably closer to 10 percent.

Undaunted, proponents of free time introduced a more ambitious measure in the US Senate. Cosponsored by Senators McCain, Feingold, and Durbin, the bill would have required broadcasters to air at least two hours a week of candidate and ballot measure programming for at least six weeks during the campaign. Stations would have to broadcast the free segments between 5:00 PM and 11:30 PM. Moreover, television stations would be required to subsidize federal candidates' television time through a system of vouchers financed by a tax on broadcasters. For the entire cycle, the proposal made available $650 million of free airtime for individual candidates and $100 million for each party.[6]

It goes without saying that the broadcasting industry strenuously opposed the McCain–Feingold–Durbin bill. Broadcast companies claimed that the law amounted to an arbitrary taking of private property (prohibited by the Fifth Amendment) and that the free-time requirement would infringe on their First Amendment free speech rights. As a result of their intense lobbying, the bill died in committee. The 2004 campaign returned to business as usual: television news coverage of the campaign was minuscule and broadcasters took in $1.6 billion from political advertisers.

The unwillingness of broadcasters to accept their public-service obligations and provide free time to candidates suggests an alternative remedy to the problem of nonsubstantive campaigns; the strategy would be to bypass broadcasters and deliver substantive information concerning the candidates' positions on the issues directly to every voter. In one scenario, nonpartisan civic groups would pose the questions, and the candidates would produce videos of their answers, which would then be assembled online and publicized. The cost of such an effort would be a tiny fraction of the total amount spent on campaign advertising in the 2012 campaign. We'll return to the theme of bypassing the media shortly.

Unlike broadcast media, newspapers and magazines cannot be required to provide minimal levels of campaign coverage. Instead, a media watchdog group or ombudsman could be established to monitor the level of substantive content in election news in print media. The results, if published each week during September and October, might attract considerable publicity and work as a necessary disincentive for editors preoccupied with the horse race. An institutionalized system for monitoring issue-oriented coverage among the major print outlets would also foster competition to be rated as the most-civic news source (and to avoid last place in the substance ratings), thus increasing editors' willingness to run issue-oriented stories in place of the horse race. If afforded coverage of their policy proposals, elected officials have a significant incentive to talk about the issues at some length. The end result would be some semblance of a genuine debate.

ENCOURAGING A MORE PARTISAN PRESS

Journalists are hardly appropriate intermediaries between voters and candidates. As paid professionals, they are more interested in getting the story right (avoiding any semblance of partisan bias) and less interested in helping voters identify the candidate who has the better ideas, programs, or track record. It is this arm's-length treatment of candidates and parties that is partly responsible for the low level of coverage accorded to issues. For instance, evaluating the strengths and weaknesses of the competing candidates' positions on global climate change would leave journalists open to charges of bias. The supply of substantive, issue-oriented coverage could be increased if news organizations were more explicit about their political preferences.

The tradition of a partisan press is not antithetical to democracy (as witnessed by several European democracies), and it is not foreign to the United States. In fact, American political campaigns originated in the early eighteenth century when activist newspaper editors allied themselves with the Democratic Republicans. The Federalists countered in 1798 by passing the Alien and Sedition Acts, but their attempts at censorship only accelerated politicization of the press. By the middle of the nineteenth century, most American newspapers were openly affiliated with a party:

> Partisan newspapers and loosely organized parties (aided by government subsidies) combined to create a hitherto unrecognized institution, the newspaper-based party, which dominated the American political scene in the

antebellum years, remained strong in the late nineteenth century, and did not disappear completely until the twentieth century. (Pasley, 2001, p. 17)

The presence of a vigorous partisan press helped create a sense of common identity among party supporters. Urgent notices in the party newspaper, as well as the availability of manpower provided by the urban machines, were especially useful when it was time to get voters to the polls. The heyday of the partisan press and strong party organizations generated the highest levels of voter turnout in American history. In the presidential campaign of 1896, Democrat William Jennings Bryan traveled the entire length of the country delivering hundreds of speeches to enthusiastic supporters. Bryan's appeal was based entirely on issues, most notably his opposition to free trade and the gold standard. The Republican campaign, masterminded by Marc Hanna (the first paid political consultant) brought in thousands of supporters to Washington, where they listened to McKinley rebut Bryan's populist positions on the issues. Both parties mobilized their supporters with brass-band parades and torch-light marches; on Election Day, nearly 80 percent of the electorate voted.

As the urban population grew and printing costs fell, newspaper publishers began to realize that they could more easily expand their circulation by shedding their partisan ties and appealing to readers on the basis of the everyday utility of their product rather than the correctness of their politics. Once mass-circulation media and professional journalism came of age, the die was cast for the current system of media politics. All it took was the advent of the direct primary and the weakening of the political party organizations for journalists to replace party leaders as the central players in the campaign.

The practice of professional journalism does not preclude the expression of partisan preferences. In fact, as we noted in Chapter 3, the public is already widely skeptical about the objectivity of reporters. No matter how scrupulously objective or balanced the coverage of events and issues is, partisans inevitably see the news as slanted in favor of their opponents. Bias is very much in the eyes of the beholder.

One occasion when the press reveals a more explicit bias is the endorsement of candidates at the end of a campaign. American newspapers have always endorsed candidates, although, as a recent study by Ansolabehere, Lessem, and Snyder (2006) notes, the manner of their endorsement has become less articulated and more candidate-oriented than party-oriented. Candidate endorsements can be seen either as an attempt at transparency (revealing the editors' preferences to the reader) or as an attempt at persuasion. By endorsing candidates, the press is casting a partisan vote. Empirical research into the effects of endorsements on reader preferences typically finds a nontrivial effect: endorsed candidates tend to do better at the polls.

The frequency with which newspapers endorse candidates suggests that the practice has no adverse impact on circulation. Newspapers do not make endorsements strategically—that is, they do not favor candidates from the majority party. Publishers do not seem to fear that readers supporting the non-endorsed candidate will cancel their subscriptions.

Endorsements may not hurt circulation, but is there a market for partisan or biased journalism? The emergence of Fox News as the cable ratings leader suggests that in a highly competitive market environment, a clear political slant allows a news organization to grow by creating a niche for itself. Recent theoretical work by economists corroborates this observation by showing that under competition and diversity of opinion among readers, newspapers will provide content that is more biased: "Competition forces newspapers to cater to the prejudices of their readers, and greater competition typically results in more aggressive catering to such prejudices as competitors strive to divide the market" (Mullainathan & Shleifer, 2005, p. 18). Thus, rational newspaper owners stand to gain by injecting more rather than less political slant or bias into their news. Perhaps newspapers that are more explicitly pro-Republican or pro-Democratic in their editorial pages can use their ideological transparency as a means of attracting readers.

No matter what the implications are for circulation and revenue, a more rather than less partisan press will have the effect of increasing the supply of issue-oriented news. At the very least, we recommend that newspapers increase the amount of editorial space devoted to their endorsements. Supporting a candidate requires a rationale; newspapers can use the occasion of their endorsement to run a series of editorials explaining why the endorsed candidate's positions are preferable to the opponent's. On the whole, the availability of newspapers balanced between Democratic and Republican bias will enable motivated readers who monitor multiple news sources to encounter both sides of the debate.

FOSTERING DIRECT COMMUNICATION BETWEEN CANDIDATES AND VOTERS

Information technology offers a promising avenue for a renewal of *direct* communication between candidates and voters. Nearly two-thirds of American adults own a smartphone, according to a 2014 Pew survey, and three-fourths of the population is connected to the Internet at home. About 240 million Americans regularly use the Internet, according to statistics compiled by the International Telecommunication Union.

Given the rapid proliferation of technology, it is not surprising that candidates and political groups have made their presence known online. From the president on down to city council members, elected officials offer a wealth of information on their websites. Visitors may browse through speeches, view television commercials, complete surveys, contribute money, or request information and assistance.

In the case of campaign websites, the evidence shows clearly that candidates provide extensive information about their positions and pledges on the issues. In the most systematic study of campaign websites to date—including all Senate elections between 2002 and 2006 and a large representative sample of House contests—the researchers found that virtually every candidate (90 percent) had a separate section dedicated to issues, and 60 percent made this information available on the opening screen (see Druckman, Kifer, & Parkin, 2009). Moreover, issue-oriented information was much more prominent than information about the candidates' personal background and biography. The contrast with media coverage of campaigns is hard to miss. A Pew Research Center study of media coverage of the 2008 campaigns, based on a sample of more than two thousand reports put out by forty-two different news sources between September 8 and October 16, found that horse-race coverage was the number one theme, accounting for 53 percent of all news. Stories about public policy made up only 20 percent of election coverage.

Although officeholder and campaign websites are a rich source of substantive information, they have yet to attract more than a tiny share of Internet traffic. Political junkies may make regular visits to whitehouse.gov and taxpayers may find necessary filing information at irs.gov, but for most Americans, seeking information about candidates or government programs takes a backseat to online pastimes like shopping or catching up on the latest baseball scores. In March 2012, for instance, the combined audience for the White House and Internal Revenue Service sites amounted to less than 10 percent of the visitors to Amazon and eBay (see Figure 11.1).

REACHING THE TECHNOLOGY GENERATION

Direct candidate-to-voter communication is likely to have the greatest impact on younger Americans. Youth make up the vanguard of Internet and mobile technology users. School-age children and young adults are considerably

FIGURE 11.1

Visitors to Selected Websites

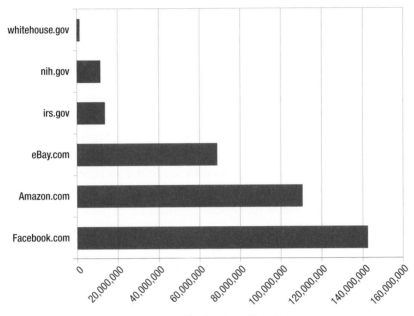

Number of monthly visitors

Source: Data from comScore.com, Retrieved March 2012.

overrepresented among people who regularly use smartphones and broadband Internet. Among eight- to eighteen-year-olds, 95 percent access the Internet at home. Not only are the young especially adept with new technologies, but they have also integrated them into their personal lives as never before.

From doing homework to chatting with friends, playing games, posting photographs, listening to or creating music, and downloading and watching the latest movies, the Internet has become a core element of contemporary youth culture. On October 2, 2012, less than ten years after the company was created, Mark Zuckerberg, the founder of Facebook, announced that the billionth person had joined his website. People under the age of thirty-four make up a third of Facebook users. The average Facebook user spends nearly an hour a day at the website, he or she is a member of twelve groups, is invited to three events each month, and posts twenty-five comments. Thus, in stark contrast to their underrepresentation in any form of political action, youth are dominant in their daily use of information technology and social media. From our perspective, the important question is whether their attraction to technology can be harnessed to stimulate a greater sense of involvement in the world of politics.

One way in which Facebook fosters political engagement is by allowing users to publicly promote a political issue or candidate. Users can create or "like" candidate's pages, for example, or post positive or negative comments about a candidate. Among the politicians with a Facebook page, Barack Obama is clearly the most popular. As of 2014, over 41 million Facebook users like Obama's page. (But many more people like the Texas Hold 'em Poker Page [71 million], Eminem [84 million], and 59 other pages on Facebook.) As we noted in Chapter 5, social media is also an important source of news. According to a 2013 Pew survey, 34 percent of Americans between the ages of eighteen and twenty-four saw news on social media "yesterday." Another survey found that 26 percent of young adults claimed to get news from Facebook or MySpace at least three days a week during the 2008 presidential primary season (Baumgartner & Morris, 2010).

More generally, young people are attracted to technology not because they seek political enlightenment but rather for social interaction and personal stimulation. If technologically enhanced political material is to catch their eye, the presentation must necessarily include popular elements of youth culture, most notably music, animation, and comic relief. As of this writing, 13 million people have watched "Obama Girl" on YouTube, and the online audience for Tina Fey's impersonations of Sarah Palin amounts to more than 10 times the audience for the live *SNL* broadcasts. Stanford researchers tested the assumption that the use of technologically rich political presentations would engage young people by producing a youth-oriented election CD for the 2002 gubernatorial campaign in California. The CD presented an exhaustive, easily searchable database about Democrat Gray Davis and his Republican opponent, Bill Simon, supplemented with a variety of interactive games, contests, and quizzes that were all designed to make the presentation especially appealing to youth. For instance, the CD featured two different "Whack-a-Pol" games in which users had to hit rapidly moving political targets (politicians or interest groups) with a hammer, a music quiz asking users to identify popular songs and associate the artists with candidates or causes, a similar celebrity quiz, and a self-administered "rate your campaign IQ" test.

What were the effects of using the CD? Even after adjusting for the overrepresentation of activist subjects among the ranks of CD users, the CD group's actual turnout rate exceeded turnout among the control group by a significant margin. CD users were also more likely to express interest in the campaign.

High-tech campaigns have the potential to mobilize youth. Moreover, unlike ordinary get-out-the-vote methods, an online campaign instills internal rather than external political motivation and is thus more likely to have a long-lasting effect on youth attitudes. Conventional mobilization campaigns, by providing the target recipient with a salient external rationale for voting, may actually impede the development of participant attitudes. At the very least, these campaigns have no effects whatsoever on the dispositions known to encourage political participation. Campaign websites place the visitor in a more active posture, at least as compared with potential voters who are targeted by telephone or door-to-door campaigns. The fact that individuals are free to explore websites on their own has important psychological implications.

Social psychologists have long known that behavior affects self-perception. Typically, individuals attribute their own actions to either dispositional (internal) or situational (external) causes. Someone who votes, for instance, may believe that she decided to vote on her own or, alternatively, that she was influenced to vote by a phone call or campaign worker. Attributing the act to internal factors contributes to *intrinsic motivation*, which is known to encourage long-term learning of the act in question. In one classic study, preschoolers who were promised a reward for drawing were later found to approach drawing materials less frequently than those who were not led to expect any reward.

The implications of the findings on intrinsic motivation for youth political participation are clear: young people who seek out and encounter campaign information of their own accord and spend time interacting with political material may come to see themselves as interested in politics. The relatively inexpensive act of visiting a political website may then open the door to more significant acts, including registering to vote and discussing the campaign with parents or friends. Thus, a relatively trivial and unobtrusive addition to one's technology space promises greater long-term payoffs than do conventional efforts at mobilization. The reason for this effect of technology use is simple: an eighteen-year-old who, in the course of playing a video game, learns that certain groups or causes he dislikes are on a particular candidate's team has a compelling basis (his actual behavior) for claiming an interest in politics. An eighteen-year-old who receives a phone call urging him to vote has some basis for claiming precisely the opposite.[7]

To sum up, the proliferation of information technology makes possible alternative forms of campaigning that cast voters in a more independent role. Consider the contrast between voters with access to online sources and those who rely on network television. The former, with minimal effort, can sample from an extensive compilation of information featuring the candidates in their own words; the latter would have access to a daily sound bite and accounts of the horse race. Rather than waiting passively, and most likely in vain, for the media to provide coverage of relevant issues, Internet users can access information that is personally meaningful. The evidence suggests that this newfound independence fosters a general sense of political involvement.

The benefits of unmediated political communication for voters are clear, but bypassing the media is just as advantageous for the candidates. They can distribute their messages widely, devoid of criticism and media analysis. Maintaining a website or Facebook page is affordable even for the smallest minor-party candidates.

Many politicians have joined Facebook to express their opinions and recruit potential supporters. Sarah Palin's Facebook page is instructive. Not only does Palin post notes on a regular basis (more than 250 as of October 2010) but fans' comments are also available, as long as they are not too controversial or critical of the candidate (Dickerson, 2010). When Palin reached her 2 millionth fan on Facebook (she now has more than 4 million), she commented "Two million! Wow! That's more than some cable news shows. Thank you all and let's keep the momentum!"

As strategic actors, candidates can be expected to take advantage of this new mode of direct campaigning by addressing a more complete range of policy positions than can be conveyed in sound bites. The fact that the Internet is just as transparent a forum as televised advertising or candidate debates makes it unlikely that Web content will be any more misleading or deceptive than standard campaign presentations are. The presence of vigilant bloggers, motivated to scrutinize every word posted by the candidates, is a powerful incentive for candidates to stay close to the facts and record in their online pitches. As the evidence on free-time appearances indicates, candidates are far more inclined to provide arguments and advocacy rather than slogans and personal attacks when they are personally accountable. In the end, unmediated communication better realizes voter independence, the breadth and depth of the policy debate, and candidates' control over their messages. These gains, significant in themselves, may ultimately be significantly augmented by the collective benefit of having a more enthusiastic and engaged citizenry.

CONCLUSION

American politics stands at a critical crossroads. For decades, candidates and elected officials depended on the news media to get their messages out—with predictable consequences. The media used their newfound influence to develop new forms of reporting that reduced candidates' control over their messages but enhanced the voice of the journalist. In the process, journalists were side-tracked from their public-service obligations, and voters were left uninformed, confused, and cynical.

The development of new technologies affords society an opportunity to escape the sideshow of combat between the candidates and the press. Voters can gain access to information that is more substantive and personally relevant than that provided by mainstream news organizations' coverage of the campaign. Technology also makes possible more-personalized forms of candidate-to-voter and voter-to-voter communication. Although there is good reason to hope that new forms of campaign communication will provide a better way to inform and engage voters, the fundamental dynamic of media politics will remain unchanged: instead of television advertising, politicians will turn to websites, Facebook pages, tweets highlighting their most recent accomplishments, and online town hall meetings to score points with voters. What will be different, however, is the substantive content of their discourse and the reduced cost of communicating with voters.

Given access to voters, candidates are unlikely to campaign on the basis of their strategies or the state of the horse race; instead, they will talk about their accomplishments and positions on the issues. Reaching voters via information technology is far less expensive than mounting a full-scale advertising campaign. The lower entry costs will make for a larger pool of candidates, a more multisided flow of information, and eventually, more-competitive elections. As we enter the postmedia era, the electoral process could well be rejuvenated.

SUMMARY

1. The system of media politics in the United States today may be seen as having two main shortcomings: (a) the absence of a substantive or policy-oriented electoral forum, and (b) the substitution of journalists and analysts for the candidates as the principal voices in the news.

2. Some scholars argue that the electorate's lack of policy information is inconsequential. According to one stream of research, most people can approximate their full-information opinions by combining simple cues with widely available psychological heuristics or shortcuts. Other scholars cite evidence that informed and uninformed opinions are frequently at odds. A significant body of research has demonstrated that when people are given the arguments on both sides of an issue, they often change their positions.

3. Suggestions for addressing the lack of a policy-oriented electoral forum include the following:
    * Increase funding for public broadcasting.
    * Require broadcast outlets to provide candidates with free airtime in the closing days of the campaign.
    * Grade news organizations on the substantive content of their programming, with the goal of generating greater awareness of the problem and improving the quality and content of the news delivered.
    * Return to a more partisan press, in which the print media would adopt a more expansive form of candidate endorsements. Since American newspapers are evenly divided in the partisan direction of their candidate endorsements, collectively these more substantial endorsements would better inform the reading public.
4. One suggestion for addressing the marginalization of candidate voices is to have candidates adopt a technology-driven system of direct or unmediated political communication to bypass the news media and communicate directly with voters, improving voters' ability to make decisions on the basis of the candidates' issue positions. Preliminary research suggests that direct candidate-to-voter communication does, in fact, increase voter interest and participation in the process.

FURTHER READINGS

Althaus, S. (1998). Information effects in collective preferences. *American Political Science Review, 92,* 545–558.

Ansolabehere, S., Lessem, R., & Snyder, J. M. (2006). The orientation of newspaper endorsements in U.S. elections, 1940–2002. *Quarterly Journal of Political Science, 1*(4), 393–404.

Bartels, L. M. (2005). Homer gets a tax cut: Inequality and public policy in the American mind. *Perspectives on Politics, 3*(1), 15–31.

Baumgartner, J., & Morris, J. (2010). MyFaceTube politics: Social networking websites and political engagement of young adults. *Social Science Computer Review, 28,* 24–44.

Druckman, J. N., Kifer, M. J., & Parkin, M. (2009). Campaign communication in U.S. Congressional elections. *American Political Science Review, 103*(3), 343–366.

Fishkin, J. (1995). *The voice of the people.* New Haven, CT: Yale University Press.

Hamilton, J. T. (2003). *All the news that's fit to sell: How the market transforms information into news.* Princeton, NJ: Princeton University Press.

Lupia, A. (1994). Shortcuts versus encyclopedias: Information and voting behavior in California insurance reform elections. *American Political Science Review, 88,* 63–76.

Luskin, R. C., Fishkin, J. S., & Jowett, R. (2002). Considered opinions: Deliberative polling in Britain. *British Journal of Political Science, 32,* 455–487.

Pasley, J. L. (2001). *The tyranny of printers: Newspaper politics in the early American republic.* Charlottesville: University of Virginia Press.

NOTES

1. The Andrade case was the basis for a prolonged legal challenge to the California three-strikes law on the grounds that the sentence constituted "cruel and unusual punishment." The US Court of Appeals for the Ninth Circuit upheld the challenge, but the California attorney general appealed the decision to the US Supreme Court. In a five-to-four vote, the Supreme Court overturned the appellate decision and reinstated the sentence.

2. The major donor was Jerry Keenan, whose contribution amounted to $2 million. Opponents of the measure were quick to point out that Keenan's motives were less than pure, his son having been convicted of drunken driving. The "Yes on 66" campaign was also the beneficiary of a $500,000 contribution from financier George Soros (whose impartiality was not questioned).

3. Making the imbalance even more striking is the fact that the population of California is roughly one-third of the total population of the remaining three-strikes states.

4. The A. H. Belo Corporation, owner of several television stations across the country, extended the free-time program to gubernatorial and congressional candidates.

5. CBS and CNN both provided ratings data for the days that they aired the candidate appearances. It is surprising that in neither case was there any evidence of significant channel switching.

6. The voucher system was based on a matching formula. Candidates who were able to raise a minimum amount of money in private contributions would receive three dollars in vouchers for one dollar of cash contributions.

7. In fact, Green and Gerber (2001) report that telephone calls encouraging young people to vote have no effect at all on standard participant predispositions.

BIBLIOGRAPHY

Chapter 1

Besley, T., & Prat, A. (2006). Handcuffs for the grabbing hand? Media capture and government accountability. *American Economic Review, 96*, 720–736.

Henrichson, C., & Delaney, R. (2012). The price of prisons: What incarceration costs taxpayers. New York: Vera Institute of Justice.

Weissburg, R., Mukamal, D., & Seagall, J. (2011). Life in limbo: An examination of parole release for prisoners serving life sentences with the possibility of parole. Stanford, CA: Stanford Criminal Justice Center.

Chapter 2

Bagdikian, B. H. (2000). *The media monopoly* (6th ed.). Boston: Beacon.

Besley, T., & Burgess, R. (2002). The political economy of government accountability: Theory and evidence from India. *Quarterly Journal of Economics, 117*, 1415–1451.

Besley, T., & Prat, A. (2006). Handcuffs for the grabbing hand? Media capture and government accountability. *American Economic Review, 96*, 720–736.

Bishop, R., & Hakanen, E. A. (2002). In the public interest? The state of local television programming fifteen years after deregulation. *Journal of Communication Inquiry, 26*, 261–276.

Brants, K. (1998). Who's afraid of infotainment? *European Journal of Communication, 13*, 315–335.

Denver, D., Hands, G., Fisher, J., & MacAllister, I. (2003). Constituency campaigning in Britain, 1992–2001: Centralization and modernization. *Party Politics, 9*, 541–559.

Gilliam, F. D., Jr., & Iyengar, S. (2000). Prime suspects: The influence of local television news on the viewing public. *American Journal of Political Science, 44*, 560–573.

Goldmark, P. C., Jr. (2001). *Old values, new world: Harnessing the legacy of independent journalism for the future* (with a report of the Fourth Annual Aspen Institute Conference on Journalism and Society, "The evolution of journalism in a changing market economy," by D. Bollier). Washington, DC: Aspen Institute.

Hallin, D. C., & Mancini, P. (2004). *Comparing media systems: Three models of media and politics.* Cambridge, England: Cambridge University Press.

Hazan, R. Y. (2002). Candidate selection. In L. LeDuc, R. G. Niemi, & P. Norris (Eds.), *Comparing democracies 2: New challenges in the study of elections and voting* (pp. 108–126). London: Sage.

Heinderyckx, F. (1993). Television news programmes in western Europe: A comparative study. *European Journal of Communication, 8*, 425–450.

Holtz-Bacha, C., & Norris, P. (2001). To entertain, inform and educate: Still the role of public television? *Political Communication, 18*, 123–140.

Iyengar, S. (1997). Overview of media-based political campaigns. In S. Iyengar & R. Reeves (Eds.), *Do the media govern?* (pp. 143–148). Thousand Oaks, CA: Sage.

Iyengar, S. & Curran, J. (2009). *Media systems, news delivery and citizens' knowledge of current affairs.* Retrieved October 1, 2010, from http://publicsphere.ssrc.org.

Kaid, L. L., & Jones, C. A. (2004). United States of America. In B. Lange & D. Ward (Eds.), *The media and elections: A handbook and comparative study* (pp. 25–59). Mahwah, NJ: Erlbaum.

Krasnow, E. G. (1997). *The "public interest" standard: The elusive search for the Holy Grail.* Briefing paper prepared for the Advisory Committee on Public Interest Obligations of Digital Television Broadcasters. Retrieved April 2, 2005, from www.mediainstitute.org/gore /STUDIES/krasnow.html.

Krüger, U. M. (1996). Boulevardisierung der Information im Privatfernsehen. *Media Perspektiven, 7*, 362–375.

Lacy, S., & Simon, T. F. (1993). *The economics and regulation of United States newspapers.* Norwood, NJ: Ablex.

McNicholas, A., & Ward, D. (2004). United Kingdom. In B. Lange & D. Ward, *The media and elections: A handbook and comparative study* (pp. 145–164). Mahwah, NJ: Erlbaum.

Polsby, N. W. (1983). *Consequences of party reform.* New York: Oxford University Press.

Project for Excellence in Journalism. (2003, April 29). *Does ownership matter in local television news: A five-year study of ownership and quality.* Retrieved March 19, 2005, from the Project for Excellence in Journalism website: www.journalism.org/resources/research /reports/ownership/Ownership2.pdf.

Project for Excellence in Journalism. (2004c). *The state of the news media, 2004: Overview— Ownership.* Retrieved March 7, 2005, from the State of the News Media website: www .stateofthenewsmedia.org/2004/narrative_overview_ownership.asp?media=1.

Sinclair Broadcast Group. (2004, October 19). *Sinclair to air "A POW Story"* (Sinclair Broadcast Group press release). Retrieved March 9, 2005, from www.sbgi.net/press /release_20041019_87.shtml.

Williams, Granville. (2003). *European media ownership: Threats on the landscape. A survey of who owns what in Europe* (Upd. ed.). Brussels, Belgium: European Federation of Journalists. Retrieved September 18, 2004, from the International Federation of Journalists website: www.ifj.org/pdfs/europeownershipupdate2003.pdf.

Zechowski, S. (n.d.). Public interest, convenience, and necessity. In H. Newcomb (Ed.), *The encyclopedia of television.* Retrieved March 10, 2005, from the Museum of Broadcast Communications website: www.museum.tv/archives/etv/P/htmlP/publicintere/public intere.htm.

Zuckerman, E. (2003, August). *Global attention profiles—A working paper: First steps towards a quantitative approach to the study of media attention.* Cambridge, MA: Harvard Law School, Berkman Center for Internet and Society. Retrieved March 10, 2005, from the Global Attention Profiles website: http://h2odev.law.harvard.edu/ezuckerman/paper .pdf.

Chapter 3

Baker, C. E. (2002). *Media, markets, and democracy.* New York: Cambridge University Press.

Baum, M. A. (2005). Talking the vote: Why presidential candidates hit the talk show circuit. *American Journal of Political Science, 49,* 213–234.

Carter, Bill. (2005, December 24). Microsoft quits MSNBC TV, but Web partnership remains. *The New York Times,* p. C1.

Crouse, T. (1972). *The boys on the bus.* New York: Random House.

Curran, J., Iyengar, S., Lund, A. B., and Salovaara-Moring, I. (2009). Media system, public knowledge, and democracy: A comparative study. *European Journal of Communication, 24,* 5–26.

D'Alessio D., & Allen, M. (2000). Media bias in presidential elections: A meta-analysis. *Journal of Communication, 50,* 133–156.

Gilliam, F. D., Jr., & Iyengar, S. (2000). Prime suspects: The influence of local television news on the viewing public. *American Journal of Political Science, 44,* 560–573.

Goldman, S., & Mutz, D. (2011). The friendly media phenomenon: A cross-national analysis of cross-cutting exposure. *Political Communication, 28,* 42–66.

Hallin, D. C. (1986). *The uncensored war: The media and Vietnam.* Berkeley: University of California Press.

Hamilton, J. T. (2003). *All the news that's fit to sell: How the market transforms information into news.* Princeton, NJ: Princeton University Press.

Iyengar, S. (1991). *Is anyone responsible?* Chicago: University of Chicago Press.

Iyengar, S., Norpoth, H., & Hahn, K. (2004). Consumer demand for election news: The horserace sells. *Journal of Politics, 66,* 157–175.

Kalb, M. (2001). *One scandalous story: Clinton, Lewinsky, and thirteen days that tarnished American journalism.* New York: Free Press.

Kaplan, M., Goldstein, K., & Hale, M. (2005). *Local news coverage of the 2004 campaigns: An analysis of nightly broadcasts in 11 markets* (Report). University of Southern California, Annenberg School for Communication, Lear Center Local News Archive. Retrieved March 19, 2005, from www.localnewsarchive.org/pdf/LCLNAFinal2004.pdf.

Klite, P. K., Bardwell, R. A., & Salzman, J. (1997). Local TV news: Getting away with murder. *Harvard International Journal of Press/Politics, 2,* 102–112.

Kurtz, H. (1999). *Media meltdown.* Annual Carlos McClatchy Lecture, Stanford University.

McChesney, R. W. (1999). *Rich media, poor democracy: Communication politics in dubious times.* Urbana: University of Illinois Press.

Patterson, T. E. (2000). *How soft news and critical journalism are shrinking the news audience and weakening democracy.* Cambridge, MA: Joan Shorenstein Center on the Press, Politics, and Public Policy, Kennedy School of Government, Harvard University.

Patterson, T. (2007). *Young people and news.* Cambridge, MA: Joan Shorenstein Center for the Press, Politics and Policy, Kennedy School of Government, Harvard University.

Pew Research Center. (2010). *The state of the news media 2010: An annual report on American journalism.* Retrieved on January 18, 2011, from the State of the News Media website: www.stateofthemedia.org/2010.

Pew Research Center. (2012). *Winning the media campaign 2012: Both candidates received more negative than positive coverage in mainstream news, but social media was even harsher.* http://www.journalism.org/2012/11/02/winning-media-campaign-2012/.

Radio Television Digital News Association (RTDN). (2013). *TV and radio news staffing and profitability survey.* https://www.rtdna.org/uploads/files/div12.pdf.

Robinson, M. (2007). *Two decades of American news preferences, Part 1: Analyzing what news the public follows—and doesn't follow.* Pew Research Center.

Rosenstiehl, T., Jurkowitz, M., & Sartor, T. (2012). *How the media covered the 2012 primary campaign.* Pew Research Center.

Sigal, L. (1973). *Reporters and officials.* Lexington, MA: Heath.

Slattery, K. L., & Hakanen, E. A. (1994). Sensationalism versus public affairs content of local TV news: Pennsylvania revisited. *Journal of Broadcasting and Electronic Media, 38,* 205–216.

Stevens, M. (n.d.). History of newspapers, Collier's Encyclopedia. Retrieved August 17, 2004, from www.nyu.edu/classes/stephens/Collier's%20page.htm.

Chapter 4

Althaus, S. (2003). When news norms collide, follow the lead: New evidence for press independence. *Political Communication, 20,* 381–414.

Althaus, S., Edy, J., Entman, R., & Phalen, P. (1996). Revising the indexing hypothesis: Officials, media and the Libya crisis. *Political Communication, 13,* 407–421.

Ansolabehere, S., Behr, R., & Iyengar, S. (1993). *The media game: American politics in the television age.* New York: Macmillan.

Arlen, M. J. (1969). *Living-room war: Writings about television.* New York: Viking.

Braestrup, P. (1977). *Big story: How the American press and television reported and interpreted the crisis of Tet 1968 in Vietnam and Washington.* Boulder, CO: Westview.

Conetta, C. (2003, October 20). *The wages of war: Iraqi combatant and noncombatant fatalities in the 2003 conflict* (Project on Defense Alternatives Research Monograph No. 8). Retrieved July 26, 2005, from the Project on Defense Alternatives website: www.comw .org/pda/0310rm8.html.

Conetta, C. (2004, February 18). *Disappearing the dead: Iraq, Afghanistan, and the idea of a "new warfare"* (Project on Defense Alternatives Research Monograph No. 9). Retrieved March 19, 2005, from the Project on Defense Alternatives website: www.comw.org /pda/0402rm9.html.

Dorman, W. A. (1997). Press theory and journalistic practice: The case of the Gulf War. In S. Iyengar & R. Reeves (Eds.), *Do the media govern? Politicians, voters and reporters in America* (pp. 118–125). Thousand Oaks, CA: Sage.

Entman, R. M. (2004). *Projections of power: Framing news, public opinion, and U.S. foreign policy.* Chicago: University of Chicago Press.

Frenznick, D. A. (1992). The First Amendment on the battlefield: A constitutional analysis of press access to military operations in Grenada, Panama and the Persian Gulf. *Pacific Law Journal, 23,* 315–359.

From the editors: The *Times* and Iraq. (2004, May 26). *The New York Times,* p. A10.

Hayes, D., & Guardino, M. (2013). *Influence from abroad: Foreign voices, the media, and U.S. public opinion.* New York: Cambridge University Press.

Karnow, S. (1997). *Vietnam: A history* (2nd ed.). New York: Penguin.

Krueger, A. B., & Laitin, D. (2004, May 17). Are we winning the war on terror? (Editorial). *The Washington Post,* p. A21.

Mermin, J. (1999). *Debating war and peace: Media coverage of U.S. intervention in the post-Vietnam era.* Princeton, NJ: Princeton University Press.

Mueller, J. (1973). *War, presidents and public opinion.* New York: Wiley.

US Department of State. (2004, June 22). *Remarks on the release of the revised patterns of global terrorism 2003 annual report.* Retrieved July 26, 2005, from www.state.gov/s/ct/rls/rm/2004/33801.htm.

Zaller, J. R. (1994). Elite leadership of mass opinion: New evidence from the Gulf War. In W. L. Bennett & D. L. Paletz (Eds.), *Taken by storm: The media, public opinion, and U.S. foreign policy in the Gulf War* (pp. 186–209). Chicago: University of Chicago Press.

Chapter 5

Abramowitz, A. I., & Saunders, K. L. (2006). Exploring the bases of partisanship in the American electorate: Social identity vs. ideology. *Political Research Quarterly, 59,* 175–187.

Adamic, L. A., & Glance, N. (2005). *The political blogosphere and the 2004 U.S. election: Divided they blog.* Paper presented at Annual Workshop on the Weblogging Ecosystem, WWW2005, Chiba, Japan, May 10–14.

Anburajan, A. (2013). Where did all the search traffic go? At http://www.buzzfeed.com/aswini/where-did-all-the-search-traffic-go#2wbjx2g.

Bimber, B. (2003). *Information and American democracy: Technology in the evolution of political power.* New York: Cambridge University Press.

Bimber, B., & Davis, R. (2003). *Campaigning online: The Internet in U.S. elections.* New York: Oxford University Press.

Boulianne, S. (2009). Does Internet use affect engagement? A meta-analysis of research. *Political Communication, 26,* 193–211.

Delli Carpini, M. X., & Keeter, S. (1996). *What Americans know about politics and why it matters.* New Haven, CT: Yale University Press.

Fiorina, M. P., Abrams, S. J., & Pope, J. C. (2005). *Culture wars? The myth of a polarized America.* New York: Pearson Longman.

Gentzkow, M., & Shapiro, J. (2010). *Ideological segregation online and offline* (Working Paper 15916). Retrieved August 15, 2010, from the National Bureau of Economic Research website: www.nber.org/papers/w15916.

Han, H. C. (2009). *Moved to action: Motivation, participation, and inequality in American politics.* Stanford, CA: Stanford University Press.

Hassanpour, N. (2014). Media disruption and revolutionary unrest: Evidence from Mubarak's quasi-experiment. *Political Communication, 31,* 1–24.

Hill, S. (2009). World wide webbed: The Obama campaign's masterful use of the Internet. *Social Europe Journal, 4,* 9–15.

Hindman, M. (2008). *The myth of digital democracy.* Princeton, NJ: Princeton University Press.

Iyengar, S. (1990). Shortcuts to political knowledge: Selective attention and the accessibility bias. In J. A. Ferejohn & J. H. Kuklinski (Eds.), *Information and the democratic process* (pp. 161–185). Champaign: University of Illinois Press.

Iyengar, S., Hahn, K. (2009). Red media, blue media: Evidence of ideological polarization in media use. *Journal of Communication, 59,* 19–39.

Iyengar, S., Hahn, K. S., Krosnick, J. A., & Walker, J. (2008). Selective exposure to campaign communication: The role of anticipated agreement, interest in politics, and issue salience. *Journal of Politics, 70,* 186–200.

Jacobson, G. C. (2006). *A divider, not a uniter: George W. Bush and the American people*. New York: Pearson.

King, G., Pan, J., & Roberts, M. E. (2013). How censorship in China allows government criticism but silences collective expression. *American Political Science Review, 107,* 1–18.

Kraut, R., Lundmark, V., Patterson, M., Kiesler, S., Mukopadhyay, T., & Scherlis, W. (1998). The Internet paradox: A social technology that reduces social involvement and psychological well-being. *American Psychologist, 53,* 1017–1031.

Krosnick, J. A. (1990). Government policy and citizen passion: A study of issue publics in contemporary America. *Political Behavior, 12,* 59–92.

LaCour, M. J.(2012). A balanced news diet, not selective exposure: Evidence from a direct measure of media exposure. Unpublished paper, University of California—Los Angeles.

Lawrence, E. D., Sides, J., & Farrell, H. (2010). Self-segregation or deliberation? Blog readership, participation, and polarization in American politics. *Perspectives on Politics, 8,* 141–158.

Lazarsfeld, P. F., Berelson, B. R., & Gaudet, H. (1948). *The people's choice*. New York: Columbia University Press.

Lelkes, Y., Sood, G., & Iyengar, S. (2014). *The hostile audience: Selective exposure to partisan sources and affective polarization*. Paper presented at the Annual Meeting of the International Communication Association.

McGee, M. (2014). *Facebook cuts into Google's lead as top traffic driver to online news sites*. At http://marketingland.com/facebook-cuts-googles-lead-top-traffic-driver-online -news-sites-report-75578.

Messing, S. (2013). *Social influence in social media*. Unpublished doctoral dissertation, Stanford University, Stanford, CA.

Messing, S., & Westwood, S. J. (2013). *Friends that matter: How social influence affects selection in social media*. Unpublished paper, Stanford University, Stanford, CA.

Messing, S., & Westwood, S. J. (2014). Selective exposure in the age of social media: Endorsements trump partisan source affiliation when selecting news online. *Communication Research, 41,* 1042–1063.

Miller, C. C. (2008, November 7). *How Obama's Internet campaign changed politics*. Retrieved November 21, 2008, from the *New York Times* blog website: http://bits.blogs.nytimes .com.

Mullainathan, S., & Shleifer, A. (2005). The market for news. *American Economic Review, 95,* 1031–1053.

A. C. Nielsen Company. (2012). *Top U.S. brands and news websites, May 2012*. At http://www .nielsen.com/us/en/insights/news/2012/may-2012-top-u-s-web-brands-and-news -websites.html.

Pew Project for Excellence in Journalism. (2010). *The state of the news media 2010: An annual report on American journalism*. Retrieved January 18, 2011, from the State of the News Media website: www.stateofthemedia.org/2010.

Pew Research Center (2005). *The Dean activists: Their profile and prospects*. At http://www.people -press.org/2005/04/06/the-dean-activists-their-profile-and-prospects/

Pew Research Center. (2011). *Press widely criticized, but trusted more than other information sources*. Retrieved December 10, 2014, from http://www.people-press.org/files/legacy -pdf/9-22-2011%20Media%20Attitudes%20Release.pdf.

Pew Research Center. (2012). *Cable leads the pack as campaign news source.* Retrieved December 8, 2014, from http://www.people-press.org/2012/02/07/cable-leads-the-pack-as-campaign -news-source/.

Pew Research Center. (2014). *How social media is reshaping news.* Retrieved August 15, 2014, from http://www.pewresearch.org/fact-tank/2014/09/24/how-social-media-is-reshaping -news/.

Pew Research Center for the People and Press. (2004). *Online news audience larger, more diverse: News audience increasingly polarized.* Retrieved August 15, 2010, from the Pew website: http://people-press.org/reports/pdf/215.pdf.

Pew Research Center's Project for Excellence in Journalism. (2010). *State of the news media: An annual report on American journalism.* Retrieved October 17, 2010, from www .stateofthemedia.org/2010.

Pfau, M. J., Houston, B., & Semmler, S. M. (2007). *Mediating the vote: The changing media landscape in U.S. presidential campaigns.* Lanham, MD: Rowman & Littlefield.

Price, V., & Zaller, J. (1993). Who gets the news? Alternative measures of news reception and their implications for research. *Public Opinion Quarterly, 57,* 133–164.

Rheingold, H. (2002). *Smart mobs: The next social revolution.* Cambridge, MA: Basic Books.

Rhoads, C. (2008, October 18). Web data offer new slant on traditional horse race. *The Wall Street Journal,* p. A5.

Robinson, M. J., & Sheehan, M. (1983). *Over the wire and on TV: CBS and UPI in campaign '80.* New York: Basic Books.

Rutenberg, J., Thompson, M. W., Kirkpatrick, D. D., & Labaton, S. (2008, February 21). For McCain, self-confidence on ethics poses its own risk. *New York Times,* p. A1.

Scherer, M. (2012). Inside the secret world of the data crunchers who helped Obama win. *Time,* November 7. Retrieved August 15, 2014, from http://swampland.time .com/2012/11/07/inside-the-secret-world-of-quants-and-data-crunchers-who -helped-obama-win/.

Sears, D. O., & Freedman, J. L. (1967). Selective exposure to information: A critical review. *Public Opinion Quarterly, 31,* 194–213.

Shambaugh, D. (2007). China's propaganda system: Institutions, processes, and efficacy. *The China Journal, 57,* 25–58.

Sherman, G. (2010, October 3). Chasing Fox. *New York Magazine.* Retrieved August 17, 2010, from http://nymag.com/news/media/68717.

Smith, T. J., III, Lichter, S. R., & Harris, T. (1997). *What the people want from the press.* Washington, DC: Center for Media and Public Affairs.

Smith, A., Schlozman, K. L., Verba, S., & Brady, H. (2009). *The Internet and civic engagement.* Pew Research Center, Washington, DC.

Sunstein, C. (2001). *Republic.com.* Princeton, NJ: Princeton University Press.

Valkenburg, P. M., & Peter, J. (2007). Online communication and adolescent well-being: Testing the stimulation versus the displacement hypothesis. *Journal of Computer-Mediated Communication, 12,* 1169–1182.

Valkenburg, P. M., & Peter, J. (2009). Social consequences of the Internet for adolescents: A decade of research. *Current Directions in Psychological Science, 18,* 1–5.

Vargas, J. A. (2008, November 20). Obama raised half a billion online. *The Washington Post.* Retrieved August 20, 2010, from http://voices.washingtonpost.com/44/2008/11/20 /obama_raised_half_a_billion_on.html.

Chapter 6

ABC News. (September 27, 2012). Romney campaign sets debate expectations low against Obama. At http://abcnews.go.com/blogs/politics/2012/09/romney-campaign-sets-debate-expectations-low-against-obama/.

Ansolabehere, S., & Iyengar, S. (1995). *Going negative: How attack ads shrink and polarize the electorate.* New York: Free Press.

Buckley v. Valeo, 424 U.S. 1 (1976).

Citizens United v. Federal Election Commission, 558 U.S. 50 (2010).

CBS News. (August 16, 2010). *Ground zero mosque debate becomes a campaign issue.* At http://www.cbsnews.com/news/ground-zero-mosque-debate-becomes-a-campaign-issue/.

CNN. (September 29, 2008). *Obama-Biden camp hype Palin's debating skills.* At http://politicalticker.blogs.cnn.com/2008/09/29/obama-biden-camp-hype-palin%E2%80%99s-debating-skills/.

CNN PoliticalTicker. (September 30, 2010). *SEIU rips Whitman at start of $5 million ad campaign.* At http://politicalticker.blogs.cnn.com/2010/09/30/seiu-rips-whitman-at-start-of-5-million-ad-campaign/comment-page-1/.

Diamond, E., & Bates, S. (1992). *The spot: The rise of political advertising on television.* Cambridge, MA: MIT Press.

Fox News. (August 11, 2012). Democrats and Republicans react to Paul Ryan as VP selection. At http://nation.foxnews.com/reaction-paul-ryan-vp/2012/08/11/republicans-and-democrats-react-paul-ryan-vp-selection.

Martin, J., & Allen, M. (2008, August 21). McCain unsure how many houses he owns. *Politico.* Retrieved on January 19, 2011, from the *Politico* website: www.politico.com/news/stories/0808/12685.html.

McConnell v. Federal Election Commission, 540 U.S. 93 (2003).

McCutcheon v. Federal Election Commission, 572 U.S. ___ (2014).

Politico. (September 30, 2012). Obama: I'm just an 'OK' debater. At http://www.politico.com/politico44/2012/09/obama-im-just-an-ok-debater-137076.html

Washington Post (June 22, 2014). At http://www.washingtonpost.com/blogs/post-politics/wp/2014/06/22/hillary-clinton-says-shes-unlike-the-truly-well-off/.

Chapter 7

Ansolabehere, S., Behr, R., & Iyengar, S. (1991). Mass media and elections: An overview. *American Politics Quarterly, 19,* 109–139.

Ansolabehere, S., Behr, R., & Iyengar, S. (1993). *The media game: American politics in the television age.* New York: Macmillan.

Arnold, R. D. (2004). *Congress, the press, and political accountability.* Princeton, NJ: Princeton University Press.

Auletta, K. (2004, January 19). Fortress Bush: How the White House keeps the press under control. *The New Yorker.* Retrieved March 28, 2006, from the New Yorker website: www.newyorker.com/fact/content/?040119fa_fact2.

Billings, E. (2004, June 2). Democrats eye fall "contract." *Roll Call.*

Brody, R. A. (1991). *Assessing the president: The media, elite opinion and public support.* Stanford, CA: Stanford University Press.

CNN. (2005, January 27). *Bush expounds on theme of freedom: President says, "I firmly planted the flag of liberty."* Transcript of the January 26, 2005, presidential press conference; retrieved July 20, 2005, from CNN's website: www.cnn.com/2005/ALLPOLITICS/01/26 /bush.

Canes-Wrone, B. (2001). The president's legislative influence from public appeals. *American Journal of Political Science, 45,* 313–329.

Clayman, S. E., Elliot, M., Heritage, J., & Beckett, M. (2010). A watershed in White House journalism: Explaining the post-1986 rise of aggressive presidential news. *Political Communication, 27,* 229–247.

Clayman, S. E., Elliot, M., Heritage, J., & McDonald, L. (2007). When does the watchdog bark? Conditions of aggressive questioning in presidential press conferences. *American Sociological Review, 72,* 23–41.

CNBC. (2009, June 16). *On the economy, Iran.* (Interview Transcript). By John Harwood. Retrieved December 8, 2014, from the CNBC website: http://www.cnbc.com/id /31393724.

Cook, T. E. (1998). *Governing with the news: The news media as a political institution.* Chicago: University of Chicago Press.

Grimmer, J., Messing, S., & Westwood, S. J. (2012). How words and money cultivate a personal vote: The effect of legislator credit claiming on constituent credit allocation. *American Political Science Review, 106,* 703–719.

Grossman, M. B., & Kumar, M. J. (1981). *Portraying the president.* Baltimore: Johns Hopkins University Press.

Hertsgaard, M. (1988). *On bended knee: The press and the Reagan presidency.* New York: Farrar, Straus and Giroux.

Kantar Media, June 5, 2013

Kernell, S. (1986). *Going public: New strategies of presidential leadership.* Washington, DC: Congressional Quarterly Press.

Kernell, S. & Rice, L. R. (2011). Cable and the partisan polarization of the president's audience. *Presidential Studies Quarterly, 41,* 696–711.

Kornblut, A. (2005, February 19). Administration is warned about its publicity videos. *The New York Times,* p. A11.

Kumar, M. J. (2003). The contemporary presidency: Communications operations in the White House of President George W. Bush: Making news on his terms. *Presidential Studies Quarterly, 33,* 366–393.

McClelland, S. (2008). *What happened? Inside the Bush White House and Washington's culture of deception.* New York: Public Affairs.

Meinke, S. R., & Anderson, W. D. (2001). Influencing from impaired administrations: Presidents, White House scandal, and legislative leadership. *Legislative Studies Quarterly, 26,* 639–659.

Nakamura, D., Gearan, A., & Wilson, S. (2013, October 23). Stung by a Twitter renegade, group in Obama administration launched sting of its own. *Washington Post.* Retrieved on March 3, 2015 from http://www.washingtonpost.com/politics/2013/10/23/3cb89d56 -3c00-11e3-b6a9-da62c264f40e_story.html

Pew Project for Excellence in Journalism. (2009). *The state of the news media 2009: An annual report on American journalism.* Retrieved on January 19, 2011, from the State of the News Media website: www.stateofthemedia.org/2009.

Rivers, D., & Rose, N. L. (1985). Passing the president's program: Public opinion and presidential influence in Congress. *American Journal of Political Science, 29*, 183–196.

Rohde, D. W., & Simon, D. M. (1985). Presidential vetoes and congressional response: A study of institutional conflict. *American Journal of Political Science, 29*, 397–427.

Speakes, L. (with Pack, R.). (1988). *Speaking out: The Reagan presidency from inside the White House*. New York: Scribner.

Stelter, B. (2009, October 11). Fox's volley with Obama intensifying. *New York Times*. Retrieved January 20, 2011, from the New York Times website: www.nytimes.com/2009/10/12 /business/media/12fox.html.

Tenpas, K. D. (2004, June 29). *President Bush's 2004 campaign travel*. Washington, DC: Brookings Institution. Retrieved March 22, 2005, from the Brookings Institution website: www .brookings.edu/dybdocroot/views/papers/tenpas/20040629.pdf.

Tulis, J. K. (1987). *The rhetorical presidency*. Chatham, NJ: Chatham House.

Vinson, D. C. (2003). *Through local eyes: Local media coverage of Congress and its members*. Cresskill, NJ: Hampton.

Chapter 8

Almond, G. A., & Verba, S. (1965). *The civic culture: Political attitudes and democracy in five nations*. Princeton, NJ: Princeton University Press.

Ansolabehere, S., Behr, R., & Iyengar, S. (1993). *The media game: American politics in the television age*. New York: Macmillan.

Ansolabehere, S., & Iyengar, S. (1995). *Going negative: How attack ads shrink and polarize the electorate*. New York: Free Press.

Ansolabehere, S., & Iyengar, S. (1998). *Message forgotten: Misreporting in surveys and the bias towards minimal effects*. Unpublished manuscript, Department of Political Science, Massachusetts Institute of Technology, Cambridge, MA.

Ansolabehere, S., Iyengar, S., & Simon, A. (1999). Replicating experiments using aggregate and survey data: The case of negative advertising and turnout. *American Political Science Review, 93*, 901–910.

Arceneaux, K., & Johnson, M. (2013). *Changing minds or changing channels: Partisan news in an age of choice*. Chicago: University of Chicago Press.

Bailenson, J., Iyengar, S., Yee, N., & Collins, N. (2009). Facial similarity between voters and candidates causes influence. *Public Opinion Quarterly, 72*, 935–961.

Bartels, L. M. (2002). Beyond the running tally: Partisan bias in political perceptions. *Political Behavior, 21*, 48–69.

Baum, M. A. (2002). Sex, lies and war: How soft news brings foreign policy to the inattentive public. *American Political Science Review, 96*, 91–109.

Baumgartner, F. R., & Jones, B. D. (1993). *Agendas and instability in American politics*. Chicago: University of Chicago Press.

Behr, R. L., & Iyengar, S. (1985). Television news, real-world cues, and changes in the public agenda. *Public Opinion Quarterly, 49*, 38–57.

Bennett, W. L., & Iyengar, S. (2008). A new era of minimal effects? The changing foundations of political communication. *Journal of Communication, 58*, 707–731.

Boyer, P. (1986). Famine in Africa: The TV accident that exploded. In M. Emery & T. Smythe (Eds.), *Readings in mass communications*. Dubuque, IA: William C. Brown.

Bullock, J. G., Gerber, A. S., Hill, S. J., & Huber, G. A. (2013). Partisan bias in factual beliefs about politics. Unpublished paper, Yale University, New Haven, CT.

Cappella, J., & Jamieson, K. H. (1997). *Spiral of cynicism: The press and the public good.* New York: Oxford University Press.

Cohen, B. E. (1963). *The press and foreign policy.* Princeton, NJ: Princeton University Press.

Converse, P. (1962). Information flow and the stability of partisan attitudes. *Public Opinion Quarterly, 26,* 578–599.

Curran, J., Iyengar, S., Lund, A., & Salovaara-Moring, I. (2009). Media systems, public knowledge and democracy: A comparative study, *European Journal of Communication, 24,* 5–26.

Dearing, J. W., & Rogers, E. M. (1996). *Agenda-setting.* Thousand Oaks, CA: Sage.

Druckman, J. N. (2001). The implications of framing effects for citizen competence. *Political Behavior, 23,* 225–256.

Druckman, J. N., & Holmes, J. W. (2004). Does presidential rhetoric matter? Priming and presidential approval. *Presidential Studies Quarterly, 34,* 755–778.

Edwards, G. C., III. & Wood, B. D. (1999). Who influences whom? The president, Congress, and the media. *American* Political Science Review, *93,* 327–344.

Eshbaugh-Soha, M., & Peake, J. S. 2005. Presidents and the economic agenda. *Political Research Quarterly, 58,* 128–137.

Eshbaugh-Soha, M., & Peake, J. S. (2008). The agenda-setting impact of major presidential TV addresses. *Political Communication, 25,* 113–137.

Eshbaugh-Soha, M., & Peake, J. S. (2011). *Breaking through the noise: Presidential leadership, public opinion, and the news media.* Stanford, CA: Stanford University Press.

Fiorina, M. P. (1976). The voting decision: Instrumental and expressive aspects. *Journal of Politics, 38,* 390–413.

Fraile, M., & Iyengar, S. (2014). Not all sources are equally informative: A cross-national analysis of political knowledge in Europe. *The International Journal of Press/Politics, 18,* 281–303.

Gilliam, F. D., Jr., & Iyengar, S. (2000). Prime suspects: The influence of local television news on the viewing public. *American Journal of Political Science, 44,* 560–573.

Hart, A., & Middleton, J. A. (2014). Priming under fire: Reverse causality and the classic media priming hypothesis. *Journal of Politics, 76,* 581–592.

Hayes, D. (2005). Candidate qualities through a partisan lens: A theory of trait ownership. *American Journal of Political Science, 49,* 908–923.

Hetey, R. C., & Eberhardt, J. L. (2014). Racial disparities in incarceration increase acceptance of punitive policies. *Psychological Science 25,* 1949–1954.

Hovland, C. L. (1959). Reconciling conflicting results derived from experimental and survey studies of attitude change. *The American Psychologist, 14,* 8–17.

Hovland, C. I., Janis, I. L., & Kelley, H. H. (1953). *Communications and persuasion: Psychological studies in opinion change.* New Haven, CT: Yale University Press.

Hovland, C. I., Lumsdaine, A. A., & Sheffield, F. D. (1949). A baseline for measurement of percentage change. In C. I. Hovland, A. A. Lumsdaine, & F. D. Sheffield (Eds.), *Experiments on mass communication* (pp. 284–289). Princeton, NJ: Princeton University Press.

Iyengar, S. (1991). *Is anyone responsible?* Chicago: University of Chicago Press.

Iyengar, S., Curran, J., Lund, A., Salovaara-Moring, I., Hahn, K., & Coen, S. (2010). Cross-national versus individual-level differences in political information: A media systems perspective, Journal of Elections. *Public Opinion, and Parties, 20,* 291–231.

Iyengar, S., & Kinder, D. R. (1987). *News that matters: Television and American opinion.* Chicago: University of Chicago Press.

Iyengar, S., Sood, G., & Lelkes, Y. (2012). Affect not ideology: A social identity perspective on polarization. *Public Opinion Quarterly, 78,* 405–431.

Iyengar, S., & Valentino, N. A. (2000). Who says what? Source credibility as a mediator of campaign advertising. In A. Lupia, M. D. McCubbins, & S. L. Popkin (Eds.), *Elements of reason: Cognition, choice and the bounds of rationality* (pp. 108–129). Cambridge, England: Cambridge University Press.

Iyengar, S., & Westwood, S. (In press). Fear and loathing across party lines: New evidence on group polarization. *American Journal of Political Science, 58.*

Johnston, R., Hagen, M. G., & Jamieson, K. H. (2004). *The 2000 presidential election and the foundations of party politics.* New York: Cambridge University Press.

Kahn, K. F. (1994). The distorted mirror: Press coverage of women candidates for statewide office. *Journal of Politics, 56,* 154–174.

Klapper, J. T. (1960). *The effects of mass communications.* New York: Free Press.

Krosnick, J. A., & Kinder, D. R. (1990). Altering the foundations of support for the president through priming. *American Political Science Review, 84,* 497–512.

Kull, S., Ramsay, C., & Lewis, E. (2003). Misperceptions, the media, and the Iraq war. *Political Science Quarterly, 118,* 569–598.

LaCour, M. J., & Vavreck, L. (2014). Improving media measurement: Results from the field. *Political Communication, 33,* 408–420.

Lazarsfeld, P. F., Berelson, B. R., & Gaudet, H. (1948). *The people's choice.* New York: Columbia University Press.

Lelkes, Y., Sood, G., & Iyengar, S. (2014). *The hostile audience: Selective exposure to partisan sources and affective polarization.* Presented at the Annual Meeting of the International Communication Association. Seattle, May 22–26.

Lenz, G. S. (2012). *Follow the leader: How voters respond to politicians' performance and policies.* Chicago: University of Chicago Press.

Levendusky, M. (2009). *The partisan sort: How liberals became Democrats and conservatives became Republicans.* Chicago: University of Chicago Press.

Lippmann, W. (1922). *Public opinion.* New York: Harcourt Brace.

Lippmann, W. (1925). *The phantom public.* New York: Macmillan.

Luskin, R. L., Iyengar S., & Fishkin, J. (2005, August). *The deliberative citizen.* Paper presented at the annual meeting of the American Political Science Association, Washington, DC.

Mason, L. (2014). "I respectfully disagree": The differential effects of partisan sorting on social and issue polarization. *American Journal of Political Science, 58,* 1–18.

McCarty, N., Poole, K. T., & Rosenthal, H. (2006). Polarized America: The dance of ideology and unequal riches. Cambridge, MA: MIT Press.

McCombs, M. C., & Shaw, D. L. (1972). The agenda-setting function of mass media. *Public Opinion Quarterly, 36,* 176–187.

Mendelberg, T. (1997). Executing Hortons: Racial crime in the 1988 presidential campaign. *Public Opinion Quarterly, 61,* 134–157.

Mendelsohn, N. (1996). The media and interpersonal communications: The priming of issues, leaders, and party identification. *The Journal of Politics, 58,* 112–125.

Miller, J. M., & Krosnick, J. A. (2000). News media impact on the ingredients of presidential evaluations: Politically knowledgeable citizens are guided by a trusted source. *American Journal of Political Science, 44,* 295–309.

Mutz, D. C., & Reeves, B. (2005). The new videomalaise: Effects of televised incivility on political trust. *American Political Science Review, 99,* 1–15.

Nelson, T. E., & Kinder, D. R. (1996). Issue frames and group-centrism in American public opinion. *Journal of Politics, 58,* 1055–1078.

Pew Research Center. (2012). *In changing news landscape, even television is vulnerable.* September 27. Retrieved March 4, 2015, from http://www.people-press.org/2012/09/27/in-changing -news-landscape-even-television-is-vulnerable/.

Pew Research Center. (2014). *Political polarization in the American public: How increasing ideological uniformity and partisan antipathy affect politics, compromise and everyday life.* June 12. Retrieved March 4, 2015, from http://www.people-press.org/2014/06/12 /political-polarization-in-the-american-public/.

Price, V., & Zaller, J. (1993). Who gets the news? Alternative measures of news reception and their implications for research. *Public Opinion Quarterly, 57,* 133–164.

Tversky, A., & Kahneman, D. (1981). The framing of decisions and the psychology of choice. *Science, 211,* 453–458.

Vavreck, L. (2007). The exaggerated effects of advertising on turnout: The dangers of self-reports. *Quarterly Journal of Political Science, 2,* 325–343.

Wattenberg, M. P., & Brians, C. L. (1999). Negative campaign advertising: Mobilizer or demobilizer? *American Political Science Review, 93,* 891–899.

Chapter 9

Ansolabehere, S. (2009). Effects of identification requirements on voting: evidence from the experiences of voters on election day. *PS: Political Science & Politics, 42,* 127–130.

Ansolabehere, S., & Iyengar, S. (1995). *Going negative: How attack ads shrink and polarize the electorate.* New York: Free Press.

Bartels, L. M., & Zaller, J. (2001). Presidential vote models: A recount. *PS: Political Science & Politics, 33,* 9–20.

Brady, H. E., & Johnston, R. (1987). What's the primary message: Horse race or issue journalism? In G. R. Orren & N. W. Polsby (Eds.), *Media and momentum: The New Hampshire primary and nomination politics* (pp. 127–186). Chatham, NJ: Chatham House.

Buchanan, B. (1991). *Electing a president: The Markle Commission research on Campaign '88.* Austin: University of Texas Press.

Dropp, K. (2014). Voter ID laws and voter turnout. Working Paper, Stanford University. Druckman, J. (2003). The power of television images: The first Kennedy–Nixon debate revisited. *Journal of Politics, 65,* 559–571.

Enos, R. D., & A. Fowler. (2014). *The effects of large-scale campaigns on voter turnout: Evidence from 400 million voter contacts* (Working Paper). Cambridge, MA: Harvard University.

Enos, R. D., Fowler, A., & Vavreck, L. (2014). Increasing Inequality: The effect of GOTV mobilization on the composition of the electorate. *Journal of Politics, 76,* 273–288.

Gerber, A. S., & Green, D. P. (2008). *Get out the vote.* Washington, DC: Brookings Institution Press.

Gerber, A. S., Green, D. P., & Nickerson, D. W. (2002, May 7). *Getting out the youth vote in local elections: Results from six door-to-door canvassing experiments.* Unpublished report, Center for Information and Research on Civic Learning and Engagement, University of Maryland, College Park, MD.

Government Accountability Office. (2014). Issues related to state voter identification laws. Publication No. GAO-14-634. Retrieved from http://www.gao.gov/assets/670/665966.

Iyengar, S., & Jackman, S. (2003, November). *Technology and politics: Incentives for youth participation*. Paper presented at the International Conference on Civic Education Research, New Orleans, LA.

Lau, R. R., Sigelman, L., Heldman, C., & Babbitt, P. (1999). The effects of negative political advertisements: A meta-analytic assessment. *American Political Science Review, 93*, 851–875.

Liptak, A. (2013). Supreme Court invalidates key part of Voting Rights Act. *New York Times*, June, 26.

Mycoff, J. D., Wagner, M., & Wilson, D. C. (2009). The empirical effect of voter-ID laws: Present or absent? *PS: Political Science & Politics*, 42, 121–126.Pastor, R. A., Santos, R., Prevost, A., & Stoilov. V. (2010). Voting and ID requirements: A survey of registered voters in three states. American Review of Public Administration, 40, 461-481.

Pew Research Center. (2007). *Modest interest in 2008 campaign news*. Retrieved on October 23, 2007, from http://people-press.org/report/364/modest-interest-in-2008-campaign-news.

Chapter 10

Ansolabehere, S., Behr, R., & Iyengar, S. (1993). *The media game: American politics in the television age*. New York: Macmillan.

Apple, R. W. (1990, September 20). Confrontation in the Gulf: Criticism of US Gulf policy growing louder in Congress. *New York Times*, p. A10.

Canes-Wrone, B., Herron, M. C., & Shotts, K. W. (2001). Leadership and pandering: A theory of executive policymaking. *American Journal of Political Science, 45*, 532–550.

Canes-Wrone, B., & Shotts, K. W. (2004). The conditional nature of presidential responsiveness to public opinion. *American Journal of Political Science, 48*, 690–706.

Eshbaugh-Soha, M. (2013). Presidential influence of the news media: The case of the press conference." *Political Communication*, 30, 545–564.

Friedman, T. (2008, April 30). Dumb as we wannabe. *New York Times*. Retrieved on January 20, 2011, from the New York Times website: www.nytimes.com/2008/04/30/opinion/30friedman.html.

Hahn, K., & Iyengar, S. (2007). History versus media management as determinants of presidential popularity. In D. Lacorne & J. Vasse (Eds.), *La Présidence Impériale. De Franklin D. Roosevelt à George W. Bush* (pp 144-60). Parise: Odile Jacob, 2007.

Huffington, A. (2000). *How to overthrow the government*. New York: ReganBooks.

Jacobson, G. (2008). *A divider, not a uniter: George W. Bush and the American people*. New York: Longmans.

Lowi, T. J. (1981). *Incomplete conquest: Governing America*. New York: Holt, Rinehart & Winston.

Lowi, T. J. (1985). *The personal president: Power invested, promise unfulfilled*. Ithaca, NY: Cornell University Press.

Neustadt, R. (1960). *Presidential power: The politics of leadership*. New York: Wiley.

Shapiro, R. Y., & Jacobs, L. R. (2000). Who leads and who follows? U.S. presidents, public opinion, and foreign policy. In B. L. Nacos, R. Y. Shapiro, & P. Isernia (Eds.), *Decisionmaking in a glass house: Mass media, public opinion, and American and European foreign policy in the 21st century* (pp. 223–245). Lanham, MD: Rowman & Littlefield.

Zaller, J. R., & Chiu, D. (2000). Government's little helper: U.S. press coverage of foreign policy crises, 1946–1999. In B. L. Nacos, R. Y. Shapiro, & P. Isernia (Eds.), *Decisionmaking in a glass house: Mass media, public opinion, and American foreign policy in the 21st century* (pp. 61–84). Lanham, MD: Rowman & Littlefield.

Chapter 11

Ansolabehere, S., Lessem, R., & Snyder, J. M. (2006). The orientation of newspaper endorsements in U.S. elections, 1940–2002. *Quarterly Journal of Political Science, 1*(4), 393–404.

Barta, C. (1996). How fair is election coverage? *Issues of Democracy (Free and Fair Elections issue), 1*(13), 12–16. Retrieved March 25, 2005, from http://usinfo.state.gov/journals /itdhr/0996/ijde/ijde0996.pdf.

Bartels, L. M. (2005). Homer gets a tax cut: Inequality and public policy in the American mind. *Perspectives on Politics, 3*(1), 15–31.

Baumgartner, J., & Morris, J. (2010). MyFaceTube politics: Social networking websites and political engagement of young adults. *Social Science Computer Review, 28,* 24–44.

Canadian Film and Television Production Association. (2002). *Assessment of the economic impact of the Canadian Television Fund.* Toronto, Ontario: PricewaterhouseCoopers. Retrieved on January 21, 2011, from www.cftpa.ca/newsroom/pdf/studies.

Carnegie Commission on Educational Television. (1967). *Public television: A program for action.* New York: Bantam Books

Department of Culture. (2009). *Appropriations conditions for Sveriges Television AB for the fiscal year 2010.* Stockholm: Government of Sweden.

Dickerson, J. (2010, August 3). Not Sarah Palin's friends: The Facebook posts Palin doesn't want you to see. Retrieved on January 20, 2011, from Slate's website: www.slate.com /id/2262544.

Domanick, J. (2004). *Cruel justice.* Berkeley: University of California Press.

Druckman, J. N., Kifer, M. J., & Parkin, M. (2009). Campaign communication in U.S. Congressional elections. *American Political Science Review, 103,* 343–366.

Editorial, Prop. 66 reform: Defeated but not deterred. (2004, November 6). *Sacramento Bee.* Retrieved September 15, 2005, from www.sacbee.com/content/opinion/story /11332538p-12247209c.html.

Federal Communications Commission. (1996, June 25). *En banc hearing of the commissioners on network proposals to provide time to presidential candidates.* Retrieved September 10, 2005, from www.fcc.gov/Reports/eb062596.txt.

Fishkin, J. (1995). *The voice of the people.* New Haven, CT: Yale University Press.

Green, D. P., & Gerber, A. S. (2001). *Getting out the youth vote: Results from randomized field experiments.* Unpublished report to the Pew Charitable Trusts, Institution for Social and Policy Studies.

Jamieson, K. H. (1997, March 11). Presentation of research. In *Free air time and campaign reform: A report of the conference held by the Annenberg Public Policy Center at the University of Pennsylvania and the Free TV for Straight Talk Coalition* (pp. 6–8). Retrieved March 25, 2005, from the Annenberg Public Policy Center website: www.annenbergpublicpolicycenter.org/03_political_communication/freetime /REP15.PDF.

Luskin, R. C., Fishkin, J. S., & Jowell, R. (2002). Considered opinions: Deliberative polling in Britain. *British Journal of Political Science, 32,* 455–487.

Mullainathan, S., & Shleifer, A. (2005). The market for news. *American Economic Review, 95,* 1031–1053.

Pasley, J. L. (2001). *The tyranny of printers: Newspaper politics in the early American republic.* Charlottesville: University of Virginia Press.

Pew Research Center for People and the Press. (2008). *Winning the media campaign.* Retrieved on February 2, 2011, from www.journalism.org/node/13307.

Pew Research Center. (2013). Twelve trends shaping digital news. Retrieved August 18, 2014, from http://www.pewresearch.org/fact-tank/2013/10/16/12-trends-shaping-digital -news/.

Pew Research Center. (2014). Cell phone and smartphone demographics. Retrieved August 18, 2014, from http://www.pewinternet.org/data-trend/mobile/cell-phone-and-smart phone-ownership-demographics/.

Popkin, S. L. (1994). *The reasoning voter: Communication and persuasion in presidential campaigns* (2nd ed.). Chicago: University of Chicago Press.

CREDITS

Text

Ch. 7: Mike McCurry, "A Day in the Life of the Presidential Press Secretary," Speech at Stanford University, May 8, 2001. Reprinted with permission of the author.

Figures

Fig. 8.6: "Political Polarization in the American Public," Pew Research Center, Washington, DC (June 2014). http://www.people-press.org/2014/06/12/political-polarization-in-the -american-public/. Reprinted with permission.

Fig. 9.7: John Sides, "Romney's Debate Win Was about Personality More than Policy," The Monkey Cage, October 11, 2012. Reprinted with permission of the author.

Photos

1 left AP Photo/J. Scott Applewhite; **1 right** AP Photo/J. Scott Applewhite; **98** CNN. (2004, April 29). Retrieved July 26, 2005, from www.cnn.com/2004/US/04/29/terror.report; **140** Courtesy of MyBarackObama.com/The Democratic Party; **142** Splash News/Newscom; **207** Cynthia Johnson/Time Life Pictures/Getty Images; **259** Photo courtesy of Shanto Lyengar. J. Bailenson, S. Iyengar, N. Yee, & N. Collins. (2009). Facial similarity between voters and candidates causes influence. Public Opinion Quarterly, 72, 935–961.

INDEX

free media time for, 336–39

free-agent, 6

image of, 283–85

media access for, 19, 45, 46–47

physical attributes of, 285

policy issues and, 286, 288–91

regulating media access to, 155–56

selection of, 6, 23, 25–28

shaping of news by, 10–12

viability of, 274, 292

voices in network news, 77

websites of, 342

See also campaigns

candidate-to-voter communication, 17–18

Canes-Wrone, B., 196, 319, 320–21

Carlson, Tucker, 327, 328

Carnegie Commission, 334–35

Carney, Jay, 202

Carter, Jimmy

　familiarity with, 286

　Ford's debate with, 189, 280–81, 303n4

　image of, 201, 228n2, 283

　Iran hostage crisis and, 315, 321–22

　media management and, 318

　popularity of, 199, 315

　press conferences, 212

　primary campaign and, 294

　priming and, 250

　Reagan's defeat of, 197, 250

Castro, Fidel, 102

CBC, subsidies and, 5

CBS

　on Bush, 92n5, 130–31

　corporate interests influencing, 41

　corporate parent of, 55

　credibility of, 61, 62, 63, 92n5

　FAIR tracking of, 106–7

　free media time and, 338, 349n5

　network newscasts by, 51–52, 57–58

　presidential coverage by, 204, 205

CBS Evening News, 57, 68, 92n9

CBS Nightly News, 58

CD, youth-oriented election, 344–45

CD tracking study, 128–29, 132, 147n2

cell phones, 109, 115, 129, 137, 238

censorship of media, 3, 101–6, 137

Center for Public Integrity, 107

Center for Responsive Politics, 26

Chalabi, Ahmed, 93–94

Challenger explosion, 210, 315

Chamber of Commerce ad campaign, 12, 223–24

Chapel Hill, North Carolina, 244

Chappaquiddick incident, 283, 303n5

character issues, 80–81, 150–51, 156–57, 253

Cheney, Dick, 3, 138

Chicago Sun-Times, 43

Chicago Tribune, 43, 60

China, 137

Chiu, D., 313

Christian Science Monitor, 43

Christie, Chris, 4

CIA leak scandal, 202

cigarette advertising, 224

Citizens United v. Federal Election Commission, 185–86

civic engagement, 119–22, 123–24, 125–26, 147n1

civil rights, 132, 169, 194, 221, 254, 257–58

Clark, Wesley, 292, 293

Clear Channel, 39

Cleese, John, 46

Clemens, Roger, 219–20

Clinton, Bill

　"Contract with America" and, 219

　debates and, 187, 189

　defeat of George H. W. Bush, 320

　election forecasting and, 273

　familiarity with, 286

　free media time to, 337, 338

　government shutdown and, 195

　healthcare reform package of, 12, 223, 224, 225

　image of, 283–84

　impeachment and, 13, 93, 179, 307, 326n2

　interpretive journalism and, 78–79

　Lewinsky scandal and, 2, 13, 69, 79, 80, 85, 87, 93, 94, 202, 210, 216, 306–7, 310, 311

　media outlet choices of, 10, 78

　NAFTA and, 319

Clinton, Bill (*continued*)
    negative advertising and, 174, 175, 176
    news coverage of, 206–7
    pool sprays, 215
    popularity of, 306–7, 310, 311, 315–16
    presidential campaign of 1992, 154,
        156–57, 164, 176, 187, 271
    presidential campaign of 1996, 174
    press secretary of, 202, 206–7
    Proposition 209 and, 321
    public opinion and, 322
    Somalia and, 15
    source credibility and, 265
    speechmaking by, 13, 210, 211
    Travelgate affair, 315–16
Clinton, Hillary
    blog post about Obama and, 131
    familiarity with, 286
    gas tax holiday proposed by, 321
    healthcare reform bill and, 224
    issue ownership and, 167
    on Obama and Wright, 141
    presidential campaign of 2008, 78,
        152–53, 156, 164, 167, 170
    primary campaign and, 294
    on wealth of Clintons, 164–65
closed party list, 27–28
closed-door strategy, 156
CLTV (Chicago), 60
CNBC, 40, 52, 198
CNN
    candidate debates sponsored by, 120
    credibility of, 62, 63
    formation of, 52, 57
    free media time and, 337, 349n5
    GDP of countries receiving more
        attention from, 33, 34
    global audience of, 57, 92n3
    online audience for, 118
    selective exposure and, 128, 134
    Sherrod story and, 322
    threat of lawsuit by, 3
    war on terrorism and, 97–98
CNN Political Ticker, 130, 177
cognitive dissonance, 126

Cohen, B. E., 244
The Colbert Report, 243
Cold War, 68, 82, 96, 164
Coleman, Norm, 136
collective-action dilemma, 11
combat stories, 77–82
Comcast, 40, 55, 60, 143
Comedy Central, 242
Commerce Department, 85
commercial television, 32–33
commercial vs. public ownership of broadcast
        media, 29–36
Committee for the Study of the American
        Electorate, 190
Communications Act of 1934, 50n6
communications director, 200, 201
Communist Party, 137
comScore, 60
confidence in the press, 61–63, 92n6
Congress
    agenda setting and, 247, 248
    campaign finance reform and, 181–82
    committee hearings, 218–20
    news coverage of, 203–4, 205, 220–22
    policy vs. electoral goals, 220–23
"Contract with America," 219, 241
Converse, P., 261
Cook, Tim, 221
Coolidge, Calvin, 211–12
Cornyn, John, 169
Corporation for Public Broadcasting, 336
corruption and watchdog function of press,
        21
Countdown with Keith Olbermann, 134
counterattack ads, 175–77
"Country I Love" ad, 163
Couric, Katie, 58
crafted rhetoric, 323
Craigslist, 55
credibility, 61–65, 259, 265
crime
    agenda setting and, 245
    as campaign issue, 72–73, 171, 175–76
    case study of coverage, 329–34
    focus on stories about, 70–71, 83, 245

framing and, 256, 257
priming and, 249
public opinion and, 16, 245, 334
racial bias in reporting of, 81–82, 257
Cronkite, Walter, 57
Crossfire, 327, 328
cross-media sources, 60
cross-ownership, 37–38, 60, 92n4
CSI, 58
C-SPAN, 218
Cuba, 102, 103, 315, 326n3
cultural identity, 169
Cutler, Lloyd, 318

Daily Kos, 124, 130
The Daily Show, 128, 242–43
Darfur, ethnic massacres in, 97
Dateline, 338
Davis, Gray, 173, 331, 344
de facto selectivity, 135
Dean, Howard, 6, 138–39, 151, 289–90, 292, 293
Deaver, Michael, 199, 201, 228n8
Deaver Rule, 228n8
debates, 186–90
    audience for, 187–88, 193n7
    Bush-Gore, 189
    Clinton-Bush, 187, 189
    eligibility for, 187
    Ford-Carter, 189
    formats, 187
    Kennedy-Nixon, 9, 149, 186
    network sponsorship of, 120
    Obama-McCain, 187
    Obama-Romney, 9
    primary campaigns and, 186
Deepwater Horizon oil spill, 3–4
DeLay, Tom, 221–22
deliberative polling, 333–34
Democratic National Convention of 1968, 154
Democratic Party
    delegate selection reform by, 23
    issue ownership of, 165–67
    Kean Commission and, 3

Rather's appearance at fund-raising event for, 61
voter allegiance to, 276
Denmark, 30
    campaign coverage regulation in, 46
    knowledge of hard news in, 35–36
Department of Defense (DOD), 101–2, 104, 109, 232
dependent variables, 231
designated media areas (DMAs), 56
Deukmejian, George, 331
Diana, Princess, 59
digital photography by eyewitness sources, 109
direct candidate-voter communication, 341–46
direct mail advertising, 178–80, 296
Disney, 55
DMAs (designated media areas), 56
documentary programming, 68
DOD (Department of Defense), 101–2, 104, 109, 232
Dole, Robert
    attack ads and, 174, 175
    Clinton's defeat of, 306
    free media time to, 337, 338
    fundamental attribution error and, 288
    immigration issue and, 170
    source credibility and, 265
door-to-door canvassing, 28, 49n3
Dr. Phil, 220
Dropp, 299
Druckman, J. N., 253
Drudge Report, 69, 85, 124, 127, 130
Dual TV Network Rule, 37
Dukakis, Michael
    image of, 283
    party allegiance and, 277
    policy issues and, 290
    presidential debates, 189
    press management and, 158
    "Willie Horton" ads and, 72–73, 170, 175–76
Duke, David, 170
Dunn, Anita, 208

Massa, Eric, 221
Masterpiece Theatre, 32
McCain, John
    campaign finance reform and, 183
    economic issues and, 233, 277
    election forecasting and, 277
    familiarity with, 287
    free media time bill and, 338
    gas tax holiday proposed by, 321
    Internet campaigning by, 138, 139
    media bias perceptions and, 128
    negative advertising and, 174
    Palin and, 78
    presidential campaign of 2000, 156
    presidential campaign of 2008, 153, 155,
        156, 158, 164, 167, 174
    primary campaign and, 294
    selective exposure and, 122
McCain–Feingold bill, 183
McCain-Feingold-Durbin bill, 338
McCarthy, Eugene, 23, 100–101
McCarthy, Joseph, 24, 218
McClellan, Scott, 202
McCombs, M. C., 244
McCurry, Mike, 202, 203, 206–7, 228n3
McCutcheon v. Federal Election
        Commission, 12, 185–86
McGovern, George, 152, 276, 294
McKinley, William, 340
McManus, Michael, 216–17
McWethy, John, 103
media effects
    agenda setting and, 13, 233, 234, 243–49
    campaigns and, 14
    framing and, 13, 254–60
    learning and, 241–43
    minimal effects, new era of, 266
    overview of, 13–18
    persuasion and, 13, 233, 260–66
    priming and, 13, 233, 234, 249–54
    research methods, 230–31, 234–40
media exposure, 235, 238, 243
media management, 15, 200–203, 312–17
media marketplace, 6, 8
    audiences, 54–65
    FCC adoption of approach, 37

local news case study, 70–71
organizational processes and routines,
        71–86
overview of, 51–54
what gets reported, 65–69, 72
media ownership, 5
    antitrust laws and, 42
    cross-ownership, 37–38, 60, 92n4
    in Europe, 41, 44
    patterns of, 28–36
    restrictions on concentration of, 37–39,
        42
media politics
    evaluating, 327–47
        direct communication between
            candidates and voters, 341–46
        free media time for candidates,
            336–39
        issueless coverage, 329–34
        overview of, 327–29
        partisan press, 339–41
        public service broadcasting, 334–36
    requirements for, 6
    as successor to party politics, 22–28
media pools, 104–6
mediality, 66
Medicare prescription drug plan, 223, 323
Meet the Press, 3–4, 198, 216
Meetup, 138
Mellman, Mark, 176
Mendelberg, T., 257–58
Mendelsohn, N., 253
message force multipliers, 217
message learning theory, 232
Messina, Jim, 143
Michigan, 162
Microsoft, 53, 60, 91n1
military officials, 102, 104–5, 106, 107, 217
Miller, J. M., 254
Mineral Management Service, 220
minimal consequences, 230
minimal effects, new era of, 266
Minneapolis, Minnesota, 49n2
minority voters, 296–97
mirror-image definition of news, 65–66, 82,
        86–87, 110

partisan polarization hypothesis, 124, 126–29

partisan press, 51, 339–41

partisanship
    presidential popularity and, 308–9, 310
    voting as an expression of, 275–76, 302n1, 303n2

Patriot Act, 99, 174

Patterns of Global Terrorism, 97–99

PBS (Public Broadcasting Service)
    audience size and, 32, 54, 66–67
    FAIR tracking of, 106–7
    free media time and, 337
    funding for, 32, 328, 335
    Hill-Thomas hearings and, 218–19
    Iraq war coverage, 107

Pelley, Scott, 58

Pennsylvania, 26

Pentagon
    as authoritative source, 7, 8, 99, 103, 108
    embedded journalists and, 106–7
    indexing the news and, 96–97, 101
    media pools and, 104–6
    message force multipliers and, 217
    as premiere beat, 84
    restriction of press access by, 102–3, 104

People and the Press, 243

Perot, Ross, 78, 319

Perry, Rick, 158, 189

Persian Gulf conflict, 109, 317
    See also Kuwait; Operation Desert Storm

personality assessments, 253

persuasion effects, 13, 233, 260–66
    receiver-related contingencies, 261–65, 264–65
    source- and message-related contingencies, 265–66

Pew Research Center
    on campaign coverage, 342
    on credibility, 61–62
    on Facebook use, 134
    on Internet usage, 114, 115, 341
    media use survey of, 243
    on online civic engagement, 125
    on partisan identity, 262, 263
    on social media as a news source, 344
    survey of Dean activists, 134

pharmaceutical industry, 16

Philadelphia, Pennsylvania, 37, 67

Philadelphia Inquirer, 43

Plame, Valerie, 202

planted questions, 212–13

Plouffe, David, 140

point-to-point communication, 113

Poizner, Steve, 172

political action committees (PACs), 181, 182

Political Communication Lab (Stanford), 147n2

political context vs. campaign effects, 270–74

political parties
    animosity between, 262–63
    campaign reform movement and, 17
    candidate selection and, 6, 23, 25–28
    media access for, 45–47
    membership in, 27, 49n1
    news credibility beliefs and, 64–65
    newspapers affiliated with, 51
    polarization, 262–65, 266, 276–77, 281
    sorting and, 262
    strength of, 22, 23, 28
    voter identification and loyalty to, 275–82, 302n1, 303n2

Politico, 150

Polsby, Nelson, 23

pool sprays, 215

pork barrel spending, 194, 220

Portugal, 30

Postol, Theodore, 105

poverty, 221, 254, 255, 256

A POW Story: Politics, Pressure and the Media, 50n9

Powell, Colin, 93, 97, 106, 107

POWs for Truth, 175

presidential communication, 199–217
    media management and, 15, 200–203
    news coverage, 203–8
    popularity and, 311–12
    press conference alternatives, 214–17
    press conferences, 211–14, 215
    speechmaking, 208–11, 228n6, 312–13

presidential elections
    forecasting, 14, 272–73, 277